D1264421

BOLTON
and the
SPANISH
BORDERLANDS

Edited and with an introduction
by John Francis Bannon

UNIVERSITY OF OKLAHOMA PRESS : NORMAN

To the late Herbert Eugene Bolton
and the host of knights and ladies
of his round table

International Standard Book Numbers:
0–8061–0612–3 (cloth); 0–8061–1150–x (paper)

Library of Congress Catalog Card Number: 64–11336

 PREFACE

THIS BOOK has several purposes. The first is to keep American historians mindful that Herbert Eugene Bolton, no matter what his other contributions to American history writing, was first and foremost the scholar who opened up the Spanish Borderlands, integrating them into the broader understanding of American history. Another is to bring into print several pieces pertinent to the Borderlands which have to date remained in manuscript. Still another is to pick up several "stray" Borderland pieces which have very real interest and value and which are not readily available. The selections are indicative of Bolton's interests in the Borderlands story and also can serve as signposts pointing to his more extensive studies. It is not a summary of either his interests or his studies. Perhaps this little volume may be of service as a Borderlands reader for students of the area and also as a historiographical aid relative to the writing of American history.

A sincere acknowledgment is due the Bancroft Library, its director, Professor George P. Hammond, and the staff for permission to print some of the bits from its collection of Bolton Papers and for the generous co-operation tendered in the assembling of materials for the introduction. Professors Kinnaird, Lawrence and Lucia, have given strong encouragement to this effort and added many bits to the documentary data and my own recollections of Professor Bolton. And special thanks should go to Miss Rita Adams for much help in preparing the manuscript and, most of all, for aiding with the proofreading and indexing chores.

John Francis Bannon

SAINT LOUIS UNIVERSITY

{ v }

CONTENTS

MAPS

INTRODUCTION

In this volume the editor has presumed to select a number of Herbert Eugene Bolton's studies and pieces which he considers both indicative and typical of the much more extensive work of this top-rank American historian. The editor has by design limited these selections to Bolton's Borderlands interests, leaving aside (save for purposes of comparison, in the case of the last number) such pieces as might touch the so-called and misnamed "Bolton thesis" on the Americas.

Actually, there never was a "Bolton thesis." Bolton did little more than propose a broader approach to American history, one which was not simply Anglo-oriented or limited to the study of the thirteen colonies to which three dozen and one states were added in time. This is not the place to discuss at length this "Bolton approach" to American history. Right or wrong, fact, fad or fancy, it is only one facet of Bolton's historical contributions. He was a diligent researcher, a prolific producer, and an untiring editor of sources long before he ventured into the controversial field of historical synthesis.

In the heat of periodic discussion about whether the Americas have had and have a "common history" (a term which was not coined by Bolton), there is the unfortunate and very real possibility that Bolton's correct place in the history of American historical writing may be obscured to the point of being overlooked. He was first and foremost the historian of the Borderlands. He may not have succeeded in his oft-professed aim to "Parkmanize" the story of the Spaniards in North America; but he certainly laid the groundwork for the Parkman of the future, if he ever appears and undertakes the gigantic task. Bolton's Borderlands studies have helped us to see and understand the totality of the American story much better. In this lies his greatest contribution to American historiography. The American story need no longer be an unrelieved, and in that measure, an unhistorical, Anglo epic.

Bolton's own work and the influence which he exerted on his many students, to complement and supplement his researches, proved to be one of those periodic breaths-of-life which have blown over and invigorated the writing of American history. The deservedly famous essay of Frederick Jackson Turner, "The Significance of the Frontier in American History," was another and earlier one. Turner personally and through his students, and their students, brought the American West into focus. Bolton broadened the concept of the West by adding another American frontier to the dimensions of the story.

The work of Turner and his school tended to limit the historians' vision unduly. The "West" for Turner was, in large measure, what has come to be termed the Trans-Allegheny, and even more specifically the Old Northwest. He was not unaware of the rest of the American story, but rarely did he venture beyond the great river of the Mid-Continent and into the Trans-Mississippi in his analyses of the frontier. The range of many of his disciples and followers has often not gone much further. Even when they do "cross the river," the frontier of which they write is almost without fail the Anglo-American forward surge westward. Too often the frontier for them, as it was for their master, has been the outer edge of Anglo advance encroaching on the actual or the supposed wilderness.

In truth, the Anglo frontiersman only occasionally met a virgin or unprepared wilderness as he pushed westward from the crest of the Appalachian highlands. This statement takes the prehistoric and historic Indian frontiers for granted. Rather it means to recall that there were white men's frontiers antedating the Anglo-American, some of them decades and others even centuries old. Further, these pre-Anglo frontiers in many instances prepared for and made possible much of the phenomenal success of the Anglo-American enterprise of the late eighteenth and the nineteenth centuries in the "West." Anglo frontiers were often second frontiers.

The more westerly of the Great Lakes, sections of the Ohio Valley, the Wabash Valley, and the great Mississippi Valley along its entire course had seen the white man, had housed him, had begun to yield to him some, at least, of their natural wealth long before the stream of Anglo-American settlers first started to trickle and then to flood down from the Appalachian watershed. The French had been there much earlier in the eighteenth century, had explored widely, had built their posts, and had begun to tap the resources. Mid-Continent was their frontier before Britisher and later Anglo-American took over.

When the Anglos pushed out to the farther edge of the Mid-Continent and beyond, they found the groundwork already laid in a good half of the area. The Spaniards had been in New Mexico almost ten years before there was a Jamestown. They had been in Florida and had extended along the Georgia coast even before their fellows in the West had gone north to settle on the upper reaches of the Río Grande. In the second decade of the eighteenth century, after the French had come in force to the mouth of the Mississippi and began to range westward, the Spaniards turned Texas into a buffer province. By that date the western flank of their northward movement had crossed the future international boundary into Arizona. And the preliminaries to the ultimate thrust to California's Golden Gate were well under way on the far western peninsula, Baja California. Thus, much of the continent had been seen and charted and even "frontierized" before the first Anglos arrived.

Francis Parkman had written of the French frontier in American history. Bolton found a Spanish frontier in the Borderlands and devoted most of his scholarly life to uncovering and interpreting it. Hubert Howe Bancroft had been an earlier pioneer, but Bolton was to be *the* historian of the Borderlands. These samplings may help to recall this fact.

§   §   §

Back in the last decade of the past century, just three years after Turner read his important paper to the American Historical Association meeting in Chicago in 1893, the University of Wisconsin professor had a graduate assistant by the name of Herbert Eugene Bolton, born in 1870 in the little town of Tomah, Wisconsin. As an undergraduate at the University, he had listened to Turner and to another future "great" among America's historians, Charles Homer Haskins, the medievalist. These men inspired young Bolton to reshape his plans for the future: instead of a career in law, which he had originally envisioned, he decided that history should be his field and a classroom, rather than a courtroom, his arena. This was all right, too, with Gertrude Janes, who, the year after he took his Bachelor of Letters degree, became his wife. In 1896 the young couple was back in Madison, and Bolton embarked on the career which would engross his energies for the next fifty-odd years.

From his Wisconsin master Bolton had caught the infectious spirit which turned history into a great adventure. From Turner, too, he learned something of that thrilling satisfaction which can come from a pioneering effort. Turner talked enthusiastically about men who opened up the great American West and in the process showed himself another kind of pioneer. In 1897, Bolton left the University of Wisconsin after his year's assistantship with a Master's degree and imbued with the spirit of the frontier and the pioneer. He had been named a Harrison Fellow at the University of Pennsylvania. During the next two years the Midwesterner was exposed to men who had already climbed into the ranks of the American "greats": John Bach McMaster, Edward Potts Cheyney, and Dana C. Munro. In 1899, Bolton received his doctor's degree—his dissertation had been a Yankee venture into Rebel-land, "The Free Negro in the South before the Civil War." Pennsylvania in those days was not yet ready for the frontier of which Turner had talked at Wisconsin.

Although he was an American historian by training and predilection, when he went to the University of Texas in 1901, after a two-year stand at Milwaukee State Normal, he found himself assigned to give courses in medieval history. Grateful for his previous work with Haskins and Cheyney, he was the department's medievalist for the next several years. Interestingly, these "medieval" years were to furnish much excellent background for a deeper understanding of the story and the people whom soon he was to make his.

At Austin a new frontier began to open before him. Later he

wrote: "At the University of Texas, while I taught Medieval History, I became interested in the Spanish background of our Southwest." Spain, indeed, had left her mark on the Texas which was all around him. Bolton was intrigued, intrigued enough to want to learn more about pre-Sam Houston Texas. In satisfying that scholar's curiosity, Bolton found "his" frontier.

Summer vacation of 1902 came and the young professor went off to Mexico on the first of what would be many, many excursions beyond the border, during which he found treasures to be mined which American historians had hardly suspected. The next summers and other archives showed how rich the lode ran. As early as the fall of 1902 he began to hint at some of his findings in *The Quarterly* of the Texas State Historical Association. In the following years more studies appeared in that journal and a number of shorter sketches went into Frederick Webb Hodge's *Handbook of American Indians North of Mexico*. The hundred and more articles on the Texas Indians won for him acclaim both as historian and ethnologist. He was showing scholars in other fields how the Mexican archival riches could contribute valuable information for their disciplines. During these early twentieth-century years Bolton's growing knowledge of the colonial Spaniards was called upon by Blair and Robertson, who were at that time assembling materials for their monumental collection of documents on the Philippines: he translated a number of pieces for this fifty-five-volume work.

But an even more important invitation came in 1906. In that year J. Franklin Jameson, at the moment directing a project for the Carnegie Institution, wrote to Bolton. Jameson was arranging for the publication of calendars of materials pertinent to the history of the United States existing in foreign archives. The University of Texas professor had shown himself the logical man to do the job in the Mexican archives. Funds were voted, and the year 1907–1908 ("fifteen consecutive months," to be more exact) found Bolton on leave in Mexico, preparing what, in 1913, became the very valuable *Guide to Materials for the History of the United States in the Principal Archives of Mexico*—still the "archive bible" for American and Mexican researcher alike.

Bolton's reputation was growing. In 1908, Stanford University was seeking a replacement for Professor Max Farrand. The department chairman, E. D. Adams, opened correspondence with Bolton. Lured by the promise of a full professorship (at a salary of $3,500) and even more by the assurance of a library budget for the acquisition of transcripts from the Mexican archives, he accepted and in the summer of 1909 moved to Palo Alto. Texans were up in arms when the news broke. They had grown both fond and proud of the scholar who was opening up a phase of their history which went back into pre-nineteenth-century "antiquity." They might not get on well with the Mexicans who lived among them, but these Texans did feel a surge of pride in their ancient Spanish background. Two years later the University of Texas tried to get Bolton back to Austin and very nearly succeeded. At this point Bolton was faced with a major decision.

Meanwhile, the University of California had entered the competition as a bidder for his services and his growing prestige as a scholar. Henry Morse Stephens, the dynamic chairman of the department of history at Berkeley, recognized that new emphasis must be given to American history in his department, and was looking for someone to do the job. Early in 1910 he wrote Frederick Jackson Turner, inviting him to join the California faculty. But Harvard, belatedly discovering that the area west of the Alleghenies might have some importance in American history, had gotten to Turner before him. Stephens then became interested in Bolton. Word was out that Bolton was thinking of returning to Texas. In August, Stephens wrote Bolton: "If we cannot have Turner, let us have Turner's most promising pupil. . . . With Turner lost, I know of no one whom I would sooner have by my side as my special colleague to handle American history than yourself." Those late 1910 months were not easy ones for Bolton. There were pleasant memories of Texas, and many warm friends both in and outside the University. But the University of California had a special allurement. It was neither the professorship nor the salary ($4,000 the starting figure); it was the fact that California had the Bancroft collection. Bolton already knew it, for more than once in his days

at Stanford he had slipped up to Berkeley to browse in that remarkable library of Mexicana and Western Americana gathered by the
amazing Hubert Howe Bancroft.

Bancroft had had an experience not unlike that of Bolton himself.
The former had decided to prepare a history of California and had
not gone far before the trail led him to Mexico and the Spanish
masters of yesteryear; Bolton's interest in Texas had the same end
result. The University of California had recently (1906) acquired
Bancroft's library of books, manuscripts, and other historical sources
and had moved the collection to the campus.

Stephens was anxious that his department make the fullest use
of the enormous research potential of these materials. On second
thought, Bolton might even prove himself better than Turner in
exploiting them. Bolton now was his man, but for a time there was
question as to whether Bolton would agree. However, when given a
firm promise that the University of California would add to the
Bancroft collection, and generously so, Bolton hesitated no longer.
In September, 1911, he moved to the Berkeley campus and began
a stay there which only his death, in 1953, ended.

Bolton brought with him to the University of California a dream,
one that had been maturing for some time past: his ambition was to
do for the Spaniards in North America what Parkman had done
for the French. He was not long on the Berkeley campus before
he had a long report on the desk of President Benjamin Ide
Wheeler—this is the first piece reproduced in this collection. A few
years later (1917) in a letter to Professor William E. Dodd, University of Chicago and a close friend through the years, Bolton
detailed his dream as follows:

> Since you mention Parkman you may be interested to know that I
> am planning to "Parkmanize" the history of the Spanish Southwest.
> I have been gathering materials and writing painful monographs
> for a long while, but one of my aims is to present the story of the
> Spanish advance into the Southwest in a series of scholarly but
> graphic sketches, much as Parkman wrote for the history of the
> French in North America. The subject is much larger and the ma-
> terials richer than he had, and with a pen equal to his one could win

immortal fame, and at the same time make money for his publishers.

My plan would be to write a volume on "The Discovery and Occupation of the West Indies," another on "Cortés and His Companions," another on "The Early Explorers in Florida and the Southeast," another on "Viceroy Mendoza," another on the "Conquerors of New Mexico," another on the "Founders of New Mexico," another on the "Struggle for the Texas and Louisiana Border," another on "The Jesuits on the Pacific Slope," another on "Louisiana under Spain," another on "The Anglo-Spanish Border," and another on "California under Spain."

Even a man of Bolton's tremendous energy could not accomplish such a vast program. Interestingly, however, many segments of this dream would be brought into being, perhaps not always in popular style, by Bolton's students. One acquainted with the "school" of historians whom he trained can quickly insert author names behind many of the volume titles listed—Ross, Lanning, Aiton, Hammond, Espinosa, Thomas, Caughey, Kinnaird, Nasatir, Dunne, Chapman, and more. The master himself did more than his share—the lengthy introductions to the source volumes which he translated and edited are regularly little narrative gems.

The first of Bolton's major works appeared in 1913. This, and in a sense very properly, was the *Guide to Materials for the History of the United States in the Principal Archives of Mexico.* His *Athanase de Mézières and the Louisiana-Texas Frontier, 1768–1780* was already in press and came out, in two volumes, the following year; a selection from the Introduction is reprinted as No. 9 in this collection. The year 1915 saw his *Texas in the Middle Eighteenth Century* off the press—it has recently been reprinted and again made widely available. That summer the American Historical Association met on the West Coast in connection with the Panama Pacific International Exposition; there were sessions in Berkeley, Palo Alto, and San Francisco. Bolton read two papers, both of which are reprinted here—No. 8 and No. 13; these were initially published in 1917 in the volume, *The Pacific Ocean in History.* Meanwhile, Bolton had contributed one of the numbers to the

"Original Narratives of Early American History" series, *Spanish Exploration in the Southwest, 1542–1706*. His old friend, J. Franklin Jameson, the general editor of the series, knew exactly where to turn when seeking a man to prepare this volume. Actually, the inclusion of such a volume in the series was an indication that Bolton's vision of the Spanish frontier in American history was leaving an impression on some, at least, within the profession.

In 1917, Bolton was chosen to give the Faculty Research Lecture at his university. This offered him the opportunity to bring another facet of his vision into focus with his "The Mission as a Frontier Institution in the Spanish-American Colonies"—included in this collection as No. 10. Two years later, in 1919, he offered telling evidence that the mission was a frontier institution with his two-volume edition of *Kino's Historical Memoir of Pimería Alta*. Years before he had discovered this Jesuit's lost manuscript history during one of the forays into the Archivo General of Mexico.

One of Bolton's rare textbook ventures saw the light in 1920, *The Colonization of North America, 1492–1783*, done with one of his first graduate students on the West Coast, Thomas Maitland Marshall. The story of this book is a rather fascinating bit of American historiography. One of the editorial critics to whom the publisher submitted the manuscript was positively scandalized—"First, the matter of proportion. Nearly, if not quite, one third of the whole is devoted to the period before 1606, that is to say, before there were any permanent English settlements in America. Nearly twice as much space is given to the early period of exploration as to the whole of the revolutionary movement from 1763–1783, which is, to say the least, impractical in any book designed as a college textbook, or at least as the first part of a history of the United States." This, of course, was tantamount to historical heresy—that American history should be begun, in depth, prior to 1607. Bolton stuck to his guns, and gradually the Macmillan people came around and published the work as originally presented, with minor corrections but without major cutting in that "offensive" first third of the volume. Now both the Spanish and the French frontiers could be brought to the attention of students of American history. Here was a first major step toward that broader approach to the American story which Bolton was already advocating.

Bolton again breached the walls of tradition in 1921. This time, with much difficulty and after not a few acrimonious exchanges with the editors, he squeezed his story into the small but important volume of the "Chronicles of America" series, *The Spanish Borderlands: A Chronicle of Old Florida and the Southwest.* In a certain sense this volume marks the "christening" of his frontier. "The Spanish Borderlands," or just plain "The Borderlands," has proved to be an accepted and enduring division of the American story. Here compressed into three hundred-odd pages was a sketch of what he hoped to do on the grand scale of a Parkman. The editors did admit that the work helped to round out the American story and to give it proper perspective. But it was only after some forceful prodding by Bolton that they initially consented to include this segment in their over-all concept of the American epic—Bolton was not above campaigning for his frontier.

The years from the middle 1920's into the middle 1930's were highly productive. In 1925 the eastern flank of the Borderlands frontier, the Georgia-Florida area, received notice in *Arrendondo's Historical Proof of Spain's Title to Georgia* and in the *Debatable Land: A Sketch of the Anglo-Spanish Contest for the Georgia Country*, done with Mary Ross. A section of the broader story is included in this volume as No. 7. This article is an excellent illustration of the defensive and international character of one, at least, of the Borderlands. Bolton developed this particular theme in an over-all view at the Boulder Conference on the History of the Trans-Mississippi West, in 1929. His address, "Defensive Spanish Expansion and the Significance of the Borderlands," is included herein as No. 2.

His next works covered large sections of the story of what he called the "West Coast Corridor" (see Nos. 3 and 6). First, there was the "California series," appearing in rapid succession—*Historical Memoirs of New California*, by Francisco Palóu, four volumes, in 1926; *Palóu and His Writings*, in the same year; *A Pacific Coast*

Pioneer and *Fray Juan Crespi, Missionary Explorer on the Pacific Coast, 1769–1774*, in 1927; *Anza's California Expeditions*, five volumes, in 1930; *Font's Complete Diary: A Chronicle of the Founding of San Francisco* and *Outpost of Empire: The Story of the Founding of San Francisco*, both in 1931. Selections from several of these, along with an earlier study of the explorations of the remarkable Fray Francisco Garcés, appear herein to illustrate Bolton's work on this "last Borderland."

Then Bolton turned to publicize his favorite Black Robe, Padre Eusebio Francisco Kino. *The Padre on Horseback* (1932) was a charming short sketch of Kino's remarkable career and *Rim of Christendom* (1936) was a full-length biography. This last is something of a historical tour de force, developed almost in its entirety from documents unworked by predecessors and unearthed in largest measure by the writer himself.

Meanwhile, Bolton had put the syllabus for his Americas course into print. *History of the Americas: A Syllabus with Maps* came out in print first in 1928 and was up-dated in 1935. Previously it had circulated on the Berkeley campus in mimeograph edition. This little work represents the "other Bolton" and his contribution to American historiography in another capacity, that not only of researcher, editor, and pioneer in relatively untrodden or little worked fields, such as the Borderlands, but now as synthesizer. Here was the Bolton "approach" to American history, not simply American history broadened to embrace the North American continent, but expanded to encompass all the Americas—North, Central, and South.

For years before Bolton came to the University of California, and down to his death in 1919, Henry Morse Stephens had initiated students into history with his famous "History 4a–b," the dramatic sweep of the development of Europe. Stephens was a master lecturer, a history "salesman" almost without peer. Bolton watched and admired his departmental chairman and began to dream a dream. Stephens did not tell the story simply of France or England or Germany; he pulled all the European past into a coherent whole, differences and national individualities, similarities and parallels; he did not claim that all his nations had a common development or history, but he did show that underneath there was much that made all these disparate peoples something which could be properly designated by the generic term "European." Bolton would not make American history only the story of the United States; he would survey all twenty-two of the Americas, show them growing up side by side, influencing one another, being influenced by Europe and reacting in not dissimilar ways, emerging as independent entities, facing and solving the varied problems of the modern world, each in its own way and yet in new ways that were American ways, characteristic of the New World which was theirs.

In 1920 a new course was listed among the departmental offerings, "History 8a–b: History of the Americas." September came. Instead of the hundred or so students whom he hoped might enroll, Bolton found the lecture hall bulging, and literally so, with ten times that number. "History of the Americas" became one of the most popular courses on the Berkeley campus. Soon Bolton's teaching assistants, the young graduate students who conducted the quiz sections for History 8a–b, grew up to be Ph.D.'s and went off to carry this fresh approach to American history far beyond the confines of California.

In 1932, Bolton was president of the American Historical Association. That December, to the Association holding its annual meeting in Toronto, he delivered his presidential address. He entitled the address "The Epic of Greater America"—it was "History 8a–b" compressed into several dozen pages. In spots his enthusiasm for his theme betrayed him into statements which he did not have the time to qualify and which opened his ideas to misinterpretation. In later years this synthesis of his was to become as controversial and controverted as the address given forty years before in Chicago by Bolton's first master in history, Frederick Jackson Turner.

The years of the 1930's were busy ones, even though the Bolton bibliography may not always indicate the fact. The department of history had grown, and administrative duties multiplied. So did the number of Bolton's graduate students. His earlier doctors were sending him some of their brightest students; others, attracted by his reputation and that of the California department of history, came to work under his direction. The famous "round table seminar" became so large that in some years it had to be broken into two groups. Still Bolton found time for his Borderlands. The fruits would not appear until after his retirement, and his re-retirement, to be perfectly exact. His *Coronado, Knight of Pueblos and Plains* (1948) and *Pageant in the Wilderness: The Story of the Escalante Expedition to the Interior Basin, 1776* (1950) were still to come, but he was already at work on them, not only reviewing the documents but also physically covering the geographical setting. This last, on-the-ground research, was one of Bolton's techniques which he helped to establish firmly into the process of the recreating of the American story. Many a day he spent on the trails of his Borderlands to ensure greater authenticity in his writings.

At the end of the academic year 1939–40, Bolton had rounded out three score and ten winters. The University statutes were mandatory: he became professor emeritus. Hale and hardy still, clear-headed and energetic as he was, retirement was difficult. To be sure, there were projects aplenty which had been pushed aside in late years and which could now be given full attention. But Bolton was restless. Something was missing. When it was all added up, the answer became clear. Missing were the students who for so many years had been such an integral part of his life: the History Eighters by the hundreds in Wheeler Auditorium, the juniors and seniors and graduate students in "History of North America," the serious Ph.D. candidates at the "round table" in the familiar seminar room in the library. He could and did meet many of these last informally, to help them complete research projects begun under his direction. But this was not enough for the man who had continued to be the teacher along with his scholarly researching and writing.

Then troubled times intervened in his favor. Death took Chapman and Priestley within a matter of months; the war came and Uncle Sam borrowed others for key assignments; the department was badly depleted. Bolton was called back to service as a lecturer. The next four years found him happy once more. But time was marching on. The war ended; old hands came back to the campus; new men were added. September, 1945, saw Bolton re-retired.

On a late December evening of that year, 1945, several hundred of his friends—colleagues, former students, admirers—gathered at the Saint Francis Hotel in San Francisco to do him honor. On this occasion he was presented with a handsome commemorative volume, *Greater America*, a collection of studies by the "second generation" of his Ph.D.'s. The "first generation" had so honored him thirteen years before, at Toronto, as he closed his year as president of the American Historical Association—the two-volume *New Spain and the Anglo-Amercian West*. This event of 1945 gave him a distinction still unique among American historians, of having been the recipient not of one, but of two *Festschriften*. The range of his American interests is mirrored in these two collections, representing the work of a few more than half of the 103 doctors whom he had trained.

The next years passed quickly. He was visiting professor on several campuses, worked on his Coronado and his Escalante, and prepared to put together the study on Salvatierra. Then on a July day in 1952, a few days short of his eighty-second birthday, he was struck down by a severe cerebral hemorrhage. Six months later, early in the morning of January 30, 1953, death came. And the United States mourned the passing of one of its great historians.

§ § §

Great men are always controversial figures. How truly great were they? Was the respect and honor paid them in life really deserved? Is the cult of their names in after years well founded, or is it too heavily weighted with emotion, or may it even be quite unjustified? And such questions could be multiplied. Actors in the human drama which is history are constantly being subjected to the process of evaluation and re-evaluation. And the men who sit in judgment, namely, the historians, are themselves not proof against like scrutiny. They, too, are subject to the process of ranking and rating.

What is Bolton's place in American historiography? What major contributions did he make to a better knowledge of the past in the area which was his field of special interest and researches? Does he deserve to be ranked among the "greats"? There is, undoubtedly, more than one answer, categoric or qualified, to this last and other questions concerning him. However, here is one!

To have opened a fresh field of investigation to and traced new research paths for students and colleagues is certainly a major service to the historical profession. To have worked this field extensively and intensively and to have inspired students to supplement and continue one's own researches is another. To have been an enthusiastic teacher and "salesman" of history is still another. To have been prominent and influential enough that contemporaries argued and latecomers still argue about one's works, ideas, and contributions would seem to raise one from the ranks of the ordinary. If such criteria, among others which could be marshaled, have any validity as measures of "greatness," then Bolton deserves such rating, for on all these counts he stands high in the history of American historical scholarship. He opened the field of the Borderlands to broadened research, a field which had been relatively little worked before him. His own bibliography and that of the men he inspired are most impressive. And possibly only one other American historian, his own first master, Frederick Jackson Turner, has been the center of as much controversy. He, at very least, is a sufficiently important figure in American historiography that periodically individuals feel it necessary to deflate his memory in order to protect present and future generations from contamination—and a certain measure of this has been done in recent years at his own University of California.

There is no intention here to claim that Bolton, his "dream," and his works were free of shortcomings and above criticism. No human craftsman can avoid them. The shortcomings, however, were most often those almost inevitable failings of the pioneer. The trail blazer regularly has so much to do in opening the path that little time is left to be more than a pioneer. Bolton spent much of his life opening paths. He found the mines of materials in the Mexican and the Spanish archives and showed how they could be worked to the great advantage of American history. Life did not give him enough years to refine all that he had mined. But even if one grants, for the sake of argument, that Bolton was not always a refiner, this does not immediately reduce him to the rank of an historiographical second-rater.

Bolton was a great man for finding and working with the sources. In a radio broadcast in 1934 he put his historian's creed in the short statement: "Before one can write the history of any event, one must first find the records on which the story must be based. No records, no authentic history!" Of course, this is not a new concept, but his insistence on living by it was one of the elements of his greatness.

Bolton has sometimes been described as primarily a narrative historian with the implied criticism that narrative history is not good history. Yet, without it and the archival work which goes into it too much of interpretative history—"conceptualization" is the reigning modern term—might turn out to be distressingly unenduring, not to say unendurable. Intellectual history, "trend" history, and other of the newer approaches still have to prove themselves before they run plain old narrative politico-socio-economic history out of business. Bolton's distinguished colleague at California, Frederic L. Paxson, in speaking of intellectual history once described it as an illusive subject, "something like trying to nail a handful of jelly to a barn door."

Bolton's frontier did not have the immediately perceived pertinence to the national story of, let us say, Turner's frontier. The Anglo-American frontiersmen and the institutions which they spread did not labor under the centuries-old handicap of being tarred with the "Black Legend." They were heroes almost before they did anything to merit such a rating and their institutions were considered as peerless, without doubt or question. One sometimes wonders if the Spaniards and their institutions may not have some indirect responsibility for the ranking which a seaboard-oriented craft, which American history writing so often is, accords Bolton. To be sure, Bolton's occasional charges of provincialism did not make warm friends for him of many United States historians who felt the sting of his criticism.

In connection with this train of thought, one might be allowed to wonder if Parkman would be the great name in American history which he continues to be had he chosen to write about the Spaniards, rather than the French? His Yankee predecessor, his equal as a storyteller, and a definitely superior craftsman, William Hickling Prescott, has never quite succeeded in outranking him. Prescott in his own and even in a later day was betimes suspect because of his great enthusiasm for the conquistadores, who for so long had to be, in the dramatic sense, the "heavies" in any Anglo-told history. Again, what might have been the rating of Frederick Jackson Turner, had he picked up Henry Morse Stephens's invitation of 1910, instead of moving to a seaboard chair? These and like questions are, admittedly, heavy with innuendos, and yet may it not be time to ask them? May it not be just a tiny bit possible that there is some "significance of sections in American history" writing?

Bolton was not simply a diligent archive-grubber nor only a facile narrator. Out of his painstaking research and extensive document-editing came ideas, concepts, views, intuitions, and even syntheses. "The Mission as a Frontier Institution" proved to be a most productive concept; so did insistence on the defensive character of the Borderlands; his "continental" perspective regarding the North American story made American history more truly American; the underlining of the tripartite character of the Spanish northward movement is a valuable insight into one of the several American frontiers.

Of course, if what happened in the Borderlands—along the Gulf of Mexico, in the Southwest, and on the shore of the Pacific—prior to the days of Manifest Destiny has only minor importance in the American story, then the man who is so largely responsible for those chapters of the American epic is proportionately inconsequential among American historians. Yet there remains a lingering suspicion that Williamsburg and Boston, Philadelphia and Charleston, New York and Baltimore must share some of the credit for having made the U.S.A. with Pittsburgh and Cleveland, Cincinnati and Louisville, Chicago and Saint Louis, Memphis and New Orleans, San Antonio and Santa Fe, San Francisco and Portland. The Midwest of Turner, the Great Plains of Webb, the Borderlands of Bolton are all integral parts of the great epic that is American history.

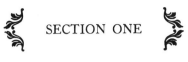

SECTION ONE

The Borderlands in American History

CHAPTER ONE

Need for the Publication of
a Comprehensive Body of Documents
Relating to the History of Spanish Activities
within the Present Limits of the United States*

BOLTON arrived on the Berkeley campus in the late summer of 1911. He came as professor of American history. One of the baits which Henry Morse Stephens had used to lure him from Stanford and to counter his possible return to the University of Texas, which at the time was strongly propositioning him, was the promise that materials, beyond the existing resources of the Bancroft collection, would be made available to him and his students for the study of the Spaniards in North America. In this report to President Benjamin Ide Wheeler,† the new professor unfolds his "dream." This is one of the earliest statements of the Borderlands project and, so to speak, a plea for the recognition of the Spanish frontier as an integral part of American history. Implementing and realizing this "dream" would be Bolton's life work. Hence, this would seem to be a most fitting selection with which to open this collection of pieces from Bolton's writings. In so far as he is important in American historiography, and he is, this piece has prime significance—it is, in a sense, his "work project" for future years.

ONE OF THE GREATEST NEEDS in the field of American History is the publication of a comprehensive body of historical materials relating to Spanish activities within the present limits of the United States. This can be demonstrated under the following heads:

* A report, Bolton to Wheeler, December 18, 1911. This report is in the Bolton Papers, Bancroft Library. It is published here with the permission of the Bancroft Library.

† Benjamin Ide Wheeler was president of the University of California from 1899 to 1919.

1. For nearly three centuries the southwestern half of the present United States constituted a portion of the Spanish possessions of North America, while for nearly half a century (1762–1800) Spain possessed the whole Trans-Mississippi West, occupying posts, conducting fur trade, and granting lands respectively as far north as Nootka Sound, the upper Missouri River, and southern Minnesota, while exerting an influence over the Indians as far northeast as Michigan. In 1821 New Spain revolted from Old Spain, and the next quarter century was a period in which the historical process in the Southwest (the region from Louisiana to California) consisted primarily of an Anglo-American movement against and across the Mexican frontier, a movement which resulted in the American conquest and settlement of the northern half of what was once New Spain.

During this long period the Spanish possessions within the limits described were an object of utmost interest in world politics, and on them turned some of the principal diplomatic contests of the period. During the same period they had an internal history in most respects quite distinct from that of the rest of the United States. This history embraced the remarkable periods of Spanish exploration and conquest; Spanish mission, presidio, pueblo, mine, and ranch; Anglo-American trapper, explorer, contraband trader, and filibuster within the Spanish domain; revolution from Spain and development under Mexican rule; and finally, Anglo-American settlement, diplomacy, and conquest. It is needless to state that this long period of Spanish occupation and the half century of conflict between the Spanish and the Anglo-American frontiers constitute a most important portion of American history, or that the subsequent development of the West—the portion of the Spanish dominions with which we are most concerned—cannot be properly interpreted without first devoting to these antecedents a complete and thorough study.

2. But this study has not yet been made, and the importance of the Spanish period in American History has not yet been duly recognized. Much more is known, for example, both to scholars and to the general public, of French than of Spanish activities in North America, and it is consequently assumed that the French influence

was the more important of the two; but the reverse of this is true. French occupation began a century later and ended half a century earlier than the Spanish, while Spain was heir to nearly half of the dominions lost by France. Spanish exploration, missionary work, industrial development, and settlement in North America at all times far exceeded those of France, a generalization which is just as true if limited territorially to districts now within the United States. But this fact is not generally known, for the reason that France in America had a Parkman, while Spain in America had none.

A more fundamental explanation of the neglect of the Spanish period and of the West generally in American history is the fact that down to recent times the history of the United States has been written almost solely from the standpoint of the East and of the English colonies. Most of the well-known names in American historiography are those of New Englanders. Examples are George Bancroft, Hildreth, Frothingham, Higginson, Schouler, Fiske, Justin Winsor, and Channing, all of whom are New Englanders and all, I believe, Harvard men. The list reflects great credit on New England and on Harvard; but it also explains their neglect of the West and consequently of Spanish influence in writing the history of the United States. In recent days Turner, of Wisconsin, has directed attention to what he calls the West; but his West is a moving area which began east of the Appalachians and has not thus far reached beyond the Mississippi Valley. He and his school have contributed very little to the history of the Southwest and the Far West. The lead in the investigation of this field must be taken by us here in the West, and it is on this field that the American history department of the University of California is concentrating its efforts.

3. Our knowledge of the history of the West, as of any other field, is limited by the available historical materials or sources from which the history is to be ascertained. Progress in developing the field beyond a certain point will depend absolutely upon adding to the body of materials already known and accessible. This point needs no demonstration. It is axiomatic.

4. From what has been said of the Spanish occupation of territory now within the United States, it is obvious that most of the materials

for the first three centuries of Southwestern and Western history exist in the archives of Spain and Mexico, whither the official reports were sent and where the records were kept. This is no theoretical assumption, but a fact that has been demonstrated by actual investigation. Research conducted in recent years has shown that the archives of Mexico and Spain are teeming with a wealth of historical materials for early Western and Southwestern history which has never before been utilized or even known of by scholars.

These investigations have principally been made by a small group of students who have devoted themselves to making lists of materials in these archives bearing upon the history of the United States.‡ A preliminary survey of the Spanish archives was made by Professor Shepherd. This is being followed up by Mr. R. R. Hill, of the Carnegie Institution, and Mr. Chapman, of the University of California. Mr. Chapman is listing the California materials in the department of the Archivo de Indias known as the Audiencia de Guadalajara, that body being for a long time the civil center of our

‡ In the first decades of the present century the Carnegie Institution of Washington sponsored and subsidized the preparation of a series of calendars of materials in foreign archives pertaining to the history of the United States, under the general editorship of J. Franklin Jameson. William R. Shepherd had, as Bolton notes, done a volume on the Spanish archives, *Guide to materials for the history of the United States in Spanish Archives, Simancas, the Archivo Histórico Nacional, and Seville* (Washington, Carnegie Institution of Washington, Publication no. 91, 1907). In that same year appeared Luis Marino Pérez, *Guide to materials for American history in Cuban archives* (Publication no. 83). Roscoe H. Hill's work, referred to by Bolton, was not published until three years after Bolton's own *Guide—Descriptive catalogue of documents relating to the history of the United States in the Papeles procedentes de Cuba deposited in the Archivo General de Indias at Seville* (Washington, Carnegie Institution of Washington, Publication no. 234, 1916). James A. Robertson had produced a slightly different sort of volume, *List of documents in Spanish archives relating to the history of the United States which have been printed or of which transcripts are preserved in American libraries* (Washington, Carnegie Institution of Washington, Publication no. 124, 1910). Charles E. Chapman, one of Bolton's early Ph.D.'s at California and for the many years thereafter a close friend and colleague, completed the work to which Bolton alludes in 1919, *Catalogue of materials in the Archivo General de Indias for the Pacific Coast and the American Southwest* (Berkeley, University of California Press, 1919).

whole West. During the past ten years, the present writer has spent much of his time in the Mexican archives and has prepared a *Guide* to materials in those archives relating to the history of the United States. It is now in the press of the Carnegie Institution. Perhaps no better way could be chosen to demonstrate the wealth of hitherto unused sources for Western history in the Mexican archives than to give a few actual examples of new discoveries made in the process of preparing the *Guide* referred to.

Speaking first of California materials, it may be stated that over three thousand card references to California documents in the Archives of Mexico were made, some of these cards representing whole volumes of manuscript documents which have never been printed or even used. Among these materials are eight volumes of original manuscripts relating to the founding and early history of the California missions, including many original letters and reports by Fathers Serra, Palóu, Crespi, Lasuén, and other prominent missionaries of the earliest days. At the time of the Portolá celebration three years ago a scholar published a biography of Portolá in which he stated that it was a regrettable fact that only one or two letters by Portolá were known, none, in fact, relating to his work in California. The truth is that at least thirty letters by Portolá regarding his work in California have been preserved and are in the archives of Mexico. Several of these were written by him while on the very trip during which he discovered San Francisco Bay. Indeed, I have exact references to what would make more than a volume of original reports and correspondence of that first expedition, practically all of which have not been published or even known.

Again, the founding of San Francisco by Juan Bautista de Anza was an important step in the development of Spanish California. However, up to the present times the barest outlines of the history of this event were known, due to a lack of material. But the archives of Mexico contain a large number of documents relative to the event that have never been used. I personally gathered four original diaries of the two Anza expeditions (only one of which had been known before), in addition to a large amount of original correspondence. Still other materials were found which were not gathered.

On the Pacific Coast voyages of the Spaniards between 1788 and 1794 there is a six-volume collection of original diaries and correspondence which have never been studied. The collection contains many documents which have never been known. Besides many diaries and extensive official reports, I recall, for example, several original letters of George Vancouver written to the Spanish authorities at Monterey, California, while Vancouver was living on his vessel in the Bay.

It has always been supposed that Fages's expedition of 1772 was the first exploration of the eastern shore of San Francisco Bay, until the discovery of a diary by the same Fages recording an expedition made almost two years earlier up the Contra Costa to the site of Berkeley, where the explorers described their view of the two bays of San Francisco and San Pablo. Among other Fages papers, of which many were found, one is a general description of the Indians of California made in 1775. This document will, when published, become one of the fundamental bases of California ethnology; yet it has never been used or known.

In a similar way I could give specific illustrations regarding the whole period of the Spanish occupation of California, for which the Mexican archives contain perhaps enough material to make two hundred volumes of original manuscripts. Of these I was able to gather only a small portion, but I secured, nevertheless, about five thousand sheets of transcripts of unpublished documents. These have been turned over to the Bancroft Library.

Turning for a moment to the background of California and to the Southwest in general, the records of the Jesuits in Lower California and Arizona call for mention. Some years ago Thwaites edited a great collection of the *Relations* of the Jesuits in "North America." They are highly important for the history of French America, including Canada and the Mississippi Valley. But they contain nothing for the Southwest, and they leave the impression that the Southwest lay outside the field of Jesuit activities. Nevertheless, there is in the archives of Mexico a great body of Spanish Jesuit records, which are of interest and importance equal and analogous to those for the French, and a study of which is necessary in order to tell the whole story of the Jesuits in North America. In other words, Thwaites' collections are not *the* Jesuit Relations, but only a part of them. Among these Jesuit papers in Mexico I discovered a complete history of the work of Father Kino and his companions in the Southwest during the period 1687–1711, written in Kino's own hand, and extended enough to make one or two good-sized volumes. This history was referred to in the eighteenth century by early Jesuit writers, but it had not been seen subsequently, and its existence had been denied by two noted modern scholars. It does exist, however, and its publication will completely change our views of many important phases of early Southwestern history. Not the least important contribution of the work is the new light it throws on the history of the attempts to get to California by land from the continent in the seventeenth and eighteenth centuries, long before upper California was actually occupied, and upon the controversy as to whether California was an island or a peninsula.

One of the best known Franciscans who labored in Arizona after Kino's day was Father Garcés. His diary of 1775 has been known, and was edited by Coues. But it was only two or three years ago that I discovered two earlier diaries by the same explorer, which throw much light on the diary of 1775, and which prove that Garcés was the real pathfinder on whom Anza relied when he made his memorable overland exploration from Sonora to Los Angeles in 1774. I also found an unknown report by Garcés upon the ethnology of the Southwest, analogous in importance to that of Fages. This enumeration of Garcés' documents does not take into account the many letters of this missionary and pathfinder which have been discovered.

On the history of New Mexico and Texas the new material is just as voluminous and just as important as that which I have but briefly described for California. Space and time will not permit me to make detailed specifications under this head, but I must refer to the extensive archive of the College of the Holy Cross of Querétaro, which contains the original records for most of the missionary work in Texas and for much of that of California and for the rest of the Southwest. It has never been used, however, except to a small degree by myself, and through me by Father Engelhardt. Again, among the Texas-Louisiana documents I discovered enough unpublished diaries of eighteenth century explorations in Louisiana and adjacent territory to make a large volume. These documents, when they become known, will put the nineteenth-century explorations of Pike and the so-called "opening of the Santa Fé Trail" in their true light.

These are but random illustrations, given offhand, to show the wealth of materials for early Western history in the archives of Mexico. It is known that those of Spain are just as rich on some periods, the two groups of repositories supplementing each other. I think no more need be said, therefore, to demonstrate the existence of a world of unused material, or to show that the early history of the Southwest and West is yet to be written. I am appending a few clippings from the galley proofs of my *Guide* to further demonstrate this point.

5. Little need be said to show that in order that these historical materials may be studied and utilized they must first be gathered and published. So long as they exist only in foreign archives they can be utilized by only a few, and then under serious disadvantages. And even if an unprinted transcript of them existed here, they could not be conveniently utilized by more than a small portion of the numerous students who would wish access to them. The only way to make them properly available, therefore, is to publish them. The publication by Margry of six large volumes of French sources on the Mississippi Valley and by Thwaites of the seventy-odd volumes of Jesuit Relations has done more than anything else to promote the study of the early history of that region. That almost nothing has been done in this regard for Spain and the Southwest is patent to all workers in the field. And it is just as clear that its undertaking is the next important step in our task.

Not all of the vast body of documents described and left undescribed are of equal importance, and not all would require publication. But the number of those of fundamental value and great human interest is immense. How many printed volumes they would make it would be difficult to estimate. But, as has already been said, a beginning on a large scale is imperative, and I have proposed undertaking a twenty-five volume collection, if the funds can be found to make it possible. We here in the West are especially interested in the West. I have suggested for the collection the title "Spain in the United States," but even under that title I should favor putting the emphasis on Spanish activities in the West and the contiguous Southwest. Nevertheless, Western history is interwoven with that of the whole country, and it must not be studied narrowly if the best results are to be secured. . . .

CHAPTER TWO

Defensive Spanish Expansion
and the Significance of the Borderlands*

IN 1929, at the University of Colorado, historians of the Anglo-American West accepted the invitation to exchange ideas and findings on their special area of interest. They talked of Indians, of cattlemen, of settlers on the rugged and challenging Plains, of wagon trains, of mines, and of many more Western topics. The men who arranged the conference chose Bolton to give one of the main addresses. One of these, Colin B. Goodykoontz, had been a Bolton pupil a number of years before and had developed an understanding and appreciation of the master's approach to American history.† The following selection is the paper which Bolton read to that gathering. Bolton had been working his Borderlands for a quarter-century, researching them, studying them, writing about them, relating them to the broader American story. This invitation offered him the opportunity to put them in their proper setting. Herein is sketched one of his synthesis concepts for the Borderlands themselves, their universal defensive character. Herein, too, he shows the Borderlands as the important points of contact between the two great civilizations of the Americas, the Anglo and the Latin, and the areas in which truly American bonds were created and bases for inter-American understanding laid. This is one of Bolton's finer pieces.

THE SOUTHERN FRINGE of the United States was once an area lightly sprinkled with Spanish outposts, and criss-crossed with Spanish trails. These Spanish Borderlands have had a picturesque, a romantic, and

* This address was originally published in *The Trans-Mississippi West*, edited by James F. Willard and Colin B. Goodykoontz (Boulder, University of Colorado, 1930), 1–42, and was reprinted in Herbert E. Bolton, *Wider Horizons of American History* (New York, D. Appleton-Century, 1939), along with several other essays.

† There is an interesting letter in the Bolton Papers from Goodykoontz. The younger man had been with Bolton at California for a year but, because of his

an important history. They had special significance as parts of the vast Spanish Empire. They are unique as the meeting place of two streams of European civilization. They have been potent factors in the inter-relations between nations.

As parts of the Spanish Empire these borderlands have been sadly misunderstood in this country. They have been regarded as typical of Spanish America, and from this erroneous assumption false inferences have been drawn regarding Spain's part in the making of Western Hemisphere civilization.

It used to be the fashion to teach our children that Spain failed; that the Spaniards did not colonize but merely explored; that they killed off all the Indians; that the Spaniards were mere gold seekers, whereas the English came to America to found homes and build commonwealths, forgetting that gold seekers have been known to establish homes and build commonwealths. A grammar school text recently published by two very distinguished university professors contains the statement, inserted without visible sign of humor, that Spain did not colonize America, but merely tried to hold it to keep other nations out.

This antithesis between the Spanish pick and the English hoe is after all somewhat fanciful and has been greatly overworked. A pioneer wrote: "There was no talke, no hope, nor worke, but dig gold. Such bru[i]te of gold, as one mad fellow desired to bee buried in the sandes, least they should by their art make gold of his bones." Surprisingly enough, this auriferous wail came not from one of Cortés' gold-seeking Spaniards, but from one of John Smith's Virginia home builders.

interest in the work of the Protestant missionaries in the "Westward Movement," Bolton suggested that he might find more materials and fuller help from Turner at Harvard. Goodykoontz went eastward, but with great admiration for Bolton and enthusiasm for his "continental" approach to American history. In 1916 he wrote that Samuel Eliot Morison, whose course on colonial America he was following and who, incidentally, was one of the Harvard dons who understood and appreciated what Bolton was trying to do for American history, had devoted two or three lectures to Spain in America. Goodykoontz also added that he had been invited to lecture in Morison's class and noted, almost with a chuckle, that "at least one class of Harvard students has heard of Kino, De León and Massanet, Aguayo, St. Denis, and other worthies."

The reason for such teaching is not far to seek. It was the inevitable result of writing United States history in isolation, apart from its setting in the history of the entire Western Hemisphere, of which the United States are but a part. It was the logical corollary of restricting the study of American history to the region between the forty-ninth parallel and the Gulf of Mexico, as though that area were an inclusive and exclusive entity, and were synonymous with America.

With a vision limited by the Rio Grande, and noting that Spain's outposts within the area now embraced in the United States were slender, and that these fringes eventually fell into the hands of the Anglo-Americans, writers concluded that Spain did not really colonize, and that, after all, she failed. The fallacy came, of course, from mistaking the tail for the dog, and then leaving the dog out of the picture. The real Spanish America, the dog, lay between the Rio Grande and Buenos Aires. The part of the animal lying north of the Rio Grande was only the tail. Let us first glance at the dog.

America was the gift of Spain and Portugal to Europe. These nations followed the discovery with a brilliant era of exploration on sea and on land. In fifty years the sons of Iberia taught the world the most stupendous geography lesson it has ever had in any half century of recorded history. For this exploratory achievement Spain and Portugal have had their due meed of praise. But here full appreciation generally ends. Few realize that, compared with their work of colonization, these epic explorations were but a minor part of what the two little nations of the Peninsula contributed to the making of the Western Hemisphere.

Surely, explorers did not build Mexico City and Lima. Surely, wild-eyed gold seekers did not found the universities of Mexico and Córdova. The old nursery tale of mere explorers must have been a myth, along with Santa Claus. Spain and Portugal followed exploration by colonization. Only a small fraction of their pioneers in America spent their time running round the map. The vast majority were merchants, planters, ranchers, soldiers, priests, and miners. Settlement by them was so rapid, so extensive, and so effective, that two-thirds of America are still Spanish and Portuguese today. The late comers, France, Holland, England, and Russia, found the ground preëmpted, and had to be content with the left-over areas and the disputed borderlands to the north—the remaining one-third.

Spain's colonies expanded by a series of frontiers, each with its own peculiar character, and each making its own contribution to American civilization. The first step in the long and steady process was the occupation of the West Indies. Here was the Mother of America. Here Spain founded tropical plantations, a strategic outpost, a commercial focus, and a base for expansion. Here she first coped with the difficult problem of native labor. Hither she transplanted the elements of her civilization before advancing to the mainland. Havana, Santo Domingo, and San Juan are symbols of the results. Columbus wrote from Isabella that although his men sickened and died, the sugar cane that he planted took root. The gigantic sugar interests of Cuba in 1929 are lineal descendants of the forty Spanish sugar mills that were being erected there in 1520.

South America was Spain's widest field of Western Hemisphere activity. From the islands colonization advanced to the Isthmus, thence south to Peru. Here the conquest was followed by permanent settlement. Spanish institutions were set up—government, cities, haciendas, churches, monasteries, and schools. The University of Lima was founded in 1551. It was no great affair in the beginning, perhaps, but neither was Harvard ninety years later, when it graduated its first class of nine pupils of about high school grade. Lima became the metropolis of the Southern Continent.

Then came Peru's mining boom. Potosí, in upper Peru (now Bolivia), became the richest mining center in the world. In 1581 it had a population of 120,000. Its wealth was astounding. This city alone spent $8,000,000 on the celebration of Philip II's accession to the throne (1556). A dead emperor was worth less than a live king. Nevertheless, three years later Potosí spent $140,000 on Charles V's funeral obsequies. Prior to 1593 the Potosí mines had paid the royal fifth on $396,000,000 worth of silver. Nor was this status fleeting.

Half a century later Potosí was still going strong, and in 1642 its citizens had $42,000,000 in cash and jewels tucked away in the local safe deposits.

Other South American areas tell a similar story. On the northern shoreline, the Spanish Main as the English called it, trading and pearl fishing stations grew into strong-walled cities. Cartagena was the home of San Pedro Claver, "sublime Apostle of the Negroes," a forerunner of Wilberforce. Farther south, Bogotá became a center of culture which still prides itself on its literary taste and its pure Castilian speech and stock. It is enough to add that in Colombia the celebrated *Varones Ilustres* was written in the sixteenth century, and that at Bogotá was operated the first astronomical observatory in America.

The conquest of Chile inspired and one of its conquerors wrote *La Araucana*, one of the great epics of all literature of all time. Here the pioneers built Santiago, and made it a Pacific Coast center of industry and culture and the seat of a great university.

The La Plata Basin was somewhat slower to develop, yet there also European civilization got a permanent hold. Early efforts to colonize the mouth of the great river were upset by the pull of Peru. Colonists planted at Buenos Aires were enticed away by the call of Bolivian silver. So Asunción, a thousand miles inland, and not Buenos Aires, became the first metropolis of the La Plata. Irala the founder hastened the process by encouraging intermarriage with the natives, setting a generous example by taking unto himself seven daughters of a powerful chief—potential oil queens they would be now.

But the broad-bosomed river and the waving pampas eventually had their way. Civilization reversed its course, and traveled down stream. Córdova, founded in a community of cowboys, became the seat of a university that has been distinguished ever since the seventeenth century. Buenos Aires, refounded in 1580, came to stay, and to grow with its two million inhabitants into the Paris of the Western Hemisphere.

The Portuguese had not been idle. The vast littoral of Brazil was carved into feudal baronies called *capitanías*. Sao Paulo, Pernambuco, Bahía and Rio de Janeiro became nuclei of European society in the sixteenth century. There, as in Spanish America, plantations, churches, monasteries, schools, and colleges were built; there poets, historians, and men of science lived and wrote. There were laid the foundations of what is now the second power in the Western Hemisphere.

In North America the Spanish pioneers were first attracted from the islands to the area occupied by the sedentary peoples. Mayas and Nahuas were brought under control, Spanish institutions were set up, and a large Spanish colony made this part of America their permanent home. Yes, Spaniards built homes. Alvarado's mansion, dating from 1524, is still a home of luxury in Coyoacán. Cortés by his will declared himself an American, and ordered that his own bones and those of all his family should return to America for eternal rest.

Here as elsewhere the Spaniards built up more than they tore down. They founded cities that still endure. They built churches, monasteries, and country mansions, on every hand. The University of Mexico was founded in 1551, simultaneously with that of Lima, and ere long its graduates were given postgraduate standing, without reduction of units or grade points, in the universities of Europe. Mexico City became the metropolis of European life and culture in all North America, a rank which it retained till near the end of the eighteenth century. In the days of the Inquisition and witch burning, not Cotton Mather of Boston, perhaps, but Sigüenza of Mexico City, was the first man of learning in the Western Hemisphere.

When the Englishman Thomas Gage visited the Aztec capital in the seventeenth century he was impressed by its wealth and refinement, and especially by the number of its coaches. In his book he tells us, "It is a byword that at Mexico there are four things fair, that is to say, the women, the apparel, the horses, and the streets. But to this I may add the beauty of some of the coaches of the Gentry, which do exceed in cost the best of the Court of Madrid and other parts of Christendom, for they spare no Silver, nor Gold, nor the best silks from China to enrich them. And to the gallantry of their horses the pride of some doth add the cost of bridles and shoes of silver." He adds, "It was a most credible report that in Mexico in my time there were above fifteen thousand Coaches," many, if not most of them, made in the same city.

Two decades were consumed in bringing Central America and southern Mexico under control. This was not a period of mining, but of agricultural and commercial economy, based on the exploitation of native labor. Then great mineral veins were discovered in the central Mexican plateau. Mining rushes followed. Spanish gold was mainly silver, and millions of this metal poured into the Spanish treasury. It was these mines and those of South America that gave Charles V and Philip II their brilliant position in Europe. By the end of the sixteenth century all the great central plateau of Mexico had been colonized at strategic points. It was a mining society, and such it has remained in many of its essential characteristics to this day. There were "strikes," "rushes," and "boom towns," the prototypes of all later ones all the way from Mexico to Alaska. Mining camps became cities; the cities became the nuclei of new provinces, and now they are capitals of states. Zacatecas, Guanajuato, Durango, Saltillo, Mazapil and Monterey, all founded in the sixteenth century, were not the work of mere explorers, but of permanent settlers and commonwealth builders, whose descendants still guide the destinies of the communities which these pioneers founded.

Beyond the mining frontier in northern Mexico, settlement edged slowly forward in the decades that followed. In Coahuila, Chihuahua, and Sonora, miners, soldiers, missionaries, and cattlemen pushed their outposts just about to the present boundary between the United States and Mexico. With minor exceptions that boundary represents roughly the northern line of Spain's effective colonization.

Thus, by the end of the sixteenth century two-thirds of America had been staked out with permanent centers of Spanish and Portuguese life, and this in the face of a mountain and desert geography which would have dismayed a people unused to mountains and deserts at home. This takes no account of areas explored, or of defensive salients that had been thrust out beyond the settled borders. The area then marked out for Hispanic America was almost the same as the area that is still Hispanic. What it lacked was added by the slow advance of the northern frontier in the seventeenth century, bringing the line of effective colonization up to the Rio Grande. The map of Hispanic America then was strikingly as it is today.

Within all that vast area, from El Paso to Buenos Aires, Hispanic American civilization continued to develop. Cities grew, commerce expanded, new mines were opened, herds grew larger, more plantations were tilled. By the end of the eighteenth century the Spanish population in America was three or four millions, and the Portuguese a million or more.[1]

And yet we say that Spain failed. But Spain and Portugal lost their colonies, some one reminds us. Yes, and so did England lose the best of hers. And the revolt of the colonies was the very best evidence of the real success of the mother countries in building up American commonwealths. Every worth-while child, when he reaches majority, sets up for himself, or at least he makes clear his ability to do so if he chooses. Anything else is a family tragedy. England raised up lusty children. Thirteen out of some thirty of them (not precisely the original thirteen) were vigorous enough to separate from the mother country and go it alone. The outcome was the United States. Spain and Portugal planted colonies, scattered over a vastly wider area than England's children. They, too, became lusty. They, too, set up housekeeping for themselves. The outcome is a score of Hispanic American nations today. Washington and his associates merely started the American Revolution; Miranda, Bolívar, San Martín, Hidalgo, Morelos, and Iturbide carried it through. England's loss of her colonies was the real mark of her success as a colonizer. By the same token, Spain's loss of her colonies was the best evidence of her success in transplanting people and civilization. Greater Spain is over here, and what a proud old mother Spain should be. Greater Portugal is over here—Brazil—and what

[1] This does not include the vastly larger native population.

a proud little old mother Portugal should be. We even trust that Mother England does not look with disdain on her grown-up children over here.

So much for the dog; now for the tail. Away up here in the Far North, thousands of miles from the Spansh centers at Mexico City, Guatemala, Bogotá, Santiago, and Buenos Aires, lay the northern fringes of the Spanish Empire—the northern borderlands. Outposts they were, but what a history they have had!

In the early years of the conquest this northern interior was a land of hope, concealing perhaps another Mexico or another Peru. It was a wonderland of romance, filled with figments of the imagination, suggested by misunderstood or jocose tales told by Indians who had a sense of humor, or who wished to pass their white visitors along.

On the Atlantic Coast, in the vast region called La Florida, there was the Fountain of Youth;[2] Cale, whose warriors wore golden helmets; Chicora, now Carolina, land of the giant King Datha. This monarch was not naturally monstrous, but in his youth he merely had been rubbed with grease and stretched. In his kingdom, too, there was a species of deer which generously fed the inhahitants on milk, thus absolving them from the primal curse of labor. There was the Queen of Cufitachiqui, land of pearls. Somewhere in the South Carolina Piedmont there was fabulous Diamond Mountain, and if you didn't believe it you could ask Sir Francis Drake.

In the west lay Gran Quivira, land whose ruler was lulled to sleep by golden bells, and whose borders were bathed by a stream in which swam fish as big as horses. Near Quivira lay Gran Teguayo and the Kingdom of the Texas. Still farther west were the Seven Cities of Cíbola, whose many-storied towns had turquoise-studded doors. Somewhere beyond the Colorado were people who lived under water; another tribe who sat in the shade of their own generous-sized ears; and still other people who did not eat their food,

[2] Not alone Spanish fancy ran astray here. Laudonnière, the Frenchman, went Ponce de León one better, for one of his scouts actually saw and conversed with men who had drunk at the Fountain of Youth, and had already comfortably passed their two hundred and fiftieth birthdays.

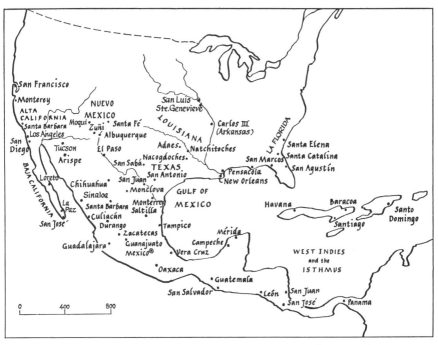

Adapted from Herbert Eugene Bolton, *History of the Americas* (new edition), 159

New Spain, 1492–1800

but lived on smells. Finally, on the western coast there were islands bearing pearls, and another whose only metal was gold; there was the Amazon Queen, the California lady with the enormous feet; and, last of these western "monstrosities," as the chronicler called them, a race of bald-headed men. Father Escobar, to whom the Indian wag recounted these wonders of the West, had a lovable human urge to believe in them. Wrong-headed persons might doubt such tales, he said, but, he reminded all such that "for any one who will consider the wonders which God constantly does perform in this world, it will be easy to believe that since he is able to create these he may have done so."

Then there were geographical notions, the offspring of a desire to get quickly to India. America tapered down toward the north like an inverted radish and brought the oceans close together. From the St. Lawrence River, or from Chesapeake Bay, a strait led to a great inland sea, or better, from ocean to ocean. Somewhere west of the upper Rio Grande the desert concealed a lake of gold, fabulous turquoise mines, and the smoke-hued Sierra Azul. And there was the north branch of the Colorado River, a second outlet, which, turning west across Nevada, merrily threaded its way through the high Sierras of California, and meandered to the ocean somewhere near San Francisco Bay.

So long as they remained untested by hard and disappointing experience, all these wonders were incentives to heroic endeavor. It was to pierce this Northern Mystery and test these tales that epic jaunts were made by eager-eyed adventurers. Under other names, these borderlands had their Columbus, their Lindbergh, their Commander Byrd.

This was "earth's high holiday." Romance was here.

> "He does not guess, the quiet-eyed
> As he goes by in his young pride,
> Who rode beside! Who rode beside!"

Not alone Lancelot, and Galahad, and Arthur, and the Maid, rode beside Lindbergh that day in May two years ago. With him were Narváez, De Soto, Cabrillo, and Coronado, too, and many another "who dared his own wild dreams to try" in these Spanish Borderlands.

Like apparitions, Narváez and De Soto flitted through the vast region called La Florida, only to find watery graves. Coronado sought wealth and fame in Gran Quivira, and returned to Mexico a broken man. Cabrillo, trusting his fate to the South Sea waves, was lured to his death by the California Lorelei. These bold adventurers gained little wealth, but their heroic marches were by no means idle jaunts or wild-goose chases. They quieted for a time the extravagant tales of great cities in the north, and taught Europe an important lesson in American geography. Each tortuous line which they left on the sixteenth century map stands for some rumor run to its lair.

Twenty years of trial put most of the yarns to rest for the nonce, and the adventurers settled back on the established frontier.

Sixteenth century Spanish expansion, with minor exceptions, had been mainly economic and missionary in its urge. Settled Indians to exploit or convert, tropical plantations, mines, stock ranches, and commerce had been the lodestones leading to new frontiers. But already another factor had entered into the process—a force which became increasingly important with the passage of time, until it became the primary motive to further Spanish advance to new areas. This factor was defense. With the exception of New Mexico, Spanish colonization in the northern borderlands was primarily defensive in its origin. In the advance into these regions missionary work was always conspicuous and important. But in the order of urgency Missions here occupied a second place, and were a means to the primary end.

The rest of Europe looked with envious eyes on Spain's monopoly in the Western Hemisphere, and registered protests. In South America Spain suffered the persistent inroads of the Portuguese from Brazil. Papal bulls and a treaty established a Line of Demarcation. Brazilian slave hunters snapped their fingers at both Pope and treaty. They raided Indian villages beyond the line, and drove back chain gangs of captives for the sugar plantations. Jesuit missionaries were sent to hold the outraged Spanish border. In reply the Brazilians stormed defenseless missions and carried off trembling neophytes. Behind these Mameluke slavers Portuguese settlers followed. On the Brazilian border Spain's frontiers gradually yielded. The Line of Demarcation was sadly bent, until it came to resemble a bow, with the old papal line as the string. And so it stands today.

On her northernmost borders Spain suffered the onslaughts of French, Dutch, English, and Russians, not all at once, but in successive clashes. Most of her expansive energy north of the Gulf and the Rio Grande was expended to meet these incursions. One by one, as occasion required, defensive salients were thrust out, like men moved forward on a checkerboard to counter the plays of an aggressive opponent.

Economic in its origin, Spain's Caribbean outpost became more and more defensive. French, English, and Dutch pirates raided treasure fleets and sacked towns. Spain replied by building walls around her coast cities, and policing the Caribbean with a naval fleet—the Armada de Barlovento.

Fifty years of prospecting and rainbow chasing in La Florida (the Atlantic mainland) proved profitless to promoters and painful to many broken heads. Philip had just decided to leave La Florida to hostile Creeks and hellish hurricanes, when French intrusion forced his hand. Ribaut occupied Port Royal, and Laudonnière settled near the site of Jacksonville. Now came Menéndez with a will strong enough to destroy the French, and a force adequate to defend the threatened coast. The awful slaughter at the French fort has echoed to the twentieth century. But the Peninsula was permanently occupied, outposts of defense were thrust up the coast to Port Royal, and momentarily even to Chesapeake Bay.

The New Mexico salient was only partially defensive in origin, but it was foreign danger that finally nerved Spain to take the cold plunge into the distant wilderness. Coronado found Cíbola disappointing. What to Friar Marcos had appeared a jeweled city, looked through the soldier's gold-rimmed spectacles like a crowded little village "crumpled all up together." Cíbola yielded no gold, the conqueror had a young bride at home, so to Mexico he returned. But time and distance encouraged new flights of fancy. From the resemblance of the Pueblos to the Aztec dwellings the region came to be called New Mexico. It was after all the "Otro México" which so many had sought. There were settled Indians to convert, and foreign danger lurked in the background. Beyond the Pueblos lay the Strait of Anian, whose western extremity the pirate Drake now claimed to have found. New Mexico therefore offered an opportunity to spread the Faith, exploit Indian labor, and protect the Empire. Ten years were spent in indecision. Then the defeat of the Armada gave the final scare, and New Mexico was colonized.

Now, like an athlete, gathering force for a mighty spring, the frontier of settlement leaped eight hundred miles into the wilderness, from southern Chihuahua to the upper Rio Grande. Thither

Oñate led his colony with paternal care. Eighty wagons creaked their lumbering way across the grim, wide desert, and seven thousand head of stock kicked up the dust over a trail miles in width. In the narrow but well-watered Rio Grande Valley the colonists settled among the Pueblo Indians. Friars built missions, soldiers warded off attacks of relentless Apaches, and civilians founded a semi-pastoral society. For two hundred and fifty years Santa Fé stood like a sentinel on the very rim of European civilization.

Another foreign head to crack popped up on the Texas horizon. Eager Franciscans, looking across the Rio Grande at the great "Kingdom of the Texas," had urged the king on. But he had no funds. Why must Spain be hurried? She was on the way; give her time and she would arrive. Ten thousand miles of actual settlements already gave her quite enough trouble and care. Then La Salle's colony intruded. Presto! Carlos roused himself, found money in another pocket, and hurried soldiers and missionaries to the border to hold the threatened land. Massanet, devout friar, and De León, seasoned Indian fighter, joined hands in defense of the realm. The French danger momentarily subsided and Texas was abandoned, only to be reoccupied when France founded Louisiana and split the Spanish Borderlands in two. Now a stronger colony was sent to the eastern Piney Woods. Los Adaes became the outpost against the French at Natchitoches. San Antonio, planted as a half-way base, became a superb missionary center, where no less than nine missions sooner or later dotted the banks of the one little San Antonio River.

For half a century Los Adaes guarded the French border; then Louisiana was ceded to Spain. There was no French danger now. "Todos somos Españoles," De Mézières told the Indians. "We are now all Spaniards." Forthwith, soldiers and missionaries, by government fiat, abandoned the border, though a few colonists held on. San Antonio, Nacogdoches, and lesser settlements had taken root and they continued to survive. These defensive outposts had held Texas for Spain against French inroads, and they made Jefferson's later claim to Texas as a part of Louisiana historically unsound.

The Louisiana cession hurled Spain from the frying pan into the fire. A small ill on the Red River was swapped for a mortal danger on the Mississippi. France had long held the Great Valley. But now the Lily came down before the Union Jack. With Canada the eastern half of the Valley went to Britain, but the western half was ceded to Spain to save it from a similar fate. To Carlos III, the energetic Spanish king, the gift looked like a White Elephant. What could Spain do with it? With settlements extending from Santa Fé to Buenos Aires she was already land poor. But arguments had no weight in the case. Louisiana, like another baby, had arrived, and must be cared for. Spain must occupy the province or the oncoming English would seize it. They had invaded Georgia and made their title good by force. In the late war they had taken Florida, too. Their buckskin-shirted pioneers were pushing over the Alleghenies, and even crossing the Father of Waters. Soon they would invade Texas, and endanger the heart of Mexico. Perhaps not all these advancing frontiersmen were quite so fear-inspiring as Mike Fink. This boastful specimen said of himself, "I can outrun, outhop, throw down, drag out, and lick any man in the country. I'm a Salt River Roarer, I am. I love the Wimming, and I'm chock full of fight."

So, reluctantly Carlos III took hold of the vast region called Louisiana, before too many Mike Finks should arrive. The French inhabitants, mourning for the tri-color, started a revolution, but Don Alejandro O'Reilly gave his firing squad a little target practice and Spain was in the saddle. The East Texas military frontier was now abandoned. Defense was concentrated on the Mississippi, and soon there was a line of posts extending from New Orleans to St. Louis.

Louisiana was not Charles III's only frontier problem. Simultaneously another arose on the Pacific Coast. Spain had long talked of advancing her settlements to Alta California. Lower California and Pimería Alta (southern Arizona) had been occupied at the end of the seventeenth century. Vizcaíno had chased elk in Carmel Valley and boosted the "fine harbor of Monterey." Zealous friars painted in glowing colors the missionary field awaiting them in the populous towns along the Santa Barbara Channel. If only the king would help, what a harvest they would reap! But there was a vast desert gap to cross, and the king always had more pressing tasks in other corners of the hemisphere. So California waited until an emergency arose.

That emergency came when Russia threatened to extend her settlements from Alaska down the Pacific Coast. Carlos III was not a man who temporized, and he proceeded to occupy Alta California. Square-jawed Gálvez organized the expedition. Its immediate purpose was to hold the harbor of Monterey, for the Golden Gate and San Francisco Bay had not yet been discovered. In command of the enterprise went Portolá. At the head of the immortal missionary band was Junípero Serra, a man remarkable among all pioneers in American history.

With vigor the plan was put into execution. San Diego was occupied as a half-way base in the summer of 1769; a year later the flag of Spain floated over Monterey Bay. Between these two strategic points a celebrated chain of missions was begun. Meanwhile Portolá discovered the Golden Gate and San Francisco Bay. Anza now opened a land route from Sonora, and a year later, in a superb feat of frontiering, he led over the same trail a colony of two hundred and forty persons to found San Francisco, on what Father Font, the diarist, called "that prodigy of nature . . . the harbor of harbors."

The Russian lever had raised the Spanish frontier one long notch; the ubiquitous English now gave it another hoist. British traders began to swarm the waters of the North Pacific. Thereupon Spain extended California even to Nootka Sound (now in British Columbia), establishing there a slender presidio and a little mission. But England shook her fist, the cards were stacked against Spain, and she withdrew to San Francisco.

Outposts so scattered called for lines of communication. Men who dared were not lacking, and Spain's frontiersmen, under the direction of the great viceroy Bucareli, proceeded to tie the border provinces together. The pathfinding energy displayed in the last quarter of the eighteenth century was scarcely less vigorous than that of the golden days of the sixteenth. Level-headed Anza had opened a route from Sonora to California. Santa Fé now became the hub of long exploratory spokes thrust out to connect the new outposts with the old. Fearless Garcés, prince of lonely wanderers, showed a way from Santa Fé to Los Angeles. Escalante, on a similar mission, made his prodigious odyssey of two thousand miles from Santa Fé through Colorado, Utah, and Arizona and back to Santa Fé. De Mézières, Vial, and their associates, blazed communication lines connecting Santa Fé with San Antonio, Natchitoches, and St. Louis. Finally, in an effort to connect Louisiana with Spain's Nootka settlement, men sent out from St. Louis ascended the Missouri River as far as the Yellowstone.

Santa Fé became more than ever a strategic outpost, but now chiefly against the Indians. Competent Anza, called to hold the New Mexico border, ascended San Luis Valley, descended the Arkansas River, somewhere in the Greenhorn Mountains met the valiant Comanche chief Cuerno Verde (hence the name Greenhorn), and proved himself to be one of the best Indian fighters who ever battled in Colorado.

Anyone who proposes to talk of Spain's decadence in the eighteenth century should first study the superb corps of men operating in her northern provinces and the defensive program which they carried through with slender resources after the Seven Years' War.

All these salients—La Florida, Texas, Louisiana, and California—in origin were defensive outposts, and so they were regarded by Spain. To hold them she utilized especially her two typical frontier institutions, the presidio and the mission.

The presidio was a soldier garrison. It might be composed of ten men or of two hundred, according to the need. Its function was to give military protection to its district, sending out detachments here, there, and yonder, scouting, chasing Indians, ejecting intruders. Temporary garrisons might occupy the merest shacks for barracks. Important and permanent presidios were provided with fortifications. The most substantial of all the northern line was that at St. Augustine. Presidios, temporary or permanent, were scattered all along the frontier of New Spain. Port Royal, San Agustín, Apalache, Pensacola, New Orleans, the Arkansas Post, St. Louis, Natchitoches, Los Adaes, San Antonio, La Bahía, San Sabá, San

Juan Bautista, Ojinaga, El Paso, Santa Fé, Janos, Tubac, Tucson, Altar, and the four in Alta California—San Diego, Santa Barbara, Monterey, and San Francisco—were the more notable of the presidios of the northern borderlands. But numerous other points, all the way from Georgia to San Francisco, were occupied for greater or lesser periods, as occasion demanded.

Beside the presidial soldier went the missionary. The mission was *par excellence* a frontier institution. The missionary was an agent not only of the Church, but of the State as well. His primary business was to save souls and spread Spanish civilization among the heathen. The heathen were to be found on the frontier, beyond the established settlements. Here was the missionary's proper field of endeavor. As soon as his pioneer work among the Indians on one frontier was done, he was expected to turn his flock over to the parish clergy and move on to a new field, farther in the wilderness.

Theoretically at least, the State was just as anxious as the Church to Christianize and civilize the heathen. But it cost money to run Indian schools (for such the missions were) and the king's money had to be spent where it was most needed. Missionary fields were unlimited, and the friars were always pulling at the rein. Not all the demands made on the royal treasury could be satisfied. Those most urgent first got attention. On the frontiers endangered by foreign foes there was a double need. Soldiers sent there could both keep out Europeans and protect the missions. Many times the sovereigns had to turn deaf ears to missionary appeals for funds and permission to go to work among outlying tribes. But when political danger coincided with missionary opportunity, the friars had their way. Then they went beside the soldier to help hold the endangered frontier for Spain, at the same time that they saved souls and spread Spanish civilization.

In fact, the friars often cleverly turned foreign danger to their own account. They saw on some international border a tribe outside the Christian fold. They begged for funds and permission to go. Neither was forthcoming. Then a rumor was heard of impending foreign aggression. Stationed on the frontier, and first to hear the rumors, the friars reported them to the viceroy. They wielded good pens, and their words carried weight. The outcome, often, was a new defensive advance of soldier and missionary to hold the border against a threatening European neighbor.

Father Hidalgo was a good example. He had been in East Texas, but with the rest of the friars had retreated to the Rio Grande. His heart yearned for his Texans. Again and again he begged for permission to return to them, but his superiors refused. Then the French played into his hands. They had founded Louisiana. If he could wave a French flag before the viceroy's eyes things would move. So he wrote a cryptic letter to the missionaries of Louisiana. It fell into the hands of Cadillac, the governor. Cadillac wanted trade with the Spaniards, and here was a chance. So he sent St. Denis, his ablest frontiersman, to confer with Father Hidalgo, and see what he could see. St. Denis crossed Louisiana and Texas, traveling nearly a thousand miles, to find the friar. When he reached the Rio Grande Hidalgo had returned to Mexico. But his associates there saw the significance of what had happened. Three of them wrote him in words to the same effect:—

"Albricias, Padre! Reward me for great news! The French are here! Now your dreams will come true! Now you will be sent back to your beloved Texans." And sent he was. It was now that East Texas was permanently occupied to keep back the French, and Father Hidalgo was among the defenders of the border.

The soldier and the missionary were the primary agencies by which defensive expansion was effected. It was all the better if civil settlers could be had, to supplement the work of the leather-jacket and the friar. So small civil colonies generally were added. Such a colony went to San Agustín, another to Santa Fé, another to San Antonio, and still others to California. The presidio and mission became nuclei around which ranchers settled on generous land grants. Retired presidial soldiers generally became settlers in the vicinity of their posts. Roman history was repeated here.

Thus these slender defensive and missionary outposts took root in the soil. As a result, nearly every stable presidio, and many missions, slowly grew into permanent settlements. Most of the old Spanish towns in the borderlands, like St. Augustine, San Antonio, Tucson, San Diego, Los Angeles, Santa Barbara, Monterey, and San Francisco have grown from small beginnings as presidios or missions or both.

Such in brief is what the borderlands were, as viewed from the standpoint of the Spanish Empire. In Madrid, in Lima, in Buenos Aires, in Mexico, they were regarded as defensive and missionary fringes. The real Spanish America lay to the south of them.

Having established these defensive salients, Spain was hard put to it to retain them. International in origin, they continued to be international in significance. As the English frontier moved westward, the Anglo-Spanish borders overlapped in a succession of areas, and one by one a series of conflicts resulted—in the Caribbean, in Georgia and Florida, in Louisiana, in Texas, in New Mexico, in California. The Anglo-American advance stopped in each case when it reached the line of effective colonization. It was the borderlands and the borderlands mainly which Spain lost to England and the United States. We have witnessed Spain's rising tide on the border; we may now follow it as it ebbs. I hold no brief for any side in the long series of contests. To the historian it is not a matter of right and wrong, but just a human tale. He should watch and try to understand the drama.

On the Caribbean fringe the English colonized some of Spain's neglected islands, and conquered Jamaica. To the English at Charleston, Guale (Spanish Georgia) was a challenge. Finding themselves "in the very chaps of the Spaniards," they proceeded on the motto, *Guale delenda est*. The Mamelucos of Brazil were emulated now by the Carolina hunters of Indian slaves. They destroyed the missions and carried off the neophytes to work on plantations. Ex-governor Moore in one campaign destroyed thirteen Apalache missions, burned Fathers Parga and Miranda at the stake, and carried off fourteen hundred neophytes as prisoners. Oglethorpe's Georgia Colony was founded more as a buffer against the Spaniards than as a philanthropic enterprise. Spain contested these inroads, but in the

Seven Years' War she was forced to give way, losing both Georgia and Florida.

At the same time, by the gift of Louisiana, Spain acquired a long frontage against the English on the Mississippi. Anglo-Americans now poured over the mountains into Kentucky and Tennessee. In the Floridas British traders, like Lachlan McGillivray, married the dusky daughters, and thus cemented their hold on the tribes. Little checked by the legal boundary, long-hunters and horse drovers began to cross into Louisiana.

During the Revolution Spain aided the American colonies against England and recovered Florida, much reduced now by the loss of the Georgia part, but increased by the scrap of old French territory which England had erected into West Florida.

By aiding the American Revolution, Spain had hastened the growth of an aggressive neighbor. Through her recovery of the Floridas, she had merely increased her burdens, by lengthening the line which she must defend. All the way from Amelia Island to Minnesota now the Anglo-Americans intruded. Having recovered Florida, Spain essayed to maintain its extreme boundaries. She denied the validity of a treaty to which she was not a party. She utilized British traders to offset the Americans. She closed the Mississippi to American commerce. She entered into intrigues with Kentuckians and Tennesseeans, offering trade in return for favors. She established a garrison in the Chickasaw country to hold the line of the Tennessee. She tried building up a buffer state, by counter-colonizing Florida and Louisiana, even coaxing in Americans, in the vain hope that they would hold back their brothers and cousins. But it was all to no avail. Spain was operating too far from her base, and in the Pinckney treaty she finally yielded the disputed area.

It is absurd to regard the outcome of this contest as merely an index of the relative strength of two civilizations, as some have done. It reveals rather the advantage of an expanding economic frontier working from an immediate base, over a defensive frontier operating at long distance from the centers of resources and population. The Anglo-American lever had a long power arm and a short weight arm; the Spanish government operated with the weight too far from the fulcrum. If the interests at stake and the distances of the contested area from the population centers had been reversed, the story would doubtless have been different.

Now the shadow of the Corsican crept over the Mississippi Valley. Napoleon unceremoniously took Louisiana out of Spanish hands. Spain was humiliated, of course, but at Madrid there was a sigh of relief at the thought of letting France be the buffer against the Frankenstein which Spain had helped to bring into existence. Then something else happened. Instead of taking charge of Louisiana himself, Napoleon sold it to the United States. The Little Corporal, for his own purposes, had shoved the American frontier one long notch nearer to the heart of Mexico.

Doggedly Spain held on. She had colonized Texas in the eighteenth century to keep the French out. She now recolonized it to keep the more feared Americans out. Adaes, the old Texas capital, was reoccupied. Garrisons or small colonies were distributed along the Camino Real from San Antonio to Adaes, on the Lower Trinity, and on the Gulf Coast. From San Antonio and from Santa Fé scouting parties went forth to work with renewed vigor among the Indians of the plains, to hold them in line against the oncoming Gringoes. Jefferson's Red River explorers were driven back. Melgares rode across the plains and defiantly ran up the Spanish flag at a Pawnee village. Withdrawing with Fabian tactics, he welcomed Pike at Santa Fé and took him a prisoner to Chihuahua.

Spain stubbornly contested Jefferson's boundary claims. The American president cast his eye over the map. Then, on every uncertain border he loyally gave his own country the benefit of the doubt. He claimed West Florida as a part of old French Louisiana, which it was; he claimed Texas as a part of old French Louisiana, which it was not, for Spain had occupied it for over a century. Jefferson even suggested that the Oregon Country might be a part of Louisiana. Such a contention could do no harm.

Diplomatic jousts followed. Napoleon was appealed to, but he refused to browbeat Spain into acquiescence in American demands. A little war on the Texas border shaved off a small slice of Spanish territory between Adaes and the Sabine River.

Then opportunity knocked at the American door. Spain's colonies rose in revolt. Hidalgo gave the Grito de Dolores. All the way from Buenos Aires to Baton Rouge the flame of revolution raged. Democracy's blood was stirred in the neighbor republic. Here was a mission. It would be glorious to spread liberty in a king-ruled country. Out of the mouths of Drake and Cromwell English and Americans had learned to talk of "Spanish tyranny." (The "Devildoms of Spain" was a later inspiration to Tennyson.) There were old scores to square. There were boundary disputes, and Spain's restrictive system made commerce with her colonies possible only by contraband. American smugglers on the Spanish borders, all the way from San Agustín to Santa Fé, and all round the rim of South America, had been thrown into Spanish dungeons.

Here was a chance. English, Irish, Scotch, Latin and nondescript Americans, encouraged by the President of the United States, in the name of liberty set up a Lone Star Republic in West Florida and an ill-starred one in East Florida. Then Madison seized West Florida to keep order and forestall England. The Grito de Dolores was echoed at San Antonio. Freedom-loving, adventure-loving, land-hungry Americans raised an army of liberation, swept Texas, and gave their lives at the Battle of the Medina.

In East Florida British influence continued. Americans encroached on Indian lands, and border troubles increased. So Jackson went in with an army. Spain, in trouble at home, her colonies in North and South America in revolt, was helpless to resist. Seeing her other colonies going, and both Floridas virtually lost, she took a price for them and legalized the title of the United States. The so-called Florida Purchase was quite as much an incident in the Spanish American Guerra de la Independencia as in the Anglo-American westward movement.

All this long border struggle availed Spain little for her immediate ends. The Wars of Independence succeeded. By 1822 most of South America, and all of Spanish North America, to Red River and the forty-second parallel, had won their independence.

The drama was now shifted from Spain to Mexico and to the region beyond Red River and the roof of the Rockies. Here the old Spanish Borderlands continued to play a leading part in inter-American relations, and more than ever they became a meeting place of two European civilizations. Mexico, less exclusive than Spain, opened a field for freer action. The thrilling tale of southwestern diplomacy, politics, and war has oft and well been told. I must limit myself here mainly to race contacts and enduring survivals.

These southwestern lands had long been a magnet to adventure and trade. The very presence of Spanish settlements rather hastened than checked the inquisitiveness of Spain's neighbors. In this way they were a cause of the very ill which they were designed to cure.

Even in early French days the Spanish outposts greatly accelerated the advance of the explorer's and trader's frontier. Everywhere in French America there were rumors of Spanish mines in the distant Southwest. Spain would be mistress of the Pacific and keep it a closed Spanish lake. She forgot that the surest way to spread the news in this old world was to whisper "Don't tell anybody." The very air of mystery bred exaggerated notions of Spanish wealth and piqued the Canadians' curiosity. Frenchmen were drawn like flies to the Spanish Borderlands. Having attracted them, Spain found difficulty in keeping them out.

Records tell of French treasure hunters way out on the New Mexico border before the end of the sixteenth century, long before Quebec was founded. From the days of Joliet and Marquette *coureurs de bois* crossed the Mississippi and headed toward Santa Fé and Coahuila. La Salle has usually been pictured as the great defender of the French against the advancing English, but he was quite as much concerned over the Spanish border far to the southwest. A prominent part of his western plan was to establish a French base on the Gulf of Mexico from which to conquer the Chihuahua mines and open a French highway across Mexico to the Pacific.

The Spanish settlements became the principal source for the French supply of horses, and from La Salle's day forward Frenchmen were drawn to the Spanish outposts, or to the Indian tribes between, to get droves of cayuses for Illinois and even for Canada. In the eighteenth century, long before the Louisiana cession to Spain, there was a veritable outburst of French energy directed toward finding a way to Santa Fé with a view to trade and prospect for mines. Several parties besides the well-known Mallet brothers succeeded in reaching their goal.

So it was with the Anglo-Americans. As they moved westward step by step from the Atlantic seaboard, they always had on their left flank a Spanish neighbor. This very Spanish presence, whether distant or less remote, was a stimulus to adventure. The Southwest was the abiding place of Romance. Adventurous Anglo-American youth, seeking the coquettish lady, hoped to find her at the end of the trail leading to Nacogdoches, to San Antonio, to Santa Fé, to Los Angeles. Returning heroes claimed to have found her. They told of dark-eyed señoritas, and of an exotic life in a foreign land, for such it was.

James Ohio Pattie, prince of braggarts, had scarcely reached New Mexico when he heroically rescued from murderous Indians the beautiful Jacova, daughter of the governor. The señorita did her part by falling head over heels in love with her gallant benefactor—so the modest Pattie tells us. Ruxton wrote a book intended to astonish stay-at-homes with mighty deeds of the American Mountain Men. There was a fandango at Taos, that gateway to New Mexico. The American beaux captured not only all the señoritas, but the señoras as well. The jealous caballeros pulled their knives. Kit Carson to the rescue! He seizes a three-legged stool, rends it limb from limb, distributes the legs, and with them, he, Dick Wootton, and LaBonté clear the room of all but the Americans and the clinging señoritas. "That's the place for me," rang the chorus back East when hot-blooded Youth read the tale.

Official explorations to the southwestern border were hastened by the presence of foreign settlements in a coveted land. Pike was sent quite as much to take a peep at New Mexico as to get topographical information about Colorado or to put his name on Pike's Peak. Jefferson, when he sent Freeman, Hunter, and Dunbar to explore Red River, was probably more interested in Natchitoches than in Red River Raft.

Southwestern trade was hastened by the presence of the Spanish settlements. On some frontiers there were none but Indians with whom to dicker. In the Southwest were Spaniards, too. If commerce could be only clandestine, the challenge merely piqued the more. Way back in the eighteenth century Anglo-Americans took up the southwestern horse and mule trade. Before the Revolution, Virginians, among them Governor Patrick Henry, obtained Spanish horses through the Pawnee Indians, or bought better stock directly from the Spanish provinces. Daniel Boone, falling for a moment from his high estate as long-hunter and scout, once at least gave "bar" and Indian "varmint" a respite while he conducted a drove of Spanish horses from Louisiana to Georgia. Philip Nolan, commonly called filibuster, was primarily horse drover, operating between the Rio Grande and the American settlements east of the Mississippi. Sometimes the stock driven by these traders was legally purchased, sometimes it was captured wild; quite as often it was stolen from the Spaniards by Indian middlemen, or by the traders themselves.

Long-haired Americans covered wide spaces to smuggle goods into New Orleans, San Antonio, and Saltillo. Santa Fé was an objective to traders long before the uninhabited stretches lying between it and St. Louis. Pike, released from Chihuahua, was a returned Marco Polo, and more than one trader's hand was made to itch by his tale of New Mexico's enticing trade, and more than one mouth to water when he wrote of El Paso's thrifty vineyards, and "the finest wine ever drank in the country . . . celebrated through all the provinces." The great Santa Fé Trail was beaten wide and deep by tobacco-chewing Missourians bound for Taos, Santa Fé, Chihuahua, and Los Angeles, because there lived señoritas who coveted calicoes, and caballeros who could pay for them in mules or silver dollars.

Accelerated adventure, exploration, and trade in the Spanish

Borderlands meant an acceleration of settlement. Behind it was the mighty push of American growth. The outcome was inevitable. The vanguard spied out the land and to them it seemed good. Trappers from the hard mountain wilderness found Taos and Santa Fé comfortable places in which to settle down. To the men of Jedediah Smith, who had crossed the dreary deserts of Utah and Nevada to California, Mission San Gabriel looked like the Promised Land, and Rogers (this was Harrison), who wrote the diary, could not have smacked his lips with greater gusto at manna from Heaven than he did at the welcoming glass of "good old whiskey," and the "dinner of fish and fowl, beans, potatoes—grapes as dessert, wine, gin, and water plenty" with which he was served by the Spaniards who, though "catholicks by profession," appeared to be "gentlemen of the first class," and who surprised the good Presbyterian by allowing him full "liberty of conscience," and even patiently indulging him while he, without a flicker of a smile, tried to correct their theology and to save their souls.

No wonder that many trappers and traders remained to settle. They had found a pleasant berth. The first comers were imperceptibly absorbed into the Spanish communities. Most of the vanguard married in the country and became members of old families. We find such on every border, in Florida, in Louisiana, in Texas, in New Mexico, in Arizona. In California, long before the Mexican War, it was a customary boast of a señorita that she would marry a blue-eyed man. Hundreds made good their vow, and before the American flag arrived nearly every California town had one or more American settlers married to heiresses, with whom they acquired landed estates. It was a story not unlike that of Oklahoma in more recent times—the landed heiress then becomes the oil queen now. Florida, Louisiana, Texas, New Mexico, and California all had their influential Anglo-American settlers while the land was still a part of Spain or Mexico. Florida had her Alexander McGillivray, William Panton, and William Augustus Bowles; Louisiana her Oliver Pollock, Daniel Clark, Philip Nolan, Daniel Boone, and Moses Austin; New Mexico, her Bents and her Kit Carson; Texas her Edward Murphy, Samuel Davenport, James Dill, William Barr, and Jim Bowie; California her Abel Stearns, John A. Sutter, Henry Fitch, and Thomas O. Larkin.

These early comers to the borderlands found the back-breaking work of pioneering already done for them. Between 1841 and the Gold Rush no less than fifteen organized caravans of overland immigrants entered California to settle. They could hardly be called pioneers. They entered an established community. Although trespassers, they were given a friendly welcome. They readily obtained supplies at the missions, ranches, and towns, and often found employment to tide them over until they were permanently established. Even the Forty-niners found the Spanish ranches an important source of supply. In Texas the American migration after 1820 was so large and so rapid that it could not be thus absorbed, and in California, during the Gold Rush, the native population was soon swamped by the invading host. But New Mexico is even yet a community that is nearly half Spanish.

Thus it is that the old Spanish Borderlands were the meeting place and fusing place of two streams of European civilization, one coming from the south, the other from the north.

Slender though these Spanish outposts were, they left their mark deep on the land. The rule of Spain has passed; but her colonies have grown into independent nations. From Mexico to Chile, throughout nearly half of the Western Hemisphere, the Spanish language and Spanish institutions are still dominant. Even in the old borderlands north of the Rio Grande and the Gulf, the imprint of Spain's sway is still deep and clear. The Anglo-American commonwealths that are their heirs have received from them a heritage with which they would not willingly part. The names of four States—Florida, Colorado, Nevada, and California—are Spanish in form. Scores of rivers and mountains and other scores of towns and cities in the southern United States still bear the names of saints dear to the Spanish pioneers. Southwestern Indians yet speak Spanish in preference to English. Many towns have Spanish quarters, where the life of the old days still goes on, and where one can always hear the soft Castilian tongue. Southwestern English has been enriched by Spanish contact, and hundreds of words of Spanish origin are in current use in speech and print everywhere along the border.

Throughout these Hispanic regions now in Anglo-American hands, Spanish architecture is conspicuous. Scattered all the way from Georgia to San Francisco are the ruins of Spanish missions. Others dating from the old régime are yet well preserved and are in daily use as chapels. From belfries in Florida, Texas, New Mexico, Arizona, and California still sound bells that were cast in Old Spain. At New Orleans the Cabildo, though standing in the French Quarter, was built in Spanish days. Likewise the old cathedral there is a heritage from Spain and not from France. These Spanish survivals from the olden time have furnished the motif for a new type of architecture in Florida and the Southwest that has become one of the most distinctive American possessions. In Florida, Texas, Arizona, and California the type is dominated by mission architecture. In New Mexico it is strongly modified by that native culture which found expression in pueblo building.

There are still other marks of Spanish days on the southern border. We see them in social, religious, economic, and even in legal practices. Everywhere in the Southwest there are quaint church customs brought from Spain or Mexico by the early pioneers. At Christmas time in San Antonio one can see Los Pastores enacted. California has her Portolá festival, her rodeos, and her Mission Play. From the Spaniard the American cowboy inherited his trade, his horse, his outfit, his lingo, and his methods. Spain is stamped on our land surveys. From Sacramento to St. Augustine nearly everybody holds his acres by a title going back to Mexico or Madrid. Most of the farms, in a wide swath along the border, are divisions of famous grants which are still known by their original Spanish names. In the realm of law, principles regarding mines, water rights on streams, and the property rights of women—to mention only a few—have been retained from the Spanish régime. From our Spanish forerunners in the Southwest we got our first lessons in irrigation, that art which has become one of our primary southwestern interests.

Among the most priceless treasures of any country are its historical records and its folklore. And what a heritage in this realm was left us by the old Spanish days! Wagner collected a hundred and seventy-seven works dealing with the borderlands and printed before the end of the eighteenth century. And this does not take into account the still unpublished treasures with which the archives of Spain and Mexico abound. These monuments of the past include narratives of heroic adventure, like the expeditons of Cabeza de Vaca, De Soto, Friar Marcos, Coronado, Espejo, and Oñate; the actual diaries of the epic journeys of dauntless men, like De León, Terán, Vizcaíno, Garcés, Anza, Escalante, De Mézières, Portolá, Serra, Crespi, and Palóu. There is Villagrá's precious metrical history of the founding of New Mexico, a thrilling tale of human exploit in a desert land. There are histories of these border provinces by Padilla, Benavides, Vetancourt, Espinosa, Arricivita, Morfi, Venegas, Kino, Ortega, and Palóu. These carefully written and beautifully printed old chronicles in many instances still stand as the authoritative word on the regions with which they deal. We Anglo-Americans, with our professed advancement in historical science, have never even caught up with them, and probably never shall.

Not the least important part of our heritage has been the Hispanic appeal to the imagination. The Spanish occupation has furnished theme and color for a myriad of writers, great and small. Lomax and Dobie, Lummis and Willa Cather, Bret Harte and Espinosa have shown that these inter-American bounds have a Spain-tinged folklore as rich as that of the Scottish border embalmed by Sir Walter Scott.

Lastly, these borderlands provide the historical background to our relations with Spain and Spanish America today. Born in international exigencies, and nurtured in race contacts, these fringes have always had vast international significance. International understanding is more than half a matter of tradition and psychology, and our national repute in Latin America and Spain even now is to a very large extent a reflection of history. Correctly or incorrectly, they remember this borderland tale.

Half of our national territory was once a part of the Spanish Empire—only the fringes, it is true, but legally a part of it, just the same. The English shouldered the Spaniards out of Georgia and Florida. Napoleon, in violation of a solemn promise not to alienate it, sold to the United States the vast area called Louisiana, embracing two-thirds of the Mississippi Valley, and only tardily, grudgingly and by force of necessity did Spain acknowledge our title.

The United States took advantage of Spain's trouble with her colonies to round out her border on the Gulf of Mexico. Yielding once more to necessity, Spain ceded to the United States all her claims to Oregon and British Columbia, as a means of retaining Texas.

Americans settled in Texas with the full consent of Mexico, and by a perfectly legal process. Friction resulted, the Americans arose in revolt, set up a republic, and extended its boundary to the Rio Grande. It matters little to Mexican psychology, unless Mexicans are rightly informed, that the Americans had serious grievances. In the face of Mexican opposition Texas was annexed. The United States tried to purchase California, but Mexico was stubborn. Then purchase was made unnecessary—the soldier accomplished what settler and diplomat had left undone. The annexation of Texas eventuated in war; the price of war to Mexico was more than half her national patrimony. Then came the Gadsden Purchase, cutting off another slice, a bargain for which Mexicans still execrate Santa Anna. Finally, in 1898, the United States by means of war shook the last of the colonies from the Spanish tree, and part of them,—Puerto Rico and the Philippines—fell into our basket.

I am not pretending here to assess or even to suggest the measure of merit or blame on either side in any instance. Wherever the balance may be, it is not surprising that Mexico remembers these border episodes. Through them all South America looked on, sympathizing with Mexico in her losses and wondering how far the process would go. Other factors enter in, but in trying to understand Latin American attitude toward us, we cannot overlook the influence of the old Spanish Borderlands, as the zone of contact, the scene of a long series of conflicts, ending in territorial transfers.

Fortunately there is another side to the shield. For a drop of gall there are two drops of cordial. If these borderlands have left some unpleasant memories between two peoples, they are partly offset by the bonds of a common inheritance. The historical ties between the borderlands and Spanish America are strong and closely drawn. Our oldest traditions run back to Spain and Mexico. Our earliest heroes are also Mexico's heroes. We teach our children many of the same hero tales that they teach their children. In the beginning Florida, New Mexico, Texas, Arizona, and California were but projections of New Spain northward. Our explorers came chiefly from a Mexican base. As Spanish heroes they went to the "far north." As our heroes they came from the "far south." But their names—De Soto, Coronado, Cabrillo, De León, Oñate, Anza, Garcés, and Escalante—are the same in either case; in the books read by their children and in the books read by our children.

Our great missionary heroes are their missionary heroes—Reynoso, Benavides, Ramírez, Casañas, Massanet, Margil, Serra, and Crespi. A year ago the State of California chose two names to represent it in the hall of fame at the capitol in Washington. One name was chosen unanimously and without dissent. That one was Father Junípero Serra. He is California's acknowledged hero. He is also Spain's hero and Mexico's hero. Two decades before he came to us he came to Mexico. His first American home was the celebrated College of San Fernando. Nine years he pursued his apostolic labors in the Sierra Gorda north of Querétaro. Once he was assigned to the Apache missions in Texas, but Fate directed his course to the farther West, and instead he went to California. Serra is a link binding Spain, Mexico, and California. In Mallorca a monument commemorates him as a Spanish hero. In Washington a statute will commemorate him as a California hero. Some day there will be a statue of him in Mexico. Then these three monuments will symbolize the common heritage of Spain, Mexico, and California. And other states have other Serras, binding them likewise to Mexico and Spain.

It is we in the borderlands who have the strongest historical bonds with our Latin neighbors. We of all North Americans best know and appreciate their brilliant minds, their generous hearts, and their delicate culture. We of all North Americans most prize the unmistakable Spanish touch which our fore-runners gave our once Spanish lands. It would be only fitting if we of the borderlands should be foremost in a fair-minded study of our common historical heritage, foremost in a study of our common problems, and foremost in making closer and stronger the bonds of true international understanding.

SECTION TWO

Approaches to the Borderlands

CHAPTER THREE

*The Northward Movement in New Spain**

THE expansion of the Anglo-American frontier had been a westward movement, working from the seaboard and tidewater back toward the mountains, then through the passes into the great valley of Mid-Continent, across the Plains, beyond other giant ranges, and on to the Pacific. "Frontier" and "westward movement" for many Americans have come to be almost synonymous terms—as though there could be no frontier which did not move westward.

In North American history there were two other frontier movements, neither of which would quite fit such a definition. The Spanish expansion, for one, was a northward movement, out of the capital of New Spain or out of islands into the Borderlands. It was every bit a frontier and quite as significant as the march of the Anglos to the west. Northward from Mexico City went the conquistador explorers; the miners and the missionaries were in the next wave, advancing under the protection of the presidial garrisons, to be followed in time by the ranchers and the settlers. This frontier in the later eighteenth century became the *Provincias Internas*, and later still it was cut up into a number of States, of the U.S.A. and of the Republic of Mexico.

This approach of the Spanish frontier to the Borderlands in time developed into a three-pronged advance, with well-defined right, left, and center. Each had its own characteristics, its own problems, and its own very specific aim or goal. In the summer of 1946, Bolton was invited to Mexico to conduct a seminar at the University. The following selection is the mimeographed introductory outline which he offered to his students. It is a fine statement embodying the clear patterns which over the years emerged as he brought his

---

* Outline for a seminar given in Mexico City in the summer of 1946. A copy of this outline is preserved in the Bolton Papers, Bancroft Library, University of California at Berkeley. It is here reproduced with the permission of the Bancroft Library.

earlier "dream" into reality. His "suggested topics" have been retained from the outline, since they in their own way highlight
personalities and developments of the broader story.

Here is the mature Bolton, after years of study, research, writing,
and, as he would be the first to admit, profiting by the accumulated
findings of his students.

FOR THE WORK of this seminar I propose a study of various phases of
the northward expansion of the frontiers of New Spain, from the
base in Central Mexico, especially in the 16th, 17th, and 18th centuries. This northward movement of population in Mexico has
played a part in the nation's history analogous in many respects to
the influence of the "westward movement" which has been so vital
a factor in the development of the United States and the Dominion
of Canada. It is similarly a remarkable panorama of frontier expansion. Ever since the Spanish conquest a large area in the north of
Mexico open for development has been a spur to the initiative of
people in the more crowded areas farther south. Frederick Jackson
Turner wrote an epic monograph on the "Significance of the Frontier" in the formation of society in English North America. It would
be interesting to consider to what extent his thesis is applicable or
inapplicable to Mexico. Such an inquiry might well result in an
interpretation of the significance of frontier expansion in Mexican
history as important as Turner's brilliant monograph. Perhaps the
scholar who some day will discover and formulate such a thesis sits
before me. Who can tell?

For our program I have in mind studies of both the processes and
the influence of this northward expansion. At the same time that we
attempt to present a view of the subject in perspective, I shall suggest topics to serve as an introduction to history in the making, as an
opportunity for each student to learn the whereabouts and the nature
of materials essential for such studies, and to make his individual
contribution.

While the ultimate objective of historical investigation may be
regarded as a search for the synthetic and the general, a person who
has never put the fabric of history under a microscope and watched
the genesis of society in process will not arrive at sound generaliza-

tions with regard to its origin and significance. Facts must go before theories. No generalization can reveal more than the merest suggestion of the full richness of the pattern and substance of the fabric which become apparent when examined in detail. Thus, although the topics proposed may at first appear small, even a minute episode, if studied with care, usually is seen to be part of much larger developments, and it may expand into surprising proportions and offer unexpected interest. A slender thread may lead to the heroine's castle.

Within broad limits, members of the Seminar will be given free choice of themes. But there is an advantage if the research of each throws light upon that of his fellow workers. Added profit will result if the subject under investigation by each bears in some way on the studies of the others. As in every important academic function, here the students are the chief personalities. The professor may suggest topics for investigation, but the essential feature of the seminar is the research done by the disciples. And so, we are here to work together, each pursuing his own inquiry, but all contributing to the common purpose of a better understanding of some aspects of the history of Mexico.

GENERAL CONSIDERATIONS

The story of the evolution of the Mexican nation is inexpressibly rich and varied, with an infinity of elements—so diversified, indeed, that it calls for a genius of the first order, with vision and knowledge of sufficient breadth to enable him to form a general concept or framework comprehensive enough to embrace and unify the manifold factors which have contributed to the making of present-day Mexico in all its principal aspects—archaeological, ethnological, geographical, religious, economic, political, social, literary or artistic. Whoever performs this task with any high degree of perfection will be an extraordinary individual.

Many scholars, chiefly Mexicans of course, have contributed prodigiously toward writing the history of this marvelous country. Nevertheless there are numerous aspects of its development which have not been adequately investigated and interpreted, but which must be taken into account in any final synthesis of the historical process by which the nation has evolved. It is for this reason that much additional research is needed, and that there is opportunity for a multitude of workers. The same could be said of any imporant country. The muse of history is notable laggard.

This will always be true. Indeed, it would be too bad if there were nothing more to be done. History could cease to be of interest if it were all written, neatly put upon the shelf in labeled categories and marked as finished. Moreover, history is never static. Fresh sources of information are constantly being discovered, and improved techniques enable us better to evaluate the older data. In the light of new materials, new methods of work, and a new outlook upon society, each generation must examine the conclusions arrived at by its predecessors. In any case, it is my sincere hope that this seminar may afford each one of us the joy of performing some task that is worth the doing.

Any comprehensive synthesis of Mexican history must take into account the factors of Mexico's geology, its physiography, its climate, its natural resources, its archaeology, its native peoples—their culture, institutions, and interrelations before the European intrusion; then the shock of the European conquest, and the four centuries of contact of European and native in the Mexican environment. The panorama is vast and offers work for many brushes.

The place where these two peoples have had longest and most vital contacts has been in southern and central Mexico, in Yucatán, in Oaxaca, in and about the Central Valley, in Michoacán and adjacent areas, where the predecessors of the Spaniards had built up high civilizations before the Europeans arrived. It was here during the conquest and in succeeding decades that the European and native elements first fused their cultures and their blood. To this region Spanish people and Spanish institutions were first transplanted within the terrain that is now Mexico. Here Spaniards and natives first found themselves in close association, side by side. Here Spanish law and government were superimposed upon native institutions but never wholly eradicated them. The two elements were complementary, one slowly modifying the other. Here was formed the first New Spain and here the first New Mexico, with vital elements drawn from each of the parent stocks. Spanish law and native custom operated side by side on the same terrain. In this respect Spain was amazingly tolerant, as can be seen on many pages of the great *Recopilación de las Leyes de las Indias.*

NORTHWARD EXPANSION

Meanwhile another chapter in Mexican history was begun. Soon the area of Spanish occupation was extended northward into regions occupied by natives representing a relatively primitive society— peoples whom the Spaniards designated by the word *Chichimecos,* a term which became descriptive of non-sedentary tribes, as distinguished from the advanced native peoples of central and southern Mexico. Here the historical process was somewhat different from what it was farther south. A rapid and elementary sketch of this northward advance of the Mexican frontier may serve to indicate the field of study which I have in mind and to suggest topics for investigation. Any one of the phases or episodes which I mention will be capable of much elaboration, and will yield results which we may not even suspect at the outset. A multitude of other topics will occur to you.

Into this vast northern area the Spaniards were drawn by a variety of circumstances and in pursuit of different objectives. They made their way into the interior in three principal columns—up the East Coast Corridor, up the West Coast Corridor, and up the Central Plateau, with frequent turns from side to side. Sometimes one of these northern salients and sometimes another was farthest from the base in Central Mexico, according to the circumstances of the moment. Preliminary excursions were early made into the north country in search of some new El Dorado—Otro México, Otro Perú. But the permanent advance of the northern frontier of Spanish occupation was first effected mainly through the exploitation of the precious metals, especially silver. It was in the Mesa Central of Mexico that the first great mining rushes of North America occurred.

Each enduring center of occupation became a focus for the formation of a permanent and complex society.

The colonization of northern Mexico was directed to a large degree by two great mountain chains, the Sierra Madre Oriental, and the Sierra Madre Occidental, stupendous and difficult barriers which divide the area sharply into three distinct geographical provinces: (1) the East Coast Corridor, a wide plain lying between the eastern sierra and the Gulf of Mexico, (2) the West Coast Corridor, a narrow plain between the western Sierra Madre and the Pacific Ocean, and (3) the Central Plateau (Mesa Central) between the eastern and the western sierras. The development of the East Coast Corridor and the West Coast Corridor was greatly influenced by water communication on the one hand by way of the Gulf of Mexico and on the other hand by way of the Pacific Ocean and the Gulf of California.

We will now briefly review in broad perspective the Spanish advance into each of these three northern salients of colonization.

THE EAST COAST CORRIDOR

Significant factors which shaped the early story of the East Coast Corridor north of La Huasteca were the sharp isolation of the region by the barrier imposed by rugged Sierra Madre Oriental; the broad plain lying in a semi-tropical zone; the cultural status of the natives of the area; the mineral deposits on the eastern slope of the mountains, especially in the north; and the exposure of the area to foreign intrustions by way of the Gulf of Mexico.

The opening chapter in the Spanish occupation of this coastwise area was furnished by Pineda, Garay, Cortés and Guzmán. Pineda projected a coast colony called *Amichel*. Pánuco became a source of Indian slaves for the tropical plantations of Cuba, Puerto Rico, and other Antilles. From the area Garay was eliminated by Cortés and succeeded by Guzmán. Don Nuño's reputation was unsavory, but instead of calling him hard names it is more profitable to ascertain what he was doing and to understand the circumstances which motivated him and others similarly engaged. One result of this early scramble for supremacy was the opening of a road from Pánuco to the capital.

After the great exploring expeditions of Coronado and De Soto into the far north and the thrilling flight of Do Campo from Quivira to Pánuco, the East Coast corridor was temporarily looked upon as a prospective overland route from Mexico City to Quivira (Kansas) and La Florida, whose colonization from a Mexican base was then contemplated. Pánuco became in the late sixteenth century the base for a long northward leap by Carbajal—he of the "Tragic Square," as Vito Alessio Robles picturesquely calls it—over unpacified country, to the region of Cerralvo, Monterrey, and Monclova. Out of this episode came the founding of Nuevo León, where mining was a primary interest.

Herdsmen followed the miners. By the middle of the seventeenth century the rich grass lands of the area that is now northern Tamaulipas were the scene of an imposing annual stock drive, in itself an inviting theme for a history or a novel. According to the chronicle of Alonso de León (published by the learned scholar Genaro García), at this period a quarter million of cattle, sheep, and goats were driven north from the vicinity of Querétaro every spring to the plains of Tamaulipas and back again to southern markets in the fall. So the "Long Drive" did not begin in Texas, nor the nineteenth century, as Gringo historians customarily assert. The great cattle drives from Texas to Kansas and Montana were but extensions of the same institution which for two centuries had been in existence farther south, and the Texas "long horns" were lineal descendants of Spanish cattle from the other side of the Rio Grande.

Among the difficulties of settlement in the East Coast Corridor were the raids of the Indians who lived on the slopes of the Sierra Madre Oriental. To help check these devastations and convert the natives the missionaries contributed many decades of dangerous and self-sacrificing labor. Notable among these apostles were the Franciscans of the Colleges of Santa Cruz de Querétaro and San Fernando de México, either of which groups would be an enticing subject for a book.

The threat of foreign intrusions into the East Coast Corridor by way of the Gulf of Mexico, together with the raids of hostile tribes from the Sierra Madre Oriental upon the settlements, led in the middle of the eighteenth century to the spectacular colonizing enterprise of José de Escandón in the province then called Nuevo Santander. His impressive achievement left marks on the region which have conspicuously endured to the present day. He founded a score or more of towns in a stretch of country which reached from the Pánuco border clear to the Rio Grande. One of them, indeed, Laredo, was established north of that stream. Most of these towns founded by Escandón are still in existence and some of them, like Victoria and Laredo, have become important cities.

The name of Escandón looms large in the history of colony-founding in North America. His prodigious achievement was recorded in voluminous manuscript records which until recently have been little used by scholars. With Escandón's colonists went Franciscan missionaries to gather the Indians into a score of missions and teach them the rudiments of Christian civilization. One of the rare chronicles of Mexico, that written by Father Santa María, deals largely with Nuevo Santander. These materials offer a tempting opportunity for the historian. Travelers by the Pan-American Highway south from Laredo who do not know the dramatic story of Escandón miss half the thrills of the trip.

Similar threats of intrusion by way of the Gulf in the period of the Wars of Independence increased the strategic importance of the East Coast Corridor and prompted its defense and colonization. This area had strategic importance in the heyday of the American filibusters in Texas. It was a point of entry for revolutionary expeditions from the outside, notably that of Xavier Mina, and it was the scene of the final overthrow of Iturbide.

In recent times the East Coast Corridor has acquired still greater significance. The discovery of petroleum in the Tampico district brought the region into the current of modern industry and yielded more wealth than was ever dreamed of by Carbajal. It is now a scene of active colonization. The control of water has made possible plantation crops on a large and profitable scale. Together these resources have increased the general prosperity of the section, with corresponding social and cultural betterment. An added asset of the Corridor has been contributed by railroad building, and by the segment of the Pan American Highway which traverses the area and puts it in the current of international travel. Coastwise communication by water has always played a part in the development of the region.

Thus the story of the colonization and development of the East Coast Corridor north of La Huasteca is a significant and fascinating one and offers a profitable field both for minute research and for synthesis. It may interest some of you.

SUGGESTED TOPICS ON THE EAST COAST CORRIDOR

The physiography of the East Coast Corridor.
The aborigines of the East Coast Corridor.
The aborigines of the Sierra Madre Oriental.
The Province of Amichel.
Garay, Cortés, and Guzmán in Pánuco.
Moscoso, Do Campo, De Luna y Arellano, and the Route to Quivira and Florida.
Carbajal's colonizing venture—"The Tragic Square."
The Tamaulipas stock drives in the seventeenth century.
Escandón and the founding of Nuevo Santander.
Franciscan missions in the Sierra Madre Oriental.
Franciscan missions in Nuevo Santander.
The Chronicle of Father Santa María.
The East Coast Corridor in the Mexican War of Independence.
The establishment of the State of Tamaulipas.
Railroad building in the East Coast Corridor.
Water control and modern agriculture in the East Coast Corridor.
Petroleum and the development of the area.
The automobile road through the Corridor and its influence on the area.
The Lower Rio Grande Valley in recent times.
Present-day colonization in the Corridor.
The development of communication with the East Coast Corridor by water.

THE WEST COAST CORRIDOR

On the Pacific Coast another corridor has given character to the development of a vast region. Few continental areas have been so sharply isolated by geography as Sinaloa, Sonora, and part of Nayarit. Lying between the Sierra Madre Occidental and the Pacific Ocean, this narrow strip of mainland became the highway to the northwest and a sea base for advance to the Orient. Culiacán, the capital of Sinaloa, was founded in 1531, only a decade after the capture of Tenochtitlán by Cortés, and just a century before the beginnings of Boston. But so rugged is the Sierra Madre Occidental that even now, after four centuries of continuous occupation by Europeans, there is a mountain stretch nearly a thousand miles long between Tepic and the United States border which seldom has been crossed by a wheel track. Of what other comparable area in North America can this be said? Lower California is still further isolated by a Gulf several hundred miles long, separating it from the mainland. This forbidding Sierra Madre Occidental has given exceptional importance to communication by water on the Pacific Ocean and the Gulf of California.

Only broad outlines of the development of the West Coast Corridor need be indicated here, and this primarily with the purpose of suggesting themes for investigation. The opening scene in the four-century drama enacted on this occidental stage was a vigorous contest for supremacy between Guzmán and Cortés. By land Guzmán opened a route up the coast to middle Sonora and began the permanent colonization of Sinaloa. By water the men of Cortés, going west, crossed the Pacific Ocean, and following the shoreline northward discovered California, whose first colony was planted by Don Hernando himself.

By way of the same Corridor Francisco Vázquez de Coronado reached the pueblo dwellers of New Mexico and Arizona and the wide prairies of Texas, Oklahoma and Kansas, thus bringing into history a vast region then called La Tierra Nueva, and now known in the United States as the Great Southwest. Soon afterward Ibarra, by an heroic crossing of the Sierra Madre Occidental, opened a pack train route from Durango to Culiacán which until the day of the airplane has been the chief means of direct communication between the two areas.

In this Corridor and the adjacent sierra a notable chain of missions was established the full length of Nayarit, Sinaloa, Sonora and into Arizona, and across the Gulf in Baja California. By way of the same Corridor and the bordering ocean, missions and colonies were projected into Alta California, beyond which Spanish mariners explored the northwest coasts of America as far as the Russian settlements of Alaska.

In all this Corridor the advance of the frontier of settlement was greatly impeded by hostile Sinaloa Indians, and farther north by Yaquis, Seris, Apaches and Yumas. In the late seventeenth and the early eighteenth centuries the Apaches, descending from the north, destroyed outposts of colonization and drove back the frontiers of civilized society from an area a hundred miles or more in width from north to south and many times that length from east to west. In this connection it is interesting to note that the Spanish line of military defense of Sonora against these warlike Apaches established in the eighteenth century became a long segment of the boundary line which was drawn between Mexico and the United States in the middle nineteenth century. That line was determined more by the Apache problem than by the question of transcontinental route which historians always emphasize.

Notwithstanding the handicaps of isolation and Indian wars in the Corridor, agriculture was successfully practiced and mines were opened which furnished the wealth necessary for building in the seventeenth and eighteenth centuries a chain of cities with substantial plazas, beautiful churches, and other cultural institutions. Of this development Rosario, Mazatlán, Culiacán, Sinaloa, Fuerte, Guaymas, Alamos and Hermosillo are examples, but they do not exhaust the list.

This West Coast Corridor and Lower California form a rich laboratory for the study of biography in relation to environment. Here operated great missionaries, like Tápia, Pérez de Ribas, Kino, Salvatierra, Serra, Palóu, Crespi, and Garcés; able soldiers like

Hurdaide, Elizondo, and the two Anzas. Here was the scene of much of the work of the distinguished Visitador General José de Gálvez, not to mention conspicuous names of more recent periods. What comparable region has had a more notable list of historical figures in colonial days?

In the nineteenth century a trunk line railroad alleviated the isolation of the West Coast Corridor and of its widely separated towns and cities. Now the automobile and the airplane have brought them close to each other and to the outside world, with results which it would be interesting to study and evaluate. Agriculture has been stimulated by impounding the waters which flow from the Sierra Madre across the plain. Vigorous commonwealths have been formed from the lands of the Corridor, and have produced significant modern leaders.

The question arises, what has been the effect of this geographical isolation, not only upon the process by which the West Coast Corridor was colonized and developed, but upon the nature of the society which has grown up in that land of tangled *monte*, swift flowing rivers, indomitable Yaquis, and fierce Apaches? What effect has this isolation had upon the social, political, economic, and cultural institutions of the area? Is Sinaloa essentially like Michoacán? If not, what are the differences, and to what extent can they be traced to the mountain barrier, on the one hand, or to contact with the Pacific Ocean on the other hand? Does this isolation help to explain the rise in Sonora of an unusually large number of military and political leaders? The social, economic, political, and cultural results of improved means of communication and modern economic techniques would form an interesting subject for study. What, for example, has been the effect of the airplane on the development of mining in the Sierra Madre Occidental?

SUGGESTED TOPICS ON THE WEST COAST CORRIDOR

The geography of the area.
The primitive inhabitants.
Guzmán and Sinaloa.

The beginnings of Culiacán.

Cortés and California.

Ibarra's epic crossing of the Sierra Madre Occidental.

Ibarra on the West Coast.

The trail between Durango and Culiacán (The route, extent of its use, methods of travel and transportation, personalities, etc.).

Early agriculture in Sinaloa (Methods, crops, labor, supply, etc.).

The early Franciscans in Sinaloa.

The Jesuits in Sinaloa.

The early Jesuits in Sonora.—The Franciscans.

Pérez de Ribas (or some other early Jesuit on the West Coast).

Hurdaide, defender of the border.

The early history of Culiacán, Sinaloa, Fuerte, Guaymas, or Alamos.

The founding and development of Hermosillo.

Early stock raising in Sinaloa (or in Sonora).

Correos (How the mail was carried in early days).

The Yaquis in the seventeenth century.

Early mining on the West Coast.

The mines of Rosario.

The mines of Alamos.

The Anzas in Sonora, father and son.

Apache raids in Sonora in the 17th and 18th Centuries.

Building the Southern Pacific Railway on the West Coast.

The influence of the Southern Pacific Railway on the development of the West Coast.

Irrigation on the West Coast (Its history and its influence on society).

The automobile on the West Coast (Developments and influence).

Sinaloa and Sonora in twentieth-century politics.

THE CENTRAL PLATEAU

Before the middle of the sixteenth century there began an imposing march of Spanish pioneers up the Central Mexican plateau, into a vast region which became the heart of the North and the scene of some of the most vital developments in the shaping of the Mexico of today. The dominant factor in the movement was the discovery and exploitation of the precious metals, especially silver. This pursuit was by no means a matter of local interest. The treasure obtained from the mines of northern Mexico and from Potosí in Perú was the basis for Spain's later sixteenth-century glory, a cause of fundamental changes in all Western Europe, and a vital factor in world history. This theme alone could be expanded into a volume. It deserves a chapter in any textbook on the history of Europe.

Beginnings of mining were early made in Nueva Galicia and other areas south of Chichimeco Country. But Zacatecas was the center of the first great mining rush in North America and the opening of a series of rushes which eventually reached California, the Rocky Mountains, British Columbia, and Alaska. At Zacatecas, Diego de Ibarra, Cristóbal de Oñate and their associates became immensely rich, the first among millionaire miners of America. Mining quickly spread from Zacatecas northwest to Durango, and in reverse direction to San Luis Potosí and Guanajuato. To administer the northern settlements a new jurisdiction called the Audiencia of Nueva Vizcaya was erected, thus delimiting the older Audiencia of Nueva Galicia, of which first Compostela, then Guadalajara was the capital. Francisco de Ibarra, first captain-general of Nueva Vizcaya, engaged in extensive prospecting tours, pushed the mining frontier northwest to Durango, Indé and Santa Bárbara, and by his spectacular march in mid-winter across the Sierra Madre Occidental reached Culiacán and attached Sinaloa to his jurisdiction. From Santa Barbara at the end of the sixteenth century Pueblo Land was re-explored, and then a few years later Oñate founded the province of New Mexico.

In all this area of the Mesa Central there were strikes, rushes, boom towns, ghost towns, and other phenomena which have characterized the spread of mining into new regions in many parts of America ever since Ibarra's day. Here in the north a mining society was formed. Farmers, cattlemen, and supply merchants followed in the wake of the miners. Soldiers accompanied them and offered protection against hostile natives. For a labor supply dependence was placed principally on Indians, either those taken north with the miners or those native of the regions where the mines were operated. Beyond the scene of the actual mining, prospectors operated in the border areas, looking for new mineral deposits and new laborers for mines already opened. Mining techniques and processes were developed, a great body of mining law evolved, through experience new offices were created for the administration of mining, the beginning of the institution of the Minería of New Spain.

Soldiers, sometimes in fortified wagons, escorted trains carrying supplies to the mines and the silver bars to Mexico. Garrisons established along the route to the mines became permanent centers of agriculture to raise provisions for the new markets in the north, thus filling in the gaps between the old settlements and the new. Soon a regular convoy system was organized to protect the silver trains from the mines to Mexico and Vera Cruz, and for the ships carrying the bullion from Vera Cruz to Spain. The convoy system in the Caribbean and the Atlantic did not begin with World War II, as some persons have imagined. For centuries this function was performed by the Armada de Barlovento, and the galleons which escorted the annual supply ships from Spain to Vera Cruz and Puerto Bello.

In succeeding decades the frontier of settlement pushed rapidly up the Central Plateau from these first mining outposts, filling in the gaps and extending the area of settlement farther and farther north. Missionaries, soldiers, farmers, and traders followed the miners. Everywhere mining promoted the development of government, agriculture, religious institutions, city building, and other symbols of civilized life.

For some time the region of Charcas, now partly included in San Luís Potosí, was a sort of No-Man's Land near the Sierra Madre Oriental, but it was not long neglected. Here, between 1550 and 1570, Matehuala, San Gerónimo, San Pedro and other settlements were founded. By 1576 San Luís Potosí, site of rich mines, had become a villa, and soon was the seat of an alcaldía mayor. Fray Espinareda played an important part in northeastward expansion. In

1566 or 1567 he made an expedition from San Martín to Pánuco, preaching to Indians on the way. As a result of his journey through the Sierra Madre Oriental he recommended the occupation of the country between Zacatecas and the Gulf of Mexico and the opening of a road from the mines to Pánuco, to provide direct communication with Spain.

For much of our knowledge of the advance of the frontier into Coahuila, Nuevo León, and across the Rio Grande into Texas we are indebted to the erudite researches of Licenciado Vito Alessio Robles, published in numerous books and monographs, especially in his two volumes on the history of Coahuila and Texas. Northeastward mining spread to Mazapil, which by 1568 became the seat of an alcaldía mayor. In that year Francisco del Cano, of Mazapil, sent by the "Very Magnificent Alcalde Mayor," went northeast and discovered Laguna de Nuevo México, long thought to be Laguna de Parras, but now by Alessio Robles identified with old Ciénega de Patos. In or about 1575 Saltillo was founded farther east, not by Urdiñola, as previously it was thought, but by Alberto del Canto. But Urdiñola later played an important part in developing Coahuila, where he met the column of pioneers led by Carbajal, grantee of the Tragic Square, who had entered the country by way of the East Coast Corridor.

The plains of San Luís Potosí and the city of Saltillo were the scenes of an interesting experience in the utilization of natives of high culture in the extension of the frontier into *tierra de guerra*. As a means of reducing these regions, the plan was adopted of planting in them Tlascaltecan Indians, to defend the settlers, and to teach the ruder tribes the elements of Christian civilization. The Tlascaltecans had proved their loyalty to the Spaniards in the days of Cortés, and this fidelity was insured by their exemption from tribute and by other privileges. Similarly, Tarascans were moved into the western regions of the Central Plateau. This whole subject of the role of sedentary Indians from the south in the northward advance of the Spanish frontier deserves a detailed study and would fill a substantial volume.

Near the end of the seventeenth century northeastward expansion in the Central Plateau pushed the frontier of settlement to the Rio Grande. Missionaries from Guadalajara led by Father Juan Larios carried the Gospel to the wild tribes beyond Parras and gathered them into missions. Colonists from Saltillo soon afterward formed the near-by settlement called Monclova, and a new province named Coahuila, or Nueva Estremadura, was founded with Monclova as its capital and Alonso de León as its first governor.

Monclova was hardly founded when foreign danger from the northeast threatened. French colonists and traders had pushed west up the St. Lawrence Valley to the Great Lakes and down the Mississippi to its mouth. Now La Salle founded a colony on the north shore of the Gulf of Mexico planning to seize the Spanish mines of Santa Bárbara in Chihuahua, and to open a French route across the Continent to the Pacific Ocean and the Orient. To meet this French threat Governor De León founded a settlement in eastern Texas, where Franciscan friars established missions among the Tejas or Cenís Indians. For many years the capital of Texas was at Los Adaes near Red River, in territory that is now in the state of Louisiana. This was the beginning of a contest for Texas between France and Spain which endured till the end of the Seven Years' War in 1763. By this time San Antonio had become the chief center of the province of Texas, and in 1772 it was made the capital.

THE MISSIONARY FRONTIER

Missionaries everywhere preceded, accompanied, or followed the secular pioneers in their northward trek into heathendom. The missionary was expected to convert the native to the Christian faith, and discipline him in the elements of civilized life and labor. The Franciscans and the Jesuits were the most active orders on the northern frontiers, the Franciscans generally being dominant in the northeast and New Mexico, and the Jesuits in the northwest.

Each missionary order provided special preparation of men for work among the *infieles*. The great training schools for Jesuit missionaries were the novitiate of Tepozotlán just outside Mexico City and the University of San Pedro y San Pablo in the capital, but other colleges were established on the frontiers, as at Durango and Chihuahua. Franciscan missionaries operated from the Convento del Santo Evangelio in Mexico City, from the Province of Jalisco in Guadalajara, from the Province of San Francisco in Zacatecas, and from the three *Colegios de Propaganda Fide* in Mexico City, Querétaro, and Zacatecas. Those in Texas all belonged to the two colleges last named. The early missions in New Mexico were operated by the Convento del Santo Evangelio in Mexico City. When mission Indians had become well indoctrinated and civilized the missions were generally secularized—that it so say, put in charge of parish priests. After the expulsion of the Jesuits in 1767, the Franciscans took over most of the remaining frontier missions, but shortly afterward the Dominicans replaced them in Lower California.

SUGGESTED TOPICS ON THE CENTRAL PLATEAU

The boundary between Aztecs and Chichimecos at the time of the Conquest.

The beginnings of Querétaro.

The opening of the mines of Zacatecas.

The founders of Zacatecas.

Life and labor in the mines of Zacatecas.

Francisco de Ibarra.

The beginnings of Durango.

The beginnings of Santa Bárbara.

The beginnings of San Luís Potosí.

The beginnings of Saltillo.

Urdiñola.

Larios and Del Bosque in Texas.

Alonso de León in Texas.

The Jesuits in Durango.

The Jesuits in the Tarahumara.

The beginnings of Parral.

The beginnings of Chihuahua (province or city).
The College of the Holy Cross of Querétaro.
The College of Guadalupe de Zacatecas.
The College of San Fernando de Mexico.
Juan de Oñate and the founding of New Mexico.
The Marquisate of San Miguel de Aguayo.

CHAPTER FOUR

Coronado in Perspective*

THE real pioneer into a large section of the future Borderlands was Don Francisco Vásquez de Coronado. Between 1540 and 1542 this young Spanish don and his companions were in the North, looking for the Seven Golden Cities of Cíbola and then for Quivira, that *Otro México* which just was not there. They uncovered lands which later men would settle and traced paths which others would follow. They were among the first to travel the West Coast Corridor; they are the first white men into Pueblo-land, where half a century later Oñate and his fellows, lay and clerical, would establish a far-flung outpost; they were the first Europeans to range the Great Plains. It is hardly surprising that Coronado would have excited Bolton's interest, even though he ordinarily left the more "obvious" figures to others in order to bring to light men equally important but who had escaped attention.

The biography, *Coronado, Knight of Pueblos and Plains*, was one of Bolton's last works, published in 1949. However, it was long in the making—the documents had been carefully studied and restudied, the route traveled and retraveled, the works of predecessors assayed, the story sketched and refined and polished. In many respects this *Coronado* shows Bolton at his typical best. The book won the Whittelsey House Southwestern Fellowship Award in the year of its publication and likewise one of the Bancroft Prizes with which Columbia University honors distinguished writing in the field of American history.

This selection not only calls attention to Bolton's longer work, but also will show the reader several of the author's characteristics

* Herbert Eugene Bolton, *Coronado, Knight of Pueblos and Plains* (New York, Whittlesey House, 1949; Albuquerque, University of New Mexico Press, 1949 [under the title *Coronado on the Turquoise Trail; Knight of Pueblos and Plains*]), 395–403. Reprinted with the permission of the University of New Mexico Press.

as a historian. There is the care to put Coronado in his over-all American setting. Bolton's keen interest in geography shows, as does a scrupulous exactness in trying to place his story in its original setting. This last led Bolton on many an extended field trip with diary or account in hand—and this not only for his Coronado biography, but also for every one of his major works. Bolton was no cloistered scholar; he was an "outdoor historian" to whom hillocks and barrancas, arroyos and waterholes, rivers and mountain ranges were all an integral element of his research.

BECAUSE CORONADO found no precious metals in the regions he explored it has been the fashion to regard his expedition as a pointless jaunt. Nothing could be farther from the truth. Exploration was a necessary antecedent to the colonization, exploitation, and social development of any part of the New World. Before the Wright Brothers invented an airplane that would work, more than one Darius Green made a flying machine that failed to function. Before Cortés and Alvarado entered the interior of Mexico and Central America, numerous apparently profitless voyages had been made around the shores of the Gulf and the Caribbean. Before the English pioneers crossed the mountains and established homes in the Ohio Valley, it was visited by a whole galaxy of Daniel Boones and by them made known to the people on the eastern seaboard as a Promised Land. In the long perspective of history no exploring expedition was entirely profitless, even if it netted no contemporary a dollar. Negatively or positively, each reconnoissance of any region helped to prepare the way for the next step in the historical process by which the New World became what it is today.

Coronado made one of the significant expeditions of that remarkable era of the opening of the Western Hemisphere by Europeans. He performed in North America a service analogous to what was done in South America by Pizarro, Almagro, Belalcázar, or Quesada; or in Middle America by Balboa, Alvarado, or Cortés. He converted the old trail up the West Coast Corridor into a well-known road that is still in use, and in its time and place just as significant as the Wilderness Road over the mountains to Kentucky. To the map of the interior of North America he added Cíbola, Tusayán, Tiguex, the Llanos del Cíbola, and Quivira, regions which were later combined by Anglo-Americans under the name of the Southwest, or the Spanish Borderlands. Historical tradition in this vast area, all the way from California to Nebraska, runs back to the reconnoissance made by the gallant conquistador.

A notable contribution of Coronado to the larger features of North American geography was the discovery of the Continental Divide—the watershed between the Pacific and the Atlantic Oceans from which two river systems run in opposite directions. Jaramillo observed and correctly stated that in the latitude where they crossed it the Divide was just east of Zuñi. He says that "all the springs, rivers, and arroyos we have found as far as Cíbola, and perhaps also those one or two days beyond, flow to the South Sea, and those farther on to the North Sea." As a matter of general interest it would be appropriate to erect a marker of the Continental Divide on the road leading east from Zuñi where Jaramillo noted the watershed, and on it record his important discovery.

It was Coronado who first acquired a relatively accurate knowledge of the width of the continent in the latitude of his travels. Contemporary maps made in Europe showed North America as very narrow in this area. Cabeza de Vaca's long journey westward from Florida to Arizona had not dispelled the notion that north of Mexico the oceans were close together. Then a new idea dawned. Coronado while he was still at Cíbola was visited by native ambassadors from the Pecos River some two hundred miles farther east, who told of the great Buffalo Plains still beyond. Don Francisco now formed a generally sound opinion regarding Cíbola's relation to both oceans. He wrote from there: "I have gained no information about the North Sea [Atlantic Ocean] nor about the one in the west, nor am I able to tell your Lordship which one we are nearest, but I should judge we are closer to the Western Sea. It appears to me that it cannot be less than 150 leagues from here to there, and that the North Sea must be much farther away." This is a definitely more accurate estimate than the one revealed by Mendoza's instructions to Fray

Marcos. The man who furnished the initial data for this important geographical news was no other than our young friend Bigotes, chief of Pecos. He deserves a place in the history of cartography alongside of Jaramillo.

After going east to far-distant Quivira, Coronado concluded that the Tiguex pueblos were "four hundred leagues from the North Sea, and more than two hundred from the South Sea, thus prohibiting all intercourse." This would put Tiguex, on the upper Rio Grande, about one-third of the distance from the Pacific to the Atlantic, which is fairly accurate, and his estimate of six hundred leagues for the total width of the continent, though still too small, was a vast improvement over some of the contemporary maps. Nor was Coronado's opinion a guess; it was based on his long journey from Arizona to Kansas, during which he and his horses had measured every mile of the way in terms of sweat, sore muscles, and bodily fatigue. If by the North Sea Coronado meant the Gulf of Mexico, as apparently is the case, his calculation of distance was not far from correct.

This idea of the immense span of the continent acquired by Coronado on the basis of his own travels was substantiated and made more exact by the contemporary expedition of De Soto from the eastern seaboard to and across the Mississippi into the regions now called Arkansas, Louisiana, and eastern Texas. Thus the approximate width of the continent was now established on the basis of actual exploration by the two armies which almost met. To the same result Zaldívar's Indian woman contributed her bit. Having fled from the Barrancas of the Panhandle, later on she reached Moscoso's men in eastern Texas, as was learned by Coronado's men after they returned to Mexico. "Thus," Castañeda remarks, "we are led to believe that we were not far from the region they discovered. . . . So it is estimated that the land in that latitude must be more than six hundred leagues wide from sea to sea"—a very fair estimate of the distance from the Gulf of California to the Gulf of Mexico. In the short space of three years these two rival explorers had made known to the world in broad outline nearly a third of the area now contained in the United

States, and in several important respects had changed current ideas regarding the entire land mass of North America and its geographical relation to the rest of the globe.

By a strange misunderstanding, recorded by Ramusio and adopted by Gómara, European map makers absurdly reversed the direction of Coronado's long eastward march from Cíbola and the order of the pueblos seen by him, transformed the River of Quivira into a lake, and then shifted the province of Quivira to the shores of the Pacific Ocean, where for several decades it roamed up and down the map. As a corollary to this blunder, Coronado's River of La Señora [the Rio Grande] was shown as flowing west into the Pacific Ocean in northern California—categorical statements by Coronado, Jaramillo, and Castañeda to the contrary notwithstanding. It is safe to say that Coronado never told Mendoza what Ramusio attributed to him. Both Ramusio and Gómara deserve a prominent place in a Southwestern joke book.

Relatively unimportant though these curious mistakes of the map makers may have been, they make it clear that Coronado and his contemporaries had contributed more to North American geography than Europeans could quickly digest. The government of Spain was partly at fault by reason of its secretive policy with respect to the work of its explorers, for after Gómara's history, little was published regarding the Coronado expedition for several decades. French, Portuguese, English, and Russian explorers in America also suffered from the ignorance of their officials in Europe.

It must not be concluded from the strange errors made by map makers that the explorers themselves did not know where they had been, or that they did not understand the relative position of their discoveries with respect to Mexico and adjacent areas. On the contrary, the chroniclers of the Coronado expedition, contemporary Mexican officials, and contemporary frontier promoters had a generally clear idea of what both Coronado and his *vis à vis*, De Soto, had done; and they made use of the new information in the discussion of problems which immediately arose. More important than the difficulty of educating Europeans was the widening of the horizon of the colonists in New Spain, who made practical use of the new data acquired.

Coronado on his march from the Barranca Grande to the Arkansas River made an interesting contribution to knowledge of the declination of the compass needle in that region and at that date. Writers hitherto have generally approached the problem of the identity of the Barranca Grande backward. Not knowing the topography of the region, in order to locate the great canyon, and noting that Coronado said he traveled by the needle, they consulted scientists regarding the declination of the compass needle in 1541. On confessedly inadequate data the scientists conjectured that the declination along Coronado's route from the Barranca Grande was some two degrees west of true north. In accordance with that guess historians placed the Barranca Grande far east and south of its true location. But the Barranca Grande was unmistakably Palo Duro Canyon. From here Coronado traveled on the high plain, near the escarpment of the Llano Estacado, which runs about eleven degrees east of true north. This happens to be about the average declination of the needle along Coronado's route for the last century, for which we have accurate data based on astronomical observations. The obvious conclusion is that it was about the same in Coronado's day. Hence his record has enabled us to answer a question for which scientists have had no reliable data.

There is a widespread impression, often expressed in print, that the horses in use by the Plains Indians in the seventeenth and eighteenth centuries were descended from the animals left behind when the Coronado expedition withdrew to Mexico. But this opinion, as Aiton states, does not appear to be well founded. In the first place, as has already been noted, among the horses taken to New Mexico by Coronado and his men there were very few mares. In the muster roll of the army drawn up at Compostela when the expedition started north, out of some five hundred mounts listed, only two mares were mentioned. There probably were others but the number apparently was small. Since mounts were at a premium they no doubt were carefully guarded in the course of the long march and at the winter camps in Pueblo Land. In the available records of the expedition there is mention of the disappearance of two or three horses besides those killed by the Pueblo Indians in the Tiguex War. Had there been others, it is reasonable to suppose they also would have been noted. Moreover, in the accounts of the Spanish expeditions to the Southwest and Kansas in the later sixteenth and early seventeenth centuries no mention is made of horses or mounted Indians, which, if encountered, would have been sure to attract attention. It would seem, therefore, that the horses ridden by the Plains Indians in the eighteenth century as far north as the prairies of Canada were descended from stock which strayed or was obtained from the Spanish settlements after the permanent colonization of New Mexico and Texas in the seventeenth century.

The notion of vast wealth in Tierra Nueva would not down. In spite of Coronado's reports, and of the emphatic testimony of his followers as to the lack of ready-to-hand riches—namely, gold, silver, and precious stones—Don Francisco was criticized for withdrawing to Mexico, and within five years of his return there was official talk of sending a new expedition to colonize Quivira. Contributory motives were the desire to relieve Mexico City of idle adventurers, including some of Coronado's own men, and fear of another intrusion from the east such as that of De Soto. The route to Quivira now proposed was the direct one by which Do Campo had fled to Pánuco and which was paralleled by Moscoso. "Of all this wealth they give great news," wrote a high official of Mexico in 1547, "and it is very proper that your Majesty should order all that country peopled. . . . Now the route is certain and the land so healthful and fertile and abounding . . . with so many provisions and so many millions of cattle which God has scattered there that it appears to me . . . another Promised Land." Do Campo's trail from Quivira to Mexico City was not more than half as long as the one followed by Coronado, hence the route proposed for a return to Kansas.

But the defense of Florida at the moment was more urgent, and to this task attention was now given. Mendoza requested Moscoso's men to return thither overland, "offering them whatever was necessary to establish themselves in that distant land," but many of them went instead to Peru. A colony for Florida was raised in Mexico in 1559, and the man chosen to lead the adventurers was no other than Don Tristán de Luna y Arellano, who had made a good record with Coronado and had high family connections. Six of his captains had been with De Soto, acquired Alabama wives, and with them now accompanied Arellano. Thus Don Tristán was a personal link between Coronado and Florida. The Do Campo–De Soto route was at first contemplated, but the expedition was finally sent by water, which under existing circumstances was more practicable. The wide gap overland was not bridged till long afterward, but the idea persisted and it was initially based on the exploits of Do Campo, De Soto, and Moscoso.

If Coronado may appear less efficient than some of his contemporary conquistadores, it is partly due to his finer sense of the rights and dignity of human beings. He was not a swashbuckler. Don Francisco had many unquestionable qualifications for leadership. When he set forth on his great expedition he was only thirty years old. With five years of American experience behind him, he was still in the bloom of early manhood, and had those precious attributes that make youth so competent, so engaging, and so enviable. He was attractive, optimistic, and unsoured by the hard knocks and disappointments that come with sordid worldly contacts. There is abundant evidence that Coronado organized his army well, and led it in an orderly manner all the way to Cíbola, Tiguex, the Buffalo Plains, and Quivira. His treatment of the Indian allies whom he took in his train was notably more humane than that practiced by some of the conquerors of the period. Mendoza's orders regarding this matter were strict, and Coronado was zealous in carrying them out. He was so successful in this particular that on the long march of more than four thousand miles, from Mexico City to eastern Kansas and back, and embracing a period of more than two years, including two cold and hungry winters in Tiguex, few Spaniards were lost and not more than thirty Indian allies were sacrificed. No other contemporary record could match this one.

Coronado was reputed by his followers to be a strict disciplinarian, even something of a martinet, and it is well known that he sometimes punished his soldiers for misconduct, especially for offenses against the Indians. But on only one occasion, so far as the available record goes, was he charged with being harsh and arbitrary with his men. This was when some of the soldiers opposed his decision to abandon conquest and return with the whole army to Mexico. When, as we have seen, some sixty men on that occasion proposed to remain in Tiguex, or to return to Quivira with Father Padilla, Coronado threatened to punish—even to hang—anyone who remained or so much as talked about remaining. He had decided to return to Mexico for what he regarded as good reasons, and now it was his duty to enforce his orders.

If Don Francisco had been an incompetent leader some of his followers might well have clamored to turn back after the shocking disappointment experienced at Cíbola, when they saw the much advertised city was nothing but a "huddle of mud huts"; and they might have done the same after new disappointments at Tiguex, or after the hardships of the first winter there. But not many faltered, and apparently nobody deserted except some of the men left with brutal Alcaráz in Sonora Valley. Without a commander who inspired confidence and enthusiasm for the gamble this could not have been true.

There is no doubt of Coronado's dash and nerve, qualities which endeared him to his soldiers, and made them willing to follow him through thick and thin. At Cíbola he led his men into battle, receiving blows and wounds which caused his comrades to despair of his life, and to admire him all the more in consequence. His conduct in the Tiguex War was brave and soldierly. It took real stamina to march with only thirty men through unknown country from the Barrancas of the Texas Panhandle five or six hundred miles to Quivira, whose ruler had been represented as a powerful monarch who commanded an army of giants and inflicted awful punishment upon anyone who opposed his will.

The testimony of Coronado's comrades was put in phrases that leave no doubt of the loyalty and admiration of his followers. Hernando del Valle declared that the general, in the course of the expedition, "suffered great hardships from hunger, cold, heat, and loss of blood from many wounds which the natives of those lands gave him and from which he was at the point of death; and many times his life was put in great peril and danger in the service of his Majesty." Juan Bermejo, royal notary of the expedition, at Cíbola saw Coronado "at the point of death, and beyond the hope of all who went with him on the expedition, because the Indians of that valley wounded him with arrows in many places." Melchior Pérez "saw that the natives of the principal pueblo of Cíbola wounded the governor . . . when he went to enter it, because he was in the vanguard. And such were the wounds and blows they gave him on his head and his body that he lost much blood; and they carried him on their shoulders as dead to the Spanish camp." Pedro de Castro testified that at Cíbola when Coronado was leading the van and encouraging his men, the natives gave him so many wounds that they thought him dead. "They carried him out in their arms and he became very ill from his wounds." Juan Pastor declared that "in all the encounters . . . Coronado, like a good captain, was always in the vanguard, and that . . . he many times came out wounded, and was at the point of death, as is notorious among the men who went in that army." All these and many more testimonials to Coronado's qualities and deeds were given in a secret and not wholly sympathetic inquiry, conducted with a view to obtaining frank expression of opinions.

CHAPTER FIVE

Preliminaries to
*"The Spanish Occupation of Texas, 1519–1690"**

MUCH of Bolton's early writing had turned on the story of the Spaniards in Texas. It was this one of the Borderlands with which he first became acquainted. Later he would see Texas, and then Louisiana, at the end of what he came to call the "East Coast Corridor." This article is a sampling of his Texas interest.

These studies began to appear as early as 1902 in *The Quarterly* of the Texas State Historical Association (later the *Southwestern Historical Quarterly*) immediately after his return to Austin from his first exploration of the Mexican archives. In the years that followed, such articles multiplied, and he also contributed many shorter ones on the Texas Indians to Hodge's *Handbook*. In 1915 came his more lengthy study, *Texas in the Middle Eighteenth Century*. This work has recently been brought back into circulation with a reprint edition.

This present article sketches the several approaches to Texas and shows that there was considerable activity in the Texas area of the Borderlands long before the definitive settlement of the province in the second decade of the eighteenth century. The Texas story, once La Salle comes into it, is well enough known; these preliminaries have often been overlooked. Hence, aside from reminding the reader that Bolton is one of the authorities on the Spanish years in Texas and that under his guidance his students (Anne E. Hughes, William E. Dunn, and Lawrence Hill, among others) began to help him in reconstructing important segments of that story, this present study has merit in its own right.

The editor would like to note that the addition to the original title of this piece is not his work. Bolton himself later added those

* *The Southwestern Historical Quarterly*, Vol. XVI (July, 1912), 1–26. With this number the journal takes this new title; it had formerly been *The Quarterly* of the Texas State Historical Association.

introductory words, "Preliminaries to," to the title of the offprint which he turned over to the Bancroft Library for preservation among his writings.

I. INTRODUCTORY

FOR A CENTURY and a half before they made definite attempts to occupy the region now called Texas the Spaniards gradually explored it, proceeding step by step from the borders toward the interior, and slowly formed ideas concerning its geography and its suitability for settlement. Viewed in this light, the final occupation of Texas at the end of the seventeenth century was by no means the sudden event, brought about by the chance settlement of the French on the Gulf coast, which it was once thought to be.

Though it is not commonly known, Texas had its share in the romance, and myth, and fable which everywhere attended the Spanish conquest in America. In Florida the Spaniards sought the Fountain of Youth; in South America the Gilded Man (El Dorado); on the west coast of Mexico the Isle of the Amazons; in Arizona and New Mexico the Seven Cities of Cíbola; on the California coast the Strait of Anian.[1] Likewise, in Texas they searched for the Kingdom of Gran Quivira, where "everyone had their ordinary dishes made of wrought plate, and the jugs and bowls were of gold";[2] for the Seven Hills of the Aijados, or Aixaos, where gold was so plentiful that "the natives not knowing any of the other metals, make of it everything they need, such as vessels and the tips of arrows and lances";[3] for the Sierra (or Cerro) de la Plata (Silver Mountain), somewhere north of the Rio Grande;[4] for the pearls of the Jumano country; and for the "Great Kingdom of the Texas," a people who, like the

[1] Bandelier, *The Gilded Man, passim.*

[2] Castañeda, Narrative, translated by Winship, in *Fourteenth Annual Report of the Bureau of American Ethnology,* I, 493.

[3] Niel, *Apuntamientos,* in *Documentos para la Historia de México,* Tercera Serie, tomo iv, 92. See also Benavides, *Memorial,* in *Land of Sunshine,* xiv, 139–40.

[4] "Un cerro dicen que hay, que llaman el de La Plata, incógnito a los que hoy viven, también lo sería a los pasados; es hacia el Norte." (León, *Historia de Nuevo León* [Mexico, 1909], 84. Diego Ramón explored the Cerro de la Platta, at the order of the viceroy, sometime before 1703. Hidalgo, Fray Francisco, "Relación de la Quivira" [MS], 65.)

Jumanos, had been miraculously converted by the woman in blue, who lived next door to the Kingdom of Gran Quivira, were ruled by a powerful lord, had well built towns, each several miles in length, and raised grain in such abundance that they even fed it to their horses.[5] All these various quests and beliefs had made the Texas country an object of interest to the Spaniards long before it became a field for political contest with France.

II. FOUR LINES OF APPROACH TO TEXAS, 1519–1678

There were four lines of approach to Spanish Texas, through the development of which a knowledge of the region was gradually unfolded: (1) From the east and south, by way of the Gulf of Mexico; (2) from the east, by way of the vast region known in early days as La Florida; (3) from the west and southwest, by way of New Mexico and Nueva Vizcaya; and (4) from the south, through the expansion of Nuevo León and Coahuila.

1. By way of the Gulf

In the course of the exploration of the Gulf coast and the search for a strait through the newly found land mass to the East Indies, Pineda, in the employ of Garay, governor of Jamaica, in 1519 ran the coast from Florida to Pánuco (Tampico) and back, and made a map which shows with substantial accuracy the entire shore line of Texas. Two years later, on the basis of this exploration, Garay was granted a province, called Amichel, comprising the whole Gulf coast from modern Alabama to Tampico, which he attempted to colonize at its southern extremity.[6] In this he was forestalled by the master *conquistador* himself, Cortes, who in 1522 founded a villa at Pánuco.[7] By 1528 two expeditions from this place explored the coasts

[5] Declaration of Juan Sabeata before Governor Cruzate, of New Mexico, at El Paso del Rio del Norte, October 20, 1683. MS.

[6] Lowery, *The Spanish Settlements within the Present Limits of the United States*, 149–53; Navarette, *Colección de Viages*, iii, 147–53, where the Pineda map is reproduced.

[7] Called San Estévan del Puerto. Bancroft, *Mexico*, II, 94–101.

northward beyond the Rio Bravo, or Rio Grande. On a later expedition, made in 1544, it is said, Father Olmos took back and settled at Pánuco the tribe of the Olives, thought by some to have been secured on Texas soil.[8] In 1553 more than three hundred survivors of a wrecked treasure fleet were cast on the Texas shore five days' march north of the Rio Grande, and escaped toward Pánuco. In 1558 an expedition destined to colonize Florida was led from Vera Cruz by Bazares. In latitude 27° 30' he landed on the Texas shore; coasting eastward, in latitude 28° 30', he discovered and took possession of a bay which he called San Francisco, and which may have been the modern Matagorda Bay.[9] Thereafter occasional voyages were made along the northern shores of the Gulf; but the Texas coast, instead of being one of the first portions of the Gulf shore to be colonized, as it would have been had Garay succeeded, was destined to be nearly the last, its settlement being deferred still two centuries after Garay's day.

2. By way of Florida

Incident to the early attempts to explore and conquer La Florida from the east, the survivors of two shattered expeditions, seeking refuge in the settlements of Mexico, entered what it now Texas, crossed large stretches of its territory, and gained the first knowledge sent to Europe of the southern and northeastern interiors. As has been intimated, so far as the crossing of Texas is concerned, both of these explorations were accidental.

Reference is made, of course, to the well known journeys of Cabeza de Vaca and Moscoso. In 1528 Cabeza de Vaca and some two hundred companions, survivors of the Florida expedition led by Narváez, were cast on the southeastern shore of Texas. After spending six years on Texas soil, and enduring the hardships of enslave-

---

[8] Prieto, Alejandro, *Historia, Geografía y Estadística del Estado de Tamaulipas* (Mexico, 1873), 16, 60; Bancroft, *Mexico*, II, 267; Manuel Orozco y Berra, *Geografía de las Lenguas*, 293, 296; J. G. Shea, *History of the Catholic Missions* (1855), 45–46; Vetancur, *Crónica* (1697), 92. There is a confusion of the names of Olmedo and Olmos in this connection.

[9] Lowery, *Spanish Settlements*, 352–57. Barcía, *Ensayo Cronológico*, fol. 28 *et seq.*; Shea, *op. cit.*, 49–50.

ment by the Indians, Vaca and three others made their way westward across the whole southwestern border of the present state of Texas, entered northern Chihuahua, and finally reached Culiacán, in Sinaloa.[10] In 1542 Moscoso led the survivors of the De Soto expedition into Texas near the northeastern corner, westward or southwestward to a point thought by Mr. Lewis to have been in the upper Brazos, and back across the Red River by essentially the same route. This journey gave the Spaniards some knowledge of the geography of northeastern Texas and of the Caddoan group of Indians then, as later, inhabiting the region. It is remarkable, in this connection, that a map based on Moscoso's exploration shows the Nondacau, Nisone, Ays, and Guasco tribes in the same general location as that in which they were found a century and a half later.[11]

3. By way of New Mexico

The third line of approach, that from the west and southwest through New Mexico, was till the later seventeenth century the principal one, and for this reason until 1685 western Texas was much better known than the southern portion, lying nearer Mexico, or than the eastern portion, commonly regarded as "old" Texas.

The Coronado expedition.—Just before the Moscoso party entered northeastern Texas, another band, led by Coronado, entered its northwestern border. Coronado had come, by way of the Pacific Slope, to New Mexico in search of the Seven Cities of Cíbola. Disappointed at what he found, and hearing while in the Rio Grande valley of a great kingdom called Quivira to the northeast, he set out in search of it across the Llanos del Cíbolo (Buffalo Plains), going, it is believed, from the upper Pecos River southeastward to the upper Colorado, thence north across the Brazos, Red, Canadian and Ar-

[10] Bandelier, *The Journey of Alvar Nuñez Cabeza de Vaca* (Trail Makers series); Hodge, *The Narrative of Alvar Nuñez Cabeza de Vaca*, in *Spanish Explorers in the Southern United States, 1528–1543.* For various critical articles relative to the route of Cabeza de Vaca, see the early files of *The Quarterly.*

[11] Lewis, *The Narrative of the Expedition of Hernando de Soto*, by the Gentleman of Elvas, in *Spanish Explorers in the Southern United States, 1528–1543.*

kansas rivers, eastward into central Kansas, and directly back to the Pecos. In the course of the expedition, northwestern Texas was traversed in four distinct paths, and the Spaniards learned of the Llanos del Cíbolo and of the wandering tribes of Plains Indians who followed the buffalo for subsistence.[12]

Incidental crossing of southwestern Texas.—After the Coronado expedition interest in our Southwest lagged for nearly four decades, when the Spaniards again gave it their attention, this time approaching it by way of the central Mexican plateau, across what is now northern Chihuahua and up the Rio Grande or the Pecos. In the course of the renewed exploration and the colonization of New Mexico, in the last two decades of the sixteenth century, several expeditions incidentally crossed the western extremity of Texas, between the Pecos and the Rio Grande. Of these expeditions the ones best known are those made by Father Rodríguez in 1581, Espéjo in 1582, Castaño de Sosa in 1590, Bonilla and Humaña about 1595, and Juan de Oñate, the colonizer of New Mexico, in 1598.[13] All this region was then a part of New Mexico, and the exploration of it was made chiefly incident to the development and exploitation of the more interesting Pueblo region in the upper Rio Grande valley.

The search for Gran Quivira.—But the subjugation of the Pueblos did not exhaust the energies of the *conquistadores*, and they turned again from time to time with all their old fire to exploit and exploration. To the east there were several points of interest. Gran Quivira was still to be sought somewhere across the Llanos del Cíbolo; adjacent to it were the Aijados, in whose country were the Seven Hills supposedly rich in gold; southeast of Santa Fé, on the upper Colorado River, were the Jumano Indians, who welcomed missionaries and afforded trade in hides, and in whose streams were found pearls. Finally, in the pursuit of these objects, still another, more

[12] George Parker Winship, *The Coronado Expedition*; Castañeda, *Narrative of the Expedition of Coronado*, edited by Hodge, in *Spanish Explorers in the Southern United States, 1528–1543*. The route, as outlined above, is that marked out by Hodge, *op. cit.*, map.

[13] Bancroft, *Arizona and New Mexico*, 74–128; De León, *Historia de Nuevo León*, 92–95; Niel, *Apuntamientos*, 91–92.

remote, rose above the horizon in the east, the "Great Kingdom of the Texas."[14]

Concerning the expeditions made in search of Quivira after Coronado's day, our information is exaggerated and unsatisfactory, but the general outline of events is fairly clear. As the record has it, about 1595 Juan de Humaña and a party of soldiers were destroyed by the Indians while returning from a search for Quivira, at a place some two hundred leagues northeast of Santa Fé, afterward known in tradition as La Matanza (the death place). It was said that they were returning laden with gold. In June, 1601, Juan de Oñate, governor of New Mexico, made the opening expedition of the seventeenth century. Accompanied by two friars and eighty men, and with a survivor of the Humaña expedition as guide, he went east-northeast and north two hundred leagues from Santa Fé, reached La Matanza, received ambassadors from Quivira, engaged in a terrible battle with the Escanjaques Indians, and returned home.[15] In 1629, when Father Juan de Salas, of New Mexico, was on the eastern plains among the Jumanos, messengers from the Aijados and Quiviras were sent to see him and accompanied him to Santa Fé to ask for missionaries.[16] In 1634 Alonso de Vaca went three hundred leagues east from New Mexico, possibly in response to the call of 1629, to a great river across which was Quivira. Finally, Don Diego de Peñalosa, an evicted and discredited governor of New Mexico, later claimed that in 1662 he had made an expedition several hundred leagues east and north, and succeeded in finding the city of Quivira. That Peñalosa made such a journey at all is doubted by most scholars,[17] but the news that he was telling the tale at the

[14] Niel, *Apuntamientos*, 91–93. Posadas, *Informe á S. M. sobre las tierras de Nuevo México, Quivira, y Tegüayo* (1686), in Duro, *Don Diego de Peñalosa*, 53–67.

[15] Niel, *Apuntamientos*, 91–92; Bancroft, *Arizona and New Mexico*, 149–50.

[16] Posadas, *Informe*, 1686.

[17] For the Peñalosa expedition, see Cesaro Fernández Duro, *Don Diego de Peñalosa y su Descubrimiento de Quivira* (Madrid, 1882); John Gilmary Shea, *The Expedition of Don Diego Dionisio de Peñalosa* (New York, 1882); E. T. Miller, "The Connection of Peñalosa with the LaSalle Expedition," in *The Quarterly*, Vol. V, 97–112.

court of France, for the purpose of getting up an expedition against Spain's possessions on the Gulf, aroused Spain in 1678 to take a livelier interest in Texas than she had before manifested, and to renewed talk of searching for Gran Quivira.

Father Benavides' proposal. In 1630, when Quivira was attracting so much attention, Father Benavides, custos of the missions of New Mexico, made a most interesting suggestion regarding the eastern country, and one which later bore fruit. Writing of the "kingdoms" of Quivira and Aixaos, he described them as rich in gold; and, as a means of subduing them, restraining the English and the Dutch, and providing a shorter route from Cuba to New Mexico, he suggested the occupation of a place on the Gulf coast known as the Bay of Espíritu Santo, shown on the maps as somewhere between Apalache and Tampico, and, as Benavides thought, less than a hundred leagues from Quivira.[18] In 1632 Benavides published another memorial urging the same plan.[19] It will be seen that nearly half a century later the Spanish government took the proposal under consideration, and had set about putting it into effect before the La Salle expedition occurred.

Expeditions to the Jumanos: News of the Texas.—Much more satisfactory is our information concerning a similar series of expeditions made in the seventeenth century to the Jumano Indians of the upper Colorado River, in the interest of missionary work, pearl hunting, trade in skins, and exploration.

The Jumanos left a most interesting and, on account of the numerous localities in which people of that name were encountered at different times, a somewhat puzzling record. They were found, for example, on the Rio Grande below El Paso, in eastern New Mexico, in central Texas on the Colorado, in southeastern Texas, on the Arkansas, and on the Red.[20] This ubiquity of the Jumanos is to be explained in part, no doubt, by the migration of the tribe to and from the buffalo plains at different seasons of the year; but it seems

[18] Benavides, *Memorial*, translation in the *Land of Sunshine*, Vol. XIV, 139–40.

[19] Duro, *Don Diego de Peñalosa*, 132.

[20] For a summary of the history of the Jumanos, see Hodge, "The Jumano Indians," in *Proceedings* of the American Antiquarian Society at the Semi-Annual

equally clear that there were at least two distinct divisions of people known to the Spaniards by the same name. The division of particular interest here is the one which, in the seventeenth century, frequented or lived upon the buffalo plains of west-central Texas and was often visited there by the Spaniards of New Mexico for the purposes indicated.

The first recorded journey to these eastern Jumanos was made in 1629.[21] Previous to that time Father Juan de Salas, of Isleta (old Isleta, near the present Albuquerque) had worked among the Tompiros and Salineros in eastern New Mexico and had come in contact with Jumano living east of these tribes and hostile to them.[22] In the year mentioned, the Jumano sent a delegation to Isleta to repeat a request previously made that he go with them to their homes to minister to their people. On being asked why they desired missionaries, they told the story, now a classic in the lore of the Southwest, of the miraculous conversion of their tribes by a beautiful woman wearing the garb of a nun, and later identified as Mother María de Ágreda, abbess of a famous convent in Spain, who declared that she had converted these tribes during a visit to America "in ecstasy."[23]

Setting out with the petitioners, accompanied by Father Diego López and three soldiers, Salas went to a point more than one hundred twelve leagues eastward from Santa Fé, where he found a multitude of Indians, wrought miraculous cures, received messengers from the Quiviras and Aixados, and returned to Santa Fé for aid

---

Meeting, April, 1910; a treatment of special phases of the subject, suggested by Hodge's paper, is contained in Bolton, "The Jumano Indians in Texas, 1650–1771," in *The Quarterly*, Vol. XV, 66–84.

[21] In 1582 Espejo had encountered Jumano living on the Rio Grande, and during the last years of the sixteenth century Jumano were under instruction by the missionaries in eastern New Mexico. Hodge, *op. cit.*

[22] Benavides, *Memorial*, 1630; Vetancur, *Chrónica de la Provincia del Santo Evangelio* (1697), 96.

[23] For the foundation of the story of the miraculous conversion of the Jumano, see Benavides, *Memorial*, in *Land of Sunshine*, Vol. XIV, 139, and Vetancur, *Chrónica de la Provincia del Santo Evangelio* (1697), 96. Secondary accounts are in Shea, *The Catholic Church in America*, I, 195–98, and Schmidt, "Ven. María Jesus de Agreda: a Correction," in *The Quarterly*, Vol. I, 121–24. For references

in founding missions among the people he had visited.[24] There is evidence that a part of the Jumanos followed the missionaries to New Mexico and were for a time ministered to in a separate mission.[25] But the period was short, and in 1632 Father Salas went again to the Jumanos on the plains, accompanied by Father Diego de Ortega and some soldiers. When Salas returned, Father Ortega remained with the Indians six months.

From now on the location of the Jumanos comes into clearer light. The place where they were found this time was described as two hundred leagues southeast of Santa Fé, on a stream called the Nueces, because of the abundance of nuts (*nueces*) on its banks. This description corresponds essentially with those of all subsequent journeys made in the seventeenth century. The stream, as we shall see, was clearly one of the branches of the Colorado River, and not improbably the Concho.[26]

to the conversion of the Texas by this mysterious person, see the letter of De León, quoted on pages 121–22; and Manzanet, *Carta*, translated by Lilia M. Casis, in *The Quarterly*, Vol. II, 311. Manzanet (Massanet) there states that while at the village of the Nabedache chief in 1690 the chief "asked me one evening for a piece of blue baize to make a shroud in which to bury his mother when she died; I told him that cloth would be more suitable, and he answered that he did not want any color other than blue. I then asked him what mysterious reason he had for preferring the blue color, and in reply he said that they were very fond of that color, particularly for burial clothes, because in times past they had been visited frequently by a very beautiful woman, who used to come down from the hills, dressed in blue garments, and that they wished to do as that woman had done. On my asking whether that had been long since, the governor said it had been before his time, but his mother, who was aged, had seen that woman, as had also the other old people. From this it is easily to be seen that they referred to the Madre María de Jesus de Agreda, who was very frequently in these regions, as she herself acknowledged to the Father Custodian of New Mexico, her last visit having been made in 1631." Father Casañas, writing in 1691 at the Nabedache village, made the comment, evidently intended to controvert the foregoing opinion, that the Indians "greatly esteem any piece of woolen cloth, especially if it is blue. This is due solely to the circumstance that the sky is of this color." *Relación*, August 15, 1691. MS.

[24] See the works of Benavides, Vetancur, and Hodge, already cited.

[25] Hodge, *The Jumano Indians*, 10–11, and works cited therein.

[26] See Bolton, "The Jumano Indians in Texas, 1650–1771," in *The Quarterly*, Vol. XV, 68–74; Posadas, *Informe*, 1686.

What occurred in the interim does not appear, but eighteen years later an expedition led by Captains Hernando Martín and Diego del Castillo visited the Jumanos on the Nueces and remained with them six months. While there two things of greatest interest occurred. The first was the gathering of a large quantity of shells (*conchos*) from the river, which, on being burned, disclosed pearls. The other was the approach of a portion of the party, after passing fifty leagues beyond the Jumano through the country of the Cuitaos, Escanjaques, and Aijados, to the borders of a people called "Tejas." "They did not enter their territory," our chronicler tells us, "as they learned that it was very large and contained many people," but a "lieutenant" of the Tejas "king" went to see Castillo. This, so far as I know, is the first information acquired by the Spaniards unquestionably concerning the people from whom Texas got its name.[27]

The arrival of Martín and Castillo at Santa Fé with pearls, at a time when the pearls of California were proving to be a disappointment, now created a new interest in central Texas. The samples were sent to the viceroy in Mexico, who at once ordered another expedition to the Nueces. It was made in 1654 by Diego de Guadalajara, with thirty soldiers, among whom was Juan Domínguez de Mendoza, thirty years later the leader of a more important expedition to the same place. Guadalajara found the Jumano in the same region where they had been encountered in 1632 and 1650. Thirty leagues farther on they had a hard fight with the Cuitaos, of whom they killed many, besides taking two hundred prisoners and rich spoils in the way of buckskins, elkskins, and buffalo hides. Still another interest in the country had arisen—that of commerce in peltry.[28]

No other specific expedition to the Jumano is recorded till that of Juan Domínguez de Mendoza, in 1684, the records of which

[27] Posadas, *Informe*; Declaration of Juan Sabeata, October 20, 1683. There is no good reason for thinking that Yejo, the Indian referred to in Castañeda's narrative of Guzmán's exploring activities on the west coast of Mexico, or the Teyas met by Coronado on the buffalo plains, were of the Texas group found in the later seventeenth century east of the Trinity River. See Winship, *The Coronado Expedition*, 472–73; Wooten (editor), *Comprehensive History of Texas*, I, 8.

[28] Posadas, *Informe*, 1686.

settle all doubt as to the location of the tribe to whom these visits were directed. But in the interim many journeys seem to have been made to them for the purpose of trade, evidence of which has just come to light in the Mexican archives. In 1683, when a delegation of Jumanos from the eastern plains visited the Spanish refugees then at El Paso, the authorities declared in writing, as evidence of the friendship of the tribe, that before 1680, when the Pueblo revolt had occurred, trade and friendship had been maintained with the Jumanos "with such security that the Spaniards, six, eight, and ten, went to their lands and villages every year to trade with these Indians" in buckskins, *teocas*, and buffalo hides.[29] We shall see that the Mendoza party in 1684 brought back nearly five thousand buffalo skins. It was later asserted that some time before this event, two Franciscan missionaries, inspired by the Venerable Mother María de Ágreda, had gone to the Texas and baptized many of their number, "their very prince" being the first to receive the faith.[30] This allusion may have been to the visits of Father Salas and his companions to the borders of the Texas early in the century, for no other record of a missionary visit to these people before 1689 is known.

4. *From the South, by way of Nuevo León and Coahuila*

While there had thus been definite progress eastward from New Mexico during the first three-fourths of the seventeenth century, and considerable contact between that province and what is now the western half of Texas, from the south, the natural line of advance from Mexico to Texas, progress was slow.

The outposts of northeastern New Spain.—In the sixteenth century, nevertheless, northeastward expansion from the valley of Mexico had been rapid. It has already been stated that as early as 1522 Pánuco had been founded by Cortes himself, and that by 1528 two expeditions from the point had explored the coasts north of the Rio

[29] "Declaración de los Yndios que vinieron á esta Plassa de armas de San Lorenço de la toma del rio del Norte," August 11, 1683. MS. Provincias Internas, vol. 35, *Expediente*, 2, p. 60.

[30] "Memorial de Fray Nicolás López acerca de la repoblación de Nuevo Méjico," April 24, 1686, in Duro, *Peñalosa*, 67.

Grande. For half a century Pánuco remained the northeasternmost outpost, but meanwhile progress was more rapid along the central Mexican plateau, where, following the line of the most promising mineral deposits, by 1565 conquests were extended as far as Parras, Saltillo, and perhaps Monterrey.

Advance was now made again along the Gulf plain. In 1576 Luis de Carabajal pursued Indians into the country north of Pánuco, and in 1579 was commissioned to conquer and settle it. The province assigned to him was called Nuevo León, and was to extend two hundred leagues north from Pánuco, a jurisdiction reaching nearly or quite to the mouth of the Colorado River. For a few years Carabajal's headquarters were at Pánuco, but in (or by) 1583 he went inland with a colony, opened the mines of San Gregorio, and founded there the city of León, now Cerralvo. This place, situated about one hundred fifty miles from the coast and only some forty from the Rio Grande (near modern Mier), was for a long time the principal settlement and the capital of the province, and was for a century, with some intervals, the northernmost outpost on the Rio Grande frontier. Shortly after founding León, Carabajal established the villa of San Luis, farther south, which in 1596 became or was succeeded by the villa of Monterrey. Subsequently various intermediate points were occupied.[31]

Temporarily a more northerly outpost than León was established. Hearing of rich mineral deposits toward the northwest, in the district called Coahuila, about 1590 Carabajal took from Saltillo supplies and a colony, opened mines, and founded the villa of Almadén where Monclova now stands. While there he was arrested by the Inquisition on the charge of Judaism and thrown into prison in Mexico, where he died. A few months after Carabajal's arrest, Castaño de Sosa, left in charge of the colony, abandoned the place and led the

[31] This summary of the early history of Nuevo León is based mainly on León, Alonso, *Historia de Nuevo León* (Mexico, 1909); Estéban L. Portillo, *Apuntes para la Historia Antiqua de Coahuila y Texas* (Saltillo, 1888); E. J. González, *Lecciones Orales de Historia de Nuevo León* (Monterey, 1887); E. J. González, *Colección de Noticias y Documentos para la Historia del Estado de Nuevo León* (Monterey, 1885); Alejandro Prieto, *Historia, Geografía y Estadística del Estado de Tamaulipas* (Mexico, 1873).

settlers off to attempt the conquest of New Mexico, crossing the Rio Grande at the Pecos and following that stream to the Pueblo region.[32] In 1603 and again in 1644 Almadén was temporarily re-occupied, but without success, and after this León (Cerralvo), where a mission was founded in 1630 and a presidio in 1653, remained the northern outpost till 1673.[33]

Frontier explorations, 1590–1665.—By the middle of the seventeenth century explorations beyond the frontier had been made on a small scale in all directions. That they were not more extensive was due to Indian troubles and the feebleness of the frontier settlements. From Cerralvo an expedition was sent eastward in 1638 to verify the report that Europeans, thought to be Dutch, were trading with the Indians near the Gulf. The party was impeded by the swollen "Camalucanos" River, had a battle with the Indians, and failed to reach the coast. A direct route to the Gulf would have taken them across the Rio Bravo, but that stream was apparently not reached, unless it was the Camalucanos. By 1653 a regular line of trade had been established between Cerralvo and Pánuco, the Rio de las Palmas (Santandér) had been re-explored, and the country twenty leagues beyond that stream traversed.[34]

To the north the Spaniards were led short distances by a desire to establish connection with La Florida, by rumors of the silver deposit called El Cerro (or La Sierra) de la Plata, and in pursuit of Indians. Soon after Sosa's expedition up the Pecos, a party of eight men from Saltillo is said to have crossed the Rio Bravo into what is now Texas, but no details of the event are known.[35] Interest in Florida is shown by the fact that in 1613 two citizens of Nuevo León, Captains José Treviño and Bernabé Casas, offered the viceroy "their persons and their property to undertake the conquest of the interior provinces of the Kingdom of León, helping thereby to expel

---

[32] León, 91–95; Bancroft, *North Mexican States*, I, 100–107. Bancroft could not determine the location of Almadén, but this point is now perfectly clear.

[33] León, *Historia de Nuevo León*, 84, 87–88, 95–98, 102, 125–27; Arlegui, *Crónica*, 85, 126–28, 228; González, *Lecciones Orales*, 26.

[34] León, *Historia de Nuevo León*, 153.

[35] Portillo, *Apuntes*, 114n. It is referred to the time of Francisco de Urdiñola the younger, who became governor of Nueva Vizcaya in 1591.

the English from La Florida."[36] Perhaps they had heard of the settlement of Jamestown six years before. To discover the Cerro de la Plata two attempts were made in 1644 and 1648 by General Juan de Zavala, but both of them were frustrated by Indian revolts. Writing of this mineral deposit in 1648 De León said: "It is unknown to those now living . . . and must have been to those in the past."[37] Summarizing in 1650 what he had accomplished by way of exploration since 1626, when he became governor, Martín de Zavala said of himself: "he has made a beginning of northern discovery, whereby he has explored more than fifty leagues with the purpose of continuing till communication is established with La Florida, and has almost certain knowledge of the Sierra de la Plata, which he intends to reach, a feat which has so often been attempted by the governors of Nueva Vizcaya and Nuevo León, but which has been abandoned because of Indian troubles."[38] It is not clear whether the fifty leagues explored toward La Florida were those covered in search of the mine or not; but in either case, the Rio Bravo was in all probability passed.

Pursuit of the Indians was a constant occupation on this frontier. From the outset slave catching for the markets and for the *encomiendas*, which in Nuevo León were generally established, had been a favorite occupation of Cerralvo, more attractive than mining.[39] In retaliation, the savage tribes made frequent raids upon the settlements, and were as often pursued beyond the frontiers by such doughty warriors as Alonso de León, Juan de Zavala, Juan de la Garza, and Fernández de Azcué. In 1653, for example, a campaign led by Garza was made jointly by soldiers of Saltillo and Nuevo León against the Cacaxtles, who were found more than seventy leagues northward from Monterrey.[40] Two years later another joint campaign was made by the soldiers of Saltillo and Monterrey against the same tribe. The troop of one hundred three soldiers, equipped

[36] González, *Lecciones Orales*, 52, citing Cavo, *Tres Siglos*; León, *Historia de Nuevo León*, 29–30, 81, 133–34, 153, 160–63, 204, 214, 219.

[37] León, *Historia de Nuevo León*, 84.

[38] Memorial presented to the king through Alonso de León. *Ibid.*, 214.

[39] *Ibid.*, 95.   [40] *Ibid.*, 221–22.

with eight hundred horses, and led by Fernández de Azcué, were supported by more than three hundred Indian allies of the Coahuila region. Going north from Monterrey, at a place twenty-four leagues beyond the Rio Bravo they encountered the enemy within a wood, surrounded them, fought all day, slew a hundred men and took seventy prisoners, themselves suffering the loss of twenty wounded. This campaign of Azcué, made against the Cacaxtles, is the first expedition to cross the lower Rio Grande of which we have definite record.[41]

Thus, by 1670 the Spaniards had barely broken over the Rio Grande frontier below the Pecos. Now, however, another forward step was taken on this border, the frontier of settlement pushed northeastward, and missionary activity extended across the Rio Grande, a movement that brought other important developments in its train. As was often the case, the pioneers in this advance movement were the missionaries; their leader was Juan Larios, a native of Nueva Galicia and a friar of the Franciscan province of Santiago de Jalisco.

The founding of Coahuila: the Larios-Bosque Expedition.—In 1670 Father Larios began missionary work on the troubled Coahuila frontier, where he seems to have remained alone for some three years. Returning to Guadalajara, in 1673 he went again to Coahuila, accompanied by Father Dionysio de Peñasco and Fray Manuel de la Cruz, a lay brother. Aided by soldiers sent by the governor of Nueva Vizcaya, they founded of the roving tribes two Indian settlements, one on the Sabinas River and one to the north of that stream. On one of his missionary trips made at this time Fray Manuel de la Cruz crossed the Rio Grande to visit the interior tribes, and barely escaped capture by the Yerbipiames, a people who from that time till the day of their extinction gave untold trouble on this border. In the next year, 1674, Antonio de Valcárcel, appointed *alcalde mayor* of the

---

[41] *Ibid.*, 228–30. There is a persistent tradition, found in many eighteenth century and nineteenth century official Spanish documents, that an expedition made in 1630 explored clear to the San Andrés (Red) and Mississippi rivers, and marked out the boundaries of the province of Texas, but the story is not well substantiated, and contains so many conflicting and impossible elements that it is self-refuting.

Coahuila district, founded on the site of the thrice abandoned Almadén a "city" called Nuestra Señora de Guadalupe, and assisted Father Larios in transferring thither his temporary missions, which included numerous Indians from across the Rio Grande. Meanwhile the friars had been joined by Father Dionysio de San Buenaventura. In 1675 Valcárcel sent Alférez Fernando del Bosque, accompanied by Fathers Larios and San Buenaventura, across the Rio Grande to explore the country and reconnoiter the tribes, and as a result of the report brought back four missions were soon established in the Coahuila district, one for each of the four groups or confederacies, which embraced tribes to the north as well as to the south of the Rio Grande.[42]

News of the Texas.—Now the Texas arose above the Coahuila horizon, just as they had appeared above that of New Mexico a quarter of a century before. In 1676 the Bishop of Guadalajara visited Coahuila, and one of the reasons which he gave in his report for favoring the four missions recommended by Bosque was the opportunity which they would afford to reach and convert a more important people beyond, the Texas, of whom he gives a most interesting account. "Coahuila," he says,

> has as a neighbor on the north, inclining somewhat to the east, a populous nation of people, and so extensive that those who give detailed reports of them do not know where it ends. These [who give the reports] are many, through having communicated with the people of that nation, which they call Texas, and who, they maintain, live under an organized government (*en policía*), congregated in their pueblos, and governed by a casique who is named by the Great Lord, as they call the one who rules them all, and who, they say, resides in the interior. They have houses made of wood, cultivate the soil, plant maize and other crops, wear clothes, and punish misdemeanors, especially theft. The Coahuiles do not give more detailed reports of the Texas because, they say, they are allowed to go only to the first pueblos of the border, since the

[42] The principal source for the history of the developments described above is a collection of documents entitled "Autos de la conquista de la Prova. hecha en este año por D. Antonio Balcarcel," etc. Some of them are printed in Portillo, *Apuntes*. They were used by me in the original in the archives of Mexico.

Great Lord of the Texas does not permit foreign nations to enter the interior of his country. There are many of these Coahuiles who give these reports, and who say that they got them through having aided the Texas in their wars against the Pauit, another very warlike nation. The Coahuiles once pacified, the Spaniards can reach the land of the Texas without touching the country of enemies.

This account of the Texas is of special interest as being the earliest extant, so far as is known, although, as we have seen, reports of them had reached New Mexico as early as 1650. One of the objective points of the Spaniards both of New Mexico and Coahuila was thenceforth the Kingdom of the Texas.[43]

Summary.—By 1676 some advance had been made into Texas from all directions. Sixteenth century explorers coming by way of the Gulf, Florida, and New Mexico had run its coasts and traversed its southern, northern, and western borders. In the seventeenth century the continued search for Gran Quivira had led to further explorations in the west and north; frequent visits to the Jumano country had made better known the country between Santa Fé and the middle Colorado, while some beginnings had been made of missionary work and settlement in the Rio Grande valley between El Paso and the mouth of the Conchos River. In addition to interest in Quivira, the Aixados, the Jumanos, the pearls of the Nueces (Colorado), and trade in peltry and captives on the plains, there had arisen a desire to reach another land reputed to be rich but as yet untrod, the Great Kingdom of the Texas. From the south, meanwhile, the frontier had slowly expanded across the lower Rio Grande through the search for the Cerro de la Plata, pursuit of hostile Indians, efforts to establish communication with Florida, and missionary work among the tribes of the Coahuila frontier. In the pursuit of this last object, interest was aroused, here as in New Mexico, in the Texas Indians.

[43] "Informe que hizo el Yllmo Senor Don Manuel Fernz. de Sta Cruz Abpo de Guadalaxa. a el Yllmo, y exmo Senor Maestro Don Fr. Payo de Rivera, Arzobispo de Mexico. . . . dando Relasion de las Tierras de Coahuila," etc., 1676. MS. in the archive of the Bishopric of Linares.

It is clear that all these forces were leading slowly but surely to the occupation of central and eastern Texas, even in the absence of the stimulus of foreign aggression. But the old interests were now all quickened by rumors of foreign encroachment, and thenceforth the various lines of advance rapidly converged and led to the settlement of the country beyond the Trinity. At the same time the El Paso district, at the other extreme of Texas, became definitely settled as a result of a counter movement from New Mexico.

III. THE COVERAGE OF THE LINES

1. Peñalosa and Plans to Occupy the Bay of Espíritu Santo

In 1678 news was received at the Spanish court that Peñalosa, the discredited governor of New Mexico already mentioned, had proposed at the court of France an expedition against New Spain. Incident to the investigation of the report, the royal secretaries brought forth Benavides's memorial of 1630, and noted his recommendation that the Bay of Espíritu Santo be occupied as a base of operations in New Mexico and Quivira and as a defense against the encroachment of foreigners. Thereupon the king asked the viceroy for a report on the geography of the country east of New Mexico and the feasibility of Benavides's plan—"what advantages would come from Christianizing the kingdoms of Quivira and Tagago [Teguayo]; what means would be needed to effect it; whether it could be done better by the way of Florida than through the Bay of Espíritu Santo; and whether any danger was to be feared from the proposals of Peñalosa."[44]

Some time before August 2, 1685, Martín de Echegaray, pilot major and captain at Pensacola, reported to the king the danger that the French might occupy the Bay of Espíritu Santo and enter thence to New Mexico. He accordingly repeated the suggestion of Father Benavides, and offered to explore the bay with a view to its occupation and to prepare a map of the coast. A *junta de guerra* approved the proposal, and on August 2 the king ordered the governor of Florida to cooperate with Echegaray. At the same time, he repeated

[44] Bolton, "Notes on Clark's The Beginnings of Texas," in *The Quarterly*, Vol. XII, 152; Duro, *Don Diego de Peñalosa*, 50–53.

the request for the report from the viceroy, which had not yet been made, "in order that from all directions may be had the desired notices with respect to all the foregoing, for the greater security and certainty of the achievement of the discovery of the said Bay of Espíritu Santo and the kingdoms of Quivira and Tagago, and of their settlement and conservation, in order thereby to make the said provinces of Florida secure from the menaces in which they stand from the corsairs and pirates who commonly infest them."[45]

2. *The Settlement of the El Paso District*

Meanwhile, the center of the province of New Mexico had been transferred to the El Paso district, where it remained till near the end of the seventeenth century. This change of base not only resulted in the planting of considerable establishments on what is now Texas soil, but also served to increase interest in the country toward the east.

In 1659, a mission, Nuestra Señora de Guadalupe, was begun at El Paso, on the south side of the river, and a small civil settlement grew up there. Before 1680 another mission, San Francisco de los Sumas, was founded some twelve leagues down the river. In 1680 the colony received a large accretion through the revolt of the Pueblo Indians of New Mexico. As a result of this event all the Spanish inhabitants and the Indians of three pueblos retreated down the river and settled at the Pass and at different points below that place on both sides of the river for a distance of twelve or more leagues. There were now in or near the valley six missions, Guadalupe, San Francisco de los Sumas, Senecú, Socorro, Isleta, and Santa Gertrudis; four Spanish villages or pueblos, San Lorenzo, San Pedro de Alcántara, San José, and Isleta; and the presidio of El Paso.

In 1683 and 1684 missionary work was temporarily extended from El Paso to the junction of the Conchos with the Rio Grande, a point then known as La Junta, among the Julimes and their allies.

---

[45] *Cédula* of August 2, 1685, printed in Duro, *Peñalosa*, 50–53. Without knowing the date of Echegaray's proposal, it can not be stated whether it was made before or after news of the La Salle expedition reached Florida. It may have been suggested by the La Salle expedition of 1682 down the Mississippi.

Already two Franciscans, Fray García de San Francisco, founder of the mission of Guadalupe at El Paso in 1659 and guardian there till 1671, and Fray Juan de Sumesta, had separately visited the Indians at La Junta, but had not remained. Requests for missionaries at Parral proving without avail, the Indians turned in 1683 to the settlement of El Paso. In response to their appeal, Fray Nicolás López and Fathers Juan Zavaleta and Antonio Acevedo went in December, 1683, to La Junta, and before the end of 1684 seven churches had been built for nine tribes, living, apparently, on both sides of the Rio Grande, and five hundred persons had been baptized. Father López tried to secure a settlement of Spaniards for the place, but failed, and within a short time the missions were abandoned on account of an uprising.[46]

3. The Mendoza-López Expedition to the Jumanos, 1684

The same appeal that led Father López to undertake missionary work at La Junta resulted in the expedition made in 1684 by Juan Domínguez de Mendoza and Father López to the Jumano Indians of the Nueces; this event, in turn, greatly increased interest in the eastern tribes, especially the Texas and Quiviras.

The principal bearer of the request for missionaries in 1683 was a Jumano Indian known to history as Juan Sabeata, who appeared before Governor Cruzate in October.[47] According to his story he and some of his people lived with the Julimes at La Junta. Part of his tribe lived six days to the eastward, on the Nueces River, which

---

[46] The above summary is based mainly on two collections of original Spanish manuscripts entitled "Auttos tocantes; al Alsamiento de los Yndios de la Provincia de la Nueba Mexico," and "Autos Pertenecientes a el alçamiento de los Yndios de la Prova del Nuevo Mexico y la entrada, Y subçesos de ella que se hiço para su recuperacion." In addition some use has been made of the church archives of Juarez. I am indebted to Miss Anne Hughes for much aid in digesting the two *expedientes*, and to Mr. J. W. Curd, for notes from the Juarez documents.

[47] This account of the Mendoza expedition is based on the original documents in the archives of Mexico. They consist for the most part of the two collections named in the note next above, and another entitled "Viage Que A Solicitud de los Naturales de la Prova. de Texas . . . Hizo el Maestre de Campo Juan Dominguez de Mendoza."

was three days beyond the place where the buffalo herds began. Among more than thirty tribes which he named as living toward the east were the "extended nation of the Humanas," the "great kingdom of the Texas," and the "great kingdom of Quivira." He told particularly of the "great kingdom of the Texas." This populous realm, which was fifteen days eastward from La Junta, was ruled by a powerful king. As for the man who had visited Castillo in 1650, he was not king, "but only the king's lieutenant." The Texas were a settled people, raised crops in abundance, and were neighbors of La Gran Quivira, so close, indeed, that they visited back and forth almost daily. From what he had heard, they would gladly welcome settlers and missionaries, for ever since Castillo's day they had been wishing for and expecting them. Even now two messengers from the Texas were waiting at La Junta for a reply to their request sent through Sabeata. A touch of interest was added to the story by the statement, on the authority of the two Texas messengers "that in that part of the east Spaniards enter by water in Houses made of trees, and maintain trade with the said Nation of the Texas."[48] It was easy for the authorities, after the menace offered by Peñalosa, to transform these "Spaniards" into encroaching Frenchmen.

Governor Cruzate was enthusiastic at the prospect of a new field for exploration, and forwarded Sabeata's declaration to the viceroy with a letter in which he stated that he would consider it a great triumph if "another New World" and "two Realms with two more Crowns" should be added to the kingdom.[49] In answer to Sabeata's request, Father López went to La Junta, as we have already seen. Shortly afterward he was followed by Maestre de Campo Juan Domínguez de Mendoza and a small band of soldiers, destined to "the Discovery of the Orient and the Kingdom of the Texas."[50]

[48] Declaration of Juan Sabeata, October 20, 1683. Sabeata added that "he who came to see said Sargento Mayor Diego del castillo when he was there was not their King, but his Lieutenant, for the King never leaves home, and lives with great authority." *Ibid.*

[49] Cruzate to the viceroy, October 30, 1683. MS.

[50] Opening paragraph of Mendoza's "Derrotero." Mendoza's "Ynstruccion" required him to undertake "the new discovery of the Jumanas and of all the other nations who are their friends." MS. in the Bancroft Collection.

On January 1, 1684, the party, accompanied by Father López, and leaving Father Acevedo to minister to the Indians at La Junta, set out for the country of the Nueces, which they found after going seventy leagues northward to the Pecos and thence forty leagues toward the east. Mendoza kept a diary of the expedition which identifies the Nueces with one of the branches of the upper Colorado, probably the Concho, and with the stream visited by the expedition of 1654, for Mendoza had himself been on that journey and recognized the place. Moreover, he had with him Hernando Martín, who had been one of the leaders of the expedition of 1650. Forty leagues from the head of the Nueces, at a stream called the San Clemente, apparently the Colorado, a temporary fort and chapel were built. During the stay of several weeks a number of Indians were baptized and nearly five thousand buffalo hides secured. The Indians asked for missionaries and settlers, and before returning Father López and Mendoza promised to return within a year prepared to grant the request.[51]

Writing to the king of this expedition Father López said:

Penetrating and mapping out their lands, both to the north and the east, I was in sixty-six other nations [besides those at La Junta], all docile and friendly toward the Spaniard, and asking also for the water of baptism, and that we should settle where it should seem convenient. . . . We were in their lands six months, sustained by the said heathen solely on the fruits of the soil. . . . Their mineral hills offer much; there are many rivers, all with different kinds of fish and abounding in nacre, from which years ago many pearl were secured. . . . And besides these nations we had ambassadors from the Texas, a powerful kingdom, where Mother María de Ágreda catechized many Indians, as she relates in her writings. . . . And we came to tread the borders of the first settlements of this nation. . . . We succeeded also in treading the lands of the Aijados nation, next to the great kingdom of Quivira, of whom Fray Alonso de Benavides makes mention, but because the said Aijados were at war with the tribes which we had in our friendship, I did not communicate with

[51] Mendoza, "Derrotero," and accompanying documents, in "Viage Que A Solicitud," etc. For further details see Bolton, "The Jumano Indians in Texas, 1650–1771," in *The Quarterly*, Vol. XV, 68–74.

them, although they were already planning to make friends with us. It [the Aijados tribe] is less than seventy leagues distant from La Gran Quivira.[52]

4. *Proposals for the Occupation of the Jumano Country, 1685–1686*

This expedition of 1684, coupled with news of Peñalosa's doings, now became the basis of an attempt to occupy the Jumano country with missionaries and soldiers, and of renewed talk by the New Mexico officials of Gran Quivira, Gran Teguayo, and the great Kingdom of the Texas.

On their return to El Paso, Father López and Mendoza both went to the city of Mexico. In a memorial of June 7, 1685, López urged, besides support for the settlements about El Paso and the missions at La Junta, the occupation of the recently explored country of the Jumanos. Sixty-six tribes, he said, northeastward from La Junta, had given obedience, and twenty additional missionaries were needed to serve them.[53] He was backed in this request by his order, for the commissary general advertised the new field in the various monasteries, and forty-six friars volunteered to go.[54] López's petition being negatived by the authorities at Mexico on account of the bad situation at El Paso, in March, 1686, he urged anew "the manifest peril threatened by delay." At present two hundred men would suffice to avert the danger, at little cost, because of the richness of the country; but later it would "be impossible to repair it with millions." He now asked, not for twenty but for fifty-two missionaries.[55] In another memorial he requested one hundred soldiers, even from the jails, and offered, on the promise of his two wealthy brothers of El Rosario, to furnish for the undertaking five hundred *fanegas* of maize, three hundred beeves, and two hundred horses.[56]

---

[52] Memorial, April 24, 1684, in Duro, *Peñalosa*, 67–74. In another account López stated that they were within twenty-five leagues of the Texas.

[53] López, "Representación," June 7, 1685, in *Viage Que A Solicitud*, 53–73.

[54] Memorial to the king, April 24, 1686, in Duro, *Peñalosa*, 67–74.

[55] "Segunda Representación," in *Viage Que A Solicitud*, 73.

[56] Memorial of April 24, 1686, in Duro, *Peñalosa*, 67–74.

His proposals were pronounced by the fiscal as "fantastic, and ideas meriting no consideration";[57] but he had already turned to the king, repeating his request, and urging especially the nearness of the country to be occupied to the Aijados, Texas, and the great kingdom of Quivira.[58]

About the same time Mendoza also addressed a memorial to the viceroy, saying that Peñalosa, under whom he had served in New Mexico, really possessed detailed information regarding Teguayo, the Sierra Azul, and the kingdom of the Texas. "And if this Peñalosa should carry out his intention, great ruin of this New Spain is to be feared, since these lands are the most fertile and fruitful of this New World." But in Mendoza lay the remedy. To avert the danger he offered, if the king would only supply him with two hundred men from the jails, to enter the eastern country again, explore as far as the North Sea, reconnoiter Gran Quivira and the kingdom of the Texas, make maps and reports, plant two presidios in the country of the Nueces, and reduce the Indians to settled life. The only expense to the crown would be that incident to arming the men and maintaining them till they should reach the Nueces, since, once there, the country would support, not two hundred, but two million; "for, besides these advantages, we have immediate recourse to the settlement of the Texas, which nation plants maize, calabashes, and beans." This memorial was perhaps written by Father López, for, besides bearing internal marks of that friar's authorship, it was sent by him to the king with "hearty commendation."[59]

5. *The La Salle Expedition and the Occupation of Eastern Texas, 1685–1690*

By this time news had been received in Mexico of the La Salle expedition to some point on the Gulf coast, and in 1686 began the series of explorations, four by sea from Vera Cruz and five by land from Monterrey and Monclova, in search, not of the French alone,

[57] *Dictamen fiscal*, May 22, 1686.

[58] Memorial of April 24, 1686. Duro, *Peñalosa*, 67–74.

[59] "Memorial del Maestre de Campo Juan Domínguez de Mendoza," in Duro, 74–77.

but (1) of the French, (2) the Bay of Espíritu Santo, and (3) the country of the Texas, which had not yet been reached.[60]

The events of this period have been so well told by Clark and Garrison that they need no more than the merest summary here. But from what has gone before, some of them will now take on a new meaning. In 1689, on the fourth of these land expeditions, De León and Father Massanet found the remains of the French settlement on Matagorda Bay, to which the name of Espíritu Santo thenceforth became attached for a reason which is now obvious. During the same expedition De León and Massanet went as far east as the Colorado River, where they were met by the chief of the Nabedache, the westernmost of the Hasinai, or Texas, tribes. After a short conference they arranged to return in the following year to found a mission for his people.[61]

Again the country of the Texas had been approached but not reached, and again was recorded a description of that promised but unseen land. On the basis of this conference, preconceived notions, and the reports made by some rescued Frenchmen who had been farther east, De León wrote in May, 1689, as follows:

The Texas ... are a very well governed (*política*) people, and plant large quantities of maize, beans, calabashes, cantaloupes, and water-melons. They say that they have nine settlements, I mean towns (*pueblos*), the largest one being fifteen leagues long and eight or ten wide. It must contain eight hundred heads of families (*vecinos*), each one having a large wooden house plastered with clay and roofed with lime, a door attached to the house, and its crops. In this way they follow one after another. ... They are very familiar with the fact that there is only one true God, that he is in Heaven, and that he was born of the Holy Virgin. They perform many Christian rites, and the Indian governor asked me for ministers to instruct them,

[60] Note the emphasis put by Father Massanet on the discovery of the Bay of Espíritu Santo as well as the search for the French. Letter to Sigüenza, in *The Quarterly*, Vol. II, 281–312.

[61] "Derrotero de la Jornada que hizo el General Alonzo de León para el descubrimiento de la Bahía del Espíritu Santo, y Población de Franceses: Año de 1689." *Memorias de Nueva España*, XXVII, fol. 1 *et seq.*; Bolton, "The Native Tribes about the East Texas Missions," in *The Quarterly*, Vol. XI, 263–66.

[saying] that many years ago a woman went inland to instruct them, but that she has not been there for a long time; and certainly it is a pity that people so rational, who plant crops and know that there is a God should have no one to teach them the Gospel, especially when the province of Texas is so large and so fertile and has so fine a climate.[62]

To this argument for occupying the Texas country, De León added the report of a rumor that there was another French settlement farther inland, in the region which he had not explored.

True to their promise, and with the co-operation of the government in Mexico, in the following year, 1690, De León and Massanet returned east with a party, reached the westernmost village of the Texas (Hasinai)[63] confederacy, near the Neches River, and founded there the first establishments in Spanish Texas.[64] This event, it is now plain, was not merely the result of the La Salle expedition, but was the logical culmination of the long series of expeditions made to the eastward from New Mexico and of the expansion of the Nuevo León–Coahuila frontier, and more especially of the quest, begun as far back as the time of Castillo and Martín, for the "great kingdom of the Texas." This is the principal explanation to be offered for the fact that the first Spanish outpost in eastern Texas was placed, not on the Bay of Espíritu Santo, where the French menace had occurred, but several hundred miles to the eastward. It was put among the Indians whom the Spaniards so long had hoped to reach.

[62] "Carta en que se da noticia de un viaje hecho a la Bahía de Espíritu Santo, y de la población que tenían ahí los franceses," in Buckingham Smith, *Documentos para la historia de la Florida.*

[63] For a discussion of the meaning and usages of the words Texas and Hasinai, see Bolton, "The Native Tribes about the East Texas Missions," in *The Quarterly*, Vol. XI, 249–76.

[64] El Paso being in what was then New Mexico.

CHAPTER SIX

*The West Coast Corridor**

BOLTON's earliest writing was, in a sense, indicative of his sojourn in Texas, when it was quite natural that his research and interests should turn to the East Coast Corridor, namely, Texas and the approaches thereto. His later move to the West Coast, to Stanford first and then to the University of California, quite as naturally tended to focus much of his attention on the left flank of the advancing frontier, which ultimately would bring the Spaniards into Alta California. In this report paper he sketches the story of the West Coast Corridor with that masterful sweep so characteristic of his thinking and writing. Life did not leave him enough years to complete the longer work which this report projected. However, the paper rounds out his concept of the approaches to the Borderlands.

THIS PAPER IS DESIGNED to outline a problem for research rather than to solve it. I have gathered from the archives of Mexico, Spain, and other countries many thousands of pages of unpublished manuscript records bearing on the development of the West Coast of Mexico, a region with a most interesting and significant history, but which has been written only in slender outline or in particular spots. My aim today is to place the area in historical perspective, though I fully realize that in a twenty-minute sketch it will be difficult to find a middle ground between bald generalizations and details which obscure the pattern.[1]

Ever since the Spanish conquest in the sixteenth century a vast

* Paper read before the American Philosophical Society, April 24, 1947. Printed in the *Proceedings* of the American Philosophical Society, Vol. 91, No. 5 (December 1947), 426–29. Reprinted with the permission of the American Philosophical Society.

[1] A generous research grant from the American Philosophical Society has enabled me to have the very competent assistance of Miss Virginia E. Thickens in listing and photostating in the archives of Mexico several thousand pages of rare original

area in northern Mexico open for development has been a spur to the initiative of people in the more crowded regions farther south. Turner wrote a brilliant monograph on the significance of the frontier in the development of society in English North America. It would be interesting to consider to what extent his thesis is applicable or inapplicable to the history of New Spain—but that is not my theme today.

The place in Mexico where European and native have had longest and most vital contact is in the southern and central areas, where the indigenous peoples had a high civilization before the Spaniards arrived. Here during the conquest and in succeeding decades, European and native first fused their cultures and their blood. Here Spanish law and government were superimposed upon native institutions, but never wholly eradicated them. The two elements were complementary, each modifying the other. In this respect Spain was amazingly tolerant, as can be seen on many pages of the great *Recopilación de las Leyes de las Indias*, or code of public law for the New World.

Meanwhile another chapter in Mexican history was begun. The area of Spanish settlement was extended northward into regions inhabited by natives representing a relatively primitive society— peoples whom the Spaniards designated by the word *Chichimecos*— a term which became descriptive of nonsedentary tribes or bands, as distinguished from the highly civilized natives of southern and central Mexico. Here the historical process was fundamentally different from what it was in the area of advanced peoples. The Chichimecos were rapidly killed off in war or by new diseases, and the terrain left open for a more purely Spanish stock. Beginning on the eastern coast north of Vera Cruz, the line separating the two types of natives indicated ran generally westward, passing a short distance above Mexico City and Guadalajara to Compostela and Tepic. The area of the nonsedentary or unstable peoples was the scene of a great panorama of frontier expansion analogous to the Westward Move-

---

manuscripts bearing on the historical development of the West Coast Corridor, which will be utilized in the preparation of a monograph on the subject.

ment in English North America dealt with by Turner and his disciples.

The colonization of northern Mexico above this line was directed to a large extent by two great mountain chains—the Sierra Madre Oriental, and the Sierra Madre Occidental—stupendous and difficult barriers which divide the area into three distinct geographical provinces: (1) the East Coast Corridor, a wide plain lying between the eastern sierra and the Gulf of Mexico; (2) the West Coast Corridor, a narrow plain between the Sierra Madre Occidental and the Pacific Ocean; and (3) the great Central Plateau, or Mesa Central, between the eastern and western sierras. The development of the East Coast Corridor was greatly influenced by the Gulf of Mexico, and that of the West Coast Corridor by the Gulf of California and the Pacific Ocean.

In pursuit of various objectives, the Spaniards made their way north in three principal columns determined by these corridors. The East Coast salient of mining and stock raising carried Spanish civilization north from the Pánuco border the length of Tamaulipas into Nuevo León and across the lower Rio Grande, where Laredo and a score of present-day towns and cities farther south are monuments to the spectacular achievements of the great colonizer Escandón in the eighteenth century. The long cattle drive which began in Tamaulipas crossed the Rio Grande and eventually reached Montana, to which the lineage can be historically traced.

The Central Plateau of Mexico was the scene of vast mining developments in Zacatecas, San Luís Potosí, Durango, Chihuahua, Coahuila, and Nuevo León, storehouses of precious metals which, together with the mines of Perú, did so much to revolutionize economic life that some day, when we really become world-minded, they will form a chapter in every general book on the making of the modern era. The Chihuahua-Coahuila frontier carried European civilization north into Texas, Louisiana, and New Mexico. Here Spanish cavalry wrestled with Apaches and Comanches long before the Yankees arrived on the scene—witness the name Greenhorn Mountains on the map of Colorado, applied in honor of a victory by Governor Anza of New Mexico over Cuerno Verde, or Green Horn, chief of Comanches, in 1776. American history has not by any means been a wholly Westward Movement.

The West Coast Corridor, the main theme of this paper, runs with minor breaks continuously north from Tepic in Mexico to Alaska. It came into history as North America's outpost toward the Orient— a character which it still maintains. From the Isthmus of Panamá was resumed the task which Columbus thought he had accomplished—the finding of a route to the East Indies. The discovery of the South Sea was followed by feverish northward exploration of the Pacific shores, with a view to reaching Cathay. Within three years after Balboa's vision from "the peaks of Darién" the entire western shore of Central America had been run from Panamá to the borders of Mexico. Now far-seeing Cortés took up the quest. Crossing the continent, he forthwith opened shipyards on the Pacific coast as a base for communication with the Orient. Five years later Saavedra, in ships built by the conqueror at Zacatula, sailed west and reached the Moluccas. But he could not get back because of contrary winds. He had discovered a stubborn handicap to commerce with the Far East.

Conflict between Spain and Portugal over the Spice Islands brought West Coast America into prominence in world affairs. Portugal had the advantage of position, so Charles V sold Spain's rights to the Moluccas, but maintained her title to the Philippines. Then, in 1542, at the same time that Cabrillo and Ferrelo ran the entire shore line of California to Oregon, Villalobos, sailing west from Mexico with a related objective, took possession of the Philippines, but was captured by the Portuguese.

King Philip now decided to make Spain's claim stick. Legazpi in 1564 sailed in two ships from Acapulco and took effective possession of the disputed islands. Urdaneta, his pilot, was first to overcome the handicap of headwinds and find a way back across the Pacific. Sailing north from the islands he entered the belt of westerly winds, reached the American shore near Oregon, and descended the west coast to Acapulco. Legazpi founded Manila in 1571. Thereafter for some two hundred and fifty years Spain's Manila galleons, conducting her trade with the Orient, followed Urdaneta's route across the Pacific and down the west coast. On the long voyage, with bad food, sailors and passengers suffered terribly from scurvy, but the galleons sometimes stopped on the Sinaloa coast to find relief from citrus fruits. The story that this cure was first discovered by Cook in 1776 is another English myth. In fact, two centuries earlier, Menéndez de Aviles, on his way from Spain to found St. Augustine in Florida, stopped at the Canary Islands for a supply of limes to prevent the ravages of scurvy.

Throughout the seventeenth and eighteenth centuries Spain's West Coast activities were largely defensive, designed to meet the threats and inroads of English, Dutch, French, and Russians in the Pacific. Operating in the North Atlantic the French and English sought the Strait of Anian as a route to Cathay. Spain's fears became realities when, in 1577, Drake passed the Straits of Magellan, raided the coasts of South America, landed on the California shore near San Francisco Bay, took possession of what he called New Albion, in the name of Queen Elizabeth, and left his calling card in the shape of a Plate of Brasse and a silver sixpence bearing the picture of her Majesty. Cavendish plundered the Manila galleon, *Santa Ana*, on the California Peninsula (1586), burning it to the water's edge. In the wake of the English and French came the Dutch (the "Pichilingues"), who threaded the Straits of Magellan before the end of the sixteenth century and soon reached the Gulf of California, where a harbor is still called the Pichilingue Bay.

To protect Spain's interests, Vizcaino now established a Spanish colony at La Paz (1596), reexplored the entire California coast (1602), and discovered Monterey Bay, another landmark in the sequence of events.

The colonization of the California Peninsula, or Lower California, was encouraged by promoting the pearl fisheries, under contracts with speculators, some of whom were experienced pearl-hunters from the Caribbean. Thus Cardona was granted the monopoly of this enterprise in California in 1614. Acting for him, Iturbi a year later made a voyage to the head of the Gulf, and on his return one of his vessels was captured by the Dutch freebooter, Spillberg, who illustrates the international character which California had now acquired. Later contracts were made with Ortega (1633), Porter y Casanate (1648), Piñadero (1664, 1667), Lucenilla (1668), and Atondo (1679). Some of them prospered, others went broke.

Finally, in 1697, the California Peninsula was turned over to the Jesuits with the protection of a small Spanish garrison. The Black Robes founded missions, established horticulture and agriculture, built substantial churches, to the admiration of globe-trotters today, and contributed to the permanent colonization of two-thirds of the difficult region, at that time dubbed in Europe the "most outlandish place in the world."

Meanwhile permanent European civilization made a steady advance up the West Coast mainland at the foot of the impassable Sierra Madre Occidental.

Guzmán had accomplished much at Culiacán, and he deserves a better place in history than the one to which he has been assigned. Ibarra, founder of Durango and Chihuahua, in 1564 crossed the Sierra Madre in a winter so severe that his horses froze to death standing in their tracks, and gave new life to the Sinaloa settlements. Soon the frontier advanced north to Sinaloa River, then to the Fuerte, the Mayo, the Yaqui, and on to the Sonora River.

The West Coast Corridor was a land of miners, cattlemen, farmers, pearl fishers, and missionaries. After a brief attempt by the Franciscans the Jesuits took over in 1591 and labored continuously on the Corridor for the next one hundred and sixty-six years—that is about as long as from the Declaration of Independence to now.

River by river, valley by valley, canyon by canyon (one of them as deep as Grand Canyon) these harbingers of Christian civilization advanced into the realm of heathendom. They gathered the natives into villages, indoctrinated them in the Faith, trained them in agriculture and the crafts, and in schools taught many of them reading, writing, and music. Under the tutelage of the patient Jesuits, barbarians who formerly had constructed only the meanest huts now built substantial and beautiful churches, some of which still stand as architectural monuments. The natives were generally well disposed toward the missionaries. But secular Spaniards exploited their labor in mines and on haciendas, and medicine men were jealous of their white competitors. The result was a series of periodic Indian revolts in which a number of Black Robes won the crown of martyrdom. But the march went on.

It was a picturesque pageant. Black Robes moved into the wilderness beside or ahead of the prospector, miner, soldier, and frontier trader. Land travel was chiefly on horseback, muleback, or on foot, and land transportation by pack train or Indian carriers. As the frontier expanded, here and there a town, a mining camp, an hacienda, a garrison was pitched on the border of settlement. Still beyond in the midst of heathendom, Christian missions were planted. As the Spaniards advanced northward, the Indians were reduced to sedentary life. When Pérez de Ribas published his *Triumphos de Nuestra Santa Fé* in 1645 the Jesuit showing for half a century of labor was most impressive. West of the Sierra Madre, in a stretch of some six hundred miles, there were now thirty-five head missions, each with from one to four towns, perhaps a hundred in all. The mission books showed a total of more than 300,000 baptisms in the West Coast Corridor to date. The presidio of San Felipe, the principal garrison, had a force of only forty-six soldiers. This fact alone "shows how completely the natives had accepted missionary control."

The chief economic resources of the Corridor were stock raising, agriculture, fruit culture, and mining. Great herds of cattle, horses, sheep, and goats roamed the plains and foothills. Prospecting for mines was a favorite pursuit. Some of the mining ventures were successful on a large scale. At Rosario, near Mazatlán, in the eighteenth century the output of gold found expression in the building of enormous and luxurious palaces, still today decorated with classic mottoes over their spacious portals. In recent times gold digging has completely undermined the old city and the palaces are falling into their own cellars.

A rich silver strike was made at Alamos, near Mayo River, in 1686. There was a grand rush, and the camp became a substantial city, now almost deserted, but leaving a costly church, a fine civic center, and solid business blocks of beautifully worked stone and marble, as a monument to the wealth and culture of a bygone day. Farther north in Sonora a score of mining towns were founded and flourished in the seventeenth and eighteenth centuries. Cananea, near the United States line, has been active and prosperous down to the present time. Just over the border from Nogales were found in the eighteenth century silver nuggets weighing tons, among the largest on record. Southern Arizona, until the Mexican War a part of Sonora, is still an important mining region.

The West Coast Corridor produced men who were men. Among them was club-footed Hurdaide of Sinaloa who was feared by hostile Indians, and to command the obedience of the most warlike chief, he had only to send out a paper stamped with his wax seal, a symbol known far and wide. On the northern border the Anzas, father and son, were long the masters of the Sonora-Arizona border—defenders of the frontier against the hostile Apaches who were a terror to civilians.

In the middle eighteenth century the Russian bear cast his shadow over Spain's holdings on the Pacific coast. Thereupon José de Gálvez, Visitor General, proceeded to colonize Upper California. Portolá led soldiers and Franciscan missionaries to settle San Diego and Monterey. Six years later a colony was raised in Sinaloa and Sonora, led overland by stalwart Anza, to occupy the great harbor of San Francisco Bay, just when the English in Philadelphia were declaring their independence. San Franciscans and Philadelphians alike commemorate that significant year, 1776, we in the West for two good reasons.

SECTION THREE

Defensive Character of the Borderlands

CHAPTER SEVEN

Spanish Resistance to the
Carolina Traders in Western Georgia, 1680–1704*

IT is often overlooked that the southeastern area of the United
States was long a Borderlands area—first an Anglo-Spanish frontier, then an Anglo-Franco-Spanish frontier, and ultimately an
American-Spanish frontier down to 1821, when East Florida was
finally ceded to the United States. In a very real sense the Florida-
Georgia area shows the defensive role which the Borderlands often
played in the broader American story. Spanish occupation of Florida
had originally been prompted by the need to defend the Strait, the
homebound route of the galleons, against enemies, the French inter-
lopers of the early 1560's and the pirates who were beginning to
operate from bases in the Bahamas. After the English moved into the
Carolinas, this continental outpost took on an even more pronounced
defensive character, now against unfriendly and, very quickly, aggressive neighbors, who coveted the land and bid for the loyalty of
the Indians living thereon.

In 1925, Bolton published his documentary *Arredondo's His-
torical Proof of Spain's Title to Georgia: A Contribution to the
History of One of the Borderlands*, and in the same year, with
Mary Ross, reworked the introduction to the source volume as *The
Debatable Land: A Sketch of Anglo-Spanish Contest for the
Georgia Country.*†

---

* *Georgia Historical Quarterly*, Vol. IX (June, 1925), 115–30.

† Mary Ross was one of the first of his students whom Bolton interested in this
frontier. Through the 1920's she contributed a number of articles on Carolina-
Georgia history to the *Georgia Historical Quarterly*. John Tate Lanning was the
next. Before turning his attention to the intellectual and educational history of
colonial Latin America, he wrote on the international and diplomatic history of
this one of the Borderlands and also on the Franciscan missionary effort there.
Philip C. Brooks dug into the end of the Spanish story with his study on the background of the Adams-Onis Treaty and on the treaty itself.

The article here reprinted highlights another aspect of that larger story and will serve to remind the reader that this southeastern area of the United States also held Bolton's attention in his significant work of uncovering and interpreting the history of the Borderlands.

SPAIN AND PORTUGAL effectually and permanently colonized the vast area from Chile to the West Indies and the Rio Grande. The late-comers, England, France, Holland, and Sweden, planted centers of expansion in the left-over areas to the northward. In her northern borderlands Spain's activities were chiefly defensive. Foreign danger there forced her into several salients before she was ready to colonize them. The French intruded into the Caribbean, Florida, Louisiana, and Texas, and border contests ensued. As the English frontier moved westward, the Anglo-Spanish borders overlapped in a succession of areas, and one by one a series of Anglo-Spanish conflicts resulted—in the Caribbean, in Georgia and Florida, in Louisiana, in Texas, in New Mexico, in California. Anglo-American aggression stopped in each case when it reached the line of effective Spanish colonization. Together these border struggles constituted a drama covering two centuries. All the acts had features in common. But each had its own peculiar incidents and characters, and each made its particular contribution to the larger theme of American history. One episode in the long story, brimful of human interest, but heretofore practically unknown, was Spain's resistance to the Charleston traders among the Apalachicolas, or Lower Creeks, in western Georgia.

For a century or more the country that now is Georgia was debatable land, contested by Spain and England. The first phase of the struggle centered on the Atlantic coast region. That area for many decades after Menéndez's day was a Spanish settlement called Guale. From St. Mary's River to the Savannah, thence northward to Santa Elena (Port Royal), little centers of Spanish influence were planted in the midst of nearly every coast tribe. Scores of devoted missionaries lived among these children of the forest, and taught them the Gospel of Christ. Small soldier garrisons protected the missionaries, and guarded the country against unwelcome neighbors. Most of the

Guale establishments were on the islands, for these are *terra firma,* while the adjacent mainland presents a wide strip of difficult swamp and marsh, which even yet is unsubdued.[1]

Spanish activity in the Georgia country was not confined to the seaboard. Occasional visits were made to the interior tribes. Westward from the Atlantic coast a line of missions stretched along the southern border all the way from Cumberland Island to Apalache. In the Apalache district, by 1655 there were nine flourishing missions, all within a few leagues of the garrison of San Luís, now Tallahassee. Traffic with the interior tribes, the hostilities of Choctaws in the west, pirate raids on the Gulf, and the inroads of English traders in the back country, all helped to increase the importance of Apalache. Military defense was strengthened, and San Luís

[1] Early Spanish activities in the southeastern portion of the United States are treated in English by Woodbury Lowery in his two-volume work on *Spanish Settlements within the Present Limits of the United States, 1513–1574* (New York, 1901, 1905); Herbert E. Bolton, *The Spanish Borderlands* (New Haven, 1921), chs. I, III, V; J. G. Shea, *The Catholic Church in the United States,* Vol. I (New York, 1886). Their place in the general history of North America is set forth briefly in Bolton and Marshall, *The Colonization of North America* (New York, 1920), 24, 40–42, 61–65, 253–57. An excellent general account in Spanish is contained in Andrés Gonzales Barcía (Cardenas), *Ensayo Cronológico para la Historia General de la Florida* (Madrid, 1723). An indication of the original documents for the period before 1543 is given by Hodge and Lewis (editors), *Spanish Explorers in the Southern United States, 1528–1543* (New York, 1907). An interesting account of the expedition of Fray Luis Cancer and that of De Luna and Villafañe is contained in Dávila Padilla, *Historia de la fundación y discurso de la provinvia de Santiago de México,* etc. (Brussels, 1625). Articles dealing especially with the early history of the Georgia coast are: J. G. Johnson, "The Spanish Period of Georgia and South Carolina History, 1566–1702" (University of Georgia *Bulletin,* May, 1923); J. G. Johnson, "The Yamassee Revolt of 1597 and the Destruction of the Georgia Missions" (*Georgia Historical Quarterly,* March, 1923); M. Ross, "French Intrusions in Georgia and South Carolina, 1577–1780" (*Ibid.,* September, 1923); M. Ross, "The French on the Savannah, 1605" (*Ibid.,* September, 1924). See also Justin Winsor, *Narrative and Critical History of America,* Vol. II (Boston, 1886); Antonio de Herrera y Tordesillas, *Historia General,* Vol. II (Madrid, 1726); John R. Swanton, *The Early History of the Creek Indians and Their Neighbors* (Washington, 1922).

became a base for advance toward Pensacola and up the Chattahoo-chee into western Georgia.[2]

These slender posts were not alone signs of Spain's desire to spread the Faith. They were evidences, likewise, of her title to a vast area in our "Old Southeast." This title was soon enough contested. From the days of Ribaut and Drake, French and English freebooters came up out of the Caribbean, traded with the natives of the interior, and raided the settlements on the coast. Then Carolina was founded. The paper boundaries of the colony reached south to the twenty-ninth degree. What cared King Charles that Spain at that very moment had, within the area granted, a chain of coast settlements a hundred and fifty miles long, stretching from San Agustín to Santa Catalina, near the Savannah? Or, incidentally, that the grant included El Paso and Santa Fé?

Carolinians now steadily encroached on the Guale settlements. Little regard had they for the restrictions imposed by the treaty of 1670. Adequate motives were furnished by race hatred and the desire for Indian slaves; willing accomplices were found in the inter-vening tribes. Step by step the Spanish frontier receded. Santa Elena was first to yield. Then, in 1680, a combined attack of Carolinians and Indians pushed the Guale outpost back from Santa Catalina to Zápala and the Altamaha. This was not enough. Six years later, after new raids of Carolinians, Indians, and buccaneers, the frontier of actual settlement withdrew to the St. Mary's. A decade and a half still later, during Queen Anne's War, it was driven back to the St. John's River.[3]

The Spaniards had been expelled from Guale. Meantime a similar

---

[2] Manuscript materials for the history of Tallahassee district in the seventeenth century are voluminous.

[3] The retreat of the Spanish frontier from Port Royal and Georgia is summed up briefly by J. G. Johnson in "The Spanish Period of Georgia and South Carolina History," *Bulletin* of the University of Georgia, Vol. XXIII, No. 9 b., and in Barcía, *Ensayo Cronológico.* A valuable discussion is given by Antonio de Arredondo, in his *Demostración Historiographica del derecho que tiene el Rey Catholico á el Terretorio . . . de nueva Georgia.* Havana, 1742. MS. This work is plagiarized in Inigo Abad y Lasierra's *Relación de el Descubrimiento, Conquista y Población de las Provincias y Costas de la Florida.* Madrid, 1912.

contest had been in progress in the hinterland. From Charleston the English traders led the onslaught. From Apalache (Old Tallahassee) the Spanish missionaries and soldiers went forth to stem the tide.

To the westward the Georgia tribes beckoned the Englishmen across the Savannah to a life of adventure and freedom, and to profitable trade in skins and slaves. The trails through their villages led to fabled mines of silver and gold, and to the shores of the great Spanish lake (the Gulf of Mexico) on which more than one English buccaneer had already sailed. Relentlessly the Carolinians advanced. In vain the Spaniards tried to hold them back. The game was played, on either side, by means of diplomacy, trade and war. The chief pawn in the sport was the Red Man between.

Each year the Carolinians visited tribes more and more remote. While from Virginia, Lederer, Batts, Fallam, Needham, and Arthur were pushing over the mountains to the Kanawah and the Tennessee, from Charleston, Woodward, Mathews, Westbrooke, and others were advancing into the Georgia back country. The two groups represented one and the same movement. Charleston was not a year old when Dr. Henry Woodward visited the "Emperor of Cufitachiqui," in western South Carolina. Four years later he crossed the middle Savannah to the Westoes. In the course of the next three years he became acquainted with the Cassatoes who lived still further west.[4]

The Spaniards were on the *qui vive*. In the very year when Woodward crossed the middle Savannah (1674) the Apalachicolas (Lower Creeks, the English later called them) opportunely asked for missionaries. There may have been some connection between the two

[4] For the early explorations of the Virginians in the West see Alvord and Bidgood, *The First Explorations of the Trans-Allegheny Region by the Virginians, 1650–1674*. For Woodward's journey to Cufitachiqui in 1670 see *Shaftesbury Papers*, 183, 201, 265, 216–17; for his expedition to Virginia in 1671, see *ibid.*, 210, 220, 300–307, 337–38, 345, 349; his visit to the Westoes in 1674 is treated *ibid.*, 441, 443, 445, 456–62. See also *Calendar of State Papers, Colonial America and West Indies*, April 10, 1677, Nos. 176, 177, 180; McCrady, *South Carolina under the Proprietary Government*, 177. For early Carolina Indian trade see Crane, V. W., "The Southern Frontier in Queen Anne's War," in *American Historical Review*, Vol. XXIV, 379–80.

events. These tribes lived on the middle Chattahoochee below the falls. They had made more than one such petition in vain, but now their voice was heard. The English danger served as a *magna vox*. So to the Apalachicola Confederacy Fray Juan Ocón and two assistants were sent in 1679 to set up the Cross at Sábacola, a village on the Chattahoochee a few leagues below the falls. Their hopes were destined to a shock. The Gran Cacique, or Emperor, of the Cavetas (Cowetas), head tribe of the Confederacy, had not been consulted. Three days after the friars arrived this potentate descended the river and ordered them out. Heavy hearted, Father Ocón and his companions withdrew to Apalache.

Hard-fisted Cabrera now became governor at San Agustín. The trouble, he concluded, was that the friars had gone to Sábacola without soldiers. So in March, 1681, two wide-brimmed Franciscans, accompanied by seven uniformed infantrymen, rowed up the Chattahoochee once more to Sábacola. In May, Father Gutiérrez wrote glowing accounts of success. He had hopes of baptizing even the Gran Cacique himself. But his dream soon faded. Within a few months the Indians became hostile, and soldiers and friars withdrew. English influence was suspected by the Spaniards. Cabrera threatened and a compromise resulted. The Christianized portion of the Sábacolas moved down the river to the junction of the Chattahoochee and the Pedernales (Flint). There they were established in the mission of Santa Cruz de Sábacola, near to the recently formed mission of the Chatots.[5]

The English tide rolled on. Carolinians fell out with the Westoes, and by 1682 this tribe had been practically exterminated. The way was open now for the English traders to the Apalachiocolas. Dr. Woodward again led the van.

Of all the early Carolinians this romantic Englishman was most

[5] For early relations with the Apalachicolas and the founding of the Sábacola mission see Castro to the King of Spain, August 22, 1639; Aranguíz to the King of Spain, September 8, 1662 (A. G. I. 50–5–10); Hita Salazar to the King, November 23, 1675; Hita Salazar to the King, March 8, 1680; Cabrera to the King, December 8, 1680; Carta de Fray Pedro Gutiérrez, May 19, 1681; Cabrera to the King, two letters, June 14, 1681; Carta de Fray Miguel Abengojar, July 3, 1681 (A. G. I. 54–5–11); same to same, October 7, 1682 (*ibid.*, Doc. no. 95).

feared by the Spaniards. By the cacique of Parris Island he had been adopted as a son. This was before Charleston came into being. By Sandford he was left on the island as a hostage. To make his sylvan life more bearable the cacique's niece was assigned to him as a housekeeper. He studied the country and learned the tongues of the natives. Months were spent in these pursuits, then Spaniards carried him to San Agustín. The English account has it that he was captured. The Spanish version is that he went of his own accord. Be that as it may, at San Agustín he found favor. He lived with the governor, became a Catholic, and was made official surgeon. Thus advantaged, he learned the secrets of the country and then awaited a chance to escape. It soon came. In 1668 the freebooter Robert Searles favored Florida with a visit. By a mirth-provoking trick he entered the harbor of San Agustín and ransacked the town. In the confusion Woodward fled to the English and with them sailed to the Antilles. Within two years he was back in South Carolina ready once more to annoy the Spaniards.

With half a dozen hardy followers, in the summer of 1685 Woodward was on the Chattahoochee, where he introduced himself to the Gran Cacique at Caveta. His presence there brought on another border clash with the Spaniards. The documents incident to it bring the Apalachicolas at that period out of hazy conjecture into the clear light of history. The Anglo-Spanish contest for western Georgia thus begun lasted till 1763.[6]

News of Woodward's doings caused a stir at Apalache. Antonio Matheos, commander there, now assumed the character of defender of the Chattahoochee River. Governor Cabrera sent soldiers to reinforce the Apalache garrison. Without awaiting them Matheos hurried west and north with a force of Spaniards and two hundred and fifty mission Indians. His primary aim was to capture Woodward and his men and punish the vassals of Spain who had admitted

[6] For troubles of the Carolinians with the Westoes, see *Calendar of State Papers, Colonial America and West Indies*, May 17, 1680, No. 1357; February 21, 1681, Nos. 26 and 27; March 7, 1681, No. 37; March 9, 1681, No. 39. For Woodward's commission see *ibid.*, May 10, 1682, No. 499; for his pardon, *ibid.*, May 23, 1682, No. 518. See also V. W. Crane, in *American Anthropologist*, N. S. Vol. XX, 331; Swanton, *Early History of the Creek Indians*, 307.

these foreigners. On his way up the Chattahoochee to the falls, where Columbus now stands, he passed through ten or more of the villages which later were known to the English as the Lower Creeks. Contrary to what the specialists have supposed, their location was very much the same as that which they occupied a century later.[7] They had not yet moved eastward to the Ocmulgee River.

Indians and Englishmen fled. Of all the chiefs Old Pentocolo, of the village of Apalachicola, alone dared risk his neck. Before he went in hiding Woodward penned a defiant note to Matheos declaring that next time he would be strong enough to stand his ground. "I am very sorry that I came with so small a following that I cannot await your arrival. Be informed that I came to get acquainted with the country, its mountains, the sea coast, and Apalache. I trust in God that I shall meet you gentlemen later when I have a larger following. September 2, 1685. *Vale*." Above the falls Matheos destroyed a half-finished stockade built by the Indians under the direction of the Englishmen. Leaving spies in the country, he returned to San Luís, after nearly a month's chase.[8]

[7] In 1799 Benjamin Hawkins carefully reported the location of eleven villages between Sauwoogelo and the Falls of Chattahoochee, within a distance of thirty-six miles, counting bends in the river. From south to north they were Sauwoogelo, Sauwoogeloochee (Little Sauwoogelo), Paláchoocle, Hitchetee, Cheauhau, Ooseoochee, Uchee, Cussetuh, Cowetuh, Tallauhassee, and Cowetuh. Matheos found most of the villages in the same places one hundred and twelve years earlier.

Matheos ascended the Chattahoochee in September, 1685, and again in December. The reports of his two expeditions supplement each other. Between the Chicassa of Sábacola el Grande he passed through eleven or more towns, all close to the river. The distance from Sábacola el Grande to Casista (Cussetuh) was ten and a half leagues. At three miles to the league this is precisely the distance given by Hawkins from Sauwoogelo (Sábacola) to Cussetuh. Clearly the towns were approximately the same stretch. Moreover, in the two lists the towns were closely identical in name and relative positions. Matheos passed through these towns: Sábacola el Grande, Jalipasle, Ocone, Apalachicola, Achito, Ocute, Osuchi (Uchee town had not yet joined the Apalachicolas) Ocmulgue, Casista, Colone, Oavetá, Tasquique; of eight the exact order is as given here; that of the other three is certain to an approximation. Thus, eight of the Lower Creek towns in 1685 were identical with eight of those in Hawkins' list, and in the same relative positions.

[8] The first expedition of Matheos is set forth in Woodward's defiant note to Matheos, September 2, 1685 (A. G. I. 58–4–23); Matheos to Governor Cabrera,

Woodward no doubt smiled as Matheos withdrew. Scarcely had the Spaniards turned their backs when the Englishmen emerged from their hiding places and began to operate once more in the Apalachicola towns. The news was carried to Matheos by the spies. So back he posted late in December with a larger force than before. Cabrera's wrath was now stirred, and he ordered Matheos, in case the Indians refused to deliver the Englishmen, to burn their towns.

This time Matheos went overland to Sábacola el Grande. Crossing the Chattahoochee there, he went by roundabout trails in an endeavor to make a surprise attack on the Englishmen. Near Caveta he confiscated from a blockhouse five hundred deerskins and other merchandise belonging to the invaders. But his efforts to capture Woodward and his men were in vain. Once more they and the natives had taken to the woods.

Aided by Chief Pentocolo, Matheos now summoned the absconding headmen to Caveta. Eight villages reluctantly responded, but the chiefs of the four northern towns stubbornly refused to appear.[9] The eight towns which submitted were pardoned. The others—Caveta, Casista, Tasquique, and Colone—were burned to ashes. While the embers were still smoking, Matheos returned homeward. Thirty disabled men he sent down the Chattahoochee in canoes. With the rest he went to San Luís by land.[10]

The destroyed towns repented, and five weeks after Matheos returned, Pentocolo was sent to ask mercy for them. But Matheos suspected crocodile tears. His suspicions were well founded, for as soon as the Spaniards left Caveta, the Englishmen once more emerged from their hiding places and continued to trade. Some of them soon returned to Charleston, leaving Woodward ill at Casista. Late in summer he too departed, carried on a stretcher by the In-

Casista, September 21, 1685; Domingo de Leturiondo to Cabrera, San Luís, Nov. 5, 1685 (A. G. I. 58–1–26. Doc. 82).

[9] The towns represented were Ocmulgue, Osuchi, Ocute, Achito, Apalachicola, Oconi, Jalipasle, and a small village not named.

[10] For Matheos' second expedition to Caveta see Matheos to Cabrera, Caveta, January 12, 1686; same to same, San Luís, February 8, 1686; same to same, San Luís, March 14; Cabrera to the Viceroy, March 19, 1686 (A. G. I. 58–4–23); Cabrera to the Viceroy, March 19, 1686 (A. G. I. 58–1–26, Doc. 102).

dians, and followed by a hundred and fifty Apalachicola braves laden with peltry.[11] On their way home four of his men were killed and plundered by Guale Indians, allies of the Spaniards. The English traders to Apalachicola were not yet safe from a flank attack.

Woodward never returned to the Apalachicolas, it seems, but he had shown the way, and next season other Carolinians went to the Chattahoochee. Cabrera sent a third expedition to capture them. When Quiroga became governor (1687) the Apalachicolas complained bitterly of the burning of their towns. Quiroga consoled them and they renewed their allegiance. But this did not keep the English out. They kept coming each season and Quiroga in turn was forced to send two expeditions to capture them. Five such campaigns had thus been made against these Carolina traders in less than five years. But they were all in vain. The Anglomen were fully protected by the natives, for they had good merchandise at low prices.

There was only one thing to be done, said Quiroga. A garrison must be established on the Chattahoochee. To build the fort, late in 1689 he sent Captain Primo de Rivera. It was placed near Caveta. At the end of two months it was completed, with stockade, parapet, ditch and four bastions. To guard it Fabián de Angulo was left with twenty soldiers and twenty Apalache Indians. In an assembly at Caveta, in the following May, the chiefs promised Angulo to join hands with the Spaniards to keep the English out. They now had "but one word and one heart," both Spanish.

The Spanish policy seemed for a moment to have succeeded. In reality it had miscarried. The burning of the towns and the establishment of a fort in their midst were designed to keep the Indians loyal and the English out. Neither result followed. Instead the

---

[11] For the repentance of the Apalachicolas, the return of the English to the Apalachicolas, and of Woodward and his men to Charleston, see Cabrera to the King, March 22, 1686; same to same, May 29, 1686 (A. G. I. 58–1–26, Docs. 104, 106); Matheos to Cabrera San Luís, May 19, 1686; same to same, May 21, 1686; Cabrera to the Viceroy, June 2, 1686; the Viceroy to the King, July 19, 1686; Junta de guerra, Mexico, July 20, 1686 (all in A. G. I. 58–4–23); Cabrera to the Viceroy, July 22, 1686; Matheos to Cabrera, August 21, 1686 (both in A. G. I. 61–6–20); Cabrera to the King, Nov. 8, 1686, with enclosures (A. G. I. 54–5–12, Doc. 39).

Indians were alienated. Most of them now abandoned their homes on the Chattahooche and moved eastward to join the Uchis on the stream now called the Ocmulgee. Thither the English promptly followed them.[12] The Ocmulgee now became known to the English as Ocheese (Uchis) Creek, and the Indians as the Creeks, or Lower Creeks. In Spanish circles, in a similar way, the Apalachicolas gradually became known as Uchis.

It is the records of a dispute which reveal this information concerning the migration of the Creeks, hitherto unknown. Quiroga asked the provincial for missionaries for the new outpost on the Chattahoochee. An argument ensued. Father Luna maintained that the Indians, afraid of the garrison, had fled east, "to find favor with English." Quiroga denied the charge. He was able to prove that some of the Apalachicolas were still on the Chattahoochee; but it is equally clear by his own admission that some of them had moved east to the Uchis. Thus is solved the mystery of the appearance of the Lower Creeks on the Ocmulgee.[13]

[12] For Spanish relations with the Apalachicolas during 1687–90 and the building of the fort, see Quiroga to the King, April 1, 1688 (A. G. I. 54–5–12, Doc. 61, published in Serrano y Sanz, *Documentos Históricos de la Florida y la Luisiana,* 219–21; Quiroga to the King, April 15, 1686; same to same, Sept. 29, 1689; same to same, June 8, 1690, with accompanying documents relative to the building of the fort (including a drawing), on the Chattahoochee (A. G. I. 54–5–12); same to same, Aug. 21, 1690 (A. G. I. 54–5–12. Doc. 13, A. B. C.).

[13] Both Swanton and Crane were unable to determine the location of the Lower Creeks before 1690. Both have left the question a matter of speculation. Swanton writes: "South Carolina documents place this tribe (the Kasihta) on Ocheese Creek in 1702, Ocheese Creek being an old name for the upper part of the Ocmulgee, and it seems probable from an examination of the Spanish documents that they were settled there as early as 1680–1685." Commenting on Matheos' report of May 19, 1686, Swanton infers that the four towns burned by Matheos were probably on the Ocmulgee. From the foregoing it is seen that his conclusion is incorrect (J. R. Swanton, *Early History of the Creek Indians,* 220–21 [Washington, 1922]). In another connection Swanton erroneously says that in 1681 the Coweta were living in the neighborhood of Butts County, Georgia. *Ibid.,* 307. V. W. Crane ("The Southern Frontier in Queene Anne's War," *Am. Hist. Rev.,* Vol. XXIV, 381) implies that the Kawita and Kasihta (which he makes synonymous with Oconee and Ocheese) were on the Oconee in 1684. It is well established by the above that they were on the Chattahoochee. For the naming of the lower Creeks see Crane, *Missis-*

The Caveta presidio was shortlived. In the summer of 1690 corsairs threatened San Agustín. Soldiers were sorely needed and the Apalachicola garrison was withdrawn. In order that the English on the "Río de Uchise" might not occupy it, the fort was destroyed and even the ditches filled in.[14]

The defection of the Apalachicolas from Spanish allegiance did not end with the desertion of their homelands. It turned into active war on the missions of Apalache and Timucua, and on the Indians there who had taken part in the burning of their towns. Englishmen lived among the Apalachicolas, stirred them up, and led them in their assaults. It made little difference that Spain and England were now allies. Torres, the new governor, launched another campaign (1694), in which fifty captives were taken.[15] A lively dispute now followed over the boundaries. Governors Smith and Blake claimed the Apalachicola country for Carolina. Torres branded the claim as preposterous. Archdale was conciliatory, but he warned the Spaniards to keep out of Apalachicola.[16]

While Spaniards fought and protested, the Carolina Indian trade grew apace. Englishmen soon passed beyond the Chattahoochee to the Alabamas and Chickasaws. The rapidity of their advance was an index of the growing demand for Indian slaves. The climax of

---

sippi Valley Historical Review, Vol. V, 339. For the identity of the Westoes see Crane, *American Anthropologist*, Vol. XX, 331.

[14] For the call for missionaries, the abandonment of the fort, and the eastward migration of the Apalachicolas, see Quiroga to the King, April 10, 1682 (A. G. I. 54–5–13. Doc. no. 32); same to same, April 18, 1692 (*Ibid.*, Doc. 36); same to same, April 20, 1692 (*Ibid.*, Doc. 42).

[15] Swanton (p. 221) citing Serrano y Sanz, gives the date of Torres' expedition as 1695, but the documents show that it was in 1694.

[16] For Apalachicola relations and boundary disputes, 1694–1700, see Torres to Governor Smith, August 5, 1694 (A. G. I. 58–1–26. No. 132). Torres to the King, March 11, 1695 (A. G. I. 58–1–26. Doc. 130, in Serrano y Sanz, *Documentos Históricos*, 224–27); Torres to the King, July 8, 1695, with related documents concerning boundaries (A. G. I. 58–1–26. No. 132); Torres to Governor Archdale, January 24, 1695 (Archdale Papers, Library of Congress); Archdale to the Governor of Florida, Jan. 24, 1696; same to same, April 4, 1698 (Archdale Papers, Library of Congress); Torres to the King, February 7, 1697 (A. G. I. 58–1–26. Doc. 131).

greed was reached while Moore was governor (1700–1702). A new impetus was given to the traffic by the settlement of the French at Biloxi.[17]

The Carolinians now found two rivals blocking the way to the Alabamas. The first obstacles to be removed were the Spaniards and Indians of Apalache. On them the Apalachicola-English raids continued. In May, 1702, they destroyed the Timucua mission of Santa Fé. To retaliate, Governor Zúñiga sent Captain Uriza with a force of Spaniards and eight hundred Indians against the Apalachicolas and their English abettors. At the very same moment Englishmen, headed by a certain "Captain Antonio," were holding war councils in Caveta. A double blow was to be struck at the Spaniards. While a fleet captured San Agustín, traders and the Apalachicolas were to destroy Apalache. In preparation for the fray a fort was built at Caveta. On the same day that Uriza left Bacuqua, "Captain Antonio" led several hundred braves forth from Achito. The two war parties met near the Pedernales (Flint). By a trick the Spanish force was defeated. The battle ground was strewn with dead and dying Apalaches; others were captured; the rest fled in dismay, leaving baggage behind. The Spanish soldiery showed nearly equal speed. All Florida was now terrorized. The Apalache settlements were ordered consolidated close to San Luís; San Agustín was put under arms; and Governor Zúñiga sent calls for help to Spain and Mexico.[18]

[17] For the Carolina Indian trade in the last decade of the century see Crane, "The Southern Frontier in Queen Anne's War," *American Historical Review*, Vol. XXIV, 379–82. See also Carroll, *Hist. Coll., of South Carolina*, II, 88–89, 107–108, 118–21; *Journal of the Council*, Dec. 12, 1699 (Photostat of transcript); E. Randolph to the Lords of Trade, in Rivers, *A Sketch of the History of South Carolina*, 443. A Carolina view of Moore's trading activities is given in a "Representation and Address," printed in Rivers, *ibid.*, 455–56.

[18] For Uriza's campaign see Iberville to Francisco Martínez, January 3, 1702, Margry, *Découvertes ea Etablissements des Français dans l'Amérique Septentrionale*, IV, 579; J. G. Shea, *The Catholic Church in the United States*, I, 459; Zúñiga to the King, September 30, 1702 (A. G. I. 58–1–27. Doc. 59); Manuel Solano to the King, October 22, 1702 (Demanda Puesta, A. G. I. 58–2–18); Francisco Romo de Uriza to Zúñiga, October 22, 1702 (*ibid.*); autos and report regarding defense at San Agustín, October 27, and November 1 (*ibid.*). The campaign was approved

Zúñiga's fears were justified. Queen Anne's War was now proclaimed in America, and blood flowed more freely. Governor Moore in person led the expedition planned against San Agustín. As he went down the coast he spread devastation. Three transplanted Guale missions were committed to the flames and three friars were captured. Thus it was that the Spanish frontier fell back another step, from the Santa María to the San Juan. The Carolinians took the city of San Agustín, but after a siege lasting nearly a month they failed to capture the sturdy stone fortress outside the gates.[19]

Moore, no longer governor, was given a chance to retrieve his lost reputation by a new campaign against Apalache—that Apalache which stood in the road to Pensacola and Mobile. In December, 1703, he set forth from Charleston. His army grew as he advanced, and when he left the Ocmulgee he had in his train fifty Englishmen and a thousand Indian allies. The Apalache mission had served the red men three-quarters of a century; now they were doomed. The first blow was struck at the frontier town of Ayubale. Father Miranda directed the defense. The fight lasted nearly all day, and the Apalaches yielded only when their ammunition gave out. Several Englishmen fell; twenty-five defenders were slain and over one hundred and fifty captured. Of this exploit Moore wrote, "I never see or hear of a stouter or braver thing done." Near Ayubale, Moore defeated Lieutenant Mexía and the garrison of San Luís. A number of prisoners taken were tortured; while Mexía looked on from the stocks, Father Parga was burned at the stake and beheaded. Shortly

---

in royal council, August 23, 1703, nearly a year after Uriza's defeat (*ibid.*). See also Mitchell's Map of 1755 (Swanton, *Early History of the Creek Indians*, plates 3 and 6); Crane, *Am. Hist. Rev.*, Vol. XXIV, 385; McCrady, *South Carolina under the Propriety Government*, 379–80; Rivers, *A Sketch of the History of South Carolina*, 199–200; Carroll, *Hist. Col.*, II, 351; Swanton, *Early History of the Creek Indians*, 120–21.

[19] For Moore's expedition against San Agustín see Rivers, *A Sketch of the History of South Carolina* (Charleston, 1856), pp. 197–204, 453–56; Crane, *Am. Hist. Rev.*, Vol. XXIV, p. 386; McCrady, *South Carolina, 1670–1719*, 378, 391; Carroll, *Hist. Col.*, II, 351–53; J. G. Shea, *Catholic Church in the United States*, 459–60; Fairbanks, *History of Florida* (Philadelphia, 1871), 174; Barcía, *Ensayo Cronológico*, 320.

afterward Mexía himself, Father Miranda, and four soldiers met a like fate. One town bought immunity with the church ornaments and ten horses loaded with provisions. Of fourteen missions this was the only one not destroyed. When Moore withdrew eastward he took with him 1400 captive mission Indians. Part of them were enslaved; the rest were established near the Savannah River, safely between Charleston and the Apalachicola allies. Moore wrote to Governor Johnson, "We have made Carolina as safe as the conquest of Apalatchia can make it."[20]

Moore's savage attack was a mortal blow to the Apalache missions. To the end of Queen Anne's War the English were free to live and trade among the Lower Creeks, whose towns—eleven in number in 1709—were now ranged along the Ocmulgee. Apalache annihilated, it was the aim of the Carolinians next to destroy Pensacola, uproot the French of Mobile, and advance to the Father of Waters. To this they devoted their energies during the remainder of the war. But herein they failed. Peace in 1714 left Pensacola and Mobile intact, and the French secure in the Alabama Basin.[21]

Then came another English setback. Suddenly Spanish influence

[20] For Moore's campaign against Apalache see Crane, *Am. Hist. Rev.*, XXIV, 386–87; Moore, "An account of what the army did under command of Col. Moore, in his expedition last winter, against the Spaniards and Spanish Indians. In a letter from the said Col. Moore to the governor of Carolina. Printed in the *Boston News*, May 1, 1704." (Carroll, *Historical Collections of South Carolina*, II, 573–76); Zúñiga to the King, March 30, 1704 (J. H. Swanton, *Early History of the Creek Indians*, 122–23); letter of Bienville to his home government (printed in Swanton, *ibid.*, 123); "Statements made in the Introduction to the Report on General Oglethorpe's Expedition to St. Augustine" (Carroll, *Hist. Col.*, II, 352–53); J. G. Shea, *History of the Catholic Church in the United States*, I, 461–62; Rivers, *Sketch*, 207–209. Le Feboure's attack on Charleston in 1706 is set forth in Rivers, *ibid.*, 210–14.

[21] For the Alabama country during the Queen Anne's War see Crane, "The Southern Frontier in Queen Anne's War" (*American Historical Review*, Vol. XXIV, 379–95); Margry, *Découvertes et Etablissements des Français*, IV. Rivers, *Sketch*, pp. 231–37, gives a report on western trade in 1709. The same is given in *Calendar of State Papers, Colonial America and West Indies, 1708–9*, p. 468. For attacks on Pensacola in 1712 see Salinas Varona to the Viceroy, January 16, and July 16, 1713 (A. G. I. 61–1–32, pp. 31–32. See also another document, *ibid.*, 89–90); Barcía, *Ensayo Cronológico*, 328.

was restored among the Lower Creeks. It was a case of poetic justice. The Yamassees had been Carolina's chief instruments in the destruction of Guale. They now headed a widespread revolt and returned to Spanish allegiance.[22] The disaffection spread west to the Creeks. They in turn drove out the English traders and moved back to their old homes on the Chattahoochee. Here was Spain's chance, and quickly she seized it. Forty Creek chiefs made solemn peace at Pensacola. Seven of them were given free passage to Mexico to swear allegiance before the august viceroy and to see the sights of the metropolis of North America. Lower Creeks gave obedience at San Agustín and made war on Carolina.[23]

For a decade now Spanish and English diplomats struggled for supremacy among the Creeks. There was many a drawn battle. At Caveta two factions were formed. Old Brimins, the "Emperor," leaned toward the English; his son, Chipacasi (Seepy Coffee), was champion of the dons. The old weapons were still used—presents, trade, whiskey, bribery, intermarriage, force. Frequently the opponents met and matched their wits at the Creek towns. Peña and his men broke even with an English party at Caveta in 1717.[24] There,

[22] The Yamassee-Creek war is treated by Crane, *Am. Hist. Rev.*, Vol. XXIV, 394; McCrady, *South Carolina under the Proprietary Government, 1670–1719*, 513–43; J. R. Swanton, *Early History of the Creek Indians*, 97–102, 225–26. Herbert L. Osgood, *The American Colonies in the Eighteenth Century*, II, 347–53. Contemporary narratives are "An account of Missionaries sent to South Carolina" (in Carroll, *Hist. Col.*, II, 537–68); "Account of the Breaking Out of the Yamassee War," Boston *News Letter*, June 13, 1715 (Carroll, *Hist. Col.*, II, 569–72); Escudero to Marqués de Monteleón, Spanish ambassador to London, Madrid, February 17, 1716. An anonymous French account of the uprising at Caveta is given in Swanton, *op. cit.*, 225–26. The episode is made the theme of a novel in *The Yamassee*, by William Gilmore Simms.

[23] For the Creek visits to Pensacola and Mexico see Salinas Varona to Governor Ayala, Pensacola, July 24, 1717 (Serrano y Sanz, *Documentos Históricos*, 238–40; same to same, September 9, 1717 (*ibid.*, 240–42).

[24] For a visit to San Agustín in 1717 by the usingulo and war chief Chislacaliche, see a letter of Governor Ayala quoted in Swanton, *Early History of the Creek Indians*, 125. For Peña's embassy to Caveta see "Diario del Viaje que hizo el Teniente Diego Peña a Apalachicola," beginning as Sávacola on September 20, 1717 (Serrano y Sanz, *Documentos Históricos*, 227–37; Barcía, *Ensayo Cronológico*, 329, 356–57, 361).

too, Juan Fernández, a few months later, tied scores with John Mus-grove.[25] Spanish influence was strengthened by a new presidio and new missions at San Marcos.[26] But in time good bargains told in favor of the English. At last, in 1725, Tobias Fitch won over Chipa-casi. It was a signal victory.[27] Nevertheless, the down-river towns—Seminoles they became—still clung to Spain. With the rest the English were in the ascendant, but till 1763 constant vigilance was the price of success.

[25] The diplomatic mission of Juan Fernández to the Creeks in 1718 is set forth at length in Barcía, *Ensayo Cronológico*, 331–40.

[26] For the presidio and the new missions at San Marcos see Barcía, *Ensayo Cronológico*, 343–46, 348; Fray Joseph Ramón Escudero to Marqués de Monteleón, London, October 20, 1743 (MS.); extract of the same quoted in Swanton, *Early History of the Creeks*, 102.

[27] The mission of Tobias Fitch to the Creeks is recounted in Newton D. Mereness, *Travels in the American Colonies* (N. Y., 1916), 175–212.

CHAPTER EIGHT

*French Intrusions into New Mexico, 1749–1752**

NEW MEXICO almost from its initial settlement at the end of the sixteenth century was a defensive bulwark on New Spain's far northern frontier. One of its original purposes was to serve as an advanced outpost against possible English use and occupation of the transcontinental Strait of Anian, which rumor had it that Drake had discovered on his swing round the world. Time proved that there was no Strait of Anian. But by the late seventeenth and early eighteenth centuries New Mexico assumed an important role, in Spanish thinking, against another threatening colonial rival, namely, France. The French had moved into the middle Mississippi Valley, and soon reports came to Santa Fe of white men on the Plains. In 1720 the Villazur expedition went northward, to be cut down on the Platte. In 1739 the party headed by the Mallet brothers, from the Illinois country, startled the Spaniards by appearing in Santa Fe.

These Frenchmen were not home for long, when more of their fellows headed for New Mexico. It is the story of these later Gallic bands, arriving with hopes of trade, that is told in this present selection.

Other than his interest in Coronado, Bolton did not work this particular Borderland very extensively; this essay is one of the few exceptions. In general, Bolton left New Mexico to his students. Hammond has worked the Oñate years; Hackett told the story of the Pueblo Revolt; Espinosa chronicled the reconquest by Vargas; Thomas has done much on the eighteenth century.

EARLY IN THE EIGHTEENTH CENTURY French *voyageurs, chasseurs,* and traders of Louisiana and Canada looked with covetous eyes toward New Mexico. To the adventurer it was a land promising gold

* This was a paper presented at the Panama-Pacific Historical Congress, July, 1915. It was published in *The Pacific Ocean in History*, edited by H. Morse Stephens and Herbert E. Bolton (New York, Macmillan, 1917).

and silver and a path to the South Sea; to the merchant it offered rich profits in trade. The three natural avenues of approach to this Promised Land were the Missouri, Arkansas, and Red rivers. But there were two obstacles to expeditions bound for New Mexico. One was the jealous and exclusive policy of Spain which made the reception of such Frenchmen as might reach Santa Fé a matter of uncertainty; the other was the Indian tribes which stood in the way. The Red River highway was effectually blocked by the Apache, mortal enemies of all the tribes along the lower valley; the Arkansas and Missouri River avenues were impeded by the Comanche for analogous reasons. It was not so much that the Apache and Comanche were averse to the entrance of French traders, as that the jealous enemies of these tribes opposed the passage of the traders to their foes with supplies of weapons. It is a matter of interest that in the nineteenth century the American pioneers found almost identical conditions in the same region.

As the fur traders and official explorers pushed rapidly west, one of their constant aims was to open the way to New Mexico by effecting peace between the Comanche and the tribes further east. In 1718–1719 La Harpe ascended the Red River and established the Cadodacho post; Du Rivage went seventy leagues further up the Red River; and La Harpe crossed over to the Touacara villages on the lower Canadian. At the same time DuTisné reached the Panipiquet, or Jumano, villages on the Arkansas, north of the Oklahoma line. Finding further advance cut off by the hostility of the Jumano for the Comanche, he tried, but without avail, to effect a treaty between the tribes.[1] Two years later La Harpe reëstablished the Arkansas post, ascended the river halfway to the Canadian, and urged a post among the Touacara, as a base for advance to New Mexico.[2] In 1723 Bourgmont erected a post among the Missouri

[1] Miss Anne Wendels, a graduate student at the University of California, has clearly shown that the Panis visited by Du Tisné were on the Arkansas River southwest of the Osage, and that Du Tisné did not, as is sometimes stated, pass beyond to the Padoucah. *French Interest in and Activities on the Spanish Border of Louisiana, 1717–1753*, Ms. thesis.

[2] Miss Wendels, in the paper cited above, has made a most careful study of the routes of La Harpe on this and his former expedition, with convincing results.

tribe to protect the fur traders there, to check an advance by the Spaniards such as had been threatened by the Villazur expedition in 1720, and as a base for commerce with New Mexico. To open the way thither he led Missouri, Kansas, Oto, and Iowa chiefs to the Padoucah (Comanche), near the Colorado border of Kansas, effected a treaty between them, and secured permission for Frenchmen to pass through the Comanche country to the Spaniards.[3]

Shortly afterward the Missouri post was destroyed by Indians, the Missouri valley was made unsafe for a number of years by the Fox wars, and French advance westward was checked. Although there are indications that in the interim traders kept pushing up the Missouri, the next well-known attempt to reach New Mexico was made in 1739. In that year the Mallet party of eight or nine men left the Missouri River at the Arikara villages, went south to the Platte River, ascended that stream, and made their way through the Comanche country to Taos and to Santa Fé. After being detained several months in friendly captivity, six or seven of the party returned, unharmed by the Spanish authorities, and bearing evidence that the residents of New Mexico would welcome trade. Four of the party descended the Canadian and Arkansas rivers, the others going northeast to the Illinois.

The Mallet party had succeeded in getting through the Comanche country to New Mexico and had returned in safety and with good prospects for trade—two important achievements. Immediately there was renewed interest in the Spanish border, on the part of both government officials and of private adventurers. At once, in 1741, Governor Bienville sent Fabry de la Bruyère, bearing a letter to the governor of New Mexico and guided by four members of the Mallet party, with instructions to retrace the steps of the latter, open up a commercial route, and explore the Far West.[4] Shortly afterward a

[3] For Bourgmont's route I follow Miss Wendels, who differs somewhat from Parkman, Heinrich, and others.

[4] *Lettre de MM. Bienville et Salmon*, April 30, 1741, in Margry, *Découvertes*, Vol. 6, 466–67; *Instructions données à Fabry de la Bruyère, ibid.*, 468–70; *Extrait des lettres du sieur Fabry, à l'occasion du voyage projeté à Santa Fé, ibid.*, 472–92; Wendels, *French Interests and Activities on the Spanish Border of Louisiana, 1717–1753.* After proceeding a short distance up the Canadian, Fabry was forced through

new military post, called Fort Cavagnolle, was established on the Missouri at the Kansas village, and the Arkansas route was made safe by effecting in 1746 or 1747 a treaty between the Comanche and the Jumano.

The effect of the treaty was immediate, and at once there were new expeditions to New Mexico by deserters, private traders, and official agents. The fact that they occurred has only recently come to light. The incidents are so unknown to history, and reveal so many important facts concerning the New Mexico–Louisiana frontier, that they deserve narration, and have therefore occasioned this paper. Their records are contained in two *expedientes* in the archives of Mexico, discovered by the present writer.[5]

Before proceeding to the narration of these intrusions, a word further must be said regarding the position of the Comanche on the Spanish border. At that time the tribe roamed over the plains between the upper waters of the Red River and the Platte, the two divisions most frequently mentioned being the Padoucah and the Laitâne, or Naitane. They followed the buffalo for a living and had large droves of horses, mules, and even burros, which they bought or

lack of water for canoes to go back to the Arkansas post for horses. Returning by way of the Cadodacho, he found that the Mallet brothers had continued toward Santa Fé on foot. Giving up the project, Fabry crossed over from the Canadian to the Red River, where he visited the Tavakanas and Kitsaiches (Towakoni and Kichai), two of the tribes which La Harpe had found on the Canadian in 1719. The further adventures of the Mallets have not come to light, but it is known that in 1744 a Frenchman called Santiago Velo reached New Mexico. He was secretly dispatched to Mexico by Governor Codallos y Rabal. R. E. Twitchell, *The Spanish Archives of New Mexico*, vol. 1, p. 149.

[5] They are: (1) *Autos fhos sre averiguar que rumbo han tiraido tires franzeses que llegaron al Pueblo de taos con la Nazⁿ Cumanche q benian a hazer sus aconstumbrados resgates. Juez El Sʳ Dⁿ Thomas Vélez Govᵒʳ de esta Provincia.* Archivo General y Público, Mexico, cited hereafter as *Autos fhos sre averiguar.* (2) *Testimonio de los Autos fhos sre a Consulta del Govᵒʳ del nuebo Mexᶜᵒ sobre haver llegado dos franzeses cargados de efectos que conduzian de la Neuba Orleans.* Archivo General y Público, México, Provincias Internas, tomo 34. These *expedientes* consist of the declarations of the intruders, correspondence concerning them, documents confiscated from them, and records of proceedings in Mexico regarding them. Additional light is shed by some documents published in Twitchell's *Spanish Archives of New Mexico*, vol. 1, pp. 148–51.

stole from the Spaniards. In order the better to exploit the buffalo and find pasturage, they lived scattered in small bands. They were bitter enemies of the Apache tribes living to the south,[6] and until shortly before had been hostile to the Jumano, Pawnee, and most of the other tribes to the eastward. Hemmed in by this wall of enemies, they had had little contact with the French, and had depended mainly upon the Spaniards of New Mexico for supplies. Their principal trading mart was Taos, where each spring they went in large numbers to attend a great fair, where they exchanged peltry and captives for horses, knives, and other merchandise.[7] In spite of this trade with the Spaniards, the Comanche were overbearing, and often stole horses and committed other depredations in the settlements. During the quinquennium of Governor Codallos y Rabal (1744–1749) they several times attacked Pecos and Galisteo, killing one hundred and fifty residents of Pecos alone. In view of this situation, Governor Vélez, the successor of Codallos, was forced to fortify and establish garrisons at both Pecos and Galisteo. Thus, the Comanche situation was already precarious before the peace with the Jumano and the coming of the French traders; and their advent made it worse.[8]

One of the trading parties which followed upon the Comanche alliance with the Jumano was among the former tribe early in 1748, but we know little of the history of the expedition. On February 27 of that year seven Comanches from a village on the Xicarilla River entered Taos and reported that thirty-three Frenchmen had come to their settlement and traded muskets for mules. All but two had gone back, but the two were waiting at the village to accompany the Comanche to the Taos fair. In consequence of the report Governor Codallos wrote the viceroy a letter in which he surmised some conspiracy between the Comanche and the French, recalled the destruc-

[6] Carlanes, Palomas, Chilpaines, Pelones, Natagés, and Faraones.

[7] Many of these facts concerning the Comanche situation are gleaned from the two *expedientes* cited above, note 5.

[8] Governor Tomás Vélez Cachupín to the Viceroy, Santa Fé, March 8, 1750, in *Autos fhos sre averiguar*, fol. 31.

tion of the Villazur expedition in 1720 through French influence, pointed out the increased danger from the Comanche now that they were securing firearms, and proposed a military post on the Xicarilla River, the avenue of approach for both the Comanche and the French.[9]

So far as we know, the party of which Codallos wrote did not enter the New Mexico settlements, but this is not true of one which arrived the following spring. Near the end of his term, early in 1749, Codallos sent his lieutenant, Bernardo de Bustamante y Tagle, to attend the Taos fair. When he returned to Santa Fé on April 12 he brought with him three Frenchmen whom the Comanche had conducted to the fair and who had requested Bustamante to take them to the capital.[10] The new governor, Tomás Vélez Cachupín, had the strangers promptly lodged in the Palacio de Gobierno and duly interrogated. Since they did not know Spanish, they were questioned through an interpreter named Pedro Soutter, who was "sufficiently versed in the French language." The formal *interrogatorio* drawn up for the purpose contained fifteen points, and was quite typical of Spanish administrative thoroughness. It asked each of the strangers his name, marital status, religion, residence, his route in coming, the country and tribes passed through, the names, location, and condition of the French settlements, their relations with the Indians, the extent and nature of the fur trade, whether the French had mines, and numerous other items of interest to the frontier Spanish authorities.[11]

The first examination of the three strangers took place on April 13, another being held subsequently. Since the first statements were in some respects confused and indefinite, due in part, it was claimed, to the inefficiency of the interpreter, and since much new light is

[9] Antonio Durán de Armijo to Governor Codallos, Taos, February 27, 1748, in Twitchell, *The Spanish Archives of New Mexico*, I, 148; Joaquin Codallos y Rabal to the viceroy, Santa Fé, March 4, 1748, *ibid.*, 148–51.

[10] *Autto* of Vélez, April 12, 1749, in *Autos fhos sre averiguar*, ff. 1–2.

[11] *Notificación y juramento de dⁿ Pedro Souter* in *Autos fhos sre averiguar*, 2–3; "Ynterrogatorio," *ibid.*, 3–4.

shed by the subsequent depositions, my nar.ative will be drawn from the two combined.[12]

As first recorded the names of the strangers were given as Luis del Fierro, Pedro Sastre, and Joseph Miguel; they later emerged as Luis Febre, Pedro Satren, or Latren, and Joseph Miguel Riballo. According to the declarations, Febre was twenty-nine years old, a native of New Orleans, and by trade a tailor and a barber. He had been a soldier at New Orleans, had deserted to Canada, going thence to Michillimackinac ("San Miguel Machina"), to Ysla Negra, Illinois (Silinue), and to the Arkansas post. Pedro Satren, forty-two years old, was a native of Quebec, where he had been a carpenter and a soldier. He had also been at Michillimackinac and at the Arkansas post, whence he had deserted after fifteen days' service. Riballo, twenty-four years old, was a native of Illinois, a carpenter by trade, and had been a soldier in Illinois and at the Arkansas post. All stated that they were bachelors and Catholics; none could sign their names. All claimed to have deserted from the Arkansas post because of harsh treatment. They had heard of New Mexico and its mines from certain Frenchmen who had returned from Santa Fé a few years before. They had been encouraged to make the attempt to reach it by the alliance made some two years before between the Jumano and the Comanche, which made it possible to go through the country of the latter. These statements illustrate clearly the effect of the safe return of the Mallet party and of the treaty between the Indian tribes.

The point of departure of the Febre party was a village of Arkansas (Zarca) Indians a short distance west of the post. From there

[12] Declarations of the three Frenchmen, April 13, in *Autos fhos sre averiguar*, 4–12; Vélez to the viceroy, June 19, 1749, in *ibid.*, 13–14; declarations of the three Frenchmen March 5, 1750, in *ibid.*, 16–20. They declared that the first of the three rancherías of Comanche comprised eighty-four tents and eight hundred persons; the second forty and the third twenty-three tents, with people in proportion. They declared that they saw five fusees among the Comanche, and that the Indians would not permit them to enter the village. The Comanche lived chiefly on buffalo, but utilized some wild cattle for food. Deposition of Febre, in *Autos fhos sre averiguar*, 6.

twelve men had set out together in the fall of 1748. Going up the Napestle (Arkansas), they passed the two villages of the Jumano, to which point French traders went regularly in canoes to trade.[13] Being conducted from here by Jumano Indians, after going one hundred and fifty leagues they reached a Comanche settlement of three villages, where they remained some time, hunting with the Indians and being asked by them to join in a campaign against the A tribe. From the Comanche settlement Febre, Satren, and Riballo were conducted, in the course of a month, to the Taos fair, whence they were taken by Bustamante to Santa Fé, arriving there six months after setting out.[14] Upon reaching Santa Fé they were dispossessed of their fusees, lodged in the Real Palacio, and set to work.

Two months later (June 19) Governor Vélez made a report of the occurrence to the viceroy which is an interesting commentary upon the economic needs of the old Spanish outpost, and of the local attitude toward intruding foreigners who could add to the economic well-being of the province. At that time, Vélez said, the strangers were working quietly and proficiently at the Real Palacio, two of them being employed as carpenters, and Febre as tailor, barber, and blood-letter. He added, "since there is a lack of members of these professions in this villa and the other settlements of the realm . . . it would seem to be very advantageous that they should remain and settle in it, because of their skill in their callings, for they can teach some of the many boys here who are vagrant and given to laziness. It is very lamentable that the resident who now is employed as barber and blood-letter is so old that he would pass for seventy years of age; as for a tailor, there is no one who knows the trade directly. These are the three trades of the Frenchman named Luis. And resident carpenter there is none, for the structure of the houses, and repeated reports which I have from the majority of the inhabitants, manifest the lack of carpenters suffered in the province." In view

[13] In the depositions the two Panipiquet, or Jumano, villages were said to comprise about three hundred warriors, and the tribe to be fierce cannibals. *Autos fhos sre averiguar*, 6–7.

[14] Depositions of Febre, Satren, and Riballo, in *Autos fhos sre averiguar*.

of these conditions, the governor recommended that the Frenchmen be permitted to remain in New Mexico, promising to deport them to Mexico City if they should give cause.[15]

The governor's report reached Mexico in due time, and on August 29 was sent to the *auditor general de guerra*, the Marqués de Altamira, the man at the capital who at this epoch had most to do with the government of the provinces.[16] In view of the indefiniteness of the declarations of the three Frenchmen, particularly in matters of Louisiana geography, he was suspicious of their honesty, and he therefore advised that new depositions be taken. On the other hand, he approved the governor's request, and advised that the strangers be allowed to remain at Santa Fé to teach their trades, on condition that they be duly watched.[17]

The auditor's advice was acted upon, and on October 3 a dispatch was sent to Governor Vélez.[18] It was in consequence of these instructions that new depositions were taken, March 5, 1750. The Frenchmen had been in Santa Fé nearly a year now, and no interpreter was necessary—at least none was officially appointed as had been the case before. The pre-eminence of Satren among the three is indicated by the fact that his was the only declaration written in full, the other two men saying little more than to subscribe to what he stated.[19]

[15] Vélez to the viceroy, June 19, 1749, in *Autos fhos sre averiguar*, 13–14.

[16] *Decreto* of the viceroy, *ibid.*, 13 (bis). It is to be noted that in the original numbers 13 and 14 are repeated in the numbering of the folios.

[17] Altamira noted especially the fact that the deserters failed, in their descriptions of Louisiana, to mention the Natchitoches and Cadodacho posts. By a misreading he understood the declarations to state that New Orleans was six hundred leagues from the Mississippi River, whereas they meant that it was that distance from Santa Fé. Altamira also misunderstood the declarations to state that the Comanche settlements were one hundred and fifty leagues from Santa Fé. What they stated was that the settlements were that distance from the Jumano villages. Altamíra, *dictamen*, in *Autos fhos sre averiguar*, 13 (bis)–16. The numerals here and below refer to folios.

[18] *Decreto* of the viceroy, September 30, 1749, *Autos fhos sre averiguar*, 15; *memorandum*, October 3, *ibid.*

[19] Declarations of Satren, Febre, and Riballo, March 5, 1750, in *Autos fhos sre averiguar*, 16–20. Satren told in his new declaration of the military post among the Canse (Kansas) and stated that this was the tribe who "defeated the Spaniards who

In his new deposition many of the shortcomings of the former were corrected and many new details added.

In the meantime seven other men from Louisiana had arrived at Santa Fé at different times. Satren declared them to be fur traders whom he knew, and that they had left Louisiana, like himself, in order to make a better living among the Spaniards.[20] Clearly, however, they were not of the party of twelve in which Satren had set out in 1748, for they left Arkansas a year later.

Among the newcomers was a Spaniard named Felipe de Sandoval, who made a deposition at Santa Fé on March 1, 1750, four days before the second declaration of Satren was given. According to his statement he had left Spain in 1742. Near Puerto Rico his vessel had been captured by the English and taken to Jamaica. After remaining there a prisoner for two years he fled on a French vessel to Mobile, going thence to New Orleans and to the Arkansas post (Los Sarcos). There he became a hunter. In all he remained in Louisiana five years.[21]

In Arkansas he learned of New Mexico through members of the Mallet party who had descended the Arkansas River. In the fall of 1749 he set out for New Mexico from the Arkansas post with six companions, one of whom was a German. Ascending the Napestle (Arkansas) River in canoes, at the end of fifty days they reached the Jumano settlement, where a French flag was flying. This tribe was at the time living in two contiguous villages of grass lodges, situated on the banks of the Napestle, surrounded with stockades and ditches. They were a settled tribe, raising maize, beans, and calabashes. According to Sandoval the two villages comprised five hundred men. At this time they were still at war with the Pananas (Pawnees). They were fierce cannibals, and while Sandoval was among them he saw them eat two captives. They had extensive commerce with the French, and a short time before Sandoval's visit they had re-

in the year twenty, to the number of twenty men, penetrated as far as this place under the command of Don Pedro de Billasur, this kingdom of New Mexico being then governed by Don Antonio de Balverde y Cosio," *ibid.*, 18.

[20] *Ibid.*, 19.

[21] Declaration by Felipe de Sandoval, Santa Fé, March 1, 1750, in *Autos fhos sre averiguar*, 21–24.

ceived presents, including a French flag, from the *comandante general* of Louisiana. They had a few horses, which they had secured from the Comanche.[22]

After remaining twenty days with the Jumano, Sandoval's party set out, accompanied by twelve Indians. They went southward and then westward for twenty days, looking for the Comanche, but did not find them. At the end of that time Sandoval's companions turned back with the Jumano, leaving him alone. Soon becoming lost, he returned, by twelve days' travel, to the Jumano. His companions had not returned there.

After remaining with the Jumano a few days, Sandoval set out again, guided by a Comanche Indian who had gone to the Jumano to trade. Ascending the Napestle (Arkansas), at the end of forty days they reached a Comanche settlement at the foot of a mountain whence flowed the Rio Case (Canse, Kansas?). Here Sandoval remained four months, hunting with the Comanche. While at the village twenty Jumano and two Frenchmen came to trade. When the Jumano returned they left the Frenchmen, who decided to accompany Sandoval to Santa Fé. In another party there arrived at the Comanche village a German and a French priest. There are indications that they were members of Sandoval's original party.[23] They, too, contemplated going on to Santa Fé, but the German, not being a Catholic, feared the Inquisition. Accordingly, after remaining nine days, they went back.

Sandoval and his two companions set out again, guided by a Comanche who was going to New Mexico to sell slaves to the Spaniards. Proceeding slowly for seven days to another Comanche village, and then three days through a difficult mountain, they reached Taos. Sandoval estimated the distance from Taos to the Jumano as twenty or twenty-five days northeast by east, and from the Jumano to the Arkansas post down the Napestle River by boat as nine days.

[22] Declaration by Sandoval, Santa Fé, March 1, 1750, in *Autos fhos sre averiguar*.

[23] In my transcript of Sandoval's declaration, it is stated that he left Arkansas with "four Frenchmen, a *sargente*, and a German," *ibid.*, fol. 21. In view of the presence of the *religionario* and the German among the Comanche, I am led to suspect that *sargente* here is a miscopy for *religionario* or *religioso*.

After taking the new depositions, on March 8, 1750, Governor Vélez reported again to the viceroy.[24] The burden of this communication, aside from a long geographical description,[25] was the danger to New Mexico arising from the new alliance between the Comanche and the tribes of the east, the danger of Comanche attacks on New Mexico, and the bad policy of Governor Mendoza in permitting the Mallet party, "who were the first who entered," to return after having spied out the land. "I regard as most mischievous the permission given to the first Frenchmen to return," he said, because "they gave an exact account and relation, informing the Governor of Louisiana of their route, and the situation and conditions of New Mexico." He was convinced, moreover, that it was French policy

[24] Governor Vélez Cachupín to the viceroy, Santa Fe, March 8, 1750, in *Autos fhos sre averiguar,* 25–31.

[25] Governor Vélez's geographical statement is of great interest as showing the outlook from New Mexico at that time. The distance from New Mexico to Louisiana was commonly regarded as about two hundred leagues to the east, that to San Antonio, "of the government of Coaguila," as one hundred and fifty southeast. To the east and southeast were the Carlanes, Palomas, Chilpaines, Natagés, and Faraones, the last two tribes living to the south. To the northwest were the Comanches and Jumanes, the latter called by the French Panipiquets. The two tribes, now allied, made cruel war upon the Carlanes and other Apache bands above named. The entrance of the French into New Mexico was facilitated by the Comanche-Jumano alliance. The Río de Napestle, "well-known in this realm," had its source in a very rugged mountain range, about eighty leagues from Taos; the Arkansas was shallow in its upper reaches, but at the Jumano village, he had learned from the French, it was large, and farther down, after being joined by the Colorado (Canadian) it was still larger. Soldiers of New Mexico, in pursuit of Comanches, and led by Don Bernardo de Bustamante y Tagle, had reached the vicinity of the Jumano, following the banks of the Río de Napestle, "on which expedition were acquired adequate reports of those regions, in the summer very delectable and pleasing, and inhabited by innumerable buffalo, which the Divine Providence created for the support of the barbarians and the greed of the Frenchmen." To the north of New Mexico, in the rugged mountains, at a distance of one hundred and fifty or two hundred leagues, were the nations of Chaguaguas, and less remote, the Yutas, with whom also the Comanche were at war. For this reason they (meaning the Comanche, I understand) went northwest, joined the Moachos and fought with the settlements of New Mexico, namely the Navajoo, Zuñi and Moqui. From reports given by the Moachos it was thought that to the northwest the sea was less than two hundred leagues distant.

which had "influenced the minds of the Jumanes or Panipiquees to make peace with the Comanches, recently their enemies, with the purpose of being able to introduce themselves by the Rio de Na- pestle, thus approaching near to New Mexico." None of the new- comers were soldiers, he said, but all were paid hunters, in the employ of fur merchants. Now that they knew the way, he feared that they would come with increasing frequency, "which to me ap- pears less dangerous to these dominions than that they should return to their colonies with complete knowledge of and familiarity with the lands inspected through their insolence." Better distribute them, he thought, as settlers in Nueva Vizcaya or Sonora, without per- mission to return, especially since all were good artisans, already at work at their trades, and since they were crack shots, and therefore would be very useful in defending the provinces against the Indians.

The governor's report reached Mexico by August, and on Jan- uary 9, 1751, Altamira reviewed the whole matter.[26] The new depositions of Satren and his companions satisfied him on geograph- ical matters. In view of what Vélez had written, he urged keeping out the French, on the one hand, and the opening of communication between New Mexico and Texas, on the other.[27] He approved, also, sending to the interior the six new intruders and others who might come later, designating Sonora as the place, because it was the most remote possible from Louisiana.[28] On January 14 the viceroy ap-

[26] On August 14 it was sent to Altamira, the *auditor general de la guerra*. On September 14 Altamira asked for the documents relating to previous French in- trusions into New Mexico, and on the 16th the viceroy ordered them furnished. *Autos fhos sre averiguar*, 25. On November 18 a *testimonio* of the governor's report was made. Memorandum, *ibid.*, 31.

[27] Altamira estimated that from Santa Fé to Los Adaes it was less than two hundred leagues, and still less from Albuquerque or El Paso, "and it would be very fitting that the transit and communication be facilitated from one province to the other, in order that with mutual and reciprocal aid of arms, intervening tribes who persecute both realms should be forced into subjection, which would be aided greatly by practical acquaintance with the watering places, pastures, and other features of that unknown intervening space," *ibid.*, 26.

[28] Altamira, *dictamen*, January 9, 1751, in *Autos fhos sre averiguar*, 25–30.

proved the recommendation, and on the 31st the corresponding dispatch was written.[29]

Two distinct parties of Frenchmen had thus entered New Mexico in less than a year by the Arkansas River. They were soon followed by others over the northern route. In the meantime the Jumano had made peace with the Pawnee (Panana) and had secured an alliance of the Comanche with the Pawnee and even with the A tribe.[30] In these arrangements the French no doubt had a hand, as in the case with the earlier Comanche-Jumano treaty.

In 1751 four traders from New Orleans reached New Mexico by way of the Missouri River, it is said, but who they were and what the circumstances of their journey has not yet come to light.[31] In the following year, however, another party came by that route concerning whom our information is quite complete. This expedition, it will be seen, had official sanction in Louisiana.[32]

On August 6, 1752, two Frenchmen arrived at the cemetery of the mission of Pecos, bearing a white flag, and conducted by Jicarilla and Carlana Apaches whom they had encountered fifteen leagues before, on the Gallinas River. They had nine horses and nine tierces of cloth, or of clothing. Father Juan Joseph Toledo, missionary at Pecos, deposited the merchandise in the convent of the mission, and at once wrote to the governor. Fray Juan was clearly not a French scholar, for the names of the strangers he wrote as Xanxapij and Luis Fxuij. In later correspondence they emerged as Jean Chapuis and Luis Feuilli (also Foissi).[33]

---

[29] *Decreto*, January 14, 1751, *ibid.*, 30. On January 25, a *testimonio* of the *expediente* was made and deposited in the archives of the Secretaría del Vireynato. Memoranda, January 14, *ibid.*

[30] According to the Spanish documents these tribes were now making war on the Kansas and Osage. *Testimonio de los Autos* (see note 32), fol. 14.

[31] *Ibid.*, 11.

[32] The account of this party is gleaned from the *expediente* entitled *Testimonio de los Autos fhos a Consulta del Gov^or del nuebo Mex^co sobre haver llegado dos franzeses cargados de efectos que conduzian de la Nueba orleans*, hereafter cited as *Testimonio de los Autos*.

[33] Fray Juan Joseph Toledo to Governor Vélez, Pecos, August 6, 1752, in *Testimonio de los Autos*, 2.

Father Toledo's message was received at Santa Fé on the day when it was written, and the *alcalde mayor* of Pecos and Galisteo, Don Tomás de Sena, who happened to be at the capital, was at once sent to conduct the Frenchmen thither. Next day he returned with the strangers and their goods. Their papers were confiscated, and on the 9th their depositions were taken, Luis Febre, who by now was "slightly versed in the Spanish tongue," acting as interpreter. From the confiscated documents, the declarations, and the related correspondence, we learn the following story of the advent of Chapuis and Feuilli into the forbidden territory.[34]

Chapuis, forty-eight years old, was a native of France and a resident of Canada. On July 30, 1751, he had secured a passport from the commander at Michillimackinac, Duplessis Falberte, permitting him to return to Illinois to attend to his affairs, and to embark the necessary goods to sell in Illinois—those later confiscated at Santa Fé. Reaching Ft. Chartres, he conferred with the commander, Benoit de St. Clair (Santa Clara in the documents), relative to opening a trade route to New Mexico, his object being to deal in fabrics. St. Clair encouraged the enterprise, and on October 6, 1751, issued a license to Chapuis and nine other men to "make the discovery of New Mexico and carry the goods which they may think proper," permitting Chapuis to carry a flag, and commanding the men not to separate till they should reach their destination. Chapuis was therefore the recognized leader of the expedition, which had a semi-official sanction. As transcribed into Spanish records, the names of the others mentioned in the license were Roy, Jeandron, Foysi, Aubuchon, Calve, Luis Trudeau, Lorenzo Trudeau, Betille, and Du Charme.[35]

Feuilli was evidently not at Ft. Chartres at the time when the

---

[34] *Decreto* of the governor, Santa Fé, August 6, 1752, *ibid.*, 9; *Obedecimiento* by Thomas de Sena, Alcalde Mayor and Capitán á guerra of Pecos and Galisteo, Santa Fé, August 7, 1752, *ibid.*, 9. *Decreto* of the governor, Santa Fe, August 8, *ibid.*, 9–10; *Juramento del Intérprete*, August 8, *ibid.*, 10.

[35] Declaration of Juan Chapuis, August 9, 1752, *ibid.*, 10–14; license signed by Benito de Santa Clara (translation), Fuerte de la Charte, October 6, 1751, *ibid.*, 8; license signed by Duplesis Falberte, Fuerte de San Phelipe de Michilimacinac, July 30, 1751, *ibid.*, 8.

Adapted from Herbert Eugene Bolton, *History of the Americas* (new edition), 161

Northern Frontier of New Spain in the Eighteenth Century

license was issued, but joined Chapuis at the Kansas (Canzeres) Indian village,[36] said to be one hundred and fifty leagues from Ft. Chartres, where for eight years he had been official interpreter in the pay of the king of France, and where, during the same period, there had been a detachment from Ft. Chartres. The Kansas detachment is called in the documents Fuerte Cavagnol.[37] Where the other eight men joined Chapuis does not appear.

[36] In his first declaration Feuilli stated that he joined Chapuis at the Kansas post, *ibid.*, 13; but in the later one he stated that he left "the city of Los Ylinueses" in October, 1751, which was about the time that Chapuis set out, *ibid.*, 36.

[37] Declaration Feuilli, *ibid.*, 13.

Chapuis set out promptly, and on December 9, 1751, was at Fuerte Cavagnol. On the way thither, or after reaching there, he passed among and traded with the Osages and Missouris, who, together with the Kansas, comprised five villages, all under French domination maintained by soldiery. At Fuerte Cavagnol, Chapuis formed a partnership with Feuilli, "to go together to Spain, under contract to arrive during the month of April near the settlements of Spain, beyond Sta Bacas," Chapuis agreeing to advance to Feuilli four hundred pounds in merchandise for the journey, on condition that if Feuilli should break the agreement he should pay Chapuis five hundred pounds. Feuilli could not sign his name. The agreement was witnessed by Pedro and Lorenzo Trudeau. On the same day Feuilli acknowledged a debt to Chapuis of four hundred and nine pounds, due in the following April, to be paid in beaver skins or other peltry, at the price current at Fuerte Cavagnol.[38]

Leaving the Kansas about the middle of March, 1752, the party continued to the Pawnee (Panana). Either there or at the Comanche[39] eight of the men turned back,[40] through fear of the Comanche, who could not be trusted. The two partners continued to the Comanche, who levied a heavy toll upon them as a condition of letting them pass, but having received liberal presents they directed them to New Mexico. From a point north of the Arkansas they were guided by an Ae Indian who had been a captive in New

[38] Agreement between Juan Chapuis and Luis Foissi, Fuerte Cavagnol, December, 9, 1751, *ibid.*, 3; acknowledgment of debt by Luis Foissi, December 9, 1751, *ibid.*, 3. Among the papers found in the possession of Chapuis and Feuilli at Santa Fe were two which throw further light on their operations. One was a letter signed by Languemin to an unnamed person, requesting him to aid Chapuis in recovering a slave sold by the former to the latter, and saying, "I have delivered thirty pounds of merchandise to the said Chapuis to give to the savages. I will give more if necessary. I would have gone myself to —— if the Truteaus had not gone up." Another was a letter by Foissi (Feuilli) to Señor Moreau to come and report what was happening in the district, *ibid.*, 4.

[39] Feuilli stated that it was four and a half months from the time of leaving the Kansas to that of arriving at Pecos, *ibid.*, 14.

[40] There is a discrepancy in the documents regarding the place where the eight turned back.

Mexico and was fleeing, and whom they induced to return with them as guide, bringing them in from the north. At the Gallinas River, fifteen leagues from Pecos, they met Jicarilla and Carlana Apaches, who conducted them to the Pecos mission, which they reached, as we have seen, on August 6, forty days after leaving the Comanche, four and one half months after leaving the Kansas, and ten months after leaving Ft. Chartres.[41]

In the course of the interrogation by Governor Vélez, Chapuis explained that his plan for trade was to convey goods up the Panana (Missouri) River by canoes, to the neighborhood of New Mexico, and thence by caravan, with horses bought from the Pawnee and Comanche. On account of risk from the Comanche, "in whom they have not complete confidence," they would escort each caravan with fifty or sixty soldiers. Feuilli stated that by leaving the Missouri to the left (*sic*), it would not need to be crossed. The other six rivers, excluding the Mississippi, he said, could be forded by horses. In a later statement Feuilli said that the goods could be taken in canoes up the Panana River to the Panana Indians, thence to New Mexico by horses bought from that tribe for the trade, a distance of three hundred leagues.[42] On being informed that their project was entirely illegal, both Chapuis and Feuilli emphatically declared that they were ignorant of the fact, and had supposed that by paying duties they might trade. Having learned that such was not the case, they begged permission to go back to report to their commander.

But their request was not granted. On the contrary, Governor Vélez decided to send the intruders to Mexico. Their goods were confiscated, put up at auction for three days, and sold to Thomas Ortiz, a cattle ranchman, for 404 *pesos*, 3 *reales*, 11 *granos*, the proceeds being devoted to defraying the expenses and conducting the prisoners to the capital. Of the amount the governor himself took one hundred *pesos* for the expenses incurred in New Mexico. On the 18th Vélez reported the incident to the viceroy, and expressed renewed fear at the Comanche alliance with the eastern

[41] Governor Vélez to the viceroy, September 18, 1752, *ibid.*, 24; declaration of Feuilli, Mexico City, November 23, 1753, *ibid.*, 37.

[42] *Ibid.*, 12, 38.

tribes. About the first of October the prisoners were sent south, in charge of Pedro Romero, of El Paso, and on October 29 they reached Chihuahua. From there they were conducted to Mexico by Lorenzo Álvarez Godoy, "muleteer of the Mexican route," who received fifty *pesos* for the service.[43]

In January, 1753, the governor's report was handed to Altamira, who in return expressed the fear that the proposed trade was a pretext for "other hidden and more pernicious ends." The matter being referred to Dr. Andreu, the fiscal, it was July before he replied. The original declarations of the Frenchmen were then handed to a translator. Meanwhile the prisoners were languishing in jail and clamoring for release. In November Andreu again took up the matter and had new depositions taken from the foreigners. They contained a few contradictions and a few additions to the former stories.[44]

Immediately after the declarations were taken, orders were issued requiring kind treatment given the prisoners, and on January 18, 1754 the fiscal gave his opinion. Since the Frenchmen had come to open up a trade route with the permission of a French official, one of them being in the pay of the French king, he recommended that the prisoners be sent at once to Spain, in order that the king might decide the matter. On the 19th this recommendation was approved by the viceroy.[45]

The French advance through the Comanchería at this time, encouraged as it was by Governor Bienville and the commandant St. Clair, gives significance to the proposal of Governor Kerlérec

[43] Governor Vélez to the Viceroy, September 18, 1752, *ibid.*, 24; declaration of Feuilli, Mexico City, November 23, 1753, *ibid.*, 14–24, 29–30, 37.

[44] *Decretos* of the viceroy, January 12, 1753; *Dictamen* of the *auditor*, January 12, 1753; *Respuesta fiscal*, July 28, 1753; *Decreto* of the viceroy, July 30, 1753; *escripto* by the prisoners; *Dictamen fiscal*, November 15, 1753; *Citación de Intérprete*, November 21, 1753; Deposition of the prisoners, November 21–23, 1753; *Notorio al Alcalde*, November 23, 1753; *Respuesta fiscal*, January 18, 1753, *ibid.*, 24–25, 32–40.

[45] *Projet de Paix et D'Alliance avec les Cannecis et les Avantages qui en Peuvent Résulter Envoyé par Kerlérec, Gouverneur de la Louisianne, en 1753*, in *Journal de la Société des Américanistes de Paris, Nouvelle Série*, vol. 3, pp. 67–76.

of Louisiana, in 1753, to break through the Apache barrier and open up trade with the more interior provinces of Mexico. In a *mémoire* addressed to the king in that year the new governor spoke of Spain's jealous frontier policy, the weakness of her outposts, and the ease with which the mines of Coahuila and Nuevo León could be conquered. As a base for securing them in case of any rupture, he proposed taking possession of the country of the Apache, at present attached neither to Spain nor France, he said. But unless peace were established between the Apache and all their numerous enemies to the eastward, access to their country would be impossible. He proposed, therefore, to remove the barrier to the Apachería by securing an alliance between the Apache and these eastern enemies. Under the existing circumstances of the French monarchy, it is not strange that the proposal was never made the basis of a program, but the fact that it was made at all is significant.[46]

These intrusions of Frenchmen into New Mexico were closely bound up, in their effect upon Spanish policy, with similar infringements upon the Texas border, which had been going on with greater or less freedom for many years, and the noise made by the incursions over the New Mexico border found its loudest echo on the Texas frontier. In 1751, when the doings of the Febre party in New Mexico were reported to the king of Spain, they were considered together with the Louisiana-Texas question. As a result of the deliberations, on June 26, 1751, it was ordered that French intruders in the Spanish dominions be prevented from returning to their country under any pretext whatsoever. The viceroy was ordered to keep vigilant watch of the operations of the French nation, and, if necessary, to order the commandant of Louisiana to abandon the Presidio of Natchitoches and Isla de los Labores, "without using the force of arms for the present, in case he should resist it, in order not to cause disturbances and obligations on those frontiers which might become paramount in Europe."[47]

[46] *Instrucción Reservada que Trajo el Marquéz de las Amarillas*, Aranjuez, July 30, 1755 (Capitulo 8 summarizes previous proceedings), in *Instrucciones que los Vireyes de Nueva España Dejaron a sus Sucesores* (Mexico. 1867), pp. 96–97.

[47] *Testimo de Autos de Pesquiza sobre comercio Ylícito y Demás que expresa el*

In the course of the next two or three years complaints regarding French aggressions on the Texas border grew apace. Barrios y Jáuregui, Governor of the province, made investigations, reported that the French were operating freely among all the tribes of north-eastern Texas, and that the Spaniards were at the mercy of the French, who absolutely controlled the natives who were held in check only by Louis de St. Denis, the younger. As offsets, Barrios proposed that Spaniards be permitted to sell firearms to the Indians, that freedom be promised to slaves escaping from Louisiana, and that a presidio be established on the San Pedro River, a branch of the Neches, from which to watch the French traders.[48]

This was the situation in January, 1754, when it was decided in Mexico to send Chapuis and Feuilli to Spain. Immediately there-after (January 21–22) the viceroy held a *junta* to consider the royal order of June 26, 1751, together with the related affairs of Texas and New Mexico. It was decided for the present to make no move to drive the French across the Red River, since it was not certain whether that stream or Gran Montaña was the boundary. For the same reason the sending of an engineer to mark the boundary, which had been suggested, was regarded as unnecessary. Barrios's proposal that Louisiana slaves be publicly offered their liberty was declared to be in bad taste, and further consideration was regarded as necessary before acting upon his plan for a presidio on the San Pedro. But Barrios was ordered to keep watch that the French should not extend their boundaries; French interpreters must be recalled from villages on Spanish soil, and Governor Barrios, "with his discretion, industry, vigilance, and prudence must try to prevent the commerce of the French with the Indians of Texas, observing what the gov-

---

superior Despacho que esta por careza de ellos, Adais, 1751. Béxar Archives, Adaes, 1739–1755; Report of Investigation of French trade by DeSoto Vermúdez, under direction of Gov. Barrios, 1752–1753, in Archivo General y Público, Mexico, *Historia,* vol. 299, *Testimonio de Autos fechos en virtud de Superior Decreto Expedido por el ex^mo Señor D^n Juan Fran^co de Guemes y Horcasitas,* etc., September 26, 1752, Béxar Archives, Adaes, 1739–1755.

[48] *Instrucción Reservada,* July 30, 1755, in *Instrucciones que los Vireyes de Nueva España Dejaron a sus Sucesores,* pp. 96–97.

ernor of New Mexico had practiced in the matter, with the idea of preventing the Indians from communicating with them."[49]

This decision of the *junta de guerra* in Mexico bore fruit in the arrest by Barrios, in the fall of 1754, of the French traders, Joseph Blancpain and his associates, on the Texas coast, near the Trinity River, and the establishment there soon after, of a Spanish presidio and mission, as means of holding back the French. Thus the whole French border question, from Santa Fé to the mouth of the Trinity, was treated as one.

The French intrusion into New Mexico found another echo in Sonora. On March 2, 1751, Fernándo Sánchez Salvador, Captain of Cuirassiers of Sonora and Sinaloa, cited the French advance westward as a reason for haste in the Spanish occupation of the Colorado of the West. He was convinced that the French traders had ulterior ends and that they would soon reach the Colorado and descend it to the South Sea unless impeded by a Spanish advance.[50]

[49] This episode is discussed at length by Bolton, in *Southwestern Historical Quarterly*, vol. 16, pp. 339–78. The connection between the *junta* of January 21–22, 1754, and the arrest of Blancpain is shown in *Expediente sobre la aprehencion . . . de tres Franceses*, Archivo General de Indias, Sevilla, Guadalajara, 103–6–23, a copy of which I secured through Mr. W. E. Dunn.

[50] Sánchez thought that the Carmelo River, of California, was a western mouth of the Colorado. *Cuarta Representación*, in *Doc. Hist. Mex.*, III Ser., vol. 3, pp. 662–63.

CHAPTER NINE

The Cession of Louisiana and the New Spanish Indian Policy*

TEXAS originally had been the defensive buffer against the French in the lower Mississippi Valley. Suddenly, in December, 1762, the situation changed interestingly. The French ceded the trans-Mississippi half of their Louisiana claims to Spain. Spain thus fell heir to another Borderland, the whole of the Trans-Mississippi, territory and problems. Louisiana, after the Peace of Paris of 1763, had to be turned into a defensive bulwark against the English.

Among the problems inherited with Louisiana the Indians bulked ominously large. Spain had first handled the Indian problem with the institutions of the encomienda and the *repartimiento* and subsequent adaptations thereof; these had been tried initially in her Caribbean islands as far back as the first years of the sixteenth century. These were transplanted to Mexico with the conquest and had worked rather well until the frontier advanced northward into Chichimeca country, in the latter half of that sixteenth century. Here the Spaniards ran into Indians who had not been conditioned to personal service or tribute-paying to native caciques. By the end of the century the missionary had begun to replace the encomendero as the agent of control. Through the seventeenth and into the eighteenth century the mission system, with missionaries protected by presidio garrisons, had worked satisfactorily. But now on the Louisiana frontier Spain ran into an even different problem with the natives. France, short on missionaries through the Valley, had resorted to other methods to ensure the friendship of the tribes. This selection sketches the "new Spanish policy" and highlights another facet of the Borderlands story.

When Spain saw that she had to be serious about her newly acquired vast province, she enlisted the good services of a very

* *Athanase de Mézières and the Louisiana-Texas Frontier, 1768–1780*, 2 vols. (Cleveland, The Arthur H. Clark Company, 1914), I, 66–79.

knowledgeable Frenchman, Athanase de Mézières. Having un-covered materials on this man and his work on the Texas-Louisiana frontier, in days when he was still primarily interested in the Texas story, Bolton, in 1914, published two volumes. As always, he prefaced his translation of the documents with a lengthy historical introduction—this selection comes from these preliminary pages.

Worthy of note is the fact that, although this work is almost Bolton's only excursion, with a major study, into Louisiana, he opened this Borderland, like New Mexico, to his students: Kinnaird, Nasatir, Caughey, and O'Callaghan have all contributed to the fuller Louisiana story.

THE FOREGOING SURVEY has presented a general view of French and Spanish relations with the principal tribal groups of Texas and western Louisiana down to the cession of the latter province to Spain, a transfer contracted for in 1762 but not completely carried into effect till 1769. This event put a new face upon several important matters.

In the first place, Spain's neighbor on the east was now England instead of France. That the new neighbor was more to be feared than the old was correctly understood by Spain from the outset.

In the second place, although jealousies continued to exist between the Spanish subjects of Texas and the French of Louisiana, and although Louisiana was attached to the captaincy-general of Havana while Texas was a province of New Spain, yet Texas now became in effect an interior province, whereas it had formerly constituted a most important frontier. This change, together with the fact that the Franciscan missions which the frontier presidios had in part been designed to protect had failed, made it possible now to withdraw the feeble defenses which for half a century had stood on the Louisiana-Texas border. Such a step was recommended by the Marqués de Rubí in 1767 and was taken by the government in 1772–1773, when the missions, presidios, and small surrounding settlements were removed to San Antonio at the order of the government.[1] Military defense was now diverted from eastern Texas

---

[1] Bolton, "Spanish Abandonment and Reoccupation of East Texas," in *Texas State Historical Association Quarterly*, Vol. ix, 68–82.

mainly to San Antonio, on the one hand, and to the line of the Mississippi River on the other. As soon as the province of Louisiana was taken over by Spain this process of change was begun by the strengthening of St. Louis. As time went on other defenses were established on the same line, and before the close of the American Revolution garrisons were recommended for eastern Iowa.[2]

The local authorities in Texas, fearing the inroads of the Red River tribes, and urging the danger of English influence among them, requested that some of the defenses to be removed from eastern Texas be transferred to the country of the Taovayas, on the upper Red River, toward which point the Panis-mahas, disturbed by the Louisiana cession, were migrating from the Missouri, and whither English firearms and other goods had already come by 1772, either through the intervening tribes or in the hands of the English themselves. This petition for a northern garrison, though much discussed by the government, was not granted.[3]

In the third place, and in many ways the most important, Spain now had on her hands an enormous new Indian problem, which underlay all the other phases of the matter. The vast horde of Louisiana tribes between the Gulf of Mexico and Canada must be brought to Spanish allegiance and kept good natured. On the southwestern frontier of Louisiana, the region with which this study especially deals, the problem was particularly complex, for Spain had not only the burden of winning and restraining the Osage and other tribes who had been enemies of the French and who might be counted on to continue their hostility toward the province of Louisiana regardless of the change of ownership, but must also bring to Spanish allegiance the Nations of the North—the Comanche, the Wichita, the Tonkawa—who had been not merely partisans of the French, but active enemies of the Spaniards. Formerly these tribes could be looked upon and treated by Spain as foreign enemies; but now they were within the very heart of Spanish territory, and, like the Apache, must be expelled, exterminated, or brought to Spanish allegiance. This part of the problem was made more difficult by the

[2] Houck, *History of Missouri*, Vol. ii, *passim*; Francisco de Leyba to Gálvez, Nov. 16, 1778, MS.; Houck, *Spanish Régime in Missouri*, I, 166, 332.

[3] See *Document* 90.

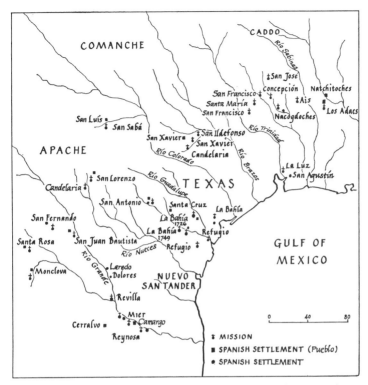

Adapted from Herbert Eugene Bolton, *History of the Americas* (new edition), 160

Texas Under Spain

fact that the strength of the Nations of the North was now being increased by that of the Panis-mahas.

Moreover, all these new tribes, from the mouth of the Sabine to Canada, must be kept hostile to the advancing English, and, so far as possible, utilized as a means of keeping English traders and adventurers from crossing the Mississippi or entering the mouths of the coast streams by way of the Gulf. Fear of English influence, even among the far southwestern tribes, had arisen with the first prospect that as a result of the French and Indian War England would secure western Louisiana. Almost immediately after the fall of Quebec this danger was urged as a reason for strengthening the far western presidio of San Sabá. On October 28, 1760, for example, the president of the Queréteran missions in Texas, who was then in Mexico, expressed to the viceroy the belief that Louisiana would fall into the hands of England, adding, "we know very well through documents and reports received before my journey, not only that the French succeed in introducing themselves among and trading with our declared enemies, but also that the English with frequency succeed in doing these things."[4] A week later Parrilla, the former captain at San Sabá, informed the viceroy that according to Apache prisoners who had escaped from the Taovayas, there were among the Nations of the North white persons, not Frenchmen—and presumably Englishmen, Parrilla concluded—who were teaching the Indians the use of weapons that answered to the description of "explosive bombs," whose purpose, it was of course imagined, was to destroy the Spaniards.[5] From now forward to the end of the Spanish régime fear that the Anglo-Americans would tamper with the southwestern tribes and invade Spanish territory was the almost constant refrain of the frontier officials. England did not get western Louisiana as a result of the French and Indian War; but she did reach the Mississippi. And if under the other supposition there was danger of English influence among the southwestern tribes, how much greater now was the danger that they would seduce the tribes ranged along the Mississippi and the easily accessible Missouri!

To meet the new and difficult situation, Spain was forced to adopt for Louisiana and the frontier of New Spain what was to her an essentially new Indian policy. In the northern provinces of New Spain reliance for Indian control had always been placed largely on the missions supported by presidial guards; and by narrowly restricting trade among the Indians in their own country an attempt had been made to force them to depend upon the missions for supplies. It is a striking fact, therefore, that just at the time when Spain was utilizing the mission as the principal means of occupying and

[4] Letter to the viceroy, in *Expediente sobre establecimiento de Misiones en la inmediación del Presidio de S^n Savas.*

[5] *Expediente sobre establecimiento de Misiones en la inmediación del Presidio de S^n Savas,* 39–40.

holding the new province of Alta California and developing there what was, perhaps, the highest type of Indian mission in the history of New Spain, in Louisiana the mission was given no part in the scheme of control. The difference is to be found in the differing Indian situations. California was inhabited by docile, unwarlike tribes, like those of the San Antonio and the lower Rio Grande regions, and of the kind with which the mission was best calculated to succeed. Louisiana, on the other hand, was inhabited by powerful and warlike tribes. In eastern Texas, Spanish missions had already been tried among them and had failed, while the French missions west of the Mississippi had never been of a kind to meet the more rigid Spanish ideal. The Louisiana Indians, moreover, from the upper Missouri to the Gulf, had long been accustomed to a system of control through fur traders and annual presents distributed in the name of the king. Finally there was already available in Louisiana a large body of traders, known to the tribes and dependent upon the fur trade for a living. To continue the French system was, therefore, but to follow the line of least resistance. It was seen from the outset, indeed, that to do otherwise would be very difficult.[6] Consequently the French method of control through the fur trade and presents, with a good many modifications in the directions of greater equity for the white men and greater humanity toward the natives, was frankly adopted, and its administration left largely in the hands of French agents. Within a few years the system was extended to include the friendly tribes of eastern Texas. The method violated many of the principles of Indian control which had been practiced by Spain in North America through more than two centuries, but it was the obvious plan to follow, and that it was adopted shows the unwonted readiness of Charles the Third to attempt any kind of reform which promised success, no matter how radical and regardless of tradition.

The general aims of the Indian policy now adopted by Spain for Louisiana and the Texas frontier have already been indicated in the statement of the problems which it was designed to meet. More closely analyzed, and including the subsidiary or incidental with the

[6] Undated letter of Ulloa to O'Conor (1768).

major, the aims were as follows: (1) to win and maintain the allegiance of the numerous tribes of Louisiana, from Canada to the Gulf coast, and including the hostile Nations of the North on the borders of Texas; (2) to keep these tribes hostile to all foreigners, and particularly beyond the influence of the English. These were the great central aims of the policy; others of less vital importance or incidental to the main purposes were: (3) to coerce the hostile tribes into friendship by cutting off supplies from all sources except those authorized by the government; (4) to exclude from the Indian villages all unlicensed persons, whether traders or vagabonds, Spanish or foreign, the worst nest of outlaws to be dealt with under this head being that infesting the Arkansas River; (5) to stop all trade with the Indians in horses, mules, and Indian slaves, forms of traffic which had caused such hardship when conducted by the French on the Spanish border; (6) to stop harmful intertribal hostilities, notably that between the Caddo and the Osage; this aim, however, did not preclude following the old policy of balance, by which one tribe was turned against another if the situation required it; (7) to prevent the escape of apostates from the missions to the unchristianized tribes; (8) to put an end to the taking of Christian captives and holding them for ransom; (9) to stop the atrocities so often perpetrated by the cannibal Karankawa upon shipwrecked mariners along the Gulf coast; (10) to do what was possible under the new plan toward realizing the Spanish ideal, so lacking in the French policy, of elevating the natives to civilized life.

The means adopted for achieving these many and varied ends were likewise many and various. As has been stated, the central means were the distribution of annual presents to the friendly tribes in the name of the king and the provision of the tribes with regularly licensed traders, to whom they could sell their furs and surplus crops, and from whom they could get their necessary supplies. The traders were as much government agents as private businessmen, for they went out under definite government instructions, looking to the best interests of the service. They must be men of good habits, and if possible, of substance. They were required to make known by formal harangues the transfer of Louisiana to Spain, and the fact that

Frenchmen and Spaniards were brothers; to proclaim to both friend and foe the clemency and the might of the new sovereign; to report all occurrences among the Indians of interest to the government, sending special couriers for the purpose if necessary; to expel all foreigners and all vagabonds, outlaws, or unlicensed subjects found among the tribes, calling upon the Indians to give forcible aid if the case required it; to treat the Indians fairly, selling staple goods at fixed and reasonable prices; to refrain from selling intoxicating liquors; to use their influence to induce the Indians to live a settled life; and to see that no Indian died without baptism. As a means of coercing the hostile tribes, traders were under strictest orders not to supply them or unlicensed traders among them with any kind of merchandise. One of the numerous modifications of the old French system was that no individual was permitted to monopolize the trade of any tribe, but this provision in after years broke down. The goods distributed by these traders were commonly supplied by wealthier merchants, under government contract, and were paid for out of the ensuing year's profits.

Supplementary means of control were the use of friendly nations as intermediaries with the hostile; the encouragement of embassies from the distant tribes to see the governors and post commanders of Texas and Louisiana (unless this became too expensive or dangerous); and the sending of ambassadors, like De Mézières, LeBlanc de Villeneufve, and Gaignard, to the distant tribes. The friendly tribes were encouraged to pillage the English traders; tribes living east of the Mississippi were induced to cross the stream and become Spanish subjects; and the Mississippi posts were increased in number and strength, as time went on, in a desperate attempt to keep out by force the English traders and adventurers. To quiet the trouble between the Osage and the Cadodacho, an effort was made to have the Arkansas recognized as the boundary beyond which neither tribe should pass.[7]

---

[7] Undated letter of Ulloa to O'Conor (1768); O'Reilly to De Mézières, Jan. 22 and 23, 1770 (three letters); De Mézières to Unzaga y Amezaga, Feb. 1, 1770 (nos. 7–10); De Mézières, Instructions to traders, Feb. 4, 1770; Unzaga y Amezaga to De Mézières, March 16, 1770 (several letters); agreement of De Mézières with

As a mark of honor and to instil patriotism, friendly tribes were provided with Spanish flags [*pabellones*]; distinguished chiefs were appointed *capitanes* or *gobernadores* and dignified by decoration with great and small medals. Notable medal chiefs depending on Natchitoches during the early years of the Spanish occupation were Tinhioüen, cacique of the Cadodacho, and the most influential Indian among the allies; Cocay, head chief of the Yatasí; and Cyxnion, chief of the Tawakoni. Brazo Quebrado, Kichai chief, and Guakan, Yatasí chief, perhaps also received medals. Among the medal chiefs depending on the governor of Texas during the same period were Sauto, or Bigotes, chief of the Hasinai tribe and head of the Hasinai Confederacy; and Gorgoritos, a Bidai, who was at the head of the Bidai-Arkokisa Confederacy.

The principal distribution points and centers of control for the western tribes were Natchitoches, the Arkansas post, and St. Louis. From Natchitoches goods and presents were distributed to the Yatasí, the Petit Cado, the Cadodacho, the Tonkawa, the Wichita, the Hasinai, and Bidai; the Arkansas and other small tribes looked to the Arkansas post; while St. Louis was the agency for the Osages and all the tribes of the Missouri and the upper Mississippi. A document dated in 1777 shows that at that time the following tribes were accustomed to go to St. Louis to receive their annual presents: Osages Pequeños, Misuris, Canzes, Nación la Republica, Hotos, Panis of the Platte, Majas, Grandes Osages, Hayuas, Sioux, Yates abuene, Renar, Sac, Puaen, Mascouten, Quicapu, Pu, Otabuas, Sotu, Peorias, and Kaskaskias.[8] In later days, after the reoccupation of Nacogdoches by Spain, that place assumed much of the former importance of Natchitoches by becoming the distribution point for most of the tribes of the Texas-Louisiana frontier.

chiefs of the Cadodacho and Yatasí, April 21, 1770; De Mézières to Unzaga y Amezaga, May 15, 1770; reports by De Mézières of his expeditions of 1772, 1778, 1779. The above paragraph is based on a study of the correspondence and reports of De Mézières during his whole career as lieutenant-governor of Natchitoches, the above cited documents being only a few illustrative ones.

[8] *Recopilación de las Naciones de Yndios del Rio Misury q*[e] *acostumbran venir a recevir regalos in este puesto*, Nov. 15, 1777. Bancroft Coll. MSs., translated in Houck, *Spanish Régime in Missouri*, I, 141–48.

It has been commonly supposed that the early Louisiana fur trade was all centered at St. Louis, and a study of this branch of it has made familiar the names of such men as La Clede, the Chouteaus, Robidoux, Lisa, and Clamorgan.[9] A parallel study of the southwestern frontier reveals a long list of equally interesting and perhaps equally important names. Among the supply merchants at Natchitoches and New Orleans during the decade between 1770 and 1780 were Juan Piseros, who at one time was creditor to the Spanish government and the missions to the amount of thirty thousand dollars; Voix, also a man of means, and his agent Joanis; Ranzon, Antonio Charbonet, and Gilbert Maxent. Among the traders and interpreters, who during the same period went among the tribes, were Le Blanc de Villeneufve, Bormé, La Mathe, Mathías le Court, Fazende, the Layssards (Jean Baptiste, and Nicolás Marafret), Lemé, De Qunidse, Sosier, Bosquet, Pichet, Barré, La Lima, Du Chesne [Dugene], Rose, Gagnée, and Gaignard.

The attachment of Louisiana to Havana while Texas was a part of New Spain, where a different system of Indian control was in vogue, led to much conflict of policy on the two sides of the frontier. The governor of Texas, the Baron de Ripperda, did his best to co-operate with the Louisiana authorities, on whom reliance was placed for the protection of Texas from the Nations of the North; but by this very fact he found himself under the suspicion of the officials of New Spain, where the Louisiana policy was not approved. Since the Nations of the North received their supplies and presents from Natchitoches, there was little self-interest to prevent them from molesting the Texas settlements; and later on, when Ripperda saw the control of the Indians slipping from his hands through their dependence on Louisiana, he requested that power to license traders, even from Louisiana, be transferred to himself. Thus things were often at cross purposes. Many parts of the policy were hard to enforce. While the Natchitoches traders were strictly prohibited from buying horses and mules from the Taovayas, that tribe frequently found a market for these animals with the contraband traders

[9] Houck, *History of Missouri*, *passim*; Chittenden, *American Fur Trade of the Far West*, I, passim.

from the Arkansas, or even with the tribes of the Missouri, and thus horse-stealing at the Spanish settlements was still encouraged,[10] while the Natchitoches merchants demanded a removal of the restrictions, in order that they might compete with the *contrabandistas* from the Arkansas.

Nor did the frontier forts and the Indian policy combined succeed in keeping the English out of Louisiana. The oncoming tide could not be restrained; indeed, its advance wave crossed the Mississippi much earlier than has commonly been supposed. This had occurred even before the American Revolution, as is clearly shown by numerous items of evidence relating to various parts of the frontier. Some of these items may be noted here.

On the southwestern border the English entered the Spanish territories by way of the coast, or went across Louisiana to various parts of the Texas frontier. Tribes as far west as the Texas border were going to the English to purchase goods as early as 1768. In 1769 four Englishmen were found living at Natchitoches. One was a man named Guillermo Ovarden [William Warden], another a man of Irish birth named Juan Cruz [John Cross?]. Several cases of shipwreck of English mariners occurred on the Texas coast in the succeeding years. In 1771 a party of them were picked up and taken to La Bahía; the next year they went overland to Natchitoches driving one hundred and thirty-three head of beef cattle and more than forty horses, purchased at San Antonio with three pipes of rum and three barrels of sugar. This transaction, of course, was authorized by the San Antonio officials. From the sugar and the rum we would infer that the Englishmen, perhaps, had come by way of the West Indies. In the same year, 1772, it was learned that English firearms and other goods were in use to a small extent among the Taovayas on the upper Red River. In that year, also, several English mer-

[10] *Expediente sobre proposiciones del Governador de Texas, Baron de Ripperda, para erección de un Nuevo Presidio y Emprender una Cruda Guerra contra los Apaches Lipanes, haciendo alianza con las naciones del Norte,* Archivo General, Mexico, *Historia,* vol. 51; *Expediente sobre la dolosa y fingida paz las Naciones del Norte; y comercio ilícito de los Franceses de la Nueba Orleans,* Archivo General, Mexico, *Historia,* vol. 93, *passim;* Journal of J. Gaignard's expedition to the Naytanes, 1773–1774.

chants were reported as residing at Opelousas, trading with the inhabitants there and with the Texas tribes and boasting that they would trade wherever they pleased. In October of the next year, 1773, the governor of Louisiana reported to the king of Spain that English traders were crossing the wilds of Louisiana and dealing with several of the Indian tribes in spite of all that he could do. In response he was instructed to entrust the task of stopping the traffic to Athanase de Mézières, lieutenant-governor of Natchitoches. In June of the next year, 1774, it was reported that Juan Hamilton and others *continued* to make journeys to the mouth of the Trinity to buy horses and mules from the Indians, who stole them from the Spanish settlements, and to go inland to the Bidai tribe, where they were causing disturbances. At the same time a certain Jerome Matalinche, said to be the agent of English merchants of Manchac, West Florida, was conducting similar trade among the tribes of the Neches River. In 1777 Gil Ybarbo, captain of Bucareli, on the Trinity River, was told by a trader among the Arkokisa that an English vessel laden with brick had stranded on Sabine Lake at the mouth of the Neches River. Going to reconnoiter, he learned that the English had been entering the Neches in small vessels and trading with the natives, having remained there in 1774 long enough to plant a crop. He found the vessel as it had been reported, and on his return picked up west of the Trinity a lost Englishman, whose name is given as Miler. These inroads of the English on the coast, it was claimed, were partly checked by the work of Ybarbo from his vantage point at Bucareli.

Writing in 1778 of the trade in firearms with the Nations of the North, Croix, the commandant-general of the Interior Provinces, declared himself opposed to it if it were not for the fact that the trade would surely pass to the hands of the English "who lose no opportunity to introduce themselves among the Indians, both for the profit gained from the barter, and for the welcome and gratitude with which the Indians receive them."

Thus there is no lack of evidence that before the close of the Revolution the English were causing a great deal of anxiety on the part of the Spanish officials, or that they were actually pushing across

Louisiana and by way of the Gulf to the borders of Texas.[11] Moreover, the indications given here regarding English activities on the southwestern frontier during the decade 1770–1780 can all be paralleled by similar data regarding Upper Louisiana, where traders from Illinois were ascending the Missouri by 1773, and were getting furs to the value of many thousand dollars a year by 1778.[12]

[11] For evidence on the matters treated in the foregoing paragraph see Ulloa to O'Conor, 1768 (undated letter); Ripperda to Unzaga y Amezaga, May 26, 1772; Ripperda to the viceroy, April 28, 1772; Joseph de la Peña to Unzaga y Amezaga, Sept. 14, 1772; Arriaga to Unzaga y Amezaga, May 30, 1774; De Mézières to Unzaga y Amezaga, June 30, 1774 and Aug. 2, 1774; reports by De Mézières of his expedition to the Taovayas, 1778; Croix to Joseph de Gálvez, Sept. 23, 1778; Bolton, "Spanish Abandonment and Reoccupation of East Texas," *op. cit.*, 117–18.

[12] Piernas to Unzaga y Amezaga, July 4, 1772 and April 21, 1773; Leyba to Bernardo de Gálvez, Nov. 16, 1778.

SECTION FOUR

The Southwest, a Mission Borderland

CHAPTER TEN

The Mission as a Frontier Institution
in the Spanish American Colonies*

In this piece Bolton offers one of his synthesis ideas to the broad American story. The interest in the Anglo-American frontier was now just short of a quarter-century old. Turner's essay of 1893 had sparked a great deal of research and writing on the American West, and more, much more was still to come. Bolton, inspired by Turner two decades before to be a pioneer, had uncovered another American frontier and was busily exploiting its riches and winning disciples to aid in the task. Even more than Turner's frontier, that of Bolton needed guideposts. One of these Bolton sought to supply in the present study.

Though a constant in the story of French expansion in North America, as Parkman and Thwaites had shown, the missionary was a quite unfamiliar figure in the Anglo-American westward movement. Americans associated the Franciscan friars with the romantic California missions and, perhaps, if they were a mite more knowledgeable, also with the pueblos of New Mexico and maybe even with the Spanish years in Texas and Florida. But for most Americans the friars added little more than atmosphere to an already quaint picture. Few Americans, for whom Daniel Boone and men like him typified the frontier, would have been so daring as to think of Serra or Benavides, Margil or Kino as frontiersmen. Yet each of them, and all their fellows in robes brown or grey, blue or black, truly were American frontiersmen, and magnificent examples of the breed. Here was a point of difference between the frontiers of Turner and Bolton. But underneath the differences were striking

* Faculty Research Lecture, University of California, March, 1917. First published in the *American Historical Review*, Vol. XXIII (October, 1917), 42–61; reprinted in *Wider Horizons of American History* (New York, D. Appleton-Century, 1939), 107–148; and also in Academic Reprints (El Paso, Texas Western College Press, 1960), with introduction by John Alexander Carroll.

similarities—Old World civilization was moving into New World rawness to turn it into something newer still.

But let Bolton tell his story!

OF THE MISSIONS in Spanish America, particularly those in California, much has been written. But most of what has been produced consists of chronicles of the deeds of the Fathers, polemic discussions by sectarian partisans, or sentimental effusions with literary, edifying, or financial intent. They deal with the heroic exploits of individuals, with mooted questions of belief and practice, or with the romance that hovers round the mission ruins. All this is very well, and not to be ridiculed, but it is none the less true that little has been said of these missions in their relation to the general Spanish colonial policy, of which they were an integral and a most important part. Father Engelhardt's learned books are a notable exception, but his view is confined closely to California, whereas the mission, in the Spanish colonies, was an almost universal establishment.

One of the marvels in the history of the modern world is the way in which that little Iberian nation, Spain, when most of her blood and treasure were absorbed in European wars, with a handful of men took possession of the Caribbean archipelago, and by rapid yet steady advance spread her culture, her religion, her law, and her language over more than half of the two American continents, where they still are dominant and still are secure—in South America, Central America, and a large fraction of North America, for fifty million people in America today are tinged with Spanish blood, still speak the Spanish language, still worship at the altar set up by the Catholic kings, still live under laws essentially Spanish, and still possess a culture largely inherited from Spain.

These results are an index of the vigor and the virility of Spain's frontier forces; they should give pause to those who glibly speak of Spain's failure as a colonizing nation; and they suggest the importance of a thoughtful study of Spain's frontier institutions and methods. Professor Turner has devoted his life to a study of the Anglo-American frontier, and rich has been his reward. Scarcely less conspicuous in the history of the Western world than the advance of the Anglo-American frontier has been the spread of Spanish culture, and for him who interprets, with Turner's insight, the methods and the significance of the Spanish-American frontier, there awaits a recognition not less marked or less deserved.

Whoever essays this task, whoever undertakes to interpret the forces by which Spain extended her rule, her language, her law, and her traditions, over the frontiers of her vast American possessions, must give close attention to the missions, for in that work they constituted a primary agency. Each of the colonizing nations in America had its peculiar frontier institutions and classes. In the French colonies the pioneers of pioneers were the fur-trader and the missionary. Penetrating the innermost wilds of the continent, one in search of the beaver, the other in quest of souls to save, together they extended the French domains, and brought the savage tribes into friendly relations with the French government, and into profitable relations with the French outposts. In the English colonies the fur-trader blazed the way and opened new trails, but it was the backwoods settler who hewed down the forest, and step by step drove back the Indian with whom he did not readily mingle. In the Spanish colonies the men to whom fell the task of extending and holding the frontiers were the *conquistador*, the presidial soldier, and the missionary.

All of these agents were important; but in my study of frontier institutions in general, and in my endeavor in particular to understand the methods and forces by which Spain's frontiers were extended, held, and developed, I have been more and more impressed with the importance of the mission as a pioneering agency. Taking for granted for the moment its very obvious religious aspects, I shall here devote my attention more especially to the mission's political and social meaning. My point of view embraces all of New Spain— all of the Spanish colonies, indeed—but more particularly the northern provinces, from Sinaloa to Texas, from Florida to California. My conclusions are based on the study of documents, unprinted for the most part, which have been gathered mainly from the archives of Mexico and Spain.

The functions of the mission, from the political standpoint, will be better understood if it is considered in its historical relations.

The central interest around which the mission was built was the Indian. In respect to the native, the Spanish sovereigns, from the outset, had three fundamental purposes. They desired to convert him, to civilize him, and to exploit him. To serve these three purposes, there was devised, out of the experience of the early conquerors, the *encomienda* system. It was soon found that if the savage were to be converted, or disciplined, or exploited, he must be put under control. To provide such control, the land and the people were distributed among Spaniards, who held them in trust, or in *encomienda*. The trustee, or *encomendero*, as he was called, was strictly charged by the sovereign, as a condition of his grant, to provide for the protection, the conversion, and the civilization of the aborigines. In return he was empowered to exploit their labor, sharing the profits with the king. To provide the spiritual instruction and to conduct schools for the natives—for Indian schools were actually prescribed and maintained—the *encomenderos* were required to support the necessary friars, by whom the instruction was given. Thus great monasteries were established in the conquered districts.

But the native had his own notions, especially about being exploited, and he sometimes fled to the woods. It was soon discovered, therefore, that in order properly to convert, instruct, and exploit the Indian, he must be kept in a fixed place of residence. This need was early reported to the sovereigns by *encomenderos* and friars alike, and it soon became a law that Indians must be congregated in pueblos, and made to stay there, by force if necessary. The pueblos were modeled on the Spanish towns, and were designed not alone as a means of control, but as schools in self-control as well.

Thus, during the early years of the conquest, the natives were largely in the hands of the *encomenderos*, mainly secular landholders. The friars, and afterward the Jesuit priests, came in great numbers, to preach and teach, but they lacked the authority of later days. In 1574 there were in the conquered districts of Spanish America nearly nine thousand Indian towns, containing about one and a half million adult males, representing some five million people, subject to tribute. These nine thousand towns were *encomi-endas* of the king and some four thousand *encomenderos*.

The *encomienda* system then, by intention, was benevolent. It was designed for the conversion and the civilization of the native, as well as for the exploitation of his labor. But the flesh is weak, and the system was abused. The obligations to protect, convert and civilize were forgotten, and the right to exploit was perverted into license. Practical slavery soon resulted, and the *encomienda* system became the black spot in the Spanish-American code. Philanthropists, led by Las Casas, begged for reform; abuses were checked, and *encomiendas* were gradually, though slowly, abolished.

This improvement was made easier by the decreasing attractive-ness of *encomiendas*, as the conquest proceeded to the outlying districts. The semi-civilized Indians of central Mexico and Peru had been fairly docile, had had a steady food supply and fixed homes, were accustomed to labor, and were worth exploiting. The wilder tribes encountered later—the Chichimecos, as they were called—were hostile, had few crops, were unused to labor, had no fixed villages, would not stand still to be exploited, and were hardly worth the candle. Colonists were no longer so eager for *encomiendas*, and were willing to escape the obligation to protect and civilize the wild tribes, which were as uncomfortable burdens, sometimes, as cub-tigers in a sack. Moreover, the sovereigns, with increasing emphasis, forbade the old-time abuses of exploitation, but as strongly as before adhered to the ideal of conversion and civilization. Here, then, was a larger opening for the missionary, and to him was entrusted, or upon him was thrust, consciously or unconsciously, not only the old work of conversion, but a larger and larger element of responsibility and control. On the northern frontier, therefore, among the roving tribes, the place of the discredited *encomendero* was largely taken by the missionary, and that of the *encomienda* by the mission, the design being to check the evils of exploitation, and at the same time to realize the ideal of conversion, protection, and civilization.

These missionaries became a veritable corps of Indian agents, serving both Church and State. The double capacity in which they served was made easier and more natural by the close union between Church and State in Spanish America, where the king exercised the *real patronato*, and where the viceroys were sometimes archbishops as well.

Under these conditions, in the seventeenth and eighteenth centuries, on the expanding frontiers of Spanish America, missions became well-nigh universal. In South America the outstanding examples were the Jesuit missions in Paraguay. Conspicuous in North America were the great Franciscan establishments in Alta California, the last of Spain's conquests. Not here alone, however, but everywhere on the northern frontier they played their part—in Sinaloa, Sonora, and Lower California; in Chihuahua, Coahuila, Nuevo León, and Nuevo Santander; in Florida, New Mexico, Texas, and Arizona. If there were twenty-one missions in California, there were as many in Texas, more in Florida, and twice as many in New Mexico. At one time the California missions had over thirty thousand Indians under instruction; but a century and a half earlier the missions of Florida and New Mexico each had an equal number.

The missionary work on the northern frontier of New Spain was conducted chiefly by Franciscans, Jesuits, and Dominicans. The northeastern field fell chiefly to the Franciscans, who entered Coahuila, Nuevo León, Nuevo Santander, New Mexico, Texas, and Florida. To the Northwest came the Jesuits, who, after withdrawing from Florida, worked especially in Sinaloa, Sonora, Chihuahua, Lower California, and Arizona. In 1767 the Jesuits were expelled from all Spanish America, and their places taken by the other orders. To Lower California came the Dominicans, to Alta California the Franciscans of the College of San Fernando, in the City of Mexico.

The missions, then, like the presidios, or garrisons, were characteristically and designedly frontier institutions, and it is as pioneer agencies that they must be studied. This is true whether they be considered from the religious, the political, or the social standpoint. As religious institutions they were designed to introduce the Faith among the heathen. Having done this, their function was to cease. Being designed for the frontier, they were intended to be temporary. As soon as his work was finished on one frontier, the missionary was expected to move on to another. In the theory of the law, within ten years each mission must be turned over to the secular clergy, and the common mission lands distributed among the Indians. But this law had been based on experience with the more advanced tribes of Mexico, Central America, and Peru. On the northern frontier, among the barbarian tribes, a longer period of tutelage was always found necessary.

The result, almost without fail, was a struggle over secularization, such as occurred in California. So long as the Indians were under the missionaries, their lands were secure from the land-grabber. The land-grabber always, therefore, urged the fulfillment of the ten-year law, just as the "squatters," the "sooners," and the "boomers" have always urged the opening of our Indian reservations. But the missionaries always knew the danger, and they always resisted secularization until their work was finished. Sooner or later, however, with the disappearance of frontier conditions, the missionary was expected to move on. His religious task was beside the soldier, *entre infieles*, in the outposts of civilization.

But the missionaries were not alone religious agents. Designedly in part, and incidentally in part, they were political and civilizing agents of a very positive sort, and as such they constituted a vital feature of Spain's pioneering system. From the standpoint of the Church, and as viewed by themselves, their principal work was to spread the Faith, first, last, and always. To doubt this is to confess complete and disqualifying ignorance of the great mass of existing missionary correspondence, printed and unprinted, so fraught with unmistakable proofs of the religious zeal and devotion of the vast majority of the missionaries. It is quite true, as Engelhardt says, that they "came not as scientists, as geographers, as school-masters, nor as philanthropists, eager to uplift the people in a worldly sense, to the exclusion or neglect of the religious duties pointed out by Christ." But it is equally true, and greatly to their credit, that, incidentally from their own standpoint and designedly from that of the government, they were all these and more, and that to all these and other services they frequently and justly made claim, when they asked for government aid.

The missions, then, were agencies of the State as well as of the Church. They served not alone to Christianize the frontier, but also to aid in extending, holding, and civilizing it. Since Christianity was the basic element of European civilization, and since it was the acknowledged duty of the State to extend the Faith, the first task of the missionary, from the standpoint of both State and Church, was to convert the heathen. But neither the State nor the Church— nor the missionary himself—in Spanish dominions, considered the work of the mission as ending here. If the Indian were to become either a worthy Christian or a desirable subject, he must be disciplined in the rudiments of civilized life. The task of giving the discipline was likewise turned over to the missionary. Hence, the missions were designed to be not only Christian seminaries, but in addition were outposts for the control and training schools for the civilizing of the frontier.

Since they served the State, the missions were supported by the State. It is a patent fact, and scarcely needs demonstrating, that they were maintained to a very considerable extent by the royal treasury. The Franciscan missions of New Spain in the eighteenth century had four principal means of support. The annual stipends of the missionaries (the *sínodos*) were usually paid by the government. These *sínodos* varied in amount according to the remoteness of the missions, and on the northernmost frontier were usually $450 for each missionary. In 1758, for example, the treasury of New Spain was annually paying *sínodos* for twelve Querétaran friars in Coahuila and Texas, six Jaliscans in Coahuila, eleven Zacatecans in Texas, ten Fernandinos in the Sierra Gorda, six Jaliscans in Nayarit, twenty-two Zacatecans in Nuevo León and Nueva Vizcaya, seventeen Zacatecans in Nuevo Santander, five San Diegans in Sierra Gorda, and thirty-four friars of the Provincia del Santo Evangelio in New Mexico, or, in all, 123 friars, at an average of about 350 *pesos* each. This report did not include the Provincia de Campeche or the Yslas de Barlovento, for which separate reports had been asked. Other appropriations were made for missionaries in the Marianas and the Philippine Islands, dependencies of New Spain.

Besides the *sínodos*, the government regularly furnished the missionaries with military protection, by detaching from the near-by presidios from two to half a dozen or more soldiers for each mission. In addition, the royal treasury usually made an initial grant (*ayuda de costa*) of $1000 to each mission, to pay for bells, vestments, tools, and other expenses of the founding, and in cases of emergency it frequently made special grants for building or other purposes.

These government subsidies did not preclude private gifts, or alms, which were often sought and secured. In the founding of new missions the older establishments were expected to give aid, and if able they did respond in liberal measure. And then there were endowments. The classic examples of private endowments on the northern frontier were the gifts of Don Pedro de Terreros, later Conde de Regla, who offered $150,000 to found Apache missions in Coahuila and Texas, and the Jesuit Fondo Piadoso, or Pious Fund, of California. This latter fund, begun in 1697, grew by a variety of gifts to such an amount that the missions of Lower California were largely supported by the increase alone. With the expulsion of the Jesuits in 1767 the fund was taken over by the government, and became the principal means of support of the new Franciscan missions of Alta California, besides being devoted in part to secular purposes. Even in Alta California, however, the royal treasury paid the wages (*sueldos*) of the mission guards, and gave other financial aid.

Finally, the Indians of the missions were expected soon to become self-supporting, and, indeed, in many cases they did acquire large wealth through stock-raising and agricultural pursuits. But not a penny of this belonged to the missionaries, and the annual *sínodos*, or salaries, continued to be paid from other sources, from the Pious Fund in California, and from the royal treasury generally elsewhere.

While it is thus true that the missions were supported to a very considerable degree by the royal treasury, it is just as plain that the amount of government aid, and the ease with which it was secured, depended largely upon the extent to which political ends could be combined with religious purposes.

The importance of political necessity in loosening the royal pursestrings is seen at every turn in the history of Spanish North America. Knowing the strength of a political appeal, the friars always made use of it in their requests for permission and aid. While the monarchs ever used pious phrases, and praised the work of the padres— without hypocrisy no doubt—the royal pocketbook was not readily opened to found new missions unless there was an important political as well as a religious object to be gained.

Striking examples of this fact are found in the histories of Texas and California. The missionaries of the northern frontier had long had their eyes on the "Kingdom of the Texas" as a promising field of labor, and had even appealed to the government for aid in cultivating it. But in vain, till La Salle planted a French colony at Matagorda Bay. Then the royal treasury was opened, and funds were provided for missions in eastern Texas. The French danger passed for the moment, and the missions were withdrawn. Then for another decade Father Hidalgo appealed in vain for funds and permission to re-establish the missions. But when St. Denis, agent of the French governor of Louisiana, intruded himself into Coahuila, the Spanish government at once gave liberal support for the refounding of the missions, to aid in restraining the French.

The case was the same for California. Since the time of Vizcaíno the missionaries had clamored for aid and for permission to found missions at San Diego and Monterey. In 1620 Father Ascensión, who had been with Vizcaíno eighteen years before, wrote, "I do not know what security His Majesty can have in his conscience for delaying so long to send ministers of the Gospel to this realm of California," and, during the next century and a half, a hundred others echoed this admonition. But all to no purpose till the Russian Bear began to amble or to threaten to amble down the Pacific Coast. Then money was forthcoming—partly from the confiscated Pious Fund, it is true—and then missionaries were sent to help hold the country for the crown. On this point Father Engelhardt correctly remarks:

> The missionaries, who generally offered to undergo any hardships in order to convert the Indians, appear to have been enlisted merely for the purpose of securing the territory for the Spanish king . . . [and] the Spanish government would not have sent ships and troops to the northwest if the Russians had not crept down the Pacific coast. . . .

The men who presumed to guide the destinies of Spain then, and, as a rule ever since, cared not for the success of Religion or the welfare of its ministers except in so far as both could be used to promote political schemes.

In this last, I think, Father Engelhardt is too hard on the Spanish monarchs. Their pious professions were not pure hypocrisy. They were truly desirous of spreading the Faith. But they were terribly "hard up," and they had little means to support religious projects unless they served both political and religious ends.

The value of the missionaries as frontier agents was thus clearly recognized, and their services were thus consciously utilized by the government. In the first place, they were often the most useful of explorers and diplomatic agents. The unattended missionary could sometimes go unmolested, and without arousing suspicion and hostility, into districts where the soldier was not welcome, while by their education and their trained habits of thought they were the class best fitted to record what they saw and to report what should be done. For this reason they were often sent alone to explore new frontiers, or as peace emissaries to hostile tribes, or as chroniclers of expeditions led by others. Hence it is that the best of the diaries of early exploration in the Southwest—and, indeed, in most of America—were written by the missionaries.

As illustrations of this kind of frontier service on the part of the missionaries we have but to recall the example of Friar Marcos, who was sent by Viceroy Mendoza to seek the rumored "Seven Cities" in New Mexico; the rediscovery of that province, under the viceroy's patronage, by the party led by Fray Agustín Rodríguez; the expeditions of Father Larios, unattended, into Coahuila; the forty or more journeys of Father Kino across the deserts of Sonora, and his demonstration that California was a peninsula, not an island, as most men had thought; the part played by Kino in pacifying the revolt of the Pimas in 1695, and in making the frontier safe for settlers; the diplomatic errands of Fathers Calahorra and Ramírez, sent by the governors of Texas to the hostile northern tribes; the lone travels of Father Garcés, of two thousand miles or more, over the untrod trails, in Arizona, California, and New Mexico, seeking

a better route to California; and the expedition of Fathers Domínguez and Escalante, pathfinders for an equal distance in and about
the Great Basin between the Rockies and the Sierras.

The missions served also as a means of defense to the king's
dominions. This explains why the government was more willing to
support missions when the frontier needed defending that at other
times, as in the cases, already cited, of Texas and California. It is
significant, too, in this connection, that the Real Hacienda, or Royal
Fisc, charged the expenses for presidios and missions both to the
same account, the Ramo de Guerra, or "War Fund." In a report for
New Spain made in 1758 a treasury official casually remarked:

> Presidios are erected and missions founded in *tierra firme* when-
> ever it is necessary to defend conquered districts from the hostilities
> and invasions of warlike, barbarian tribes, and to plant and extend
> our Holy Faith, for which purposes *juntas de guerra y hacienda*
> are held.

It is indeed true that appropriations for missions were usually made
and that permission to found missions was usually given in councils
of war and finance.

The missionaries counteracted foreign influence among their neophytes, deterred them from molesting the interior settlements, and
secured their aid in holding back more distant tribes. Nearly every
army that was led from San Antonio, Texas, in the eighteenth century, against the hostile Apaches and Comanches, contained a strong
contingent of mission Indians, who fought side by side with the
Spaniards. Father Kino was relied upon by the military leaders of
Sonora to obtain the aid of the Pimas, his beloved neophytes, in
defense of the Sonora settlements. When he was assigned to California, in company with Salvatierra, the authorities of Sonora protested, on the ground that, through his influence over the natives, he
was a better means of protection to the province than a whole company of soldiers. When a Spanish expedition was organized to attack
the Apaches, Kino was sent ahead to arouse and enlist the Pima allies.
When the Pimas put the Apaches to flight, it was Kino to whom
they sent the count of the enemy's dead, recorded by notches on a

pole; on the same occasion it was Kino who received the thanks of citizens and officials of the province; and, when doubt was expressed as to what the Pimas had accomplished, it was Kino who rode a hundred miles or more to count the scalps of the vanquished foe, as evidence with which to vindicate his Pima friends.

The very mission plants were even built and often served as fortresses, not alone for padres and neophytes, but for near-by settlers, too. Every well-built mission was ranged round a great court or patio, protected on all sides by the buildings, whose walls were sometimes eight feet thick. In hostile countries these buildings were themselves enclosed within massive protecting walls. In 1740 President Santa Ana wrote that Mission Valero, at San Antonio, Texas, was better able to withstand a siege than any of the three presidios of the province. This of course was only a relative excellence. Twenty-two years later the same mission was surrounded by a wall, and over the gate was a tower, equipped with muskets, ammunition, and three cannon. At the same time the mission of San José (Texas) was called "a castle" which more than once had been proof against the Apaches.

Not only were the missionaries consciously utilized as political agents to hold the frontier but they often served, on their own motion, or with the co-operation of the secular authority, as "promoters" of the unoccupied districts. They sent home reports of the outlying tribes, of the advantages of obtaining their friendship, of the danger of foreign incursions, of the wealth and attractions of the country, and of the opportunities to extend the king's dominion. Frequently, indeed, they were called to Mexico, or even to Spain, to sit in the royal councils, where their expert opinions often furnished the primary basis of a decision to occupy a new outpost. As examples of this, near at home, we have but to recall Escobar, Benavides, and Ayeta of New Mexico, Massanet, Hidalgo, and Santa Ana of Texas, Kino of Lower California, and Serra of Alta California. Thus consciously or unconsciously, directly or indirectly, with or without secular initiative, the missionaries served as most active promoters, one might even call them "boosters," of the frontier.

But the missionaries helped not only to extend and hold and promote the frontier; more significantly still, they helped to civilize it.

And this is the keynote of my theme. Spain possessed high ideals, but she had peculiar difficulties to contend with. She laid claim to the lion's share of the two Americas, but her population was small and little of it could be spared to people the New World. On the other hand, her colonial policy, equalled in humanitarian principles by that of no other country, perhaps, looked to the preservation of the natives, and to their elevation to at least a limited citizenship. Lacking Spaniards to colonize the frontier, she would colonize it with the aborigines. Such an ideal called not only for the subjugation and control of the natives, but for their civilization as well. To bring this end about the rulers of Spain again made use of the religious and humanitarian zeal of the missionaries, choosing them to be to the Indians not only preachers, but also teachers and disciplinarians. To the extent that this work succeeded it became possible to people the frontier with civilized natives, and thus to supply the lack of colonists. This desire was quite in harmony with the religious aims of the friars, who found temporal discipline indispensable to the best work of Christianization.

Hence it is that in the Spanish system—as distinguished from the French, for example—the essence of the mission was the *discipline*, religious, moral, social, and industrial, which it afforded. The very physical arrangement of the mission was determined with a view to discipline. The central feature of every successful mission was the Indian village, or pueblo. The settled tribes, such as the Pueblo Indians of New Mexico, or the Pimas of Arizona, could be instructed in their native towns, but wandering and scattered tribes must be assembled and established in pueblos, and kept there, by force if necessary. The reason why the missions of eastern Texas failed was that the Indians refused to settle in pueblos, and without more soldiers than were available it was impossible to control them. It was on this question that Father Serra split with Governor Neve regarding the Santa Barbara Indians in California. To save expense for soldiers, Neve urged that the friars should minister to the Indians in their native rancherías. But the missionaries protested that by this arrangement the Indians could not be disciplined. The plan was given up therefore, and instead the Indians were congregated in great pueblos at San Buenaventura and Santa Barbara. Thus, the pueblo was essential to the mission, as it had been to the *encomienda*.

Discipline called for control, and this was placed largely in the hands of the missionaries. The rule was two friars for each mission, but in many instances there was only one. The need of more was often urged.

As a symbol of force, and to afford protection for missionaries and mission Indians, as well as to hold the frontier against savages and foreigners, presidios, or garrisons, were established near by. And thus, across the continent, from San Agustín to San Francisco, stretched a long and slender line of presidios—San Agustín, Apalache, Pensacola, Los Adaes, La Bahía, San Antonio, San Juan Bautista, Rio Grande, San Sabá, El Paso, Santa Fé, Janos, Fronteras, Terrenate, Tubac, Altár, San Diego, Santa Barbara, Monterey, and San Francisco—a line more than twice as long as the Rhine-Danube frontier held by the Romans, from whom Spain learned her lesson in frontier defense.

To assist the missionaries in their work of disciplining and instructing the neophytes, each mission was usually provided with two or more soldiers from the nearest presidio. To help in recovering runaways—for the Indians frequently did abscond—special detachments of soldiers were furnished. The impression is often given that the missionaries objected to the presence of soldiers at the missions, but as a rule the case was quite the contrary. What they did object to was unsuitable soldiers, and outside interference in the selection and control of the guard. It is true, indeed, that immoral or insubordinate soldiers were deemed a nuisance, and that since the presidials were largely half-breeds—mestizoes or mulattoes—and often jailbirds at that, this type was all too common. But in general military aid was demanded, and complaint of its inadequacy was constantly made. On this point the testimony of Fray Romualdo Cartagena, guardian of the College of Santa Cruz de Querétaro, is valid. In a report made in 1772, still in manuscript, he wrote,

> What gives these missions their permanency is the aid which they
> receive from the Catholic arms. Without them pueblos are fre-

quently abandoned, and ministers are murdered by the barbarians. It is seen every day that in missions where there are no soldiers there is no success, for the Indians, being children of fear, are more strongly appealed to by the glistening of the sword than by the voice of five missionaries. Soldiers are necessary to defend the Indians from the enemy, and to keep an eye on the mission Indians, now to encourage them, now to carry news to the nearest presidio in case of trouble. For the spiritual and temporal progress of the missions two soldiers are needed, for the Indians cannot be trusted, especially in new conversions.

This is the testimony of missionaries themselves. That protection was indeed necessary is shown by the martyrdom of missionaries on nearly every frontier—of Father Segura and his entire band of Jesuits in Virginia in 1570; of Father Saeta in Sonora; of Fathers Ganzábal, Silva, Terreros, and Santiesteban in Texas; of Fathers Carranco and Tamaral in Lower California; of Father Luis Jayme at San Diego (Alta California); of Father Garcés and his three companions at Yuma, on the Colorado; and of the twenty-one Franciscans in the single uprising in New Mexico in 1680. But these martyrdoms were only occasional, and the principal business of the soldiers was to assist the missionaries in disciplining and civilizing the savages.

As teachers, and as an example to new converts, it was the custom to place in each new mission three Indian families from the older missions. After a time the families might return to their homes. As Father Romualdo remarked: "It is all the better if these families be related to the new, for this insures the permanence of the latter in the missions, while if they do flee it is easier to recover them by means of their relatives than through strangers."

Notable among the Indians utilized as teachers and colonists in the northern missions were the Tlascaltecans, of Tlascala, the native city of Mexico made famous by Prescott. Having been subdued by Cortés, the Tlascaltecans became the most trusted supporters of the Spaniards, as they had been the most obstinate foes of the "Triple Alliance," and, after playing an important part in the conquest of the Valley of Mexico, they became a regular factor in the extension of

Spanish rule over the north country. Thus, when San Luis Potosí had been conquered, colonies of Tlascaltecans were set to teach the more barbarous natives of that district both loyalty to the Spaniards and the elements of civilization. In Saltillo a large colony of Tlascaltecans was established by Urdiñola at the end of the sixteenth century, and became the mother colony from which numerous offshoots were planted at the new missions and villages further north. At one time a hundred families of Tlascaltecans were ordered sent to Pensacola; in 1755 they figured in the plans for a missionary colony on the Trinity River, in Texas; two years later a little band of them were sent to the San Sabá mission in western Texas to assist in civilizing the Apaches; and twenty years afterward it was suggested that a settlement, with these people as a nucleus, be established far to the north, on the upper Red River, among the Wichita Indians of Texas and Oklahoma. To help in civilizing the mission Indians of Jalisco, Sinaloa, and Sonora, the Tarascans of Michoacán were utilized; further north, the Opatas, of southern Sonora, were sent into Arizona as teachers of the Pimas; to help in civilizing the Indians of California, Serra brought mission Indians from the Peninsula.

Discipline and the elements of European civilization were imparted at the missions through religious instruction, through industrial training, and, among more advanced natives, by means of rudimentary teaching in arts and letters.

Every mission was, in the first place, a Christian seminary, designed to give religious discipline. Religious instruction, of the elementary sort suited to the occasion, was imparted by a definite routine, based on long experience, and administered with much practical sense and regard for local conditions.

Aside from the fundamental cultural concepts involved in Christianity, this religious instruction in itself involved a most important means of assimilation. By the laws of the Indies the missionaries were enjoined to instruct the neophytes in their native tongues, and in the colleges and seminaries professorships were established to teach them. But it was found that, just as the natives lacked the concepts, the Indian languages lacked the terms in which properly to convey the meaning of the Christian doctrine. Moreover, on some frontiers there were so many dialects that it was impossible for the friars to learn them. This was pre-eminently true of the lower Rio Grande region, where there were over two hundred dialects, more than twenty of which were quite distinct. On this point Father Ortiz wrote in 1745:

> The ministers who have learned some language of the Indians of these missions assert that it is impossible to compose a catechism in their idiom, because of the lack of terms in which to explain matters of Faith, and the best informed interpreters say the same. There are as many languages as there are tribes, which in these missions aggregate more than two hundred. . . . Although they mingle and understand each other to some extent, there are twenty languages used commonly by the greater number of the tribes. And since they are new to us, and there are no schools in which to learn them, and since the Fathers are occupied with ministering to the spiritual and temporal needs of the Indians, and in recovering those who flee, the Fathers can hardly be held blameworthy for not learning the native languages.

For these reasons, on the northern frontier instruction was usually given in Spanish, through interpreters at first, and directly as soon as the Indians learned the language of the friars. In the case of children, who were the chief consideration, this was quickly done. And thus incidentally a long step toward assimilation was accomplished, for we all know the importance of language in the fusing of races and cultures. The firmness of the hold of the Spanish language upon any land touched by Spain, however lightly, has often been noted. It was partly, or even largely, due to this teaching of the native children at the missions.

The routine of religious discipline established by the Franciscans in the missions taken over from the Jesuits in Sonora, in 1767, was typical of all the Franciscan missions, and was not essentially different from that of the other orders. It was described by Father Reyes, later Bishop Reyes, as follows:

> Every day at sunrise the bells call the Indians to Mass. An old Indian, commonly called *mador*, and two *fiscales*, go through the

whole pueblo, requiring all children and unmarried persons to go to the church, to take part in the devotion and silence of the Mass. This over, they repeat in concert, in Spanish, with the minister, the prayers and the Creed. At sunset this exercise is repeated at the door of the church, and is concluded with saying the rosary and chanting the *salve* or the *alavado*. The *mador* and the *fiscales* are charged, on Sundays and feast days, to take care to require all men, women, and children to be present at Mass, with their poor clothes clean, and all washed and combed.

The very act of going to church, then, involved a lesson in the amenities of civilization. There was virtue then as now in putting on one's "Sunday clothes."

On these days [Father Reyes continues] Mass is chanted with harps, violins [all played by the natives], and a choir of from four to six [native] men and women. In Lent all have been required to go to Mass daily. . . .

On Palm Sunday, at the head missions (*cabeceras*), that feast is observed with an image and processions. After Easter, censuses are made to ascertain what ones have complied with the Church. In the first years it seemed impossible to us missionaries to vanquish the rudeness of the Indians, and the difficulties of making them confess, and of administering communion. But lately all the young men and some of the old have confessed. In the principal pueblos, where the missionaries reside, many attend the sacraments on feast days. On the Day of Santa María the rosary is sung through the pueblo. On other occasions they are permitted to have balls, diversions, and innocent games. But because they have attempted to prohibit superstitious balls and the scalp dance, the missionaries have encountered strong opposition from the [secular] superiors of the province, who desire to let the Indians continue these excesses.

They contributed, no doubt, to the war spirit, and thus to the defense of the province against the Apaches.

If the mission was a Christian seminary, it was scarcely less an industrial training school. Father Engelhardt writes:

It must be remembered that the friars came to California as messengers of Christ. They were not farmers, mechanics, or stock breeders. Those who, perhaps, had been engaged in such pursuits, had abandoned them for the higher occupation of the priest of God, and they had no desire to be further entangled in worldly business. In California, however [and he might have added, quite generally] the messengers of the Gospel had to introduce, teach, and supervise those very arts, trades, and occupations, before they could expect to make any headway with the truths of salvation. . . . As an absolutely necessary means to win the souls of the savages, these unworldly men accepted the disagreeable task of conducting huge farms, teaching and supervising various mechanical trades, having an eye on the livestock and herders, and making ends meet generally.

The civilizing function of the typical Spanish mission, where the missionaries had charge of the temporalities as well as of the spiritualities, was evident from the very nature of the mission plant. While the church was ever the center of the establishment, and the particular object of the minister's pride and care, it was by no means the larger part. Each fully developed mission was a great industrial school, of which the largest, as in California, sometimes managed more than two thousand Indians. There were weaving rooms, blacksmith shop, tannery, wine-press, and warehouses; there were irrigating ditches, vegetable gardens, and grain fields; and on the ranges roamed thousands of horses, cattle, sheep, and goats. Training in the care of fields and stock not only made the neophytes self-supporting, but afforded the discipline necessary for the rudiments of civilized life. The women were taught to cook, sew, spin, and weave; the men to fell the forest, build, run the forge, tan leather, make ditches, tend cattle, and shear sheep.

Even in New Mexico, where the missionaries were not in charge of the temporalities—that is, of the economic interests of the Indians—and where the Indians had a well-established native agriculture, the friars were charged with their instruction in the arts and crafts, as well as with their religious education. And when the custodian, Father Benavides—later Bishop of Goa—wrote in 1630, after three decades of effort by the friars in that province, he was able to report fourteen monasteries, serving fifty-odd pueblos, each with its school, where the Indians were all taught not only to sing, play musical instruments, read, and write, but, as Benavides puts it, "all the trades and polite deportment," all imparted by "the great industry of the Religious who converted them."

In controlling, supervising, and teaching the Indians, the friars were assisted by the soldier guards, who served as *mayor domos* of the fields, of the cattle and horse herds, of the sheep and goat ranches, and of the shops. In the older missions, even among the most backward tribes, it sometimes became possible to dispense with this service, as at San Antonio, Texas, where, it was reported in 1772, the Indians, once naked savages who lived on cactus apples and cotton-tail rabbits, had become so skilled and trustworthy that "without the aid of the Spaniards they harvest, from irrigated fields, maize, beans, and cotton in plenty, and Castilian corn for sugar. There are cattle, sheep, and goats in abundance," all being the product of the care and labor of the natives.

The results of this industrial training at the missions were to be seen in the imposing structures that were built, the fertile farms that were tilled, and the great stock ranches that were tended, by erstwhile barbarians, civilized under the patient discipline of the missionaries, assisted by soldier guards and imported Indian teachers, not in our Southwest alone, but on nearly every frontier of Spanish America.

The missionaries transplanted to the frontiers and made known to the natives almost every conceivable domestic plant and animal of Europe. By requiring the Indians to work three days a week at community tasks, the Jesuits in Pimería Alta—to give a particular illustration—established at all the missions flourishing ranches of horses, cattle, sheep, and goats, and opened fields and gardens for the cultivation of a vast variety of food plants. Kino wrote in 1710 of the Jesuit missions of Sonora and Arizona,

> There are already thrifty and abundant fields . . . of wheat, maize, frijoles, chickpeas, beans, lentils, bastard chickpeas (*garabanzas*), etc. There are orchards, and in them vineyards for wine for the Masses; and fields of sweet cane for syrup and panocha, and with the favor of Heaven, before long, for sugar. There are many Castilian fruit trees, such as figs, quinces, oranges, pomegranates, peaches, apricots, pears, apples, mulberries, etc., and all sorts of garden stuff,

such as cabbage, lettuce, onions, garlic, anise, pepper, mustard, mint, etc.

Other temporal means [he continues] are the plentiful ranches, which are already stocked with cattle, sheep, and goats, many droves of mares, horses, and pack animals, mules as well as horses, for transportation and commerce, and very fat sheep, producing much tallow, suet, and soap, which is already manufactured in abundance.

An illustration of some of the more moderate material results is to be had in the following description of the four Querétaran missions in Texas, based on an official report made in 1762.

Besides the church, each mission had its *convento*, or monastery, including cells for the friars, porter's lodge, refectory, kitchen, offices, workshops, and granary, usually all under a common roof and ranged round a *patio*. At San Antonio de Valero the *convento* was a two-story structure fifty *varas* square with two *patios* and with arched cloisters above and below. The others were similar.

An important part of each mission was the workshop, for here the neophytes not only helped to supply their economic needs, but got an important part of their training for civilized life. At each of these four missions the Indians manufactured *mantas, terlingas, sayales, rebozos, frezadas,* and other common fabrics of wool and cotton. At Mission San Antonio the workshop contained four looms, and two store-rooms with cotton, wool, cards, spindles, etc. At Concepción and San Francisco there were three looms each.

The neophytes of each mission lived in an Indian village, or pueblo, closely connected with the church and monastery. Of those of the four Querétaran missions we have the fullest description of the pueblo at Mission San Antonio de Valero. It consisted of seven rows of houses built of stone, with arched porticoes, doors, and windows. There was a plaza through which ran a water-ditch, grown with willows and fruit trees. Within the plaza was a curbed well, to supply water in case of a siege by the enemy. The pueblo was surrounded by a wall, and over the gate was a tower, with embrasures, and equipped with three cannon, firearms, and ammunition. The houses were furnished with high beds, chests, metates, pots, kettles, and other domestic utensils. The pueblo of San Antonio was typical of all.

Agricultural and stock-raising activities had increased since 1745. At the four Querétaran missions there were now grazing 4,897 head of cattle, 12,000 sheep and goats, and about 1,600 horses, and each mission had from 37 to 50 yoke of working oxen. Of the four missions San Francisco raised the most stock, having 2,262 head of cattle and 4,000 sheep and goats. Each mission had its ranch, some distance away, where the stock was kept, with one or more stone houses, occupied by the families of the overseers; the necessary corrals, farming implements, and carts; and tools for carpentry, masonry, and blacksmithing. Each mission had well-tilled fields, fenced in and watered by good irrigating ditches, with stone dams. In these fields maize, chile, beans, and cotton were raised in abundance, and in the *huertas* a large variety of garden truck.

This picture of the Texas missions is interesting, but in magnitude the establishments described are not to be compared with those in Paraguay or even in California, where, in 1834, on the eve of the destruction of the missions, 31,000 mission Indians at twenty-one missions herded 396,000 cattle, 62,000 horses, and 321,000 hogs, sheep, and goats, and harvested 123,000 bushels of grain, and where corresponding skill and industry were shown by the neophytes in orchard, garden, wine-press, loom, shop, and forge.

The laws of the Indies even prescribed and the missions provided a school for self-government, elementary and limited, it is true, but germane and potential nevertheless. This was effected by organizing the Indians of the missions into a pueblo, with civil and military officers, modelled upon the Spanish administration. When the mission was founded the secular head of the district—governor, captain, or alcalde—as representative of the king, formally organized the pueblo, appointed the native officers, and gave title to the four-league grant of land. In constituting the native government, wisdom dictated that use should be made of the existing Indian organization, natives of prestige being given the important offices. Thereafter the civil officers were chosen by a form of native election, under the supervision of the missionary, and approved by the secular head of the jurisdiction.

The civil officers were usually a governor, captain, alcaldes, and alguacil, who by law constituted a cabildo, or council. The military officers were a captain or a *teniente*, and subalterns, and were appointed by the secular head, or by a native captain-general subject to approval by the secular head. The military officers had their own insignia, and, to give them prestige, separate benches were placed in the churches for the governor, alcalde, and council. In Sonora there was a *topil*, whose duty was to care for the community houses— a sort of free hostelry, open to all travellers, which seems to have been of native rather than of Spanish origin. The Indians had their own jail, and inflicted minor punishments, prescribed by the minister. Indian overseers kept the laborers at their work and, indeed, much of the task of controlling the Indians was effected through Indian officers themselves. Of course it was the directing force of the padres and the restraining force of the near-by presidio which furnished the ultimate pressure.

This pueblo government was established among the more advanced tribes everywhere, and it succeeded in varying degrees. It was often a cause for conflict of jurisdiction, and in California, where the natives were of the most barbarous, it was strongly opposed by the missionaries. It has been called a farce, but it certainly was not so intended. It was not self-government any more than is student government in a primary school. But it was a means of control, and was a step toward self-government. It is one of the things, moreover, which help to explain how two missionaries and three or four soldiers could make an orderly town out of two or three thousand savages recently assembled from diverse and sometimes mutually hostile tribes. So deeply was it impressed upon the Indians of New Mexico that some of them yet maintain their Spanish pueblo organization, and by it still govern themselves, extra-legally. And, I am told, in some places even in California, the descendants of the mission Indians still keep up the pueblo organization as a sort of fraternity, or secret society.

§   §   §

In these ways, then, did the missions serve as frontier agencies of Spain. As their first and primary task, the missionaries spread the

Faith. But in addition, designedly or incidentally, they explored the frontiers, promoted their occupation, defended them and the interior settlements, taught the Indians the Spanish language, and disciplined them in good manners, in the rudiments of European crafts, of agriculture, and even of self-government. Moreover, the missions were a force which made for the preservation of the Indians, as opposed to their destruction, so characteristic of the Anglo-American frontier. In the English colonies the only good Indians were dead Indians. In the Spanish colonies it was thought worth while to improve the natives for this life as well as for the next. Perhaps the missions did not, in every respect, represent a twentieth-century ideal. Sometimes, and to some degree, they failed, as has every human institution. Nevertheless, it must not be forgotten that of the millions of half-castes living south of us, the grandparents, in a large proportion of cases, at some generation removed, on one side or the other, were once mission Indians, and as such learned the elements of Spanish civilization. For these reasons, as well as for unfeigned religious motives, the missions received the royal support. They were a conspicuous feature of Spain's frontiering genius.

CHAPTER ELEVEN

Kino in Pimería Alta*

DURING his probings into the Archivo General de la Nación of Mexico, back in the early years of the century, Bolton first became acquainted with Padre Eusebio Francisco Kino, who has often been called "his favorite Black Robe." In Volume 27, Sección de Misiones, he stumbled on a manuscript—431 pages with a fourteen-page table of contents. It proved to be Kino's *Favores Celestiales*, a work which his missionary successors often referred to, but which had come to be thought lost. The manuscript told the fascinating story of almost a quarter-century on the far northwestern frontier of New Spain in the late seventeenth and early eighteenth centuries. Bolton determined that he would one day translate and publish this precious piece—this he did in two volumes in 1919. The work brought Kino into focus as one of the most active and very typical of Spain's missionary frontiersmen.

Over the years Bolton gathered more Kino materials, further searching Mexican archives, carrying his quest to Europe into Old World and Jesuit archives, visiting the Tyrol, where Kino, still a lad by the name of Chini (the original Italian form of his name), grew to manhood. In 1932 there was a stir of interest in Arizona to honor this pioneer padre; the late Professor Frank Lockwood of the University of Arizona was one of the prime movers. Bolton contributed a delightful little sketch, *The Padre on Horseback*,† to further the movement. Four years later appeared a full-length biography of Padre Eusebio Francisco, *Rim of Christendom*.

In many respects Kino was a prize laboratory specimen to prove the validity of Bolton's analysis of 1917 in "The Mission as a Fron-

* *Kino's Historical Memoir of Pimería Alta.* 2 vols. (Cleveland, The Arthur H. Clark Company, 1919); reprinted, 2 vols. in one, Berkeley and Los Angeles, University of California Press, 1948, pp. 49–65.

† San Francisco, The Sonora Press, 1932; reprinted in 1963 by the Loyola University Press, Chicago, with introduction by John Francis Bannon.

tier Institution." Besides being a remarkable missionary, the Jesuit was explorer, builder, trail-breaker, cattleman, Indian agent, and more. This selection is a short sketch of some of his achievements.

AT THIS POINT Father Kino takes up in detail the story of his career in America in his *Favores Celestiales*, which is printed hereinafter, and the remainder of this sketch will therefore be brief. As soon as he learned that the conversion of California had been suspended, he asked and obtained permission to go to the Guaymas and Seris, with whom he had dealt during his voyages from California to the mainland. Leaving Mexico City on November 20, 1686, he went to Guadalajara, where he secured special privileges from the Audiencia. Setting forth again on December 16, he reached Sonora early in 1687, and was assigned, not to the Guaymas as he had hoped, but to Pimería Alta, instead.

Pimería Alta included what is now northern Sonora and southern Arizona. It extended from the Altar River, in Sonora, to the Gila, and from the San Pedro River to the Gulf of California and the Colorado of the West. At that day it was all included in the province of Nueva Vizcaya; later it was attached to Sonora, to which it belonged until the northern portion was cut off by the Gadsden Purchase.

Kino found Pimería Alta occupied by different divisions of the Pima nation. Chief of these were the Pima proper, living in the valleys of the Gila and the Salt Rivers, especially in the region now occupied by the Pima Reservation. The valleys of the San Pedro and the Santa Cruz were inhabited by the Sobaipuris, now a practically extinct people, except for the strains of their blood still represented in the Pima and Papago tribes. West of the Sobaipuris, on both sides of the international boundary line, were the Papagos, or the Papabotes, as the early Spaniards called them. On the northwestern border of the region, along the lower Gila and the Colorado Rivers, were the different Yuman tribes, such as the Yumas, the Cocomaricopas, the Cocopas, and the Quiquimas. All of these latter spoke the Yuman language, which was, as it is today, quite distinct from that of the Pima.

When Kino made his first explorations down the San Pedro and the Santa Cruz Valleys, he found them each supporting ten or a dozen villages of Sobaipuris, the population of the former aggregating some two thousand persons, and of the latter some two thousand five hundred. The Indians of both valleys were then practicing agriculture by irrigation, and raising cotton for clothing, and maize, beans, calabashes, melons, and wheat for food. The Papagos were less advanced than the Pimas and Sobaipuris, but at Sonóita, at least, they were found practicing irrigation by means of ditches. The Yumas raised crops, but apparently without artificial irrigation. Much more notable than the irrigation in use at the coming of the Spaniards were the remains of many miles of aqueducts, and the huge ruins of cities which had long before been abandoned, structures which are now attributed by scientists to the ancestors of the Pimas.

Father Kino arrived in Pimería Alta in March, 1687,[1] and began without the loss of a single day a work of exploration, conversion, and mission building that lasted only one year less than a quarter of a century. When he reached the scene of his labors the frontier mission station was at Cucurpe, in the valley of the river now called San Miguel. Cucurpe still exists, a quiet little Mexican pueblo, sleeping under the shadow of the Agua Prieta Mountains, and inhabited by descendants of the Eudeve Indians who were there when Kino arrived. To the east, in Nueva Vizcaya, were the already important *reales*, or mining camps, of San Juan and Bacanuche, and to the south were numerous missions, ranches, and mining towns; but beyond, in Pimería Alta, all was the untouched and unknown country of the upper Pimas.

On the outer edge of this virgin territory, some fifteen miles above Cucurpe, on the San Miguel River, Kino founded the mission of Nuestra Señora de los Dolores (Our Lady of Sorrows), at the Indian village of Cosari. The site chosen was one of peculiar fitness and beauty. It is a commonplace to say that the missionaries always selected the most fertile spots for their missions. This is true, but it is more instructive to give the reason. They ordinarily founded

---

[1] It may be of interest to note that this was the very month of La Salle's assassination in the wilds of Texas.

their missions at or near the villages of the Indians for whom they were designed, and these were usually placed at the most fertile spots along the rich valleys of the streams. And so it was with the village of Cosari.

Near where Cosari stood, the little San Miguel breaks through a narrow cañon, whose walls rise several hundred feet in height. Above and below the cañon, the river valley broadens out into rich *vegas* of irrigable bottom lands, half a mile or more in width and several miles in length. On the east, the valley is walled in by the Sierra de Santa Teresa, on the west by the Sierra del Torreón. Closing the lower valley and hiding Cucurpe, stands Cerro Prieto; and cutting off the observer's view toward the north rises the grand and rugged Sierra Azul. At the cañon where the river breaks through, the western mesa juts out and forms a cliff, approachable only from the west.

On this promontory, protected on three sides from attack, and affording a magnificent view, was placed the mission of Dolores. Here still stand its ruins, in full view of the valley above and below, of the mountain walls on the east and the west, the north and the south, and within the sound of the rushing cataract of the San Miguel as it courses through the gorge. This meager ruin on the cliff, consisting now of a mere fragment of an adobe wall and saddening piles of debris, is the most venerable of the many mission remains in all Arizona and northern Sonora, for Our Lady of Sorrows was mother of them all, and for nearly a quarter of a century was the home of the remarkable missionary who built them.[2]

From his outpost at Dolores, during the next quarter century, Kino and his companions pushed the frontier of missionary work and exploration across Pimería Alta to the Gila and Colorado Rivers. By 1695 Kino had established a chain of missions up and down the valley of the Altar and Magdalena Rivers and another chain northeast of Dolores. In April, 1700, he founded, within the present state of Arizona, the mission of San Xavier del Bac, and within the next two years those of Tumacácori and Guebavi within the present state

[2] The ruins of the Mission of Dolores are on Rancho de Dolores, on the hill directly overlooking the residence of the owner. They were visited by the writer in 1911.

of Arizona. Kino's exploring tours were also itinerant missions, and in the course of them he baptized and taught in numerous villages, all up and down the Gila and the lower Colorado, and in all parts of northern Pimería.

Kino's work as missionary was paralleled by his achievement as explorer, and to him is due the credit for the first mapping of Pimería Alta on the basis of actual exploration. The region had been entered by Fray Marcos, by Melchior Díaz, and by the main Coronado party, in the period 1539–1541. But these explorers had only passed along its eastern and western borders; for it is no longer believed that they went down the Santa Cruz. Not since that day—a century and a half before—had Arizona been entered from the south by a single recorded expedition, while, so far as we know, not since 1605, when Oñate went from Moqui down the Colorado of the West, had any white man seen the Gila River.[3] The rediscovery, therefore, and the first interior exploration of Pimería Alta was the work of Father Kino.

Not to count the minor and unrecorded journeys among his widely separated missions, he made at least fourteen expeditions across the line into what is now Arizona. Six of them took him as far as Tumacácori, Benson, San Xavier del Bac, or Tucson. Six carried him to the Gila over five different routes. Twice he reached that stream by way of Santa Cruz, returning once via Casa Grande, Sonóita, the Gulf of California and Caborca. Once he went by way of the San Pedro, once from El Saric across to the Gila below the Big Bend, and three times by way of Sonóita and the Camino del Diablo, along the Gila Range. Two of these expeditions carried him to Yuma and down the Colorado. Once he crossed that stream into California, and finally he reached its mouth.

East and west, between Sonóita and the eastern missions, he crossed southern Arizona several times and by several trails. In what is now Sonora he made at least half a dozen recorded journeys from Dolores to Caborca and the coast, three to the Santa Clara Mountain to view the head of the California Gulf, and two to the coast by

---

[3] Father Kino is authority for the statement that before his day the Spaniards of New Mexico had traded with the Sobaipuris of the San Pedro Valley.

then unknown routes south of the Altar River. This enumeration does not include his journey to Mexico, nor the numerous other trips to distant interior points in what is now Sonora, to see the superior mission authorities.

After 1699, aside from his search for souls in the Pimería, Kino's most absorbing quest was made in search of a land route to California. Since the days of Cortés and Cabrillo many views had been held regarding the geography of California, some regarding it as a peninsula and others as an island. Kino had been taught by Father Aygentler, in the University of Ingolstadt, that it was a peninsula, and had come to America firm in this belief; but in deference to current opinion, and as a result of certain observations of his own, he had given up the notion, and as late as 1698 he wrote of California as "the largest island of the world." But during the journey of 1699 to the Gila occurred an incident that caused him to turn again to the peninsular theory. It was the gift, when near the Yuma junction, of certain blue shells, such as he had seen in 1685 on the Pacific coast of the Peninsula of California, and there only. If the shells had come to the Yumas from the South Sea, he reasoned, must there not be land connection with California and the ocean, by way of the Yuma country? Kino now ceased his work on the boat he was building at Caborca and Dolores for the navigation of the Gulf, and directed his efforts to learning more about the source of the blue shells. For this purpose he made a journey in 1700 to San Xavier del Bac. Thither he called the Indians from all the villages for hundreds of miles around, and in "long talks" at night he learned that only from the South Sea could the blue shells be had.

This assurance was the inspiration of his remaining journeys. In the same year, 1700, he for the first time reached the Yuma junction, and learned that he was above the head of the Gulf, which greatly strengthened his belief in the peninsular theory. In the next year he returned to the same point by way of the Camino del Diablo, passed some distance down the Colorado, and crossed over to the California side, towed on a raft by Indians and sitting in a basket. Finally, in 1702, his triumph came, for he again returned to the Yuma junction, descended the Colorado to the Gulf, and saw the sun rise over its head. He was now satisfied that he had demonstrated the feasibility of a land passage to California and had disproved the idea that California was an island.

In estimating these feats of exploration we must remember the meager outfit and the limited aid with which he performed them. He was not supported and encouraged by several hundred horsemen and a great retinue of friendly Indians as were De Soto and Coronado. On the contrary, in all but two cases he went almost unaccompanied by military aid, and more than once he went without a single white man. In one expedition, made in 1697 to the Gila, he was accompanied by Lieutenant Manje, Captain Bernal, and twenty-two soldiers. In 1701 he was escorted by Manje and ten soldiers. At other times he had no other military support than Lieutenant Manje or Captain Carrasco, without soldiers. Once Father Gilg, besides Manje, accompanied him; once two priests and two citizens. His last great exploration to the Gila was made with only one other white man in his party, while in 1694, 1700, and 1701 he reached the Gila with no living soul save his Indian servants. But he was usually well supplied with horses and mules from his own ranches, for he took at different times as many as fifty, sixty, eighty, ninety, one hundred and five, and even one hundred and thirty head.

The work which Father Kino did as a ranchman, or stockman, would alone stamp him as an unusual businessman, and make him worthy of remembrance. He was easily the cattle king of his day and region. From the small outfit supplied him from the older missions to the east and south, within fifteen years he established the beginnings of ranching in the valleys of the Magdalena, the Altar, the Santa Cruz, the San Pedro, and the Sonóita. The stock-raising industry of nearly twenty places on the modern map owes its beginnings on a considerable scale to this indefatigable man. And it must not be supposed that he did this for private gain, for he did not own a single animal. It was to furnish a food supply for the Indians of the missions established and to be established, and to give these missions a basis of economic prosperity and independence. It would be impossible to give a detailed statement of his work of this nature, but some of the exact facts are necessary to convey the impression. Most of the facts, of course, were unrecorded, but from those available it is learned that stock ranches were established by him or directly under his supervision, at Dolores, Caborca, Tubutama, San Ignacio, Imuris, Magdalena, Quiburi, Tumacácori, Cocóspera, San Xavier del Bac, Bacoancos, Guevabi, Síboda, Busanic, Sonóita, San Lázaro, Saric, Santa Bárbara, and Santa Eulalia.

Characteristic of Kino's economic efforts are those reflected in Father Saeta's letter thanking him for the present of one hundred and fifteen head of cattle and as many sheep for the beginnings of a ranch at Caborca. In 1699 a ranch was established at Sonóita for the triple purpose of supplying the little mission there, furnishing food for the missionaries of California, if perchance they should reach that point, and as a base of supplies for the explorations which Kino hoped to undertake and did undertake to the Yumas and Cocomaricopas, of whom he had heard while on the Gila. In 1700, when the mission of San Xavier was founded, Kino rounded up the fourteen hundred head of cattle on the ranch of his own mission of Dolores, divided them into two equal droves, and sent one of them under his Indian overseer to Bac, where the necessary corrals were constructed.

Not only his own missions but those of sterile California must be supplied; and in the year 1700 Kino took from his own ranches seven hundred cattle and sent them to Salvatierra, across the Gulf, at Loreto, a transaction which was several times repeated.

And it must not be forgotten that Kino conducted this cattle industry with Indian labor, almost without the aid of a single white man. An illustration of his method and of his difficulties is found in the fact that the important ranch at Tumacácori, Arizona, was founded with cattle and sheep driven, at Kino's orders one hundred miles across the country from Caborca, by the very Indians who had murdered Father Saeta at Caborca in 1695. There was always the danger that the mission Indians would revolt and run off the stock, as they did in 1695; and the danger, more imminent, that the hostile Apaches, Janos, and Jocomes would do this damage, and add to it the destruction of life, as experience often proved.

Kino's endurance in the saddle was worthy of a seasoned cowboy. This is evident from the bare facts with respect to the long journeys which he made. When he went to the City of Mexico in the fall of 1695, being then at the age of fifty-one, he made the journey in fifty-three days between November 16 and January 8. The distance, *via* Guadalajara, is no less than fifteen hundred miles, making his average, not counting the stops which he made at Guadalajara and other important places, nearly thirty miles per day. In November, 1697, when he went to the Gila, he rode about seven hundred or eight hundred miles in thirty days, not counting out the stops. On his journey in 1698 to the Gila he made an average of twenty-five or more miles a day for twenty-six days, over an unknown country. In 1699 he made the trip to and from the lower Gila, about eight or nine hundred miles, in thirty-five days, an average of ten leagues a day, or twenty-five to thirty miles. In October and November, 1699, he rode two hundred and forty leagues in thirty-nine days. In September and October, 1700, he rode three hundred and eighty-four leagues, or perhaps one thousand miles, in twenty-six days. This was an average of nearly forty miles a day. In 1701, he made over four hundred leagues, or more than eleven hundred miles, in thirty-five days, an average of over thirty miles a day. He was then nearing the age of sixty.

Thus we see that it was customary for Kino to make an average of thirty or more miles a day for weeks or months at a time, when he was on these missionary tours, and out of this time are to be counted the long stops which he made to preach to and baptize the Indians, and to say mass.

A special instance of his hard riding is found in the journey which he made in November, 1699, with Father Leal, the Visitor of the missions. After twelve days of continuous travel, supervising, baptizing, and preaching up and down the Santa Cruz Valley, going the while at the average rate of twenty-three miles (nine leagues) a day, he left Father Leal at Batki to go home by carriage over a more direct route, while he and Manje sped "á la ligera" to the west and northwest, to see if there were any sick Indians to baptize. Going thirteen leagues (thirty-three miles) on the eighth, he baptized two infants and two adults at the village of San Rafael. On the ninth he rode nine leagues to another village, made a census of four hundred

Indians, preached to them, and continued sixteen more leagues to another village, making nearly sixty miles for the day. On the tenth he made a census of the assembled throng of three hundred persons, preached, baptized three sick persons, distributed presents, and then rode thirty-three leagues (some seventy-five miles) over a pass in the mountains to Sonóita, arriving there in the night, having stopped to make a census of, preach to, and baptize in, two villages on the way. After four hours of sleep, on the eleventh he baptized and preached, and then rode, that day and night, the fifty leagues (or from one hundred to one hundred and twenty-five miles) that lie between Sonóita and Busanic, where he overtook Father Leal. During the last three days he had ridden no less than one hundred and eight leagues, or from two hundred and fifty to three hundred miles, counting, preaching to, and baptizing in five villages on the way. And yet he was up next morning, preaching, baptizing, and supervising the butchering of cattle for supplies. Truly this was strenuous work for a man of fifty-five.

Another instance of his disregard of toil in ministering to others may be cited. On the morning of May 3, 1700, he was at Tumacácori, on his way to Dolores, from the founding of Mission San Xavier del Bac. As he was about to say mass at sunrise, he received an urgent message from Father Campos, begging him to hasten to San Ignacio to help save a poor Indian whom the soldiers had imprisoned and were about to execute on the following day. Stopping to say mass and to write a hurried letter to Captain Escalante, he rode by midnight to Imuris, and arrived at San Ignacio in time to say early mass and to save the Indian from death. The direct route by rail from Tumacácori to Imuris is sixty-two miles, and to San Ignacio it is seventy. If Kino went the then usual route by the Santa Cruz River, he must have ridden seventy-five or more miles on this errand of mercy in considerably less than a day.

Kino's physical courage is attested by his whole career in America, spent in exploring unknown wilds and laboring among untamed savages. But it is especially shown by several particular episodes in his life. In March and April, 1695, the Pimas of the Altar Valley rose in revolt. At Caborca Father Saeta was killed and became the proto-martyr of Pimería Alta. At Caborca and Tubutama seven servants of the mission were slain, and at Caborca, Tubutama, Imuris, San Ignacio and Magdalena—the whole length of the Altar and Magdalena Valleys—the mission churches and other buildings were burned and the stock killed or stampeded. The missionary of Tubutama fled over the mountains to Cucurpe. San Ignacio being attacked by three hundred warriors, Father Campos fled to the same refuge, guarded on each side by two soldiers. At Dolores Father Kino, Lieutenant Manje, and three citizens of Bacanuche awaited the onslaught. An Indian who had been stationed on the mountains, seeing the smoke at San Ignacio, fled to Dolores with the news that Father Campos and all the soldiers had been killed. Manje sped to Opodepe to get aid; the three citizens hurried home to Bacanuche, and Kino was left alone. When Manje returned next day, together they hid the treasures of the church in a cave, but in spite of the soldier's entreaties that they should flee, Kino insisted on returning to the mission to await death, which they did. It is indicative of the modesty of this great soul that in his own history this incident in his life is passed over in complete silence. But Manje, who was weak or wise enough to wish to flee, was also generous and brave enough to record the *padre's* heroism and his own fears.

In 1701 Kino made his first exploration down the Colorado below the Yuma junction—the first that had been made for almost a century. With him was one Spaniard, the only other white man in the party. As they left the Yuma country and entered that of the Qui-quimas, the Spaniard, Kino tells us in his diary, "on seeing such a great number of new people," and such people—that is, they were giants in size—became frightened and fled, and was seen no more. But the missionary, thus deserted, instead of turning back, dispatched messages that he was safe, continued down the river two days, and crossed the Colorado, towed by the Indians on a raft and sitting in a basket, into territory never before trod by white men since 1540. Perhaps he was in no danger, but the situation had proved too much for the nerve of his white companion, at least.

And what kind of a man personally was Father Kino to those who knew him intimately? Was he rugged, coarse fibered, and adapted by nature to such a rough frontier life of exposure? I know of no portrait of him made by sunlight or the brush, but there is, fortunately, a picture drawn by the pen of his companion during the last eight years of his life, and his successor at Dolores. Father Luis Velarde tells us that Kino was a modest, humble, gentle, ascetic, of mediaeval type, drilled by his religious training to complete self effacement. I should not be surprised to find that, like Father Junípero Serra, he was slight of body as he was gentle of mind.

Velarde says of him:

> Permit me to add what I observed in the eight years during which I was his companion. His conversation was of the mellifluous names of Jesus and Mary, and of the heathen for whom he was ever offering prayers to God. In saying his breviary he always wept. He was edified by the lives of the saints, whose virtues he preached to us. When he publicly reprimanded a sinner he was choleric. But if anyone showed him personal disrespect he controlled his temper to such an extent that he made it a habit to exalt whomsoever maltreated him by word, deed, or in writing. . . . And if it was to his face that they were said, he embraced the one who spoke them, saying, "You are and ever will be my dearest master!" even though he did not like him. And then, perhaps, he would go and lay the insults at the feet of the Divine Master and the sorrowing Mother, into whose temple he went to pray a hundred times a day.[4] After supper, when he saw us already in bed, he would enter the church, and even though I sat up the whole night reading, I never heard him come out to get the sleep of which he was very sparing. One night I casually saw someone whipping him mercilessly. [That is, as a means of penance.] He always took his food without salt, and with mixtures of herbs which made it more distasteful. No one ever saw in him any vice whatsoever, for the discovery of lands and the conversion of souls had purified him. These, then, are the virtues of Father Kino: he prayed much, and was considered as without vice. He neither smoked nor took snuff, nor wine, nor slept in a bed. He was so austere that he never took wine except to celebrate mass, nor had any other bed than the sweat blankets of his horse for a mattress, and two Indian blankets [for a cover]. He never had more than two coarse shirts, because he gave everything as alms to the Indians. He was merciful

4 The allusion is to the name of the mission, Nuestra Señora de los Dolores.

to others, but cruel to himself. While violent fevers were lacerating his body, he tried no remedy for six days except to get up to celebrate mass and to go to bed again. And by thus weakening and dismaying nature he conquered the fevers.

Is there any wonder that such a man as this could endure the hardships of exploration?

Kino died at the age of sixty-seven, at Magdalena, one of the missions he had founded, and his remains are now resting at San Ignacio, another of his establishments. His companion in his last moments was Father Agustín de Campos, for eighteen years his colaborer and for another eighteen years his survivor, as I recently learned from the church records of San Ignacio. Velarde describes his last moments in these terms:

> Father Kino died in the year 1711, having spent twenty-four years in glorious labors in this Pimería, which he entirely covered in forty expeditions, made as best they could be made by two or three zealous workers. When he died he was almost seventy years old. He died as he had lived, with extreme humility and poverty. In token of this, during his last illness he did not undress. His deathbed, as his bed had always been, consisted of two calfskins for a mattress, two blankets such as the Indians use for covers, and a pack-saddle for a pillow. Nor did the entreaties of Father Agustín move him to anything else. He died in the house of the Father where he had gone to dedicate a finely made chapel in his pueblo of Santa Magdalena, consecrated to San Francisco Xavier. . . . When he was singing the mass of the dedication he felt indisposed, and it seems that the Holy Apostle, to whom he was ever devoted, was calling him, in order that, being buried in his chapel, he might accompany him, as we believe, in glory.[5]

The words of that eloquent writer, John Fiske, in reference to Las Casas, Protector of the Indians, are not inapplicable to Father Kino. He says:

> In contemplating such a life all words of eulogy seem weak and

[5] I have seen no confirmation of Father Benz's story that Kino was killed by rebel Indians. From what is said here it seems altogether improbable. See *Catholic Encyclopedia*, VIII, 660.

frivolous. The historian can only bow in reverent awe before . . . [such] a figure. When now and then in the course of centuries God's providence brings such a life into this world, the memory of it must be cherished by mankind as one of its most precious and sacred possessions. For the thoughts, the words, the deeds of such a man, there is no death. The sphere of their influence goes on widening forever. They bud, they blossom, they bear fruit, from age to age.

CHAPTER TWELVE

*The Black Robes of New Spain**

KINO may have been Bolton's "favorite Black Robe," but, as he probed deeper into the Borderlands story, he found many of Kino's Jesuit brethren along the way. Kino's close friend and associate, Padre Juan María Salvatierra, successful founder of the Baja California missions, he planned to memorialize; but this dream, like so many others, he did not have the years to realize. In 1934, however, he did have the opportunity to brief the tale of Black-Robe exploits in New Spain in one of his fine broad-sweep studies.

In the early paragraph Bolton again alludes to an ambition, which had long been his, to "Parkmanize" the story of the Spaniards in North America. He sketched the outline in his letter to Professor Dodd, cited in the introduction to this volume. He briefed the story in his lecture series to the Lowell Institute of Boston during the winter of 1920–21—eight in number. And his *The Spanish Borderlands* was another foretaste of what he hoped was to come. But even great men have a mortal life span.

With the Black-Robe story, as with so many of his other Borderlands projects, he inspired many of his students to implement his vision. Shiels, Dunne, McShane, Harry Johnson, Tichenor, Treutlein, Ewing, Downey, and the present editor sought to fill in parts of the picture; and, after Bolton's retirement, Kinnaird, his successor at the University of California, had other students continue the work.

FOR ME TO APPEAR before the American Catholic Historical Association to speak on the subject of the Jesuits is no less than rash. But I come with the utmost humility—even more than I felt when I started

* Paper read at the Fifteenth Annual Meeting of the American Catholic Historical Association, Washington, December 29, 1934. Published in *The Catholic Historical Review*, Vol. XXI (October, 1935), 257–82; reprinted in *Wider Horizons of American History* (New York, D. Appleton-Century, 1939), 149–91.

to write my paper. My presence here is an evidence of a sincere if a feeble endeavor to learn something of the stupendous achievements of the Black Robes in Spanish North America, and to indicate in broadest outline a field of study which a group of us are modestly cultivating.

I

No phase of Western Hemisphere history reveals greater heroism, and few have greater significance, than that of the Jesuit missions. The story of the Black Robes in Paraguay and other parts of South America has been told by many writers. The deeds of the Jesuits in New France have been made widely known to English readers by the scintillating pages of Parkman, the monumental documentary collection edited by Thwaites, and the scholarly monographs of Kellogg and a host of Canadian scholars.

It would be presumptuous for me to attempt greatly to modify what the brilliant New England historian wrote. Indeed, aside from its limited geographical horizon and the Puritan assumptions on which it is based, the chief fault to be found with the literary masterpiece is its title. Parkman called his classic *The Jesuits in North America*, meaning only those of New France. In the book there is scarcely a hint that there were any Jesuits in colonial America except those who labored in Canada and the Mississippi Valley. He wrote so brilliantly that he conveyed to lay readers a grossly erroneous impression; for, because of Parkman's facile pen, nine out of ten persons in English speaking circles, when they hear the phrase "the Jesuits of North America," think instinctively and exclusively of the Black Robes of New France; and many of them would be surprised and perhaps skeptical if told that there were any Jesuits in colonial days other than those of which Parkman wrote. But the Black Robes of New France were by no means the only sons of Loyola in the North American colonies. Indeed, they were not the earliest nor the largest group, for they were long preceded and greatly outnumbered by those of New Spain. The French Jesuits suffered martyrdoms which made them justly famous among the martyrs of all the missionary world. But they were not the sole nor even the most numerous Jesuit martyrs in colonial North America, for they were far exceeded numerically by the Black Robe martyrs of Nueva España.

Judged by their own criteria, the Canadian Jesuits were not by any means the most successful sons of Loyola in colonial America. The primary aim of the missionary was to save souls. To baptize a dying babe nearly any of them would go through fire and water. Their first measure of success was the number of baptisms solemnized, the number of pagan mortals brought into the Christian fold. Thus computed, the success of the Canadian Jesuits was relatively small. This was no fault of theirs. They labored in a most difficult land, where Satan and his imps were particularly rampant. The Black Robes of New France counted their conversions by hundreds, or at best by thousands; those of New Spain, working in a more propitious field, numbered their baptisms by hundreds of thousands, or even by millions. And their achievements in other directions were similarly disparate. Do not misunderstand me. These comparisons are by no means made to exalt one group of noble men in order to disparage another group equally worthy. They are intended merely to bring to the attention a momentous episode in North American history which has remained obscure. The height of one great mountain can best be realized by comparing it with another great mountain of known elevation. The imposing stature of the Jesuits of New France is widely known because they had Parkman as their historian. The Spanish Jesuits in North America await their Parkman.

There is space here only to sketch in broadest outline the two hundred year sweep of Jesuit missionary work in New Spain. What I say will be the more impressive if it is borne in mind that each page of mine calls for at least a full-length volume, each of which in turn must rest on many volumes of documentary materials, known to exist, but most of which have not been printed.[1]

[1] In preparing a sketch so broad and so general as this one, it has not been deemed advisable to give specific citations to all the materials drawn upon. Besides the general authorities such as Florencia, Pérez de Ribas, Alegre, Manje, Kino, Venegas, Baegert, Pfefferkorn, Decorme, Astrain, and Bancroft, extensive use has been made of documentary materials from foreign archives, most of which are still unpublished. It is a pleasure to acknowledge here the stimulus which I have received in

II

The pioneer Jesuits in North America labored on the Atlantic seaboard, all of which was then comprised in the vast region called La Florida.[2] Father Martínez, the first Black Robe to arrive, was martyred by a Georgian chief in September, 1566, just sixty years before Lallemand and his band entered Canada. Father Segura and his followers were slain near Chesapeake Bay not far from the site where the English settled thirty-seven years later. Virginia history thus opened not with the founding of Jamestown, but with giving to the world eight Jesuit martyrs. The Black Robes who escaped the Virginia massacre and a Carolina revolt were soon transferred to a happier field. Mexico, or New Spain, was made a Jesuit province. Pedro Sánchez came from Europe as Provincial with fifteen companions, who were soon joined by the Florida survivors. In the fall of 1572 Sánchez and his band reached Mexico City, and began an unbroken work of almost two centuries. Sánchez was a "sturdy beggar" and a gifted man of affairs. Generously endowed by private citizens, the viceroy, and the city, the Jesuits soon had a substantial residence and a church. More Black Robes came from Spain, an American novitiate was opened, and recruits were drawn from the "flower of Mexico."

For nearly a score of years effort was directed mainly toward establishing educational institutions, for which the young Order was already famous.[3] Four colleges and a seminary were followed by the great Colegio Máximo of San Pedro y San Pablo, which received its papal charter sixty years before Harvard opened its doors, and soon took its place as one of the three or four leading universities in all America. Father Ratkay, fresh from Europe in 1680, just before

my study of Jesuit history from my former students, the Reverend Dr. William Eugene Shiels, S.J., the Reverend Dr. Jerome V. Jacobsen, S.J., and the Reverend Dr. Peter M. Dunne, S.J.

[2] Their story has just been told in an excellent volume by the Reverend Dr. Michael Kenny, S.J., entitled *The Romance of the Floridas*.

[3] The Reverend Dr. Jerome V. Jacobsen, S.J., will soon make known this important chapter in the history of America in a book, now awaiting publication, entitled *Educational Foundations of the Jesuits in New Spain*.

Philadelphia was founded, remarked that it had fifteen hundred students and a respectable debt of $40,000. Schools and colleges outside Mexico City were established in quick succession, at Pátzcuaro, Valladolid, Oaxaca, Puebla, Vera Cruz, and other places. Some of them were maintained especially for the natives. Conversion evidently bred humility, for one of the young chieftains became a professor, and taught for more than forty years in the college of San Gregorio. Such were some of the foundations and ministries of the Black Robes in and near the capital of New Spain, among Spaniards and sedentary Indians, in the early years of their apostolate. Two decades had not passed when they began to push beyond the border to found missions among the less civilized tribes—the work in New Spain for which they ultimately became most famous.

Their maiden effort in missions *entre infieles* was at San Luís de la Paz, where they were sent to help tame the wild Chichimecos, those people who terrorized the highway leading from the capital to the mines of Zacatecas. Under the gentle influence of the Black Robes roving Indians turned to village life, warriors became farmers, and the roads were made safe. Spaniards settled in the vicinity, and the present city of San Luís de la Paz is the result. Thus the first Jesuit mission among the wild Indians of Mexico was typical of all: it became the nucleus of a Christian colony and a center of civilization.

The Chichimec mission was but a step toward the great heathendom of Nueva Vizcaya, that immense jurisdiction embracing all the country beyond Zacatecas, and extending a thousand miles or more, to New Mexico and California. Before the Jesuits arrived Spain had made considerable beginnings toward the occupation of this vast Northwest. Coronado had opened a road to Cíbola, Guzmán and Ibarra had conquered Sinaloa, thousands of cattle roamed the plains, haciendas flourished here and there in the fertile valleys, and silver mines were thinly scattered through the mountains of Durango.

Jesuit Land, for such the Northwest might well be called, comprised the modern districts of Nayarit, the four great states of Durango, Chihuahua, Sinaloa, and Sonora, Baja California, and part of Arizona, a domain larger than all of France. And the Black Robes did not merely explore this vast area, they occupied it in detail. This extensive region was chiefly a mountain country. It embraced four rather distinct geographic areas: the Central Plateau, the Sierra Madre, the Coastal Plain, and the California Peninsula, each with features which greatly influenced Jesuit activities. The Central Plateau, seven thousand feet high in southern Durango, gradually slopes northward and extends to and beyond the Rio Grande. On the west this tableland is walled in by one of the roughest portions of the entire Western Hemisphere—so rough indeed that south of the United States border there is a stretch of nearly a thousand miles which has never yet been crossed by a wheel track. On its precipitous western slope this Sierra Madre is cut by numerous rivers which tumble through immense barrancas—veritable Grand Canyons—some of them several thousand feet deep and many miles long. The Indians of this vast expanse were of various linguistic stocks and of many tribes. They occupied fairly definite areas, but with a few exceptions they did not lead a wholly sedentary life. For food most of the mainland peoples within the area raised maize, beans, and calabashes by primitive methods; the Peninsula Indians practiced no agriculture at all. The natives of the mainland coast and the foothills were the most numerous, the most docile, and offered the best missionary field.

The pioneer missionaries in Nueva Vizcaya were the Franciscans. But the sons of Loyola now entered the district (1591), and became almost its sole evangelists during the next century and three quarters. Then the Franciscans came back. In two wide-fronted columns the Jesuits marched northward up the mainland, one up the eastern and one up the western slope of the imponderable Sierra Madre, meeting generally west of the Continental Divide. At the end of the seventeenth century they crossed the Gulf and moved in a third phalanx into the Peninsula of California.

River by river, valley by valley, canyon by canyon, tribe by tribe, these harbingers of Christian civilization advanced into the realm of heathendom. They gathered the natives into villages, indoctrinated them in the Faith, trained them in agriculture and the simpler crafts, and in schools and seminaries taught many of them reading, writing, and music. Under the tutelage of the patient Jesuits, barbarians who formerly had constructed only the meanest huts now built substantial Christian temples, some of which still stand as architectural monuments. The natives were generally well-disposed toward the missionaries. But secular Spaniards exploited their labor in mines and on haciendas; and native priests were jealous of their white competitors. The result was a series of periodic Indian revolts in which a score or more of Black Robes in New Spain won the crown of martyrdom. But the march went on.

It was a picturesque pageant. Black Robes moved into the wilderness beside or ahead of prospector, miner, soldier, and frontier trader. Land travel was chiefly on horseback, muleback, or on foot, and land transportation by pack train or Indian carriers. As the frontier expanded, here and there a town, a mining camp, an hacienda, a garrison was pitched on the border of settlement. Still beyond, in the midst of heathendom, Christian missions were planted. As the Spaniards advanced northward, the Indians were reduced to sedentary life or were driven back. The spread of European civilization in North America was not by any means wholly a westward movement.

At the head of the Jesuit province of New Spain was the provincial, resident at Mexico City. Missions were grouped into rectorates under rectors, and these in turn into larger districts, under visitors. In regions near the capital the provincial himself customarily made the visitation. In the eighteenth century the office of visitor-general or vice-provincial was utilized. Few provincials ever found it possible to inspect the entire province.

The central feature of the mission was the pueblo, or permanent Indian village. The Black Robe went into the wilds seeking out heathen, making them his friends, telling them the Gospel story, baptizing the children of such parents as were willing, and adults who were dangerously ill. But this did not suffice. In order properly to indoctrinate the whole body of natives, drill them in the rudiments of Christian civilization, and give them economic stability, they were assembled in pueblos, or towns, organized to achieve these aims. If the natives already lived in a permanent and compact village, there the mission was established. There the work of "reduction" had already been done. With the wilder tribes pueblo forming was often a difficult task, for they preferred to live in freedom in caves or huts. The mountain Tarahumares especially opposed reduction to pueblo life.[4] As a nucleus of a new pueblo, it was the practice to bring a few families of Christianized Indians from an older mission, to help tame and domesticate the raw recruits. Customarily each Jesuit missionary had charge of three pueblos, a *cabecera* and two *visitas*.

The heart of the mission and the pride of the padre was the church. Near by was the residence of the pastor. Close at hand, perhaps in another quadrangle, were the houses of the Indians which constituted the pueblo. In a fully developed mission there were carpenter shops, blacksmith shops, spinning and weaving rooms, corrals for the stock, fields, irrigation ditches, and everything going to make a well ordered and self supporting agricultural unit. All this was supervised by the missionary himself, assisted sometimes by a lay brother expert in the mysteries of farm and shop.

At first the buildings were of the most flimsy character. These in time were replaced by more substantial houses, larger and more beautiful churches, generally of adobe but sometimes of stone. In hostile country it was customary to erect a strong protecting wall around the pueblo, or at least around the missionary's residence, and to provide it with military towers. Such a mission was a veritable

---

[4] The difficulties of gathering these mountain people into pueblos are set forth by Father Joseph Neumann in a letter written during his first months among them: "Our labors consist in converting and baptizing the natives, in founding settlements, in persuading the Indians to leave their caves and scattered hovels and to adopt a civilized life, and in forming them, so to speak, into a corporate body. We compel them to live in villages near the churches, which we build in convenient locations where the country is more open. This is a very difficult task. For,—to explain their character a little—while these people were still heathen . . . they were accustomed to live, not in groups, but separately, one from another. With their wives and children they dwelt in mountain caves or in huts built of straw, which seemed more suitable for catching birds than for human habitation." (Letter to an unknown Father, Sisoguichic, Feb. 8, 1682.)

frontier stronghold. To help supervise the labor of the Indians, keep them in order, punish minor offenses, and drill the neophytes in the rudiments of civilized life, native officers were appointed— governor, captain, alcalde, topil, mador, chief herdsman, head muleteer, head plowman, etc. According to their respective spheres, some of these functionaries were named by the missionary, others by the provincial governor or some other secular representative of the king.[5]

Religious teaching of the neophytes included a daily routine of drill in the catechism, prayers, and sacred music. Many a missionary was as proud of his native choir and orchestra as of his church.[6]

[5] Father Pfefferkorn, long a missionary in Sonora, thus describes the functions of the *madores* in a book which he wrote after the Jesuit Expulsion: "In each pueblo there were also one or two *mayori* or, as the Spaniards say, *madores*, who had the supervision of the grown children and at the same time the care of the sick. For this office Indians were chosen who from their known behavior gave promise of being faithful and careful. . . . They assembled the children daily for attendance at Mass and the Christian service, and during it they watched that order and decency be maintained. They also visited daily all the houses in the pueblo to see if there was anybody ill within. If they saw that anybody was in the least danger they immediately informed the pastor, who then had a look for himself and acted according to the circumstances. Marriages, which for most important reasons were arranged as soon as the age of the Indians permitted, were usually managed by the *mayor*. He chose the pair whom he thought suited to one another and presented them to the pastor. The latter inquired into the views of both parties and if they agreed the marriage took place." Pfefferkorn describes also the functions of pueblo governors, alcaldes, and fiscales. (*Beschreibung des Landschaft Sonora*, Cologne, 1795.)

[6] Pfefferkorn writes as follows: "In all the missions of the Opatas and Eudebes, also in some among the Pimas, Solemn High Mass was celebrated on Sundays and feast days. Some of the choirs consisted of Indians who were so skillful in singing that many European churches might well wish such choristers. I had eight of them in my mission of Cucurpe, four men and four women. Among the latter one especially was noted for her incomparable voice. In the missions of the Opatas and Eudebes there were also Indians who performed with very agreeable harmony on musical instruments and who during Mass played in the pauses when the singers stopped. Mine practiced so diligently under my direction that they accompanied the singers with violins, harps, and zithers. In this way we celebrated in my mission not only Mass, but in the evening, after the completion of the Christian Doctrine and the saying of the Rosary, we sang the Litany of Loretto and the *Salve Regina*, accompanied by instruments."

Promising youths were trained as altar boys, and as *temastianes* or catechists, to help drill the neophytes. Several of the central missions—those at San Felipe, Mátape, Parral, Chihuahua, and other places—had seminaries designed to give the temastianes the necessary training for their tasks. The religious life of a mission included attendance at Mass, the regular prayers, the Sunday sermon, confession, and the celebration of Church holidays with processions, pageantry, and other suitable exercises, in imitation of the Spanish settlements. These religious fiestas, often attended by the Spaniards of the vicinity, were combined with the jollities of secular sports— foot races, horse races, bull fights, and other healthful releases for the nervous system. On his own testimony one Black Robe, at least, is known to have engaged in a race with his Indians—he on horseback, they on foot—and to have been beaten.

III

The pioneer Jesuit in Nueva Vizcaya was Gonzalo de Tapia, of eternal fame.[7] With one companion in 1591 he crossed the perilous Sierra Madre. His precise destination was San Felipe, on Sinaloa River, then the very last outpost of European civilization in northwestern New Spain. San Felipe became and long continued to be the Jesuit capital on the Pacific Coast. Taking their lives in their hands, the two apostles undertook their gigantic task. Their touch was magic. Within six months several pueblos had been formed and more than a thousand natives baptized. Undaunted by poisoned arrows and yawning chasms, Tapia recrossed the Sierra to Mexico for additional help. More workers came, other thousands were converted, new pueblos established and better churches built.

Four years passed, and the Faith was taking firm root on Sinaloa River. But in the same degree, the chronicler tells us, the wrath of Satan grew. Tapia was marked for destruction. Nacabeba, a native medicine man, who saw his power waning, brained Father Gonzalo with a war club and celebrated his triumph with pagan orgies. Tapia

[7] His inspiring career has recently been made known to English readers through the excellent biography by Father William Eugene Shiels, entitled *Gonzalo de Tapia* (*1561–1594*).

thus became the proto-martyr of Jesuit New Spain. It was a terrible shock to the Black Robes, but the work went on. The confidence of the natives regained, conversions struck a new pace. By the end of the first decade there had been 10,000 baptisms, and the Jesuits had eight missions with substantial churches serving thirteen pueblos along Sinaloa and Mocorito Rivers.

People sometimes raise their eyebrows at such stories of wholesale baptisms at the beginning. But the explanation is simple. Infant heathens were baptized without catechism, the same as children of Christians. When the padres first arrived there was a large crop of infants awaiting them. Thereafter baptisms proceeded at a slower rate, for the annual increment of babes was smaller than the first accumulation; and older children and adults must first be instructed.

Almost simultaneously the Black Robes began their work on both slopes and in the heart of the Sierra Madre. With a gift of $22,000 from Governor del Rio and others, a college was established in Durango in 1593–94. By the end of the century six Jesuits of this house were founding missions among the Acaxees in Topia, among the Tepehuanes in central Durango, and at Parras among the Laguna tribes of Coahuila. Here was a field as large as that of Sinaloa.

Father Santarén became the saint of Topia; but Ruíz did not fall far behind him in prowess and fame. Together they assembled crowds, destroyed heathen idols, built churches, and baptized thousands. At first the natives were friendly. But Topia was a mining district, Indian labor was exploited, and a typical revolt followed. The Acaxees took up arms, murdered Spaniards, burned churches, and devastated mining towns. In the crisis Father Ruíz performed a prodigy. Eight hundred Acaxees besieged forty Spaniards at San Andrés. The beleaguered settlers struck back. In one of the sorties Ruíz marched ahead of the soldiers protected only by his Crucifix. "Clouds of arrows were discharged at the holy man, but not one struck him," we are told. The chronicler regarded this as evidence of divine protection—a scoffer might suspect bad native marksmanship.

Governor Urdiñola rushed from Durango with soldiers to relieve the siege. But Santarén became the hero of the episode. Going almost alone among the hostiles, by diplomacy he won them over and marched back to Topia at the head of a thousand natives bearing a cross and the white flag of peace. There was a love feast and the Indians rebuilt their churches. The conversion now spread to the Xiximes and other tribes, where there were baptisms by added thousands. The name of Santarén is still a household word in all that western Sierra, where he has become a legendary figure.

Fonte and Ramírez had parallel success in central and northern Durango among the virile Tepehuanes. Other evangelists turned northeast and founded missions in the famous lake region of Coahuila called Parras. The Lake People were docile and the progress of the Black Robes was flattering. But like other missions, those of Parras had their full measure of pioneer troubles. Smallpox carried off four hundred neophytes in 1608, shortly before Jamestown's "starving time." The Nazas River went on a rampage, destroyed the church of one mission, forced the people to flee from another, and nearly cost the life of a Black Robe. First it was too wet, then too dry. Drought was followed by famine. But in spite of these calamities baptisms multiplied to thousands, and Parras became a precious jewel in Loyola's crown.

The scene now shifts back to Sinaloa.[8] On nearly every frontier the Black Robes found and relied on some secular champion. Such were Del Rio and Urdiñola in Durango. More famous in this role was Hurdaide, defender of the Faith in Sinaloa, contemporary of Canada's Champlain, of Virginia's John Smith, and of Plymouth's John Alden. His appointment as Captain at San Felipe was a decisive event in Sinaloa history and in Jesuit annals. For nearly three decades this bandy-legged soldier ruled the Pacific Coast like a mediaeval Count of the March. El Capitán, as he was known, was famous far and wide for the wax seals with which he authenticated his orders. Any naked Indian messenger bearing a bit of paper stamped with these symbols had safe passage among friends or foes.

Hurdaide's part was to make safe the northward advance of the Black Robes. The Sinaloa River vineyard had been firmly planted by Tapia and his successors. But the way to the Fuerte, the next

---

[8] In a forthcoming book on the Jesuit missions of Sinaloa Rev. Dr. Peter M. Dunne has taken up the story where Father Shiels left off.

main stream north, was blocked by hostile Suaquis, Sinaloas, and Tehuecos. One by one El Capitán subdued these tribes, by methods which were sometimes harsh and always spectacular. Fathers Ribas, Méndez, and Villalta followed where Hurdaide led. Ribas made his name enduring at Ahome, Villalta baptized four hundred Sinaloas the very first day, Méndez gleaned a similar harvest, and within a year the whole river valley west of the mountains had been added to Christendom. By placating the sturdy Yaquis and subduing the defiant mountain Tepahues, El Capitán next opened the way to Mayo River. Venerable Father Méndez, once more in the vanguard, headed a procession of Black Robes, three thousand children were baptized within two weeks, and seven pueblos were founded in a stretch of eighteen leagues. The 30,000 Mayos had come into the fold.

All the North Country now received a terrific shock, and mountain streams of Durango ran red with the blood of missionaries and settlers. In the Tepehuán missions the Black Robes had labored with gratifying success for more than two decades. Pueblos had been formed, churches built, thousands of Indians baptized. Then suddenly the Tepehuanes, led by a self-styled Messiah, rose in savage rebellion. In the fall of 1616 the natives of Santa Catalina sprung the trap and murdered Father Tobar. Two hundred Spaniards fell at Atotonilco, one of the victims being the Franciscan Father Gutiérrez. At Santiago Papasquiaro Fathers Orozco and Cisneros, with some Spanish families, were brutally slain in the cemetery. At Zape nearly a hundred victims fell, including Fathers Alavez, Del Valle, Fonte, and Moranta. Santarén, the saint of Topia, who happened to be in the vicinity, also went down in this bloody uprising. Soldiers hurried north, punished the rebels, gathered up the remains of the martyred missionaries, and took them to Durango, where they were buried with solemn honors. The Tepehuán rebellion was at an end. Undaunted, new Black Robes entered the field, and the missions were restored.

On the West Coast the missions now entered upon the period of their greatest prosperity. The Tepehuán revolt had caused uneasiness in Sinaloa, lest the still heathen Yaquis should join the rebels.

Instead they welcomed the Black Robes in their own territory and became one of the most faithful Christian communities. Ribas moved up the map once more and became the apostle to this dauntless tribe, among whom he set up the Cross in May, 1617. Four thousand children and five hundred adults were baptized within a few weeks. More workers came, eight missions were founded, and soon most of the populous tribe were converted. As a granary for sterile California, these Yaqui missions later played a distinctive role.

From the Yaquis it was but a step to the Lower Pimas and Opatas, higher up on the Yaqui River, where flourishing missions were begun in 1620, year of the Mayflower. Venerable Méndez, like Daniel Boone, ever on the frontier, went into the mountains to the Sahuaripas. Azpilcueto, at Batuco, was a fighting padre long remembered in this region. Hostile neighbors threatened to kill him and drive away his fellow Jesuits. "Hurry up" was the message he sent them; then he coolly awaited their approach. When he fired a musket and brandished a machete they turned and fled, to return soon afterward as loyal neophytes. By now the Sinaloa-Sonora missions had reached impressive proportions. Baptisms there in 1621 alone were over 17,000. As a consequence of the great expansion a new rectorate was formed in the north with its capital at the Yaqui town of Tórin, where the thick-walled old Jesuit church on the hill, today in ruins, looks like a Roman fortress. The rectorate at this time employed eleven Black Robes, and embraced 60,000 Mayos, Yaquis, and Lower Pimas. On the whole West Coast there were 86,340 converts in fifty-five pueblos. Three years later the number was estimated at more than 100,000.

Several veterans now left the scene. In 1620 Ribas retired, after sixteen years on the coast, to become provincial in Mexico and to write his great history. Six years later died Martín Pérez, veteran of all the West, for he had come with Tapia, the Founder. At the same time Sinaloa lost by death its matchless soldier, El Capitán Hurdaide. Few regions in America have had more colorful pioneers than these. Notwithstanding the loss of the Old Guard—or perhaps because of it, for Old Guards have a way of becoming impedimenta—the boom in the West continued. At Chínipas, high up in the barranca-gouged mountains, Julio Pascual won several thousand converts. In 1623 he was joined by Father Martínez. As he climbed the mountain trail to his new destination, Martínez unwittingly rode to his death. A week after his arrival both he and Pascual were martyred by the hostile Chief Cambeia. The Chínipas mission was now closed, to be reopened four decades later.

Martyrdom but fanned the apostolic flame. The Black Robes now pushed into Valle de Sonora, and to the upper waters of the many-forked Yaqui, thus carrying the Gospel to the border of the lands of the Apaches and the Upper Pimas. Valle de Sonora, site of Coronado's ill-fated San Gerónimo, was the most historic spot in all that mountain-girt region. It is from this charming little valley, peopled by gentle and industrious Opatas, that the vast state of Sonora gets its name. Father Castaño came here to live among the Opatas in 1638, shortly after Roger Williams fled to his Rhode Island wilderness. Within a year Castaño had baptized three thousand natives, who lived in pueblos which still bear the names by which they then were known. More Jesuits came. Soon the northernmost missions, mainly of Opatas, were formed into a new rectorate,[9] where seven Jesuits were ministering to fourteen pueblos, and in which already there had been a total of more than 20,000 baptisms. *Fervet opus,* the chronicler wrote.

Paraguay itself could scarcely match this evangelical record. When Ribas published his famous *Triumphos de Nuestra Santa Fe* in 1645, the showing for a half century of labor was most impressive. West of the Sierra, in a stretch of some six hundred miles, there were now thirty-five head missions, each with from one to four towns, perhaps a hundred in all. Each of the head missions and many of the visitas, or substations, had fine churches, prosperous farms and well-stocked ranches. The mission books showed a total of more than 300,000 baptisms in the West to date. The presidio of San Felipe, the principal garrison, had a force of only forty-six soldiers. This fact alone, Bancroft remarks, shows how completely the natives had accepted missionary control.

Again the scene shifts. The Jesuit frontier west of the Sierra

[9] This was in 1646.

Madre had far outrun that on the eastern slope, a fact which may
be explained in part by three circumstances. The Tepehuán revolt
had caused a setback on the Central Plateau; hostile Tobosos and
Conchos made mission life precarious there; and the field was partly
covered by the Franciscans, who were active on the right flank of
the Jesuits. But the Black Robes now made a new thrust forward,
to work among the Tarahumares, those fleet-footed mountain people
who lived on both slopes of the Sierra Madre in western Chihuahua.
Before his martyrdom Fonte had made a small beginning there,
and another nibble at the same bait was taken in 1630. Nine years
later the Tarahumar missions were begun in earnest. Meanwhile
the prosperous mining town of Parral was founded (1632) and
became for a century the residence of the governors of Nueva Vizcaya. For that reason it played a vital part in subsequent Jesuit
history.

Gerónimo Figueroa and José Pascual launched the New Deal
for the Tarahumares in 1639 (year of the Fundamental Orders of
Connecticut), when they founded missions on Conchos River north
and west of Parral. A corps of Black Robes followed in their train,
reaped a large harvest, and by 1650 carried the Cross north and west
to the upper Yaqui River in Tarahumara Alta. But they had come
to a most difficult frontier, quite different from that of Sonora. The
incursions of wild Tobosos made life unsafe for priest, secular, or
neophyte. Then the Tarahumares themselves, led by haughty Chief
Tepóraca, rose in revolt, destroyed several missions, murdered
Father Godínez (Beudin) at Papigóchic, and massacred all the
Spanish settlers at the nearby town of Aguilar. The city of Guerrero
marks the approximate site today. In a second onslaught Father
Basile was decapitated and hanged to a cross. Legend has it that
as he expired his spirit, in the form of a beautiful child, was seen to
issue from his mouth and ascend to Heaven attended by two angels.
Thus was lengthened the list of Jesuit martyrs. With a courage
which commands more than admiration, the Black Robes reoccupied
the southern missions. But with Papigóchic destroyed, Tarahumara
Alta, the region of the high Sierra, was still solidly heathen.

For two decades the Tarahumar field remained stationary. Then another forward movement was begun in 1673. This, by the way, was the very year when Marquette reached the Mississippi River. French and Spanish Black Robes were approaching each other from opposite sides of the continent. The Tarahumara Alta missions were now reopened. Apostles Tardá and Guadalajara entered the Sierra as far as Yepómera and Tutuaca. The region was inconceivably difficult; mountains and barrancas were inexpressibly rough; only the hardiest men could endure the winter cold. Yet the missions flourished. Eight Jesuits in Tarahumara Alta were serving 4,000 natives in thirty-two pueblos in 1678, and within the next four years more than thirty new churches were built.

New names now appear on the honor roll. Foronda and Picolo, Neumann and Ratkay led a procession of Black Robes from Italy and North Europe who greatly vitalized the work. For ten years they toiled on in the midst of privation and danger. Then another revolt burst forth. There was a gold rush to Santa Rosa, and Spaniards summoned the Indians to forced labor. It was the story of Papigóchic repeated. In 1690 the natives murdered Fathers Foronda and Sánchez, expelled the rest of the Black Robes from the Sierra, and destroyed six mountain missions.[10] But peace was restored, the fearless Jesuits returned to their mountain exile, and rebuilt their churches "larger and better than before." Seven years later peace was disturbed by an outburst of native wizardry. This was precisely the time when witchcraft was epidemic in New England. If we can believe the evidence, broom voyages then were more numerous than airplane flights today. Feminism seems to have been at the zero hour in Tarahumara, for nothing is said of witches. But many wizards were captured and executed, for Spaniards were as silly as Englishmen or Germans of their day. The result was another uprising. Rebels destroyed four mountain missions and again the Jesuits fled. War was followed by the submission of the natives, and the return of the Black Robes to their posts.

It had been a bitter conflict. However, says Father Neumann, who was in the midst of it all, not half of the Tarahumar nation had

[10] Yepomera, Tutuaca, Cahurichic, Tomochic, Mátachic, and Cocomorachic.

taken up arms or deserted Christianity.[11] The whole situation was now changed by a new Indian policy. Henceforth little effort was made to move Tarahumares from their mountain homes to the plains. Henceforth they remained peaceful, and the Jesuits went forward with their apostolic labors among them. The circumstance carries a moral—the transplantation policy had been a mistake from the outset.

On the eastern edge of the Tarahumara, Chihuahua became a flourishing city and the seat of a Jesuit college, where a lay brother wrote a widely used treatise on medicine. Among the colorful Black Robes in the Tarahumara at a later date was Glandorff, who served some forty years at Tomochic. Famous for his gentle sanctity, he was even better known as the great hiker. He was afraid of a horse, but he could climb a mountain like a goat, and in a cross-country run would put a mule to blush. He was a marvel even to the fleet-footed Tarahumares, who even today have worldwide renown for their own speed and endurance. According to legend Glandorff had magic shoes. An Indian servant worn with travel fell exhausted. Glandorff loaned him his moccasins and behold, he sprang up revived as if from a refreshing sleep, and without further halt continued his journey! This happened not once but many times. So runs the diverting legend.

Other frontiers were pushing forward. The Chínipas missions, after a blank of four decades, were restored by the Italians Prado and Pecoro in 1676, just when Tardá and Guadalajara were reviving the work in Tarahumara Alta. At the end of four years they had gathered into pueblos and converted 4,000 Indians. Square-jawed Salvatierra now joined his countrymen in the district, and became its most distinguished missionary. One of his exploits was his descent into the mammoth canyon of Urique, in size and awesomeness a close competitor of the Grand Canyon of the Colorado. His naïve account of the adventure is refreshing. With a Cerocahui Indian he set forth to visit the stupendous gorge. The guide told him he could ride three leagues, then he would have to walk. This

---

[11] Joseph Neumann, *Historia Seditionum*, etc., Prague. No date on the title page. The preface is dated April 15, 1724.

admonition proved unnecessary. "On seeing the precipice," says Salvatierra, "such was my terror that I immediately asked . . . if it was time to dismount. Without waiting for an answer I did not dismount but let myself fall off on the side opposite the precipice, sweating and trembling all over from fright. For there opened on the left a chasm whose bottom could not be seen, and on the right rose perpendicular walls of solid rock." He was on a mantel shelf suspended in mid-air. This account by Father Juan in 1684 should help deflate the egotism of twentieth-century "discoverers" of Urique canyon.

For ten years Salvatierra labored in the mountains, then went humbly to Guadalajara as college president. Seven years later, when on the way to Lower California, he made a flying trip to his beloved Guazápares, just in time to help check another rebellion. Not Salvatierra alone, but Fathers Ordaz and Illing likewise won fame in this war, one as a valiant defender of his mission, the other as an equally brave peacemaker. Each one left a precious legend in the land of the Chínipas.

The northwestward tide was now deflected. By this time the Black Robes had established Christianity in the Sierra Madre and on both its slopes, all the way from southern Durango to northern Chihuahua, and from Culiacán to the Arizona border. On the northeast they were blocked by the Apaches as by a Chinese wall. But the way was open to the west and northwest, in Lower California and in Pimería Alta, where large and friendly populations lay still beyond the rim of Christendom. To cultivate these extensive vineyards now came Kino, Campos, Salvatierra, Ugarte, and a valiant host of only less notable figures. Conspicuous among them all was Kino, Apostle to Pimería Alta. He arrived there in March, 1687, the very month when La Salle met his tragic death in the wilds of Texas. He was just well started when the Pimas destroyed several missions and martyred Father Saeta at Caborca. But for a quarter-century he kept on. He personally baptized more than 4,500 Indians.[12] His mission farms and ranches became the most prosperous

[12] Not 40,000, as every writer insists on saying, because they follow Ortega, who misread Kino's manuscript.

in all Sonora. His demonstration that Lower California was a peninsula, not an island, reversed stubborn opinion. Of Pimería Alta he
was not only Apostle, but also explorer, ethnologist, cartographer,
defender, cattle king, and historian.

With his dream of converting Lower California, Father Kino
infected Salvatierra, who translated the vision into reality. The
peninsula was assigned to the Jesuits on condition that they finance
it themselves. In return they were made practically autonomous,
like their brethren in Paraguay. Aided by the giant athlete Ugarte,
Salvatierra raised and organized the celebrated Pious Fund, which
is still in existence. Thus financed, he maintained a little fleet of
transports which plied back and forth across the Gulf, carrying livestock and other supplies for barren Lower California, obtained
chiefly from the mainland Black Robes. By the time of his death
he and his associates had founded seven flourishing missions among
almost savage Indians, on a rocky tongue of land scarcely capable of
sustaining civilized life.

Ugarte now carried the Cross to the hostile people on the lower
end of the Peninsula, where the names of Carranco and Tamaral
were added to the already long list of Jesuit martyrs. In the mid-
century new foundations were made in the north, until nearly a
score of successful missions were in operation, and many thousand
Indians were settled in pueblo life. During their stay of seventy
years in Lower California, more than fifty Black Robes, all told,
labored in exile in this barren cactus patch.

The last three Lower California missions were made possible by
a Borgian heiress. The tale is told that when she made the gift she
was asked in what country she wished the missions established.
"In the most outlandish place in the world," she replied. The Jesuits
consulted their atlases and returned the answer: "The most outlandish place in all the world is California." Of course, this is just
a story.

The early eighteenth century witnessed a great shortage of missionaries. European wars drained the Spanish treasury. Then came
a remarkable revival. In the far south the Black Robes took over the
difficult Coras of Nayarit. In the north a new missionary host,

mainly Germans, entered the field on both sides of the Gulf. In Sonora and Pimería Alta the Jesuit annals record the eighteenth-century labors of Black Robes with the very un-Spanish names of Bentz, Fraedenberg, Gerstner, Grashofer, Hoffenrichter, Hawe, Keller, Klever, Kolub, Kürtzel, Middendorff, Miner, Nentwig, Och, Paver, Rhuen, Sedelmayr, Segesser, Slesac, Step, Steiger, Wazet, and Weis. In Lower California in these days labored Baegert, Bischoff, Consag, Ducrue, Gasteiger, Gordon, Helen, Link, Neumayer, Retz, Tempis, Tuersch, and Wagner, all of non-Spanish extraction. In the transplantation of Christian culture to Western America these North Europeans played a distinctive part. Zealous missionaries, they were especially conspicuous as teachers of material thrift and a well-ordered life.

By these men Kino's old missions were restored and new ones founded. Keller and Sedelmayr retraced some of Kino's trails to the Gila and the Colorado Rivers. They, Consag, and Link revived Kino's plan to extend missions to the Colorado, and to supply Lower California by a land route around the head of the Gulf. In the midst of their labors the Pimas rose once more in rebellion, and killed Tello at Caborca and Rhuen at Sonóita. The West Coast martyrs now numbered one more than a score.

A large missionary province, the result of many years of development, was like a tree. The fresh growth was near the top. So it was with the Province of New Spain. The roots of the plant were the central organization in Europe and Mexico. The colleges and other permanent foundations at the principal centers on the way north represented the trunk. As time went on, this trunk gradually became bare of missionary verdure. Between Durango and Pimería Alta in the eighteenth century there were missions in all stages of evolution, some already secularized, others old and stable, but without new blood from heathendom; still others, on the periphery, filled with the vigor characteristic of youth.

The Jesuits had always labored under a degree of insecurity due to causes other than Indian revolts. Frequently there was pressure for secularizing the missions, a step which was contemplated in the system. This pressure came from bishops for various reasons, from the government which wished to collect tribute, or from secular neighbors who were greedy for Indian lands or the right to exploit Indian labor. In the middle eighteenth century the missions of the Tepehuanes and Tarahumara Baja were thus turned over to the parish clergy.

Then came the final blow—the Expulsion. For reasons best known to himself and his advisers, Carlos III decided to expel the Jesuits from the whole of the Spanish empire. The edict fell in 1767. All missionaries and other Black Robes in New Spain were arrested, dispossessed, hurried to Vera Cruz, carried to Spain, imprisoned there, or distributed in other lands. Many of the expatriates died of disease or hardship on the way. Some of the missions thus left vacant were secularized, others were put in charge of the Franciscans. Here is where Serra comes into the California story. A work of two centuries was at an end. But the service of the Black Robes to the land of their toil did not cease even now. Many of them spent their prison hours writing of the country they loved. Clavigero composed his history of California, Baegert his *Nachrichten*, Pfefferkorn his book on Sonora, Ducrue his story of the expulsion from the Peninsula. These and other works were published. Still others remain in manuscript and await the modern historian, for whom they will constitute a fresh fountain of inspiration and knowledge.

IV

Thus far this paper has been devoted to sketching in broadest outline the work of the Jesuits in New Spain, with special reference to the northward advance of the missionary frontier. The deep significance of it all would call for another paper of equal or greater length. There is space here for only a few observations.

The Black Robe story is one of Homeric quality. It is filled with picturesque men, like Santarén, who vied with the Pied Piper of Hamlen; Ruíz, who was arrow proof; Azpilcueto, who bluffed an Indian horde with blunderbuss and machete; Contreras, who led the defense of Cocóspera against an Apache attack; Kino, the hard-riding cowman; Glandorff, the Black Robe hiker with the magic shoes. The tale is full of diverting humor and of exalting edification.

The actors were human beings, who either had a sense of humor or were humorous because they lacked it.

The missionaries were the adventurers of the seventeenth and eighteenth centuries, successors to the conquistadores of an earlier day. They traveled vast distances, coped with rugged nature and the fickle savage, performed astounding physical feats, won amazing victories over mountains, rivers, hunger, cold, and thirst.

Missionary life demanded the highest qualities of manhood—character, intelligence, courage, resourcefulness, health, and endurance. Missionaries were called upon to face physical dangers and hardships almost beyond belief. They went among heathen without escorts, into places where soldiers dared not tread. They were liable at any time to hear the blood-curdling war whoop or to see the destroying fire by night. They were ever at the mercy of the whims of sensitive Indians, or of jealous and vengeful medicine men. Even to baptize a child was often perilous, for if it died the death might be charged to the "bad medicine" of the padre. Martyrdom was always a very distinct possibility. Most Black Robes came to America hoping to win this glorious crown, many still coveted it after seeing real Indians, and when martyrdom stared them in the face they met it with transcendent heroism.

Their hardest trial, more to be feared than death, was loneliness, for they lived many leagues apart and saw their own kind only at long intervals. Hence they treasured visits from distant neighbors, and looked forward with the eagerness of a homesick boy to the church dedications and celebrations which brought them for a brief time together; or to the annual journey to a neighbor mission to fulfill their religious obligations.

Not every Black Robe was fit for service in the missions. Some lacked the temperament or the physical stamina, some could not learn the Indian languages. Such were given employment of a different sort. More than one Jesuit who found himself unsuited for the frontier was sent to be professor or president in some college in softer surroundings. Many of these Jesuits had in their veins the best blood of Europe. Such were Hernando Tobar, grand-nephew of Viceroy Mendoza; Pedro Velasco, relative of another viceroy;

Ratkay, the Hungarian noble who had been a page at the Court of Vienna; and Salvatierra, son of a noble house of Spain and Italy. The Black Robes belonged to their age. They had an unfaltering faith in God and His omnipotence. Miracles were not only possible, but often passed before their eyes. They believed in and talked much of predestination. Indeed, they recognized it every time they came upon and baptized a dying ancient. The man and his wife, each two hundred and fifty years old, who were baptized by Ribas, were clear examples of this exercise of divine mercy, by which two lives were extended till the evangelist arrived.

Being theologians and spiritual practitioners, the Black Robes were naturally interested in all religious and spiritual phenomena. True to their day, they believed not only in a personal God, but also in a personal Devil, the same Devil so well known to Cotton Mather. The missionaries saw all around them patent evidence of the malice and of the mischief done by His Satanic Majesty and his obedient imps. They believed in signs and portents. Eclipses, earthquakes, epidemics, and all unusual phenomena were interpreted as divine or diabolic manifestations, with supernatural cause and significance. Witchcraft was taken for granted by seventeenth-century Jesuits, and its evils were often encountered, just as was the case in Puritan New England and in all contemporary Europe. Spaniards brought with them all the European phraseology of witchcraft, and the usual machinery for rooting it out.

A catalogue of the manifold services of the missionaries would be long and varied. In their daily routine, like the monks of old, they performed the most menial tasks. They cooked, washed, plowed, planted, harvested, handled stock, made adobes, built houses and erected churches. They served as nurses and doctors in the huts of the natives. During epidemics they were called from pillar to post, lacking time even to eat or sleep. "For in these missions," says Father Neumann, "there is but one craftsman: the missionary himself. He alone must serve both himself and others. He must be cobbler, tailor, mason, carpenter, cook, nurse for the sick—in a word, everything."

The Black Robes converted the natives to Christianity, baptizing in New Spain alone, before the expulsion, probably not less than two millions. They also brought to the Indians the rudiments of Christian civilization, teaching them decent habits, agriculture, stock raising, the handicrafts, building, and myriad other things. The less civilized natives were the ones most remolded by mission life.

A comparison will again help us. The Jesuits of New France played a highly important part in the religious, educational, and social life of the French part of the colony. But by reason of circumstances beyond their control, they did relatively little toward transforming the society of the Indian population of the vast areas over which they traveled. The Jesuits of New Spain, on the other hand, were primary agents during a century and three-quarters in the transformation of a large native population from a roving to a sedentary life, with attendant cultural changes. Indeed, a considerable part of the inhabitants of Western Mexico today are descended from ancestors, on one side or the other, who got their first contact with European civilization as neophytes in a Jesuit mission. That this was possible in one case and not in the other was due largely to the contrasting views of the respective nations under whom the Jesuits worked. Spain considered the Indian worth civilizing as well as converting, and proceeded with zeal and firmness to bring it about. In the process the missionaries were the government's best collaborators.

The Black Robes performed many services for the border Spaniards as well as for the neophytes. The mission was the agricultural unit for a large part of frontier Spanish America. There the missionary organized and directed most of the agricultural labor. The mission not only raised produce for its own subsistence, but from the surplus it supplied neighboring soldiers, miners and cattlemen with agricultural products. The missionaries, by gentle means, subdued and managed the Indians, went as diplomats to hostile tribes, and helped to pacify the frontier in time of trouble. The mission itself, with its fortified plant and its usually loyal native defenders, often served as a bulwark against hostile neighbors. Regarding frontier matters, religious or secular, including international relations, the missionaries helped to mold the opinions of central officials, and were often called to Mexico, or even to Spain and Rome, to give advice. Instructions issued from Europe on such matters were both shaped and interpreted by the men on the frontier, for they were the ones who best knew conditions.

The importance of the Black Robes as teachers and founders of colleges has been touched upon in earlier paragraphs. Their scholarly services were not confined to teaching. They wrote learned books on a great variety of subjects. Incidentally to their frontier work they were explorers, cartographers and ethnologists. Ribas declared them linguists by divine gift, and certain it is that they did much to reduce to grammar and to preserve the languages of many tribes, some of which have long since disappeared.

Finally, the Jesuits were the principal historians of early Western North America. Pérez de Ribas, Kino, Venegas, Alegre, Ortega, Baegert, Pfefferkorn and the author of the *Rudo Ensayo* all wrote chronicles which will never be displaced. The Black Robes of New France left us as a legacy the famous Jesuit *Relations* which were assembled by Cramoisy and put into English by Thwaites. These ample records of life in the wilderness are justly celebrated among the treasures of pioneer days in heathen America. They constitute a precious body of historical literature. Equally precious in quality and vastly greater in bulk are the similar Jesuit writings left behind by the Black Robes of New Spain. Most of these have yet to be assembled and edited, a gigantic task toward which a few students are now directing their attention.

SECTION FIVE

The Last Borderland: California

CHAPTER THIRTEEN

The Early Explorations
of Father Garcés on the Pacific Slope*

FROM the selections in the previous section one might be led to conclude that Bolton had "sold out" to the Black Robes and overlooked the importance of the Franciscans in the Borderlands story. This was far from true. The sons of Saint Francis shared equally in his interest. No one could propose to write the Georgia-Florida chapter or the Texas chapter and certainly not the California chapter of the Borderlands epic and bypass the friars.

One of Bolton's early pieces, here reprinted as a preliminary to the California chapter, studied one of the more fascinating, if somewhat elusive, of the great Franciscan frontiersmen. Fray Francisco Garcés was, in a sense, a worthy successor to Kino, both at Misión San Xavier del Bac and on the trail. As a matter of fact, his exploits on the trail surpassed those of the "Padre on Horseback." Garcés is an important farther southwest Borderlands figure. His connection with California is almost as great—his pathfinding activities made possible the ultimate land route from Sonora into the new province.

This paper of Bolton not only offers fine evidence of his meticulous craftsmanship, but also shows how significant were his pioneer searches into the archives of Mexico. Many a document, or body of documents, with prime pertinence to American history was brought to the knowledge of historians thereby. One can almost say that, had Bolton written nothing, his name would still deserve to be an honored one in American historiography. He, too, was a "pathbreaker" par excellence.

IT IS THE POPULAR OPINION in the country at large, inculcated by uninformed writers of school histories, that Spanish activities within

* This was a paper presented at the Panama-Pacific Historical Congress, July, 1915. It was published in *The Pacific Ocean in History*, edited by H. Morse Stephens and Herbert E. Bolton (New York, Macmillan, 1917), 317–30.

the present limits of the United States reached their climax with the founding of St. Augustine and Santa Fé. The fact is, however, that from 1519 to the opening of the nineteenth century, Spain continued steadily to extend her frontiers northward, and that the last third of the eighteenth century was a period of as great advance as any other of equal length after the death of Cortés. This activity involved not only the founding of new missions and settlements and the occupation of new military outposts, but embraced also an extensive series of explorations, quite as vast and important for territory now within the United States as the earlier expeditions.

Before the end of the sixteenth century Spanish settlement spread northward from the West Indies into Florida, and in northern Mexico to a line roughly drawn from the mouth of the Rio Grande, through Cerralvo, Parral, and San Juan de Sinaloa. In the course of the seventeenth century and the first half of the eighteenth, the wide interstices were filled in, and another tier of provinces was carved out in the north—New Mexico, Coahuila, Texas, Nuevo Santander, Sonora, and Baja California—a series of jurisdictions extending from the Pacific Ocean nearly to the middle of the present state of Louisiana.

In the course of this work of frontier colonization, the country which had been hurriedly run over in the early sixteenth century was gradually re-explored in greater detail. On the northern borders Kino reached the Gila, Keller and Sedelmayr crossed it, Castillo and Guadalajara reconnoitered the middle Colorado of Texas, Oñate crossed the Arkansas, Villazur reached the North Platte, and Bustamante y Tagle went well down the Arkansas, while the whole southeastern quarter of Texas, east of Eagle Pass and south of San Sabá, was quite thoroughly explored.

But as late as 1769 the interior of Alta California was practically unknown, the California coast had not been run by a recorded exploration since Vizcaíno, the Utah Basin was all but untrod by white man, the trail from Santa Fé to the Missouri had been little used by Spaniards since 1720, the whole northern half of Texas was almost unknown to recorded exploration, and direct communication had never been established between Santa Fé and San Antonio, or between El Paso and San Antonio. To retrace these forgotten trails on the borders of the settled portions of New Spain, and to push far beyond the borders by water to Alaska, and by the land to the Sacramento, the San Joaquín, the Utah Basin, and even to the upper waters of the Missouri, was the exploratory work of the Spaniards in the later eighteenth century.

One of the noteworthy figures in this work was Fray Francisco Hermenegildo Garcés, a Franciscan missionary of the College of Santa Cruz de Querétaro. After the expulsion of the Jesuits from Pimería Alta in 1767, fourteen Querétarans were sent to take their places. Among them was Father Garcés, who was assigned to the mission of San Xavier del Bac, then and still standing nine miles south of Tucson. It was his position at this northernmost outpost, combined with his rare personal qualities, that brought him into prominence in the new wave of frontier advance. His principal contributions to the explorations of the period were (1) to reopen the trails made by Kino, Keller, and Sedelmayr, to the Gila and through the Papaguería, (2) to serve as pathfinder across the Yuma and Colorado deserts, and as guide for Anza to the foot of the San Jacinto Mountains, when he led the first overland expedition from Sonora to California, and (3) to discover a way from Yuma to New Mexico, and across the Mojave desert to Los Angeles and the Tulares, and between these two points by way of the Tejón Pass. Altogether, his pathfinding, accomplished without the aid of a single white man, covered more than a thousand miles of untrod trails, and furnished an example of physical endurance and human courage that have rarely been excelled.

But the place of Garcés in southwestern exploration in general has been well established through the scholarly work of Dr. Coues, and he needs no eulogy from me. The occasion for reopening the subject arises from the discovery of much new material regarding Garcés since Coues published the diary of 1775 in 1900. No attempt will be made to do over again what Coues has done so well; and the emphasis of this paper will be directed to the three following points: (1) Recent accessions to original manuscript materials relating to the early explorations of Father Garcés. (2) The new light shed by these materials upon Garcés' early explorations in general, and upon his journey of 1771 in particular, and, (3) The importance of Garcés in the opening of an overland route to Los Angeles.

Up to the present our knowledge of the explorations of Father Garcés has been confined almost wholly to what is contained in Arricivita's *Crónica Apostólica* and the diary of the fifth and last expedition—that edited by Coues. For the fourth expedition made with Anza, Bancroft had access to an abridgment of a diary made by Anza, and Eldredge had Anza's diary in one of its completer forms. For the first four expeditions the sole guide of Coues was what is contained in Arricivita and the summary of Anza's diary given by Bancroft.

In addition to Arricivita and the Anza diary of 1774, known to Bancroft and Eldredge, and the diary of the fifth expedition (1775–1776), we now have, from the Mexican archives, the following manuscript materials:

(a) Diary of Garcés of his expedition of 1770.[1]

(b) Diary of Garcés of his expedition of 1771.[2]

(c) Diary of Garcés of his expedition of 1774.[3]

(d) Diaries of the 1774 expedition by Anza and Father Juan Diaz.[4]

(e) A summary by Garcés of his first four expeditions.[5]

[1] *Diario que se ha formado por el Viage hecho á el Rio Gila quando los Yndios Pimas Gileños me llamaron á fin de que baptisase sus hijos que estaban enfermos del Sarampión.*

[2] *Diario que se ha formado con la ocasión de la entrada que hiço a las naciones Gentiles.*

[3] *Diario de la entrada que se practica de orden del Exmo Sr Vi Rey Dn. Antonio María Bucarely y Ursua producida en Junta de Guerra i real acienda a fin de abrir camino por los rios Gila y Colorado para los nuebos establecimientos de San Diego y Monte Rey,* etc.

[4] *Diario que forma el Padre Fr. Juan Diaz Missionero Apoco. del Colegio de la Sta Cruz de Querétaro, en el viage, que hace en compañia del R. P. Fr. Fran^{co} Garcés para abrir camino desde la Provincia de la Sonora á la California Septentrional, y el puerto de Monterrey por los Rios Gila y Colorado,* etc.

[5] *Copia de los noticias sacadas, y remitidas por el P^e Predicator Fr Fran^{co} Garcés de los Diarios que la formado en los quatro entradas praticadas desde el año de 68 hasta el presente de 75 á la frontera septentrional de los Gentiles de Nueva España.*

(f) A special ethnological report by Garcés based on the fifth expedition, and supplementary to the diary edited by Coues.[6]

(g) A great quantity of correspondence of Garcés, Anza, Díaz, and others relating to the general question of northward expansion from Sonora between 1768 and 1776, of which Garcés' explorations formed a part.

All of this new material referred to was discovered in the archives of Mexico by the present writer between the years 1903 and 1908. Much of it was made available through the present writer to Richman for use in his history of California, but Mr. Richman's study of the work of Garcés was so incidental that, practically speaking, the materials thus far have not been utilized for the purpose in question.[7]

As I have stated, for the first three expeditions of Garcés—those of 1768, 1770, and 1771—Arricivita has been our sole guide. Regarding the first, he made it known that Garcés went west and north through the Papaguería to a village on the Gila, but did not indicate what or where the village was. Coues inferred from what Arricivita states that the ranchería visited on the Gila was a Pápago village. But we now know, from the diary of 1770 that the ranchería was the Pima village of Pítaque, a short distance below Casa Grande, and was the village of the head chief of the Pimas.

Regarding the route and the extent of Garcés' expedition to the Gila in 1770, Coues was able only to conjecture that it extended to some point below the modern Sacatón. But from the diary we are now able to fix the precise limits, both where he struck and where he left the Gila, as well as the names and locations of most of the places visited between these points. Garcés reached the Gila at Pitac, just below Casa Grande. From there he passes through Pitiaque, Saboy, Uturitic and Napcut, before reaching Salt River; and below that stream through Suta Queson, around the Gila Bend through Tucabi and Ogiatogia to San Simón y Judas de Uparsoitac, at the western elbow of the Great Bend of the Gila. From there he returned south-

---

[6] Report by Father Garcés to Fray Diego Ximénez, in *Copia de barios Papeles del R. P. Fr. Fran^{co} Garcés, Missionero en la Pimería alta.*

[7] They are being utilized by Professor Charles E. Chapman for his forthcoming work, *The Founding of Spanish California.*

east to San Xavier, "travelling half lost" among the Pápago villages.

Such in briefest *résumé* is the light shed by the new documents on the first two expeditions of Father Garcés. Much more important, as a step toward California, than either of the foregoing expeditions, was that of 1771; and much more considerable is the new light shed upon it by our new materials. Of this expedition Arricivita, though he had a diary, gave a most confused account, and Coues added strangely to the confusion. Neither they nor any one else has hitherto shown that Garcés was the first white man to succeed in crossing the Colorado desert over which Anza made his way in 1774. Bancroft was not even sure whether Garcés crossed the Colorado River or not; Coues was convinced that he crossed the Colorado, but was completely at sea as to his itinerary.

So badly indeed has this expedition been treated, and so little has its importance been recognized, that nothing will serve, even in a twenty-minute paper, short of a general restatement. A mere correction or supplement here and there, as in the case of the earlier journeys, will not suffice.

The first two expeditions had been made for missionary purposes, and with a view to extending the missionary frontier to the Gila. Garcés' enthusiastic reports had much to do with advancing the project in Mexico, and he was soon given to understand that its success was certain. Consequently, he undertook another expedition, to search for the best sites for the new establishments and to prepare the heathen for the coming of the friars.

Leaving mission San Xavier in charge of a supernumerary, on August 8, 1771, with one horse and three Indian guides, he journeyed west. The first stage of the journey was through the Papaguería to Sonóita, a deserted outpost which had been established by Kino in 1699, and abandoned as a result of a massacre in 1750. On the way he passed through Ca Cowista, Pipia, Aiti, El Camoqui, Estojavabi, Cubba, El Aquitum, and Zonai. It had been the principal purpose of Garcés to go to the Gila Pimas, but at Cubba he heard that the Yumas were friends of the western Pápagos; and since he had promised while on the Gila to go to see the Yumas, and since the Pimas were hostile to that tribe, he concluded that this was his opportunity to make them a visit.

The Indians at Sonóita raised objections to his passing on, but these were overcome, Garcés says, "by means of divine providence, the good will of the governor, and my firmness and tenacity"; and leaving his mission Indians and apparatus for saying mass at Sonóita, on August 17 he again set out for the west.

To the foot of the Gila Range he was still on a known road, for it had been travelled several times by Father Kino. But it was a terrible trail, none the less—a forbidding, waterless desert, which has since become the graveyard of scores of travellers who have died of thirst, because they lacked the skill and endurance of a Kino or a Garcés. Its terrors have justly given it the name of Camino del Diablo, or Devil's Highway.

After passing Tinajas Altas, the tanks in the mountain top discovered by Kino, instead of turning north along the eastern flank of the Gila range, as Kino had always done,[8] Garcés passed the range and headed west over an unknown desert along the sand dunes near the present international boundary, planning to go directly to the Colorado. But, being met by some Pimas, he was induced by them to go first to the Gila. Accordingly, on the 21st he turned north and on the 23d reached the Gila, about ten leagues above its mouth, and east of the Gila range, which he evidently crossed on the way. Turning down the river he went through the Narrows, passed the Noragua village below, and at ten o'clock at night arrived at the Yumas, opposite the junction.

From this point, it is clear, Garcés was much confused as to his whereabouts, and Arricivita and Coues were equally confused. Though Garcés was now near the junction of the Gila and the Colorado, he did not know it, and for many days he continued down stream thinking he was on the Gila, and looking for the Colorado. While on his next journey, in 1774, he discovered his mistake, and confessed it, both in his diary and his *Noticias*. His reason for making

[8] According to Ortega, Father Sedelmayr in 1750 returned from the lower Colorado to Sonóita across the Yuma Desert (*Hist. del Nayarit*, 452–53).

the mistake, he says, was "because in those days there had been such heavy rains, the like of which had not been seen for many years, that the Gila was greatly swollen," consequently when he reached the Colorado he saw no increase in the size of the stream he was following.

Next day the principal chief of the region, with a great throng, came across the river with presents, and offered to accompany Garcés on his journey and back to his mission. This chief was Ollyquotquiebe, the Yuma later known as Salvador Palma, and a prominent figure in the next decade's history. But in his diary Garcés calls him a Pima, Arricivita so records him, and others have followed suit; the consequence is that Palma has been first introduced into history in 1774, in connection with the Anza expedition, instead of in 1771, when he became known to Garcés. But in his *Noticias* Garcés corrects this error as well as the foregoing.

There will be no space for relating the incidents of Garcés' journey from this point, and I must be content merely to indicate his route. He asked to be taken to the Colorado, and twice the chief took him thither, and down the river to San Pablo (Pilot Knob), but, as he had missed the junction, and as the stream looked no larger than before, Garcés refused to believe what was told him. "I did not recognize the fact," he says in his *Noticias*, "that I was travelling along the banks of the Colorado, nor would I believe, in view of the many lies which I have noted in the Indians, that those further down were their enemies. But [later] I learned both of these facts."

The Indians tried to dissuade him from going below, among their enemies, and on the third day the chief deserted him. Three times Garcés set out, alone or with guides who deserted, and three times he was forced to return to the Yumas at San Pablo opposite Pilot Knob.

Finally, on September 1, he set out a fourth time, and on the fourth of the month was at a village which he named Santa Rosa. It was visited again by Garcés in 1774 and in 1775; and from the three diaries we are able to fix its location as about at Ogden's Landing.

In the course of the next twelve days Garcés toiled on under ex-

treme difficulty, and reached the mouth of the Colorado River
at tidewater, near Heintzelman's Point. On the fifth he started south
from Santa Rosa, got lost, and went close to the river. On the sixth
he ascended a hill forming a sort of plain overlooking the river
bottom, then went to the river and camped. On the seventh and
eighth he made little progress because of lagoons and swamps. On
the ninth he was where the river turns west, but was forced to go
east to get round the lagoons. During the next four days he was so
hindered by lagoons and mud that on the thirteenth he decided to
turn back to the nearest watering place, give his horse two days' rest,
and then make a final try for the sea and the Quiquimas, a tribe
living below the Yumas. Travelling northward all night, at daybreak he stopped, when his horse ran away, maddened by hunger
and thirst. Giving the animal up for lost, Garcés travelled north
on foot all day, but at night, by good luck, his horse appeared on the
scene by another route.

We are now in a position to see how confused Arricivita and Coues
were in regard to Garcés' course up to this point. On the basis of a
statement by Arricivita, Coues writes with confidence: "Next day,
the 13th, he [Garcés] followed a trail and saw smoke on the other
bank; but being unable to cross he continued down the river westward *nearly to the junction of the Gila with the Colorado*,[9] till the
lagunas and *tulares* prevented his reaching that point, and he turned
southward." Coues continues: "At this date Garcés was in the vicinity
of Yuma, for the first time in his life. His course down the Gila is
easy to trail, as a whole but not in detail. Now that he turns south,
we have more difficulty in tracing his movements from the imperfect
and somewhat confused account in Arricivita."

Thus, it is clear that Coues supposed Garcés to have been descending the Gila all the time from August 23 to September 13—over
three weeks—and he says his route "is easy to trail, as a whole." We
have seen, however, that Garcés was on the Gila but one day, August
23, when he reached the junction, and that on September 13, when
Coues thinks he reached the Colorado, he had been on that stream
for three weeks and was now near its mouth. Garcés, however, was
himself laboring under the same error, and confessed it later in his

[9] The italics are mine.

Noticias, wherein he wrote: "I afterward learned with certainty that from the morning of the 24th till I left the Yumas, which was on the 14th or 15th of October, I was on the banks of the Río Colorado and in its vicinity." The ease with which Coues followed Garcés for three weeks down the Gila when he was in reality on another stream indicates that he was not looking for trouble.

To resume Garcés' journey. Having recovered his horse, on the 15th he retraced his steps toward the south. Next morning, the 16th, he encountered some Cajuenche Indians, from across the river, fishing in the lagoons. They took him to their camp, fed him, guided him to the river three leagues away, made two rafts, and carried him, horse, and baggage, across the stream, to a large settlement, which he called Las Llagas de San Francisco, in honor of the day, September 17, a part of which he spent there. This settlement, Las Llagas de San Francisco, was the traveller's farthest point south, and from the diary of 1775, when Garcés again visited the place, it was clearly at the head of tidewater, near Heintzelman's Point.

The next stage of the journey of Father Garcés was northwestward, parallel with the Cócopa Mountains, to and beyond San Jacome, his last base of operations before returning to the Yumas at Pilot Knob. For this portion of the route we have (besides the diary of 1771, the *Noticias,* and Arricivita) the diaries of 1774, which enable us to fix several points of the route with approximate precision. Of these points the cardinal ones are Cerro Prieto, San Jacome, Santa Rosa de las Laxas, El Rosario, and Santa Olalla. It must be remembered that Garcés was lost, thought the stream he had crossed was the Gila, and was constantly looking for the Colorado, as well as for new tribes.

On the night of the 16th he was "entertained" at Las Llagas by a powwow which kept him awake all night. On the 17th he set out west with guides to find the Colorado, but they deserted. Camping out alone, he continued on the 18th through *tulares* and swamps to a place near the Sierra, where he saw seabirds. But on the 18th he returned, perforce, to Las Llagas.

Here the Indians offered to guide him back to his mission by way of the sand dunes along the gulf. But he insisted on going on to find the Colorado, unaware that it was this which he had crossed. He set out westward, but "the guide obstinately turned north," and on the 21st he reached a large lagoon, many leagues in length, over which Garcés was towed on a raft, and which he called San Matheo. From Laguna de San Matheo he went three leagues to another large lagoon or bayou, near the Sierra, then returned. Continuing on the 22d up the west bank of Laguna de San Matheo, with the Sierra on his left, on the 23d he passed a black mountain (Cerro Prieto) standing alone, near a dirty, salty arroyo, with a deep bed, which he called San Lino. On the 24th he visited a village called La Merced, to the southwest, and on the 25th returned to San Jacome, near the arroyo and the black mountain.

The approximate location of San Jacome, Garcés' last base of operations westward and northward, is clear. It is evident from the foregoing that since leaving Las Llagas he had travelled parallel with the Cócopa Mountains. It is unsafe to pin one's faith to the shifting lakes and bayous of the Colorado flood plain, but the lake which he crossed on a raft corresponds well with Lake Jululu, sometimes wet and sometimes dry. Arroyo San Lino was clearly New River: the lone black mountain was Cerro Prieto, near the same stream, and still bearing the name which Garcés gave it. San Jacome, therefore, is fixed by Garcés' diary as near the New River and Cerro Prieto, and here its deserted site was found by the Anza expedition in 1774.

From San Jacome as a base, Garcés now worked westward and northward several days. Before he set out he was given clear reports of the Spaniards seven days away, at San Diego, and saw Indians who had visited them. He was also told of Indians near a large body of water, three days west and beyond the Sierra, and he determined to find them. The people, or the water, or both, he was not sure which, were called Maqueque, or Maquete.

On the 26th he went west with guides, who deserted when he refused to go northeast to find water. "But," says Garcés, "the scarcity of water did not bother me, since I thought the Colorado River must be very near, because I was near a sierra to the west." He continued alone to the mountain, therefore, but finding no water was forced to return to San Jacome, travelling during the night and part of the next day.

On the 28th he set out again to find the Maqueques, and travelled northwest all day and all night over a dry, level plain, absolutely without water. At daybreak he found himself in sight of the Sierra Madre, with smaller mountains apart from it. The main range, he said, ran northwest, and then turned southward, almost forming a figure seven (7). Northwest and north of him he saw two openings or passes in the mountains. He had discovered the foot of the San Jacinto Mountains and San Felipe Pass, which led Anza to Mission San Gabriel three years later.

Being in sore straits for water, he dared not try to make the passes nor go further west. He turned east two leagues, therefore, to look for water. Failing to find it, he was forced to retrace his steps to San Jacome, which he reached at noon on the 31st. The inference is that he and his horse had been without water three and one-half days. This may be impossible.

The exact point reached by Garcés on the morning of September 29th may not be determinable; but its approximate location is clear. He had travelled from San Jacome all day and all night over level country, and with a good horse might well have made fifty miles or more. He had gone northwest to a point where the Cócopa Mountains no longer obstructed his view of the Sierra Madre and the two passes. The principal points to be determined, then, are how far north he got, and whether he crossed the Cócopa range, or continued east of it till he passed its northern extremity.

That he did not cross the range is implied in the diary of 1771 itself, and is made clearer from the diaries of the 1774 expedition. That expedition passed San Jacome and Cerro Prieto, and ten leagues beyond crossed the Cócopa Mountains south of Signal Mountain.[10] As soon as the range was passed the large body of water now called Lake Maquata was discovered. Garcés commented on it at length, but gave no hint that he had seen it before. Three days later[11]

[10] March 5.   [11] March 8.

the expedition reached Pozos de Santa Rosa de las Laxas.[12] This is our clue to Garcés' "farthest north," for when he arrived there in 1774 he wrote in his diary: "On my last journey, on September 29, I reached a point about three leagues east of this place." The water called Maqueque, which Garcés tried to reach beyond the Sierra, was doubtless the modern Lake Maquata, which seems to preserve the very name it had then.

The confusion of Coues over the whole matter may be illustrated at this point. He writes: "On the 28th Garcés appears to have been near the mouth of the (Colorado) River, or at any rate near tide-water" for at dawn next day he discovered the Sierra Madre, and saw "a very large gap or opening in the mountains, which he thought was the entrance of the Rio Colorado into the sea." This was the day, it will be remembered, when Garcés discovered the foot of the San Jacintos and San Felipe Pass, a fact which is easily proved by the diaries of 1774 taken together with that of 1771.

Having already consumed my allotted space, I must hasten over the return journey of Father Garcés. After making two more attempts to reach the Maqueques, on October 3 he turned northeast to Santa Olalla, north to Santa Rosa and the sand dunes, thence east and northeast to the Yumas at San Pablo. San Pablo, Santa Olalla, and Santa Rosa are all points passed through by the Anza expedition in 1774, and their approximate location is well established.[13]

At Los Muertos, above San Pablo, he learned that a state of war existed between the Yumas and the Gila tribes, and he decided in consequence to make his way back to Sonóita by way of the lower Colorado. Descending the river on the 12th, he crossed it on the 13th, and spent the day making preparations to pass the horrible desert. On the 14th he continued south, then turned southeast to the sand dunes. On the 17th he struck his outward trail at the foot of the Gila Range. In crossing the Yuma desert by way of the sand dunes he had accomplished a feat which Kino had three times tried in vain.

[12] Wells of Santa Rosa of the flat rocks, which have been identified by Eldredge as Yuba Springs, four miles north of the boundary line.

[13] See Eldredge, *The Beginnings of San Francisco*, I, Ch. IV.

The significance of this arduous journey, made by a lone man with a single horse, is greater than would appear from a glance at the map. By the time Garcés got back to Caborca he estimated that he had travelled 300 leagues, or 780 miles, not counting the windings. He had crossed the Yuma desert in two places, a feat never before recorded. He had opened a new trail from the head of tidewater to upper California; on his return he had crossed the terrible Colorado desert for a distance of nearly a hundred miles.

The relation of Garcés' undertaking to the Anza expedition and to the opening of an overland route from Sonora to Los Angeles is especially important. In 1769, according to Palou, Anza had offered to undertake the task, but was not encouraged. But the return of Garcés brought the matter to a head. After talking with Garcés, on May 2, 1772, Anza renewed his proposal, using as his principal argument the information which Garcés had acquired. He emphasized the fact (1) that the Indians where Garcés had been, told of white men not far beyond, and whom they had seen; (2) that beyond the Colorado River Garcés had discovered a Sierra Madre, hitherto unseen from the east, but which must be that beyond which was San Diego; (3) that the desert was much narrower than had been supposed, and the difficulties from lack of water therefore much less. "In view of this," he continued, "this Reverend Father and I concluded that the distance to Monte Rey is not so enormous as used to be estimated, and that it will not be impossible to compass it." He closed by requesting that if the plan should be approved Father Garcés might be permitted to go with him.

The viceroy was greatly interested, and he asked Garcés to make a special report and send his diaries. He did so, and they had much to do with securing favor for the project. Approval was given, and, as is well known, early in 1774 Anza made the memorable expedition which opened a route from Sonora to San Gabriel Mission, thence over Portolá's trail to Monterey. Garcés came with Anza as guide, and it is significant that from the foot of the Gila range to the foot of the San Jacintos—all the way across the two terrible deserts—Anza followed approximately the trail which had been made known to white men by the intrepid missionary of San Xavier del Bac.

From the standpoint of mere pathfinding, between San Xavier and Los Angeles, by Anza's route, it would be fair to say that Kino made known the way from San Xavier (near Tucson) to the foot of the Gila Range; Garcés across the Yuma and Colorado deserts; and Anza over the California mountains. Of all these stretches the most difficult by far was the Colorado desert.

Such, in brief, are the history and the significance of the early explorations of Father Garcés. The last and greatest one has been made well known by Coues.

CHAPTER FOURTEEN

Fray Juan Crespi
*with the Portolá Expedition**

DURING the half-dozen years from 1925 into 1931, Bolton was magnificently productive. It was his "California period." In 1926 came the four Palou volumes, in 1927 the Crespi diaries, in 1930 the five volumes on the Anza expeditions, and in the next year the Font diary and the excellent *Outpost of Empire: The Story of the Founding of San Francisco*. This last won for its author the gold medal of the Commonwealth Club of California—*Rim of Christendom* would receive like recognition five years later. From these volumes this and the following selection have been chosen to indicate this part of Bolton's contributions to the Borderlands epic. This one is taken from the summary introduction with which he regularly prefaced his publication of the source materials.

In a shorter article of 1927, Bolton called Fray Juan Crespi "a California Xenophon." The allusion is most apt, for the friar was precisely this for the first land expedition into Alta California—he was principal historian as well as chaplain. Crespi preceded Portolá and Serra to San Diego; then went north with the commander to the Bay of Monterey and to a find more wonderful still, the Bay of San Francisco; later with Fages he explored the shores of that new-found harbor.

Here is the first part of that story, in short compass—a "teaser," perhaps, which will lead the reader to seek the whole in the volume from which it has been taken.

THE OCCUPATION of Alta California in 1769 was one of the dramatic episodes of American colonial history. For over two hundred years

* Selection from the Introduction to *Fray Juan Crespi, Missionary Explorer on the Pacific Coast, 1769–1774* (Berkeley, University of California Press, 1927), xvii–xxxii. The Introduction to this volume, 124 pages long, was published separately in that same year as *A Pacific Coast Pioneer* (Berkeley, University of California Press, 1927).

Spain had contemplated the step but had been busy with more important affairs. Now and again the region beckoned, but it was far remote. Cabrillo made known the merits of San Diego Bay. The multitude of intelligent natives which he encountered on the Santa Barbara Channel offered an enticing field for missionary labors. Drake and Cavendish threatened the western end of the mythical Strait of Anian, and caused misgivings for the security of Spain's commerce on the Pacific. The ravages of scurvy made havoc with the crews of the Manila galleons as they came clock-wise down the Pacific coast. The merits of lime juice as an antiscorbutic were not yet known, and California was often talked of as a health-giving vegetable garden for sailors returning from the Philippines. Vizcaíno, sent to explore, reconnoitered and over-advertised Monterey Bay. But still Alta California was not occupied. The province was not needed and Spain was too busy elsewhere. And so for another century and a half the Land of Sunshine was chiefly a matter of conversation and romance.

Then the Russian Bear threatened and the situation changed. In the seventeenth century the Muscovites had crossed Siberia and opened trade with China. Early in the eighteenth century Bering made his stupendous voyages into the North Pacific. He discovered Bering Strait, coasted the American mainland, and initiated the fur trade. In a twinkling his voyages were followed by a rush of fur traders to the Aleutian Islands. Within a few years posts were established on Bering, Unalaska, Kodiak, and other islands, for a distance of nearly a thousand miles. Aleuts and sea otters now paid awful tribute to the gold-thirsty men of the North. Though trading activities were as yet confined largely to the Aleutian archipelago, alarming rumors reached the Spanish court of an impending southward push of the Russians.

It was time to act. And action was assured by the presence of two remarkable men on the northern frontier of Mexico. One was José de Gálvez, the energetic visitor-general of New Spain; the other was Junípero Serra, the fiery head of the Franciscan missions of Old California. The decision to move came early in 1768. On January 23 a royal order was sent to Viceroy Croix to resist any aggressions of the Russians that might arise. This command, which coincided with the views already arrived at by the visitor-general and the viceroy, reached Gálvez as he was on his way to Lower California.

While settling affairs on the Peninsula, Gálvez organized the historic expedition that was sent forth to hold Alta California. Specifically it was designed to establish garrisons at San Diego and Monterey, and to plant missions, under military protection, to convert and civilize the natives. The general command was entrusted to Portolá, governor of the Peninsula, and the missionary work to Father Serra. In a spectacular expedition the enterprise was carried out in 1769. The *San Carlos* under Vicente Vila and the *San Antonio* under Juan Pérez conducted a portion of the colony by sea, the rest marched overland from Lower California in two detachments.

Owing to errors in latitude made by the earlier explorers the vessels sailed too far north in their search for San Diego Bay. The *San Antonio*[1] reached port after fifty-four days at sea. Slower still, the *San Carlos* was one hundred and ten days on the way, and when she entered the harbor her crew were too ill from scurvy and lack of fresh water even to lower the boats. A weary fortnight was spent chiefly in caring for the sick and burying the dead. The supply ship, the *San José*, on which hopes were pinned, was never heard of again after her departure from port in Lower California.

The land parties were more fortunate. Provisions for the journey, horses, mules, and cattle were assembled at Vellicatá, a post eighteen leagues beyond Santa María, the northernmost of the old Jesuit missions.[2] The first of the overland parties waved goodbye at Vellicatá on March 24, 1769. It was led by Captain Rivera, commander of the company of Loreto. He had twenty-five leather-jacket soldiers (*soldados de cuera*), three muleteers, and some forty Indians from the old missions, equipped with pick, shovel, ax, and crowbar, to

[1] Also called *El Príncipe*.

[2] Villicatá, or Vellicatá, was the point of departure of the Portolá expedition from Old California. At the time Rivera and Crespi went through it was an Indian village where no mission had been founded as yet. Shortly afterward Serra and Portolá arrived from the south and founded at the site the Mission of San Fernando de Vellicatá, the first, last, and only mission on the Peninsula founded by the Franciscans. It was taken over by the Dominicans in 1773. It is now in ruins.

Adapted from Herbert Eugene Bolton, *History of the Americas* (new edition), 162

Alta California, 1769–1823

open the roads through the mountains and across arroyos. As chaplain and diarist went Father Juan Crespi, principal historian of the expedition. To the timid natives along the route the armored Spaniards were an apparition. Rivera's men were declared to be "the finest horsemen in the world, and among those soldiers who best earn their bread from the august monarch whom they serve." The *cuera*, which gave them their name, was a leather jacket, like a coat without sleeves, proof against the Indians' arrows except at very close range. For additional armor they had shields and chaps. The shields, carried on the left arm, were made of two plies of bull's hide, and would turn either arrow or spear. The leather chaps or aprons, fastened to the pommel of the saddle, protected legs and thighs from brush and cactus spines.

The way was difficult and long, but the hours were shortened by the joy of discovery. For the first eight days the trail was that followed by the Jesuit Father Linck three years before. Thereafter, for over two hundred and fifty miles, the route was now explored by white men for the first time. Like De Soto, like Coronado, Rivera and his men were pathfinders. Frequently water had to be carried in barrels and skin bags (*botas*), for the Peninsula is dry. More than once the animals had to halt for the night without water, and sometimes there was no fuel for a camp fire. Several nights were made shivery by the screaming of a mountain lion. Much of the way was over rugged mountains. The wild Indians did no harm, but occasionally they were threatening. When the Spaniards reached the coast it rained, and the men spent uncomfortable nights in water-soaked clothing. At last the difficult journey came to an end. On the 13th of May scouts from a height saw the masts of the two vessels anchored in San Diego Bay. Next day their joy was mixed with sadness; the welcome salutes and the fond embraces were offset by news of the horrible inroads made by scurvy into the ranks of the sea party.

Just one day after Rivera and Crespi reached San Diego, Portolá and Serra set out from Vellicatá. The season was better, the trail had been broken, and the journey was quicker than Rivera's, even though it may have lacked some of the romance. On the last day of June, after a march of six weeks, the wayfarers reached San Diego. Serra said Mass, the Te Deum was sung, and artillery roared salute from the new outpost of Church and State. This first band of Spanish pioneers on the soil of Alta California, when all were assembled, comprised one hundred and twenty-six souls; twenty-three of the original number had perished on the vessels or after landing; of the mission Indians some had deserted on the way, reluctant to leave home. On Sunday, the 16th of July, Serra preached to a group of naked natives made happy by little trinkets from his stock, and dedicated the mission of San Diego de Alcalá. Nearby the presidio of San Diego was founded. New California had been ushered into history.

The port of Monterey was still to be protected. Indeed, it was the main objective. Portolá therefore sent the *San Antonio* back to Mexico for men and supplies; then, leaving the *San Carlos* at anchor for want of a crew, he continued up the coast by land to complete his task without the aid of the vessels. The march began on the 14th of July, two days before Serra formally founded his mission of San Diego. Ahead rode Ortega and his scouts. Next came Portolá, Fages, Costansó, Father Crespi and Gómez, six Catalán volunteers, and the Indian sappers. Now followed the pack train in four divisions, each of twenty-five loaded mules, with muleteers and a soldier guard. In the rear came Captain Rivera, the rest of the soldiers, and friendly Indians driving the *caballada*—the herd of spare mules and horses.

Portolá and his band jogged northward along the coast by a route practically on the line of the railroads today. Most of the way pasture and water were plentiful and the Indians numerous and friendly. At Santa Ana River a sharp earthquake was felt. "It lasted about half as long as an Ave María, and about ten minutes later it was repeated, though not violently." It was from this circumstance that the inconstant Santa Ana was long called the Río de los Temblores. Other shocks occurred during several days, until the Los Angeles River was crossed. Without great difficulty the coast was followed past San Luís Obispo to a point near the southern line of Monterey County. But here the way was blocked by the rugged Sierra de Santa Lucía, whose steep cliffs overhang the sea, and a halt of several days was necessary while Rivera and the scouts sought a way through the mountains.

An opening was found by clambering up the steep slopes along San Carpoforo Creek. The way was continued then to the north and northeast for about fifty miles, across Nacimiento and San Antonio rivers, and down Kent Canyon to Salinas River, which was reached at the site of King City. This march through the Sierra de Santa Lucía was one of the hardest stretches of country encountered anywhere by the early explorers of the West. With grim humor Crespi wrote, "The mountains . . . are inaccessible, not only for men but also for goats and deer." Arroyos flowing down the deep gorges had to be crossed innumerable times. From a high peak near San Antonio River nothing but mountains could be seen in any direction. Sea and valley were completely lost to view. "It was a sad spectacle for us, poor wayfarers, tired and worn out by the fatigues of the long journey." Some of the soldiers by now were disabled by the accursed scurvy. "All this tended to oppress our hearts," said philosophic Crespi; "but, remembering the object to which these toils were directed, and that it was for the greater glory of God through the conversion of souls, and for the service of the king, whose dominions were being enlarged by this expedition, all were animated to work cheerfully."

When the scouts who went ahead looked down the Salinas Valley they thought they saw the ocean. The men now "all bestirred themselves, supposing that the goal toward which we were marching was only a short distance away, for our desires traveled faster than we," says Costansó. But it was an illusion. Six more days' march were necessary before the roar of the sea was heard at Monterey Bay. The shore was approached with breathless anticipation. Vizcaíno had told of a "fine harbor." But none was found, and Portolá, bewildered, concluded that some mistake had been made, and that the harbor must be farther north. So north he continued up the coast. As the men pressed on through the spacious forests, they saw, rank upon rank, the sheer, ruddy trunks of giant timber, and they called this new tree the *palo colorado*. This is the first historical mention of the famous California redwood. At Half Moon Bay they saw the Farallones, Point Reyes, and Cermeño's (Drake's) Bay; this they recognized at once, for the old pilot Cabrera Bueno had made it better known than any other point on the north coast.

Plainly, they had passed Monterey and were a long distance out of their course. So crossing Montara Mountain they pitched camp at San Pedro Point, to rest and debate what should be done. Ortega, chief scout, was sent ahead to try to reach Point Reyes. Next day, food being nearly exhausted, some hunters struck into the mountains northeast of the camp to look for game. The chase, or perhaps only the hope of it, led upward until presently they came out on a clear height and beheld a great quiet harbor to the east and north.

These hunters were the first white men to report a glimpse of San Francisco Bay. Ortega returned a few hours behind the hunters, with the news that his way to Point Reyes was cut off by a roadstead that led into the estuary described by the hunters—a noble harbor that was almost land-locked, so near together stood the two titanic pillars of its one gate, open to the sunset ocean. Crespi, who saw it next day, had a sense of its importance. "In a word," he said, "it is a very large and fine harbor, such that not only all the navy of our most Catholic Majesty but those of all Europe could take shelter in it."

The Indians near the Golden Gate had told Ortega that two days' march to the north there was a ship in a harbor. The hungry wayfarers concluded, or dared to hope, that the vessel was the *San José*, or perhaps the *San Carlos*, with provisions. So Portolá decided to push on and find the ship. His way up the coast was cut off by the newly-discovered channel, so he decided to go round the obstacle, by swinging south.

On the 4th of November the way-worn party descended to the bay at Palo Alto. From here Ortega and eight men were sent out to attempt to reach Point Reyes by going round the estuary. The worthy scout explored the bay to its southern extremity, but he succeeded in getting north only to the neighborhood of Hayward. Either from this point or while on the Peninsula Ortega saw the passage through the Golden Gate and the three islands within the strait—Alcatraz, Yerba Buena, and Angel. Retracing their route along the coast they again reached Point Pinos and Monterey Bay. They planted two crosses, one near Carmel River and the other on the bay shore, and continued to San Diego.[3]

[3] A good deal of debate has been indulged in as to whether Ortega saw the entrance to the harbor. Unquestionably he saw it, for the records of the Portolá expedition plainly tell us so. From camp at San Pedro Point he was sent north to explore, with Point Reyes as an objective. After going "about three leagues" he reached the "end or head of the estuary" which the hunters had described. There his way was blocked by a "very noble and very large harbor, . . . on the parallel of thirty-eight degrees." There were "three islands within the strait which connects with the ocean between some high mountains"—the pillars of the Golden Gate. On the basis of Ortega's reports of his visit to the Golden Gate and of his tour around to the Contra Costa, Costansó, engineer and mapmaker, drafted a map of

Though he was one of the lesser personages of this historic expedition, Sergeant Ortega should not be passed by without further mention. He does not need my testimony, for Junípero Serra gave him a eulogy that will fix his place in history. Ortega joined Portolá's division of the California expedition, following or rather guiding the governor all the way to San Diego. Up to that point, of course, they were following Rivera's trail, and Rivera's work as pathfinder need not be minimized in an effort to exalt Ortega. From San Diego northward Ortega was the real pathfinder. His work can best be set forth in Serra's own words:

> The Sergeant went with the expedition, and as soon as we came to the end of a short stretch of road which some of the soldiers knew because they had been over it on a preceding expedition, the governor appointed him to go every day accompanied by a soldier to explore the route that we were to take on the following day. And thus he continued for the space of more than a month that our journey lasted, going three times over the road which the rest of us traveled but once. He went to look for the watering place and the camping site, returned with the information, and then went with all the party to the place selected. The soldier who accompanied him was sometimes relieved but the Sergeant never. The danger of going in this way among heathen people who were now resisting us, as we learned afterwards, kept me in constant anxiety; and, in fact, on some occasions his escape in safety could be attributed only to the saints of his devotion.
>
> After our arrival at San Diego, where everybody was surprised at the manner in which we had come, the departure from that port in search of the harbor of Monterey was determined upon. The Sergeant never left off serving in the same office; and especially when they went out in various directions to look for the harbor, it was he who penetrated farthest in the examination of the estuaries of San Francisco, looking for a passage to the other shore.

Ortega's fame as Portolá's chief scout in the discovery of San Fran-

---

San Francisco Bay that was strikingly accurate, showing the passage to the ocean, and two arms of the bay, between the Point Richmond and Alviso of today. (See Crespi's *Diary*, entry for Nov. 3; Crespi to Palóu, Feb. 6, 1770; Ortega to Palóu, Feb. 9, 1770.)

cisco Bay is not unmerited. Portolá, commander; Crespi, diarist; Ortega, scout.

At San Diego affairs had gone badly. Fifty persons had died and the rest were homesick. During Portolá's absence they had had a serious brush with the natives, who had pillaged their huts and stripped the invalids of their garments. Provisions were scarce, and there was even talk of abandoning the enterprise. But Rivera was dispatched to Loreto for stock and supplies, and the pioneers held on as if they knew the full meaning of their fortitude. In the crisis Serra's faith was superb. "What I have desired least is provisions," he wrote. "Our needs are many, it is true; but if we have health, a tortilla, and some vegetables, what more do we want? . . . If I see that along with food hope vanishes I shall remain together with Father Juan Crespi and hold out to the last breath."

But relief was at hand. The supply ship came. To the eyes of the friars, who kept an unceasing vigil of prayer for nine days, and to the discouraged Portolá, the white sails of the *San Antonio* cleaving the clear blue twilight must have seemed as the wings of some heavenly visitant, more beautiful than ever ship before had spread to the beneficent wind. Alta California had been saved from the danger of abandonment. Another expedition to Monterey was successful and the presidio and mission of San Carlos were founded there (1770), near the spot where one hundred and sixty-eight years before Father Ascensión had said Mass under a spreading oak tree. "Let thanks be given to His Divine Majesty for the achievement of what has cost so many steps and toils," wrote Crespi, who had shared in all of them.

The Russian menace had been met. Spain's frontier had been advanced eight hundred miles. That the event was of more than local import was generally felt, and the news of it, hurried to Mexico by special courier and dispatch boat, was celebrated at the capital. "His Excellency [the Viceroy] wanted the whole population forthwith to share the happiness which the information gave him, and therefore he ordered a general ringing of the bells of the cathedral and all the other churches, in order that everybody might realize the importance of the Port of Monterey to the Crown of our monarch, and also to give thanks for the happy success of the expedition; for by this means the dominion of our king had been extended over more than three hundred leagues of land." To give the event signal emphasis the viceroy ordered a solemn Mass of thanksgiving sung in the cathedral, and attended in person with his whole viceregal court.

CHAPTER FIFTEEN

Juan Bautista de Anza, Borderlands Frontiersman*

IF Kino was Bolton's favorite among the Black Robes, Juan Bautista de Anza without much question had that rating among his captains. This Creole frontiersman, born and bred on the northwestern edge of the Spanish advance, son of a presidio commander, combined many of the rugged traits which appealed to his rugged biographer. Anza's father had been a friend and co-worker of the Jesuits before Charles III of Spain decreed their expulsion (1767) from his American Indies. Young Junior had grown up with the *padres*. Circumstances in his mature years, in Sonora and California and later as governor of New Mexico, cast him with the *frailes*; he was their friend and co-worker. He played a major role in establishing Spain in her last Borderland, truly the "outpost of empire."

In this preface one is treated again to the fine sweep of Bolton's historical vision. Interesting to note is the author's care to place "his" Spaniards in proper American perspective, one of the great aims which inspired his life as scholar and teacher.

THE SEVEN YEARS' WAR gave North America a new map. French rule there was ended. England advanced to the Gulf of Mexico, the Mississippi River, and the Canadian prairies. Spain found herself in possession of Louisiana, and frowning at England across the Mississippi. Carlos III, Spain's able sovereign, faced grave problems. From the Gulf of Mexico to the Gulf of California, clear across the continent, stretched a hostile Indian frontier, as long and as difficult as the Rhine-Danube line which Rome defended against the Germanic peoples in the early Christian era. English frontiersmen pressed against the Louisiana border. Russians threatened Spanish domination on the Pacific Coast.

* *Anza's California Expeditions.* 5 vols. (Berkeley, University of California Press, 1930), I, v–xii.

Here was work enough for any monarch. With characteristic energy, Carlos III adopted vigorous measures. To meet the Indian problem he sent Rubí and O'Conor to arrange a line of presidios extending from Gulf to Gulf. To hold back the English he occupied Louisiana and fortified the line of the Mississippi. To ward off the Russian danger he sent Portolá and Serra to occupy the harbors of San Diego and Monterey.

It was the needs of this Pacific Coast frontier that called forth from comparative obscurity Juan Bautista de Anza. The posts established in New California were symbols of possession, but they were little more. Isolated, and ill supported from a distant sea base, the new province needed overland communication with the settled mainland of Mexico, and a stronger colony to hold the threatened land. Anza responded to the call. The genius and devotion with which he served his country in this time of need made him a distinguished figure. His performance of the strenuous tasks to which he was assigned revealed him in his true proportions—a man of heroic qualities, tough as oak, and silent as the desert from which he sprang.

Anza's influence was not confined within the boundaries of a single nation. His theatre of action embraced an area vast enough for an empire. His achievement was a significant factor in the long contest of European peoples for the domination of a continent. Among the men who helped to plant European civilization on the shores of the Pacific Ocean Anza occupies an honorable place. First to open a route across the Sierras and first to lead a colony overland to the North Pacific shores, he was the forerunner of Mackenzie, Thompson, Lewis and Clark, Smith, Frémont, the Forty-niners, and all the eager-eyed throng who since have yielded to the urge of Westward Ho. His monument is the Imperial City which stands beside the Golden Gate and looks out across the Western Sea.

First it was necessary to find a way from Sonora to New California. To perform the difficult feat of opening a route Anza was commissioned, and he accomplished it with consummate skill. One public service rendered by the soldier marked him out for another. Just when he had achieved his great success, the need of defending the recently discovered bay of San Francisco was fully realized. As soon as he returned to Mexico, therefore, Anza was appointed to raise a colony and lead it to California over the road he had opened. This task he performed with even greater brilliancy than the former one. He had now completed in outline the work begun by Portolá.

Anza therefore stands forth in the double capacity of explorer and colony leader. In his first expedition he made a definite contribution to Western path finding. For full six hundred miles he was a trail breaker. His journey to and from Monterey covered more than two thousand miles. To go to Mexico City to report his work to the viceroy and return to his post involved a horseback journey of an additional three thousand miles. He had earned his title of "the hard-riding captain."

As colony leader Anza's achievement was even more notable. With slender equipment he organized and conducted a large company of men, women, and children some sixteen hundred miles, from the Sinaloa mainland to Monterey. When it left its last rendezvous at Tubac his colony comprised two hundred and forty persons. On the first day out from that post a woman paid the extreme price of motherhood. But this was the only death during the whole journey, and to offset the loss three infants were born on the way and all reached their destination safe and sound. This is a remarkable record, never excelled—perhaps never equalled—in all the history of the great pioneer trek of peoples to the Pacific Coast before, during, or after the Gold Rush. Anza's brilliant success can not be attributed to the ease of the journey, for it was made amid varying conditions of drought, cold, snow, and rain. The march of sixteen hundred miles from Culiacán to Monterey, in which only one human being was lost, was so difficult that it cost the lives of nearly a hundred head of stock which died of hardship on the way.

A comparison may be suggestive. Lewis and Clark, thirty years later, made their famous journey from St. Louis over the Rockies to the Pacific Ocean. As an exploratory achievement this great feat was comparable to what was accomplished by Anza during his first expedition. But here the parallel ends. If, on their return to Missouri, Lewis and Clark had raised and equipped a colony of two hundred and forty persons, and then led them brilliantly over the same trail to the mouth of the Columbia River to hold the country against some foreign power, the work of these famous men would have been analogous to that performed by Anza during his second California expedition. But they did not follow their exploration with colony leading. As an explorer Anza stands beside Lewis and Clark. As a colony leader it is difficult to find anyone in Anglo-American annals with whom to compare him.

Anza did not perform these feats without competent aides. A whole galaxy of frontier leaders ride beside him over the pages of the records. Two of his associates, Fray Francisco Garcés and Fray Juan Díaz, soon afterward took their places in the list of California's seven missionary martyrs. On the first expedition these two friars accompanied Anza as diarists. Garcés was already famed for his wandering among the tribes, having crossed the Colorado River and reached the Cocopah Mountains. On his return from California he boldly opened a new trail across Arizona to the Jalchedun tribe, above Yuma.

The Kit Carson of the first expedition was Juan Bautista Valdés, a soldier who had already been in California with Portolá. From Mexico City this dare-devil rode fifteen hundred miles to carry the viceroy's orders to Anza. Joining the expedition to San Gabriel, from there on horseback he carried the diaries and dispatches to Mexico, riding for much of this distance alone. Four thousand miles in the saddle was Valdés's contribution to opening a road to California.

On the second expedition Father Pedro Font went as chaplain, diarist, and astronomer. As chronicler he was superb, and the record which he kept of this expedition is unsurpassed in all the long history of exploration in the Western Hemisphere. Garcés also accompanied Anza on this expedition as far as the Yuma junction. Separating from the party there, unaccompanied by any white man he opened a trail to the Mohaves, thence west to Los Angeles and San Joaquin Valley and east to the Hopi Pueblos of northeastern Arizona. Father Eixarch, gentle soul, was left alone at Yuma till Anza's return. He had a unique experience there, and he wrote for us a detailed and appealing story of the simple beginnings of the Yuma mission—indeed, one of the best of all diaries of a missionary at his daily task.

Then there was the runaway guide, Sebastián Tarabal. This ubiquitous Indian had fled from Mission San Gabriel, crossed the mountains, and reached Sonora shortly before Anza set forth. He arrived just in time to serve as a guide during Anza's first journey. Thereafter he became Man Friday to Father Garcés, and on his second journey accompanied him up and down the Colorado River and thence across the forbidding Mojave Desert to California. "El Peregrino" this wanderer appropriately came to be called. He is a picturesque figure in the story of pioneer days in the Far West.

Both Anza expeditions were made possible by the co-operation of the great Yuma cofot, Salvador Palma. This powerful chief led and held his people and his neighbors in friendship with Anza, generously furnished him supplies, and four times assisted him in the difficult task of crossing the wide Colorado River. Without Palma's aid Anza's work could not have been accomplished, for, as the sequel proved, the Yumas controlled the gateway to California.

Lieutenant Joaquín Moraga played a more enduring role. Second in command, he took a distinguished part in conducting the settlers to Monterey. And when Anza left the colony at Monterey it was Moraga who led it to San Francisco, established it there, and for years was its chief and mentor. In California he left a name that still resounds.

Behind all these actors, directing the frontier drama, stood Bucareli, the great Viceroy of Mexico. It was Bucareli who carried out the policies of Carlos III and Gálvez. It was Bucareli who worked most heroically to keep the distant California posts from being starved out of existence. It was Bucareli who with such devotion planned with Anza and furnished him the means for making his expeditions. It was Bucareli who most anxiously awaited reports of Anza's progress, who was most thrilled by news of his successes, and who so eagerly hurried the tidings from Mexico City across the Atlantic to the anxious king in Madrid. In the founding of California Bucareli looms large.

Anza showed the qualities of a true frontier leader. On the long, hard journeys he handled his stock with judgment and his people with tender care. He inspired his followers with loyalty. When failure stared him in the face, through lack of horses to carry them across the sand dunes, his men volunteered if necessary to follow him on foot to California and even to death itself. Uncomplaining, the men, women, and children of his colony followed him over the still longer trail amid excessive hardships. And when at Monterey they parted from Anza, they wept as if saying good-bye to a beloved father.

Few episodes in early American history are so well documented as these Anza expeditions. In the diaries and correspondence we learn the actualities of path finding and of colony leading. The records of distances and natural features are so accurate and vivid that one can retrace the whole trail, day by day, camp by camp. With this explicit information there is no need of romancing, for the realities were more stirring than fiction. Seen through the eyes of the participants, dependable water holes become matters of life and death. On the very weeds eaten by the pack mules might hang the fate of empire. The equipment which the colonists carried reflects the culture which they transplanted in the wilderness. We learn with intimate detail what clothes they wore, the food they ate, the drinks they drank, the sermons they heard, the tents they lived in, the daily order of march, their troubles with unruly mules, the instruments they used for taking latitudes. The "new historians" will thrill to learn that Anza's soldiers could not eat frijoles on the trail because they carried no pots in which to cook them.

The diaries afford us a vivid cross section view of conditions at the time, on the whole Pacific Coast for a stretch of sixteen hundred miles. From Culiacán to Horcasitas Anza and his people passed through towns already old. At Horcasitas the travelers entered a wide uninhabited plain. A hundred miles further north lay a string of pueblos in the Magdalena and Santa Cruz valleys. Thereafter, from Tucson to San Francisco Bay, a distance of more than a thousand miles, the only European settlements along the trail were four slender missions and the presidio of Monterey—with a total of probably less than a hundred Europeans or half-castes.

These records mirror the Indian situation in the same sixteen-hundred-mile stretch. For ethnologists as well as for geographers and historians they constitute a precious fountain, without a competitor for the period. Tribe by tribe the natives pass before us in review. On the Magdalena, Altar, and Santa Cruz rivers, the Upper Pimas were living in missions. Half civilized, they had entered the class of *gente de razón*. On the Gila dwelt unconverted Pimas, Opas, and Cocomaricopas. Between these two groups were the partly Christianized Pápagos. All the foregoing, especially the mission Pimas, were subject to incessant Apache raids. Farther west, on the Colorado, lived the Yumas, Cajuenches, and other agricultural tribes of considerable stability. In the California Sierra and along the trail clear to Suisun Bay, only non-agricultural peoples were encountered. Notable among them all were the canoe builders of the Santa Barbara Channel, and the basket-making Nochis further north. Such records, giving us vivid glimpses of Indian life and customs, are indispensable to ethnologists, at the same time that they help the historian to understand the missionary's problem of managing, feeding, converting, and civilizing his wards.

CHAPTER SIXTEEN

Escalante Strikes for California*

THE first, or the Garcés, selection in this section was marginal to and yet closely connected with the California story. The same can be said of the present little study. In the year that Juan Bautista de Anza was leading the founding colony to San Francisco in 1776, California was the goal of another band of Spaniards. Fray Silvestre Escalante and his companions did not reach the Pacific Coast, but their explorations in the Great Basin did have significance in the development of the Borderlands. They had hoped to open a road from Santa Fe to the new California capital at Monterey. Their progress through the still largely uncharted area between the Rockies and the Sierra Nevada brought the vast Great Basin region into the ken of the masters of the Borderlands.

Bolton's last work, *Pageant in the Wilderness* (1950), told this Escalante story in greater detail. The present article sketches the highlights of that memorable journey of exploration and is included in this collection in order to recall another Bolton contribution to the history of the Borderlands. The piece, incidentally, was first presented as a memorandum to the National Park Service, on whose advisory board for historic sites, buildings, and monuments he served for many years. Several of his doctors he directed into the history division of the National Park Service, where they helped to carry on the Borderlands tradition.

THE SOUTHWEST offers a rich and varied historical supplement to the scenic and recreational assets of its national parks and monuments. Of all sections of the United States except Florida it has the longest written record. It has been the meeting place of several dis-

* *American Planning and Civic Annual: 1939*, pp 266–73. The present editor has taken the liberty of changing the title of this article, which originally appeared as "Escalante Way—An Opportunity for the National Park Service." Reprinted with the permission of the American Planning and Civic Association, Washington, D.C.

tinct peoples: the Pueblo Indians, the non-sedentary tribes, the Spaniards, the early Anglo-Americans, and recent contingents. The natives still occupy essentially the same localities in which the Europeans found them, and retain the fundamentals of their early civilizations. Indian and Spaniard have lived here side by side for three and a half centuries; neighbor to both for a century has dwelt the Anglo-American. While all have borrowed from each other, each group retains its characteristic qualities; each has made its peculiar contribution to the most interesting and in some respects the finest culture in the United States.

The history of the Southwest has been colorful. The region has always been a borderland, between nomad and sedentary native, European and Indian, Spaniard and Frenchman, Spaniard and Anglo-American, Mexican and Southwesterner. Its history embraces sharply distinctive epochs, each with its outstanding characteristics: the long period of Indian occupation, the interplay of the Pueblos and their primitive neighbors, the Spanish explorers, the search for fabulous kingdoms, the Spanish settlers and missionaries, the Pueblo Revolt and reconquest, the establishment of the Mexican regime, the Yankee fur hunter and caravan trader, Texas dreams of empire, the United States conquest, the federal explorers, the day of the cattleman, the Indian wars, the railroads, the mines, the development of the Southwest as a Mecca for archeologists, ethnologists, historians, novelists, poets, and artists.

All these phases of Southwestern history offer materials for enriching any program for the development of national parks and monuments. Nor have they by any means been overlooked by our National Park Service. Indeed, quite the contrary is the case. Nevertheless, the historical values of the region have scarcely been tapped.

Instead of discussing all the general aspects of history in the national parks and monuments, I propose to confine myself chiefly to a single illustration, one which has a very direct bearing on an immediate interest today and which will serve as an example of one historical episode out of many. One of the important projects under consideration by the National Park Service at this moment is the establishment of an Escalante National Monument. It has, therefore, seemed to me appropriate to set forth the historical basis for the name chosen for the area, and at the same time by the story itself to illustrate the way in which scenic and recreational assets of a park or monument are enriched by historical association.

Remarkable among North American adventures in the later eighteenth century, that time of remarkable adventures in the Southwest, was the expedition made by Father Escalante from New Mexico into the Great Basin in 1776, the year of the declaration of independence by the English colonies. The aim of the expedition was twofold. The government in Spain—for all this country then was a part of Spain's empire—desired to open direct communication between old Santa Fe and recently founded Monterey in Upper California. Escalante himself had visions of Indian missions in the farther West, beyond the Colorado River. Objectives coincided and forces were joined. The governor of New Mexico contributed provisions for the journey; Escalante furnished ideas and driving power. Nine men besides himself made up his little party. Father Domínguez, the other friar, was Escalante's superior, and he furnished riding horses and pack mules, but actually he was Escalante's faithful follower. It is for this reason that the subordinate and not the official is remembered. Don Pedro de Miera y Pacheco went along as map maker. Two others in the party, Pedro Cisneros and Joaquín Laín, merited the title of "don"; the rest were of humbler castes, halfbreeds or Indians. One who knew the Yuta tongue went as interpreter. This proved to be highly important, for all the way through the regions that are now Colorado, Utah, and Arizona, till after the explorers crossed the Colorado on the homeward journey, all the natives encountered were of Yuta stock. Miera made astronomical observations, and drafted a map of curious interest. Escalante himself kept a superb diary which gave the heroic odyssey its place in history. The expedition was made, as Escalante requested, "without noise of arms," and barter with the Indians for gain was forbidden.

To the right and left as they marched along, the eyes of these "splendid wayfarers" beheld much of the most impressive scenery of the Great West, two-thirds of a century before any of it was viewed by Frémont the Pathfinder. The journey covered some two thousand miles, and lasted five months of almost continuous horse-back travel. Its memory is one of the precious historical treasures of four States today—New Mexico, Colorado, Utah, and Arizona. To this list a fifth State should be added, for the objective of the expedition was the opening of a new route to California.

The start was made at Santa Fe, then a city already as old as Pittsburgh is now. Mounts were fresh and riders exuberant with the prospect of adventure. Northwest the travelers rode across the Rio Grande, up the Chama, over the San Juan and its numerous branches, to the Dolores at Mancos, down that stream through southwestern Colorado, skirting the Mesa Verde wonderland. Doubt arose as to the choice of routes, and lots were cast. Chance voted for a wide detour to visit a Comanche band called the Sabuaganas, so east the explorers turned, over Uncompahgre Plateau, and north down Uncompahgre River to the Gunnison.

To here Escalante and his followers were in known country; henceforward they were pathbreakers until after they crossed the Colorado on the return journey. On they rode, east and north over majestic Grand Mesa. Here, among the Sabuaganas, they picked up two young Laguna Indians, so called because they lived on Laguna de los Timpanogos (now Utah Lake). Homeward bound, these new guides led the explorers on another long detour, down Buzzard Creek, over Battlement Plateau, across the Colorado at Una, up the steep sides of Roan Mountain, down the narrow gorge of Douglas Creek, to White River at Rangeley, and still north over a desert plateau to the ford of Green River above Jensen, Utah. The crossing of the stream was made only a few hundred yards from the now famous Dinosaur Quarry, but of these mammoth relics Escalante seems to have had no inkling.

West they now turned, up Duchesne River, and other Wasatch Mountains to Lake Utah at Provo, where the Laguna guides lived. The boys had come home. There under the shadow of imposing, snow-covered Timpanogos Mountain, Escalante spent three days, one of the longest stops of the entire journey. Autumn was advancing, and with new guides the Spaniards continued southwest two hundred miles or more to Black Rock Springs. They were now near the latitude of Monterey, and the plan was to strike west. But here, on October 5, snow fell, and all hope of crossing the great Sierras to California vanished.

So they set their faces toward Santa Fe. Continuing south they discovered and described the sulphur Hot Springs at Thermo, crossed the great plain now called Escalante Desert, entered Cedar Valley, descended Kanarra Creek, climbed Black Ridge, dropped down to Virgin River, and entered the summerland now affectionately called "Dixie." But they could not stop to bask in its autumn sunshine, so onward they urged their sore-footed mounts.

Unaware of the existence of amazing Zion Canyon just a few miles to the northeast, they skirted precipitous Hurricane Ridge, continued south forty-five miles, across the Arizona boundary, into Lower Hurricane Valley, and climbed the cliffs by a trail which a century later became known to the Mormons as Old Temple Road, because down it they hauled timber for the building of the temple at St. George. On the arid plateau, burning with thirst, they swung east twelve miles and southeast six, finding a welcome draught at some natural tanks on the edge of a cedar-covered ridge. They were at Cooper's Pockets. Here the Indians told them of a great chasm ahead—the Grand Canyon of the Colorado. So they swung sharply north and northeast, to find a crossing of which the natives had told them. A hard march of forty miles carried them over Kanab Creek near Fredonia. Forty more miles east and northeast took them once more across the Utah line.

Before them for a hundred miles lay the toughest part of the whole journey. They were now on the edge of the area of the proposed Escalante Monument. Buckskin Mountains, the low ridge to the east, looked innocent enough, but to cross their rugged hogbacks almost overtaxed both horses and men. Swinging south and east, they skirted stupendous Vermillion Cliffs. To find a ford across the Colorado cost two weeks of anguish and of transcendent toil. The gorge of Navajo Creek was scarcely easier, as is well known to anyone who has tried it. And in the weakened condition of the men and horses, the long, dry desert thence to Oraibe seemed to stretch out interminably. It is on this segment of the trail, near Kaibito Springs, that explorers have recently been looking for a reputed Escalante inscription.

It is always darkest just before dawn. Supplies obtained from the none-too-friendly Hopis renewed waning strength and revived drooping spirits. From Oraibe home the way was well known. Zuñi, Escalante's own mission, was the next station on the road; and thence, after a brief rest, the familiar trail was followed past Inscription Rock, Acoma the Sky City, Laguna, Isleta, and up the fertile pueblo-dotted valley of the Rio Grande to home and friends. The start had been made on July 29. The day before the wayfarers dismounted in the Plaza at the Governor's Palace the church bells of Santa Fe rang in the New Year.

The high point of this great adventure was the crossing of the Colorado River, a feat which well merits a little more detail. After negotiating Buckskin Mountains, Escalante turned south across the Arizona line, up Coyote Canyon, and down House Rock Valley, then swung northeast along the base of Vermillion Cliffs to the Colorado right at the site of Navajo Bridge. Continuing five miles upstream, he crossed the mouth of Paria River, halted on the bank of the Colorado near a standing rock (Piedra Parada), and with grim humor named the camp Sal-si-puedes, "Get out if you can!" The Standing Rock is still there and is now called "the Urn" because of its shape. The camp was square at the place where Lee's Ferry was established a century later.

Here, at Salsipuedes, Escalante spent a whole week in an attempt to get across the river. Two swimmers were sent to see if they could find a way out over the cliffs on the eastern shore. They swam across the river naked, with their clothing on their heads, lost it in midstream, and returned to camp in a state of nature, without making the reconnaissance. Next day the explorers made a raft of logs, Escalante and others boarded it, and propelled it with poles four yards long, which did not reach the bottom. In three attempts they failed even to reach midstream because the wind drove the raft back to land. Miry banks on both shores were considered dangerous for the animals. So this ford was abandoned. Escalante had missed his best chance.

Four more days were spent in camp here at Salsipuedes while scouts looked for a route and a better ford upstream. Food was running low, and a horse was killed to supply the lack. On November 1 Escalante and his party ascended Paria River Canyon a league and a half, made camp, and the men nearly froze in the night. Next day the climb of half a league up the Paria Canyon wall to the top of the Mesa cost the adventurers three hard hours. Four leagues northeast "through rocky gorges" and across difficult sand dunes took them to Sentinel Rock Creek. Camp San Diego, made here, was "near a multitude of barrancas, little mesas, and peaks of red earth which . . . looked like the ruins of a fortress."

Going forward, on November 3, they swung down Sentinel Rock Creek to the Colorado and tried another crossing, called by Escalante the ford of the Cosninas. Here Camp Carlos was pitched high on the mesa above the river. The descent to the Colorado was so scarped that two mules which got down to the first ledge could not get back even without their packs. While the Padres watched operations from their perch on the mesa, horses were somehow taken down to the river and across it by swimming. The problem again was not how to cross the stream, but how to get out through the cliffs on the other side. Two men, Juan Domingo and Lucrecio Muñiz, were sent to look for an exit and did not return. The horses in camp on the mesa went without water that night.

November 4 was another day of anxiety for the wayfarers, and hunger stalked in their midst. The horseflesh had been exhausted, and the diet of the Padres was reduced to toasted cactus leaves. In spite of the dangerous descent, that night men and horses, driven by thirst, somehow slid down the canyon walls to the river to get water. In the process some of the animals were injured by slipping and rolling long distances. Before dark Juan Domingo returned without having found an exit. Lucrecio was still absent, and it was feared he was lost, or perhaps had been killed by Indians.

San Carlos was now counted out along with Salsipuedes, for no way up the east canyon wall could be discovered. So, on November 5, Escalante and his party continued upstream, leaving Andrés Muñiz to wait for his brother Lucrecio. This was another grilling day. The explorers traveled a league and a half north, up ridges and down barrancas, descended into a very deep canyon, climbed out of it by an Indian trail, continued north some four miles, found pasture and water at Warm Creek, and pitched camp at a place called Santa Romana near the Utah line. It rained all night and some snow fell.

Next day Escalante moved forward three leagues, and was stopped by renewed rain, wind, and hail "with horrible thunder and lightning." Then, turning east for half a league, he found the way blocked by cliffs, and halted at San Vicente, high up on the mesa above the river, some two or more miles north of the Utah line. Before night Lucrecio and Andrés arrived, safe and sound, but with no encouraging news regarding a ford.

Here at San Vicente a third attempt to cross the river succeeded, and made immortal both the incident and the place. Cisneros examined the ford and the way out, and pronounced them both good. But the problem now was to get horses and baggage down from their eerie perch on the lofty mesa, for the river could be reached only by a very deep side canyon. This side canyon now came into history, and Escalante literally made his mark on the face of the land.

Here are the words of the historic record. "In order to lead the animals down the side of the canyon mentioned," says the diary, "it was necessary to cut steps in the rock for a distance of three varas, or a little less,"—only about nine feet, but tremendously important under the circumstances. Those historic steps cut in the rocks are still to be seen.

The diary continues: "The rest of the way the animals were able to get down, though without pack or rider. We descended the [side] canyon [using the steps cut in the rocks], and having travelled a mile [down the side canyon] we descended to the river and went along it downstream about two musket shots . . . until we reached the place where the channel was widest, and where the ford appeared to be." Here they crossed the river without great difficulty. Evidently the Padres were not great swimmers, for the others helped them over, guiding their horses.

So the ford was passable and the Padres were across the Colorado—with their precious diary! But some of the men in charge of the baggage were still in camp at San Vicente, a mile or more away, perched on the mesa as if suspended in mid-air. They were now sent for. The method for getting the baggage down was unique. Mules without packs could descend the side canyon by sliding and using the steps cut in the rocks. But descending with loads was another matter.

The faithful diary tells us how they did it. They let the packs down over the cliffs. "We notified the rest of the companions who had remained at San Vicente," says Escalante, "that with lassoes and reatas they should let the pack saddles and other effects down a very high cliff at the wide bank (*ancón*) of the ford, bringing the animals by the route over which we had come." That is to say, the animals were to descend from the mesa by the steps cut in the rocks, the baggage being carried to the edge of the cliff near the ford and let down by lassoes and reatas. The artist has something to work on here. Escalante continues: "they did so, and about five o'clock they finished crossing the river, praising God our Lord, and firing off a few muskets as a sign of the great joy which all felt at having vanquished a difficulty so great and which had cost us so much travail and delay." They had made one of the historic river-crossings in North American history.

Since first reaching the Colorado at Lee's Ferry (Salsipuedes), the wayfarers had spent thirteen hard days, tried the river at three places, and zig-zagged along its western banks for fourteen leagues, or some forty fearful miles, before they could get across. The Padre's Crossing is a justly celebrated spot in the history of early adventure in the Southwest. But few persons ever see it, for it is still nearly as inaccessible as it was in 1776.

This extraordinary feat of exploration through the Great West, accomplished "without noise of arms" by Escalante and his little band, has tremendous historical value which can be utilized by the Park Service. Much of this value might be realized by designating an Escalante Way through the four States of New Mexico, Colorado, Utah, and Arizona, and this without special expense for road building by the Park Service or by any other agency. A map of Escalante's route, projected on the road maps of these four States, shows that even now the motorist can follow exactly, or with surprisingly close approximation, almost the entire Escalante itinerary of two thousand miles. The most inaccessible portion of the route is that between Lee's Ferry and Kaibito Springs. In other words, we have the constituent elements of an Escalante Way already built, and they merely await synthesizing in a map, and under a unifying name.

Escalante and his party passed through or near many of the conspicuous natural features of the Great Basin and the Southwest, a considerable portion of which are now embraced in our National Park System. A visitor to the parks and monuments of this vast region will find his interest and profit greatly enhanced if, as he travels from park to park or monument to monument, he knows the thrilling story of Escalante.

One of the increasing difficulties of national park administration is that these areas are becoming over-crowded with visitors at the height of the seasons, and relief is being sought in supplementary attractions easily accessible from the park areas. Much relief of this kind could be found by utilizing to the full the historical assets of the regions within or adjacent to the parks and monuments.

The Escalante Way would be a string on which a whole rosary of national park jewels could be strung by the motorist in the West. The trail starts from Santa Fe, one of the most historic spots in all the Western Hemisphere. Going north it passes through or close by a whole line of historic Pueblos. Capulin National Monument, Wheeler National Monument, Mesa Verde National Park, Aztec Ruins, Yucca House, Hovenweep, Natural Bridges, the Arches, and Colorado National Monument are close at hand as one follows Escalante north. Coming south and east from central Utah, between Cedar City and Santa Fe the Escalante Way would run right along the main street of national parks and monuments. Near at hand on one side of the trail or the other, within easy reach, lie Cedar Breaks, Bryce Canyon, Zion National Park, Pipe Spring, Grand Canyon, Rainbow Bridge, Rainbow Lodge, Wupatki, Sunset Crater, Walnut Canyon, Montezuma's Castle, the Hopi Pueblos, Canyon de Chelly, Petrified Forest, Zuñi, Chaco Canyon, El Morro, Acoma the Sky City, Laguna, Isleta, and the historic Tiguex pueblos, not to men-

tion other attractions within or outside of the park areas along the
Way. This enumeration is illustrative rather than exhaustive.

A map of the Escalante Way might be printed, showing in colors,
or in appropriate symbols, the Escalante Trail and the corresponding
highways. On the reverse side a brief and vivid account of Escalante's
historic feat would accentuate interest and multiply the profit as well
as the pleasure of the traveler. Gasoline companies or other private
agencies would perhaps be glad to print and distribute such a map.
Markers of Escalante's campsites or the scenes of outstanding episodes in the expedition, with appropriate data, might be erected
along the Way.

The Escalante Expedition is but a single example chosen out of
many romantic, interesting, and important episodes and phases of
Southwestern history which could be drawn upon to supplement the
scenic and recreational values of the national parks and monuments
and to put these areas in their historical setting. Any one of the
epochs of Southwestern history which I have mentioned above would
furnish a long list of episodes and subjects capable of utilization. If
such a program were to be developed, the descriptive bulletins such
as are now issued by the Park Service might properly include a considerable amount of material regarding the history of the regions
within and roundabout each national park or monument.

The study of history in its broader meaning has a high cultural
value for the simple reason that culture is nothing more nor less than
the epitome and the resultant of human experience. The rich materials of history are lying all around us, and one of the things
needed is to make our citizens history conscious. The Park Service
has made a magnificent contribution toward this end through the
creation and intelligent administration of its archeological and historical parks. And it seems to me that much might be done to supplement the utilization of historical materials within the individual
parks, by co-ordinating them with the broader historical resources of
adjacent areas. If my simple suggestions should appear to be out of
order so far as the National Park Service is concerned, as they may
well be, possibly they may be of interest to the American Planning
and Civic Association, whose province and vision are all-embracing.

SECTION SIX

The "Other" Bolton

CHAPTER SEVENTEEN

The Epic of Greater America *

In the year 1932 Bolton was president of the American Historical Association. At the annual meeting of the association, held in December of that year at Toronto, he delivered his presidential address, the famous "The Epic of Greater America." Much has been written and still is being written about this statement of the broad approach to American history which was proposed therein. As has been mentioned in the introduction to this volume, there is sometimes a tendency to think of Bolton almost exclusively as "the Americas man." In many ways he would have welcomed this identification, even though resenting some of the interpretations of his thought which make him say and hold things which were not his intent. In other ways he would have been less pleased to have his more significant work, that on the Borderlands, relegated to second place.

The inclusion of this essay in the present volume is more for the convenience of the reader than for reasons of its direct pertinence to the theme of this volume. And yet there is a relationship, for from his extensive Borderlands studies came some of the inspiration out of which his broad approach to American history developed. Just as his Borderlands had to be brought into perspective regarding the larger Spanish empire, so was it necessary to bring Spaniards and Portuguese, Frenchmen, and the other non-Anglo colonials into the picture, in order that American history might be viewed in its proper perspective.

Hence, here is the "other" Bolton, the "Americas" Bolton, to match the more fundamental, the more enduring, the unimpeachable scholar, Bolton of the Borderlands.

I

The membership of the American Historical Association used to

* *American Historical Review*, Vol. XXXVIII, No. 2 (April, 1933), 448–74.

consist almost exclusively of residents of the United States. At the time when it was formed a more exact name for the organization would have been "The United States Historical Association." In recent years the situation has changed. The interests of the body have greatly expanded, and membership has come to include numerous citizens of other American countries, especially of Canada. This widening of the clientele and of the outlook of the Association, together with the holding of the present annual meeting in a Canadian city, would seem to give special fitness to a presidential address dealing with some of the larger aspects of Western Hemisphere history. I have therefore chosen for my subject this evening, The Epic of Greater America.

There is need of a broader treatment of American history, to supplement the purely nationalistic presentation to which we are accustomed. European history cannot be learned from books dealing alone with England, or France, or Germany, or Italy, or Russia; nor can American history be adequately presented if confined to Brazil, or Chile, or Mexico, or Canada, or the United States. In my own country the study of thirteen English colonies and the United States in isolation has obscured many of the larger factors in their development, and helped to raise up a nation of chauvinists. Similar distortion has resulted from the teaching and writing of national history in other American countries.

It is time for a change. The increasing importance of inter-American relations makes imperative a better understanding by each of the history and the culture of all. A synthetic view is important not alone for its present day political and commercial implications; it is quite as desirable from the standpoint of correct historiography.[1]

For some three hundred years the whole Western Hemisphere was colonial in status. European peoples occupied the country, trans-

[1] This is so patent that it hardly needs demonstration, and for the future I foresee generally in practice two types of school and college courses in American history: an introductory, synthetic course, embracing the entire Western Hemisphere, analogous to courses in general European history; and courses in the history of the United States or of any other individual nation. In fact, a movement in this direction is well under way.

planted their cultures, and adapted themselves to the American scene. Rival nations devised systems for exploiting natives and natural resources, and competed for profit and possession. Some of the contestants were eliminated, leaving at the end of the eighteenth century Spain, Portugal, England, and Russia as the chief colonial powers in America.

By this time most of the European colonies in America had grown up; they now asserted their majority. In the half century between 1776 and 1826, practically all of South America and two-thirds of North America became politically independent of Europe, and a score of nations came into being. Eventually, the entire Western Hemisphere, with minor exceptions, has achieved independent nationality. Since separation from Europe these nations alike have been striving on the one hand for national solidarity, political stability, and economic well-being, and on the other hand for a satisfactory adjustment of relations with each other and with the rest of the world.

Our national historians, especially in the United States, are prone to write of these broad phases of American history as though they were applicable to one country alone. It is my purpose, by a few bold strokes, to suggest that they are but phases common to most portions of the entire Western Hemisphere; that each local story will have clearer meaning when studied in the light of the others; and that much of what has been written of each national history is but a thread out of a larger strand.

II

Columbus drew the curtain of the American stage not for Spaniards alone, but for all the European players. This navigator himself seems to have been international, if we may judge from the number of his birthplaces. His daring voyage set in motion a race for the Orient in which several nations took part. The Cabots for England reached the shores of northeastern America and returned home with boats smelling of fish. Portuguese adventurers, sailing around Africa, reached India and set up an empire there. Spain, finding the American continent in the way, sought a route through or around the unexpected nuisance. When Magellan found a southern strait for Spain, Verrazano and Cartier for France, and Thorne for England, in imitation, scurried to find a passage further north. Spain set the fashion; the others tried to keep the pace.

Discovery was followed by exploitation and colonization. This, likewise, was not a matter of one nation, but of many. Spain and Portugal led the way. They not only explored and exploited, but they colonized extensively and permanently, and their experience was utilized by later comers. In rapid succession Spain occupied the West Indies, Central America, Mexico, and all South America except the eastern seaboard. There Brazil is an imposing monument to tiny Portugal. On the mainland Spaniards first settled among the advanced peoples—Mayas, Aztecs, Pueblos, Chibchas, and Incas. These natives were easiest to conquer, were most worth exploiting, and their women made the best cooks. It happened, too, that most areas of advanced primitive culture were regions rich in mineral deposits.

The dominant position of Spain and Portugal in America at the end of the sixteenth century was truly remarkable. No other European power had established a single permanent settlement. Portugal monopolized the Brazilian seaboard. Spain had colonies all the way from Buenos Aires to the Rio Grande. Two-thirds of the Western Hemisphere was then Hispanic, and so it has remained to this day. Spain's exalted position in the New World at the time is illustrated by the enemies who then rose up against her.

The North European countries and France founded no permanent American colonies in the sixteenth century. But all were interested in expansion in similar ways. All took to the sea. All desired a share in the trade of America and the Far East. All tried to break down the monopoly of Spain and Portugal. All made intrusions into the Caribbean and the South American mainland. Britons braved winds and ice floes in an effort to find a Northwest Passage. French sea dogs, Dutch sea dogs, and English sea dogs alike plundered vessels and sacked towns all round the Hispanic American periphery. In defense Spain adopted a commercial fleet system, formed a West

Indian armada, and walled her towns on the Caribbean coasts. One of these stanch old defenses tourists see today at Cartagena. The fortifications at Havana and St. Augustine had a similar origin. The French intruded into Carolina, Florida, and Brazil, but were effectively expelled from all three. Raleigh attempted to found colonies in Carolina; his Orinoco project sent him to the block. Drake became a millionaire by plundering Spaniards, was crowned Great Hioh by the Indians near San Francisco Bay, and talked of a New Albion in California, long before there was a New England on the Atlantic Coast.

Then a new chapter opened. At the dawn of the seventeenth century North Europe and France began to found permanent colonies in the Caribbean and on the North American mainland. Being latecomers, they established themselves in the leftover areas. We Saxon Americans today may regard our respective countries as Promised Lands, reserved for God's chosen people. But our Saxon ancestors froze and starved in them primarily because their Hispanic contemporaries were firmly intrenched in the sunnier climes. The latecomers made vigorous and long-continued attempts to get a foothold on the whole Atlantic seaboard of South America, but found the way blocked by the Portuguese. This is one of the chapters we forget.[2]

The favorite colonies of the latecomers at the outset were those planted in the Caribbean and Guiana. French, Dutch, English, and Danes settled side by side in the Lesser Antilles, jostled each other, and warred with Spain. They established tropical plantations, trading stations, and buccaneering bases. Till the end of the century, investors' profits were vastly greater here than on the mainland. In 1676 the immigrant population of little Barbados alone was larger than that of all New England.

But the future for these newcomers was in the northern continent, with its wide expanse, and its unappropriated back country. Here North Europe and France might hope to achieve something of the renown and a fraction of the wealth which Hispanic Europe had won

---

[2] England striped the Spanish Main (northern South America) with sea-to-sea grants which on the map look just as imposing as the more familiar grants in North America.

in Mexico and South America. So France, Holland, Sweden, and England all planted colonies on the northern main.

The details need not detain us. France occupied Acadia, the St. Lawrence Valley, the Alabama and Mississippi basins, and the Canadian prairies. The Swedes and the Dutch settled on the Delaware and the Hudson. England founded subtropical plantations in the South, diversified colonies on the Dutch and Swedish foundations, a coastwise and industrial society in New England, fishing stations in the northeastern waters, and fur-trading posts about the shores of Hudson Bay. New England was redolent of fish and brimstone; New France at first was largely a matter of skins and souls—the skins of beaver and the souls of the heathen.

Thus by the end of the seventeenth century European colonies and trading posts formed a fringe like a figure eight clear around the rim of both Americas, from Hudson Bay to the head of the Gulf of California. Middle America was occupied from ocean to ocean, and long salients had been thrust into the interior of the wider continental areas. England alone had not thirteen but nearly thirty colonies in the islands and on the Atlantic seaboard, strung all the way from Guiana to Hudson Bay. As commonly used, the phrase "Original Thirteen" has been very misleading and even pernicious. It does not mean the original colonies at all, but the original states of the American Union.

In these peripheral regions of the two continents the Europeans settled on the land, adjusted themselves to the American environment, devised systems for utilizing natural resources, and transplanted European cultures. Governments were set up, cities founded, religious institutions perpetuated, schools and colleges begun. The universities of Mexico and Lima date from 1551, the Jesuit College of Quebec, ancestor of Laval University, from 1635, Harvard from 1636, William and Mary from 1695, and Yale from 1701. Till near the end of the eighteenth century not Boston, not New York, not Charleston, not Quebec, but Mexico City was the metropolis of the entire Western Hemisphere.

Likenesses in the colonial systems were more striking than differences. All the nations entertained mercantilistic views of colonies—that is to say, they were for the benefit of their own people. Government at first was of the contemporary European pattern, adapted to the American frontier. Nearly every mother country revived in America some vestige of feudalism—Spain tried the encomienda, Portugal the *capitanía*, Holland the patroon system, England the proprietary grant, France the seigniory.

In all tropical areas Negro slavery was common. Native policies varied according to the natives. Indian tribes were everywhere used as buffers against European rivals. Intractable Indians were everywhere driven back or killed off. Sedentary tribes were subdued, preserved, and exploited. In New Spain they were held in encomienda; in South Carolina, Brazil, and Dutch America, and in the island colonies generally they were enslaved; in New France and in mainland English America they were utilized in the fur trade. Europeans who came without their women married native girls. Half-breeds were numerous in Hispanic and French America, and squaw men were the rule on all French, Dutch, and English frontiers. In the Chickasaw nation in 1792 a fourth of the one thousand heads of Indian families were white men, mainly English. Today French, English, and Scotch "breeds" are numerous in Manitoba, Labrador, and northern California, and dark-cheeked oil queens are popular with white men in Oklahoma.

In one respect the Indian policies of the Latin countries differed essentially from those of the Saxons. The Latins considered the Indian worth civilizing and his soul worth saving. This was due largely to the influence of the Church. So in Brazil, Spanish America, and New France the missionary played a conspicuous role. There Franciscans, Dominicans, Augustinians, Jesuits, and other orders labored on every border, and founded Indian missions and Indian schools. The brilliant Parkman made widely known the heroic work of the Jesuits in New France. Less famous in Saxon circles is the equally heroic and vastly more extensive work of the Jesuits in Spanish and Portuguese America. In colonial Mexico alone there were probably ten times as many Jesuits as in New France.

III

Beginning on the rim of the continent, these European settlers pushed into the interior, opening new mines, new missions, new plantations, new farms, new trading posts, new administrative jurisdictions. Sometimes the advance to the hinterland was a westward movement, sometimes it was eastward, sometimes southward, sometimes northward. Everywhere contact with frontier environment and native peoples tended to modify the Europeans and their institutions. This was quite as true in the Latin as in the Saxon colonies.

Colonial expansion involved international rivalry. This, too, embraced the entire hemisphere. In Saxon America the story of the "struggle for the continent" has usually been told as though it all happened north of the Gulf of Mexico. But this is just another provincialism of ours. The southern continent was the scene of international conflicts quite as colorful and fully as significant as those in the north.

Minor rivalries occurred in Guiana, where France, Holland, and England exploited the region side by side. England for a century tried without success to break into the Spanish Main, and called into being the viceroyalty of New Granada. Into Portuguese America the French and Dutch intruded with great vigor and dogged tenacity.

But the major contest for territory in the austral continent was between Brazil and her Spanish neighbors to the west and south. Here an empire equal in area to the Mississippi Valley was at stake. By papal grant and royal treaty Portugal was restricted to a narrow strip on the Atlantic shore. So said the documents. But this delimitation made little difference in fact. Snapping their fingers at decrees and treaties, hardy Brazilians pushed their frontiers rapidly west, founded Portuguese settlements in the interior, and plundered Spanish outposts on the Paraguay border. The Brazilian drive toward the Andes strongly resembles the westward movement in the United States and Canada.

Spain contested these inroads. In resisting them the Jesuits played a dramatic part. Their Paraguay missions became a buffer province to restrain the aggressive Portuguese. From middle Paraguay they extended their reductions above the great falls of the Paraná. There for twenty years they prospered, and then the Portuguese hammer fell upon them. Within three years thousands of mission Indians were carried off as slaves to Brazil. With the remainder—twelve thousand neophytes—Father Montoya and his associates fled helter-skelter in river craft five hundred miles down the stream, skirting through tropical forests the ninety miles of falls and rapids that broke navigation. This stirring episode antedated by more than a hundred and twenty years the Acadian expulsion which it somewhat resembled, and it determined the fate of a territory vastly greater in size. Striking new root in the south, the Jesuits defended that border for another century, sometimes by open warfare. The left bank of the lower Plata was another scene of long continued give and take. Brazil edged south at her neighbor's expense, but Spain managed to hold the region that became the Republic of Uruguay. The middle eighteenth century saw the border contest come to a head. With English backing, Portugal had the advantage. In 1750 by treaty Brazil was given a boundary much like that of today. Thus the Line of Demarcation, fixed in the time of Columbus and Cabral, was sadly bent, and Brazil came to occupy nearly half of South America.

There was another chapter in this story. To restrain the Portuguese from further encroachments and to keep out the threatening English, who had now occupied the Falkland Islands, Spain established the viceroyalty of La Plata, with its capital at Buenos Aires. This was one of the significant American events of 1776. It did much to determine the destiny of the southern continent.

The scene now shifts to the top of the map. Here again the story has been distorted through a provincial view of history. The contest for North America is usually represented as falling between 1689 and 1763, confined chiefly to the valleys of the Ohio and the St. Lawrence, and ending on the Plains of Abraham. But this is far too restricted a view. The story neither began on the Ohio nor ended at Quebec.

In eastern North America territorial rivalry began with the first intrusions of other Europeans into Spanish possessions in the Caribbean. In the sixteenth century the intruders merely barked at the

Spaniards' heels. In the seventeenth century, long before 1689, important transfers of territory were effected both in the islands and on the mainland. By settlement of unoccupied islands, England, France, and Holland absorbed many regions stubbornly claimed but neglected by Spain. England conquered Jamaica, and the French took western Haiti. On the mainland, both Virginia and South Carolina were settled by England in the face of Spanish resistance; Swedes on the Delaware and Dutch on the Hudson soon found themselves in the maw of the British empire. For decades the buccaneers ravaged Spain's Caribbean shores. Jamaica was the focus; Seitz has given us a telling refrain:

> Ho! Henry Morgan sails today
> To harry the Spanish Main,
> With a pretty bill for the Dons to pay
> Ere he comes back again.

For this harrying Morgan, like Drake, was knighted.

Then followed the more militant rivalry which Parkman has so brilliantly depicted as the *Half Century of Conflict*. It was a death grip of England not with France alone but with both France and Spain for eastern North America. On the American mainland fur trade and Indian alliances played a significant role. In the Caribbean and Georgia the Anglo-Spanish contest still raged. Not only Louisbourg and Quebec, but also Cartagena, Porto Bello, Havana, and St. Augustine, were targets for English cannon.

The long struggle was marked by five European wars. In each of them nearly all international frontiers were war zones—the Caribbean, the Spanish Main, the Florida-Georgia border, Acadia, Hudson Bay. In the contest Carolinians duplicated on a smaller scale in Georgia and Florida the savage Portuguese raids on the Spanish missions of Paraguay. In one campaign an ex-governor of South Carolina destroyed thirteen Spanish missions, burned Fathers Parga and Miranda at the stake, and carried off more than a thousand mission Indians. Bit by bit England shaved off both borderlands. France yielded her claims to Hudson Bay, Newfoundland, and Acadia; Oglethorpe's intruding colony broke Spain's hold on Georgia. But "Old Grog" Vernon's disaster in the War of Jenkins's Ear checked English designs on the Spanish Main. There Spain remained intact, for yellow fever was a faithful ally of the Dons. Incidentally, through Washington's brother, who served in the Cartagena campaign, this war gave the United States a name for its national shrine, Mt. Vernon.

The final clash with France in this chapter of history came when English settlers threatened the French hold on the Ohio Valley. The classic story needs no repetition here. Leaden plates and a line of posts signalized French determination to hold on. France was encouraged by four years of success; the tide turned when Pitt took the helm for England. With Wolfe's victory on the Plains of Abraham, French rule in mainland North America ended.

But the close of French rule did not remove the French people. Here historians often forget. The French settlers remained, continued to be pathfinders in the West, and their prolific descendants today constitute a third of Canada's population. Yankee institutions have edged across the line into British North America. As an offset, French Canadians have pushed south and contributed greatly to the economic life of New England.

The end was not yet. The contest for the continent did not close with the Portuguese drive for the Andes, with the absorption of Spain's Caribbean islands, nor with England's victory at Quebec. Western North America was similarly involved. International rivalry was quite as much a feature of western as of eastern America, even in colonial days, and its story cannot properly be separated from the other. The stage for the contest for the continent was as wide as the hemisphere and its adjacent seas. It was international rivalry that brought into existence as organized communities nearly all the Spanish borderland areas of the Southwest and the Pacific Coast. These stirring episodes, if treated at all, have been considered only as local history, but they are a part of the general theme. They are no more local history than is the struggle for the St. Lawrence and the Mississippi Valley.

On her northern borderland Spain's expansion was largely defensive. The French intruded into Carolina and Georgia, Menéndez expelled them, and founded Florida. Into Texas Spain was forced by a later French intrusion. La Salle founded his short-lived colony on the Gulf as a base for seizing the mines of Mexico, not primarily, as Parkman says, to hold back the English. Spain, roused to action, planted temporary settlements in the Piney Woods of eastern Texas. Iberville founded Louisiana, split Spain's Gulf possessions in two, and France again threatened the western country. But Spain came back. By a counter stroke she now permanently settled Texas. In the course of the contest the Marqués de Aguayo marched a thousand miles, at the head of cavalry raised at his own expense, restored Spain's posts beyond the Trinity, and returned to the Rio Grande on foot, through loss of nearly five thousand horses in a blizzard. Aguayo saved Texas for Spain and made Napoleon's pretension and Jefferson's claim to the province as a part of Louisiana an historical joke. During the same international episode in which Aguayo recovered Texas for Spain, the French advance up the Platte River was met by a Spanish gesture from Santa Fe toward occupying the region which is now eastern Colorado.

Louisiana tells a similar story. The Seven Years' War gave North America a new map west of the Mississippi as well as east of it. At the end of the struggle Spain found herself in possession of half of the former patrimony of France, and frowning at England across the Father of Waters. Acquired by Carlos III in the stress of conflict, Louisiana was occupied and developed by Spain primarily as a buffer province to hold back first the English and then the Anglo-Americans.

Upper California was likewise a child of international rivalry. Jesuit missionaries had carried the Spanish frontier into Arizona and Lower California. There it stood. Then the Russian Bear threatened. Bering explored the North Pacific and Russians planted posts in Alaska. So Spain moved up the map once more. Portolá and Serra planted garrisons and missions at San Diego and Monterey. A few days before the Declaration of Independence was proclaimed in Philadelphia, San Francisco was founded on the Pacific Coast. It was planted as an outpost to hold the northwestern border of

Spain's vast empire, a realm which extended from the Strait of Magellan to the Golden Gate. Though less a matter of bullets, the founding of San Francisco was as much a part of world history as was Wolfe's victory at Quebec. It was another of the significant events of 1776.

IV

Then came the American Revolution. This too was by no means a local matter. It lasted half a century—from 1776 to 1826—and it witnessed the political separation of most of America from Europe. The event was perhaps inevitable. Spain, Portugal, and England had founded vigorous colonies. They grew up and asserted their majority. The revolutions were the surest signs that the mother countries had succeeded. Thirteen of the English colonies led the way; Spanish and Portuguese America followed. Throwing off their status as wards, English, Spanish, and Portuguese colonists set themselves up as American nations. Viewed thus broadly the American Revolution takes on larger significance.

Of the revolt of the thirteen English colonies little need be said before this audience. The causes were inherent in the situation. Beginning as a struggle for redress of grievances, it quickly became a war for independence. Soon the contest became international, a fact which determined the outcome. France, Spain, and Holland joined the colonial cause against England. Spain drove the British soldiery from the lower Mississippi and recovered the Floridas. In the final victory the French navy played a decisive part. The treaty of peace was a shock to European monarchs. It recognized not only a Western Hemisphere nation, but a nation with a democratic form of government. Through hostility to England the rest of Europe had contributed toward the ultimate loss of all colonial America and toward the undermining of the monarchical system.

The independence of the United States was not fully assured by the surrender at Yorktown. For the next third of a century European interests in the Mississippi Valley were a menace to the continued independence and the growth of the new republic. The shadow of Europe lay deep over the West. The infant nation was not born a giant, and many persons of prominence thought it would fail. European powers looked on with interest. If the young upstart ceased to exist, they would be on hand to share the estate; if it survived, they would check its growth and dominate its fortunes. The danger was averted only by the jealousy and the long conflict among the Europeans themselves, and by the vigor of American growth. Spain threatened the Southwest. England occupied an analogous position north of the Ohio. France was more dangerous than either. She hoped to dominate the Ohio Valley, or even to separate it from the United States. In this she failed, but by browbeating Spain, Napoleon regained Louisiana. Then, suddenly, his colonial plans having changed, he sold it to the United States for a song. The shadow of France in the West was dispelled.

The revolt of thirteen of the thirty British colonies laid the foundation not of one but of two English-speaking nations in North America. One was the United States; the other was the Dominion of Canada. Before 1776 Canada was mainly French in race stock. The settlers who now arrived made up the first large English-speaking element in the country. In the revolt of the colonies the people were far from unanimous. Only thirteen of the provinces joined, though appeals were made to all. The Maritime Provinces, Quebec, the two Floridas, and the island colonies all stood by the mother country. Even in the thirteen a third of the people were opposed to the revolution.

Under harsh treatment by the separatists, thousands of these loyalists emigrated during and after the war. Going to Halifax became a well-recognized pursuit. Some settled in the old Maritime Provinces, and others in newly formed New Brunswick. Still others flocked to Upper Canada—the Ontario of today. So British Canada was largely American in origin. These United Empire loyalists, founders of this city[3] and a multitude of others, were Canada's Pilgrim Fathers. It was they who did the most to shape the history of the vast domain north of the United States. The small seed of empire which they planted beside the French colony has grown to be the great Dominion of Canada.

[3] Toronto, where this address was delivered.

Two American nations had been founded. But the revolution had only started. At the end of the eighteenth century only a small patch on the American map had won its independence from Europe. Portugal still ruled Brazil, and Spain's power was intact all the way from Patagonia to the borders of Oregon. But the revolution went on.

A third of a century behind the English colonies those of Spain and Portugal rose in revolt. In the two cases there were similarities and contrasts. The causes were in many respects alike. In both movements independence was achieved through outside aid. The area involved in Hispanic was ten times that in English America, and the population several times larger. In Hispanic America there were vastly greater obstacles to united action than in English America. Mountains and distance gave more effective isolation. As a consequence there were separate revolutionary movements in the different areas, and several nations resulted.

External influences played a prominent part in bringing the revolution about. England and France, trade rivals of Spain, plotted the liberation of her colonies. Subversive French philosophy penetrated Spanish America in spite of all efforts to keep it out. Young Creoles were educated in Europe. English and American contact through smuggling spread liberal ideas. The revolt of the English colonies, the French Revolution, and the independence of Santo Domingo furnished examples. Napoleon started the ball a'rolling by seating his brother Joseph on the throne of Spain. Spanish American resistance to the usurper soon changed into a war for separation.

Independence came to Brazil without bloodshed. Here as in Spanish America, Napoleon set things in motion. When he threatened to depose the Braganzas in Portugal, John, Prince Regent, fled with his court to Brazil. By his liberal policy he stirred new life in the quiescent colony. Brazil became a kingdom, John returned to Portugal and left his son Pedro as regent. Brazil and Portugal now grew apart. Ordered home, Pedro refused, raised the *Grito de Ypiranga*, declared for independence, and became emperor (1822).

The wars of independence in Spanish South America were an imposing military drama. Miranda the Precursor led the way in

Venezuela. Bolívar the Liberator assumed his mantle. For fifteen years this brilliant figure moved back and forth across the continent, setting up republics, defeated here, winning victories there. Then for a time the revolution was nearly stamped out. But Bolívar had a way of coming back. Aided by British volunteers—veterans released after Napoleon's fall—he crossed the Andes where they are thirteen thousand feet high, routed the royalists, and completed the revolution in the North. This Washington of South America well merited his title of *El Libertador*. In the North the dominating figure of Bolívar gave unity to the war. In the South there was less cohesion, but the cause prevailed. By 1816 the Argentine was practically free. Dr. Francia expelled the royalists and set up a republic in Paraguay. In the Banda Oriental Artigas, the picturesque Gaucho chieftain, laid the foundations of Uruguayan nationality. The rebel forces of the North and the South now closed in on Peru, the last royalist stronghold. San Martín, greatest soldier of the South, forged a new army at Mendoza, made a stupendous march over the Andes where they are twelve thousand feet high, and completed the revolution in Chile. Then, with fresh forces, carried north in a fleet commanded by a British admiral, he defeated the royalists at Lima, and turned his army over to the Liberator. Bolívar ascended the Andes, created the Republic of Bolivia, and ended the war in Spanish South America. Bolivia commemorates his name.

Simultaneously with these epic events North America ended the rule of Spain. Hidalgo rang the Liberty Bell and sounded the *Grito de Dolores*. Mexican school boys still bless him because he raised the cry precisely at midnight, for in order to be sure to celebrate the right day, both the fifteenth and the sixteenth of September are national holidays. The Philadelphia bell ringer was not so considerate. Hidalgo raised an armed mob, defeated the royalists, and seized government stores. Routed at Guadalajara, he fled north, was captured, and executed at Chihuahua. Rayón rose and fell. Then emerged Morelos, mule driver priest, the chief military figure in the war. His astounding victories were followed by a declaration of independence.

The revolt had spread like a flash to the northern provinces of

New Spain, where it was given special character by the proximity of the United States. It must be remembered that at this time the Floridas, Texas, all the Southwest, and California were still parts of Spain. Occurrences there which in the nationalistic mold have been regarded as local events, in this larger perspective are seen to be important phases of the history of the New World.

The people of the United States favored the Mexican revolution. They had recently fought one themselves, and were flattered by the imitation. They were interested in the spread of democracy, in Mexican commerce, and in Mexican land. Sam Houston of Tennessee, long before he became famous in Texas, offered to join the revolutionary cause there in return for real estate. There were boundary disputes between the United States and Spain, and now was a good time to settle them. So Mexico found many a helping hand. President Madison encouraged a revolution in West Florida, but when a republic was erected there he seized the district to keep order and to forestall England, for the War of 1812 was now in progress. In East Florida Madison fostered another short-lived revolt, with a similar purpose in view. Carolinians and Georgians ravaged the province but were expelled. Texas was "liberated" by a volunteer army raised in the United States, but was reconquered by Spain.

Meanwhile in Mexico the revolutionary congress fled from place to place, much as the Continental Congress had done before it. Heroic Morelos was captured and executed. But the revolt, now stamped out in the center, was kept alive on the frontiers. Here Western Hemisphere history was being made. Mina revived the spark by a raid from Texas. Andrew Jackson embarrassed Spain by invading East Florida, for Bahama Britons threatened. Uncle Sam took advantage of Spain's predicament to acquire title to both Floridas, which he already held by military force,[4] and to negotiate the boundary line of 1819. General Long led new expeditions from the United States into Texas, and set up a temporary republic. Galveston Island continued to be a base for proclamations and revolutionary raids. Bouchard, by an expedition that sailed all the way from Argen-

---

[4] Brazil similarly seized Uruguay during the revolutionary disturbances, but relinquished it a few years later.

tina, tried in vain to arouse contented California. On the far southern border of Mexico Guerrero kept up a guerrilla warfare.

Iturbide now brought the struggle to a climax. Sent by royalists to crush Guerrero, he joined hands with the rebel instead, and ended the rule of Spain. Then, making himself emperor, he carried the war of liberation into Central America. He in turn was soon overthrown, and the republic of Mexico was established, though shorn of the Floridas, eastern Texas, and Central America. The American Revolution had been fought and won. It did not end at Yorktown.

It was these events that called forth the Monroe Doctrine and that make it intelligible. European monarchs looked askance at the large crop of American republics. After the overthrow of Napoleon, that mutual insurance society at one stage called the Holy Alliance was formed to restore legitimate sovereigns. It essayed this task in Spain and in Italy, and then discussed the reconquest of Spanish America. Just then Russia took an aggressive position regarding Northwestern America. The czar declared the North Pacific a closed sea. In reply Monroe issued his famous dictum, denouncing further colonization of America by Europe and all plans to restore monarchy here. Russia now withdrew all claims below 54° 40′—hence the phrase later used as a campaign slogan—and the allies gave up their plans to restore Spanish rule in America. England's precise part in this episode is still a subject of debate.

In most of the new Hispanic states independence was followed by disorder—like the "Critical Period" in the history of the United States, or like Tennessee when Sevier and Tipton were ludicrously chasing each other around the map. The turbulence was due to political inexperience, social antipathies, geographical barriers, and sectional or personal ambitions. But the struggle was not meaningless chaos. In the long period of strife, cleavage in politics usually centered on fundamental issues: centralism versus federalism; civilian rule versus militarism; privilege versus opportunity.

Disorder led to one-man power. Mysterious Francia in Paraguay, bloody Rosas in Argentina, and venal Santa Anna in Mexico are examples of *caudillos* or military chiefs who thus became dictators. The struggle for nationality in Spanish America during the first half century after independence is typified by the fortunes of Mexico. There disorder and inexperience led not only to dictatorship but also to foreign invasion and loss of territory. Mexico's career was given special character, and made more difficult, by proximity to the "Colossus of the North." Canada had a similar experience with her neighbor.

V

Saxon America again occupied the center of the Western Hemisphere stage. All of Europe and America anxiously watched the drama. By the time the Hispanic states were established their territorial limits were fairly well fixed except on the north. The Spanish republics fitted into the *audiencia* districts of the old viceroyalties, whose outlines were already determined. Since independence there have been many boundary disputes in Hispanic America, Brazil has taken good-sized bites out of her neighbors' domain, but there have been few major transfers of territory.

Quite different was the case in Saxon America. When independence came to the United States and the Loyalists founded British Canada, most of North America above Mexico was still in the raw. Spain's holdings north of the Rio Grande were mainly defensive and missionary outposts. Beyond these, the major portion of the continent was Indian country, still in the fur trade stage. It lay in the pathway of several expanding peoples. It was an outpost of four empires, each of which contributed its pioneers. It was their land of opportunity, and it was anybody's prize. The ultimate domains of the three principal North American nations were still to be hammered out. The shaping of them was a primary interest of the Hemisphere for the next half century. Western North America was still largely a matter of frontiersmen and international politics. The spoils to be divided were the Spanish borderlands and the open spaces of the Great West and Northwest. It was an affair of all North America, not of any single nation. The outcome no one could predict, patriotic historians to the contrary notwithstanding.

In this elemental process of shaping national zones the two English-speaking peoples moved westward side by side. In each there was a succession of frontier types. In both cases the vanguard were the fur men. The United States frontier nosed its way like a wedge between British America on the right flank and Spanish America on the left. Besides being the crux of international relations, both border zones were areas of cultural influence, quite as significant as that of the isolated frontier.

Into the Pacific Northwest, British and American fur men raced across the continent. These "splendid wayfarers" profited by the commerce in skins, marked out spheres of influence for their respective nations, prepared the way for fixing boundaries, and were harbingers of permanent civilization. The British traders moved west from two eastern bases, and represented principally two great organizations. The Hudson's Bay Company at first had held close to eastern shores. In the mid-eighteenth century it was forced inland by French rivalry in the back country and by criticism at home.[5] Then it found a rival in the St. Lawrence Valley. Scotch settlers entered the fur trade at Montreal, formed the Northwest Company, and pushed boldly west. Mackenzie, McGillivray, McDougal, and all the rest—they have been called the "Clan of the Macks." South of the Great Lakes they competed with American traders, and beyond the Mississippi they invaded the territory of Spain. In the Minnesota country and on the Missouri the Americans found them intrenched in the Louisiana Purchase. In the Canadian prairies the Nor'westers engaged in a life and death struggle with the Hudson's Bay Company. Rival posts were planted on every important stream. Price wars and bloodshed ensued, and tribal relations were sadly upset. But important explorations resulted; the Rocky Mountains were soon reached, and Mackenzie descended his fluvial namesake to the Arctic Ocean.

The next step was across the northern Rockies. Mackenzie again led the way and rivals followed. Spaniards from St. Louis ascended the Missouri, and Lewis and Clark crossed the mountains to the

---

[5] It is interesting to note in passing that Samuel Hearne for the Hudson's Bay Company explored the copper mine country at the very same time that Daniel Boone reached the Mississippi. The two west-moving columns were neck and neck.

Lower Columbia. For the Nor'westers Fraser established posts in Fraser River Valley and David Thompson got a toe-hold on the upper Columbia in regions which are now British Columbia, Idaho, and Montana. Fraser's New Caledonia posts were the first permanent English speaking settlements on the Pacific Coast of America. Close behind the Nor'westers went Astor's men, and when Thompson descended the Columbia to its mouth he found Astoria established there. For the moment he was forestalled.

Then the American fur men had a setback. To them the War of 1812 was disastrous all along the border from Detroit to Astoria. Indians around the Lakes generally joined the British, and American traders fell back. Manuel Lisa and his associates retreated down the Missouri. Astoria was sold to the Nor'westers to prevent its capture by a British war vessel.

Canadian fur men were now confident. Why not restore the good old boundary of the Quebec Act, and extend it west? Urged by the traders, the British peace commissioners at Ghent proposed just this, demanding the cession of most of the country north of the Ohio, Missouri, and Platte rivers. The Oregon country was already in their hands. It would have been a pretty slice of territory. But quite the contrary happened, and the Canadians in turn got a setback. By the treaty British fur men were excluded from the United States, American traders replaced them around the Lakes, and the boundary was run along the forty-ninth parallel to the Rockies. Another great chapter in the story of the map was finished. As the Americans saw it, the shadow of Britain in the Upper Mississippi Valley had been removed. Canadians express it differently.

West of the Rockies the Canadians were still far ahead. Spain traded her rights to Oregon for those to Texas and withdrew south to 42°. Then Mexico took Spain's place. England and the United States arranged for joint occupation of the Oregon country—a seven-hundred-mile stretch from California to 54° 40'. In that vast region the legal rights of the two nations were now equal. But *de facto* the advantage was clearly with the British, for the Astorians had sold out, and left the British in control. Nor'westers now consolidated with the Hudson's Bay Company, a western capital was placed at Ft. Vancouver,[6] and Dr. McLoughlin took charge. For nearly two decades now this white-haired dictator controlled most of the fur business of the Pacific Northwest, all the way from San Francisco to Alaska and eastward to the Rockies. His counterpart at Sitka was Baránof. These two fur barons were the monarchs of all Northwest America.

The American fur men had better luck in Mexico. Forestalled by the British traders in the Oregon country, they pushed southwest and west across the Great Valley, and into the Rockies. Everywhere west of Louisiana and south of 42° they were intruders on Mexican soil. Most of our American explorer heroes of the Far West, from Smith to Frémont, were in reality belated explorers of a foreign country. For a quarter century after 1820 these trespassers roamed the western wilds, profiting by the fur trade, and "discovering" the mountain passes—which Spaniards had discovered long before. Into the Great Basin they entered simultaneously by way of the Platte River and the Rio Grande.

These mountain men were exemplars of manifest destiny. They wandered through Mexican lands, sometimes with but more generally without permission, unconscious of their character as unwelcome intruders, or arrogantly resentful of dark skinned people who spoke a foreign tongue and disputed the "inalienable right" of Americans to do as they pleased. Most of the fur gatherers were restless adventure lovers—rolling stones who gathered no moss, nor can we say that they got a very fine polish in the process of rolling. But they were endowed with that physical energy, that fondness for a life of half savagery, and that detachment from locality which fitted them for the great task which titanic Nature had set for someone.

Below the impresario Americans, who as partners managed large affairs, and beside the rank and file of reckless Americans who went as hired men or free trappers, there were the more numerous French *engagés*. These hardy souls, half European, half Indian, still formed the backbone of the western fur trade both in Canada and the United

[6] Across the river from the site of the present city of Portland.

States. One such has given his name to Provo, another to Laramie, another to Pierre's Hole. Western Canada is similarly peppered with place-names commemorating the deeds of the French. These half-breeds did the humbler tasks of rowing, packing, skin curing, and camp duty. They served as guides into the wilderness, for their ancestors for generations had led the van, whether under English, French, Spanish, or American rule. Just as the American cowboy learned his trade from the Spanish *vaquero*, so the American fur trader borrowed his methods and his lingo from the French *métis*. *Bourgeois*, the word for manager, in the mouth of the mountain men became *bushwa*, for boss.

These American fur men were by no means monarchs of all they surveyed. In the southern Rockies and in the Great Basin they found Mexican traders everywhere ahead of them. They tried to push into jointly-owned Oregon, but found their way blocked by the Hudson's Bay Company, safely intrenched in Snake River Valley. Climbing the Sierras, they descended the western slopes into California. There, in the Sacramento Valley, they found the streams trapped by Russians from Ft. Ross and by McLoughlin's brigades from Ft. Vancouver. A Hudson's Bay settlement encountered by the Americans in the valley, and for obvious reasons called by them French Camp, is still in existence near Stockton and still bears the same name.

The Americans had been beaten, not only to the Pacific Northwest, but to northern California as well. Both they and the men of H. B. C. were unwelcome trespassers on the soil of Mexico. The international contest was not yet over. The map was not yet made. The ultimate fate of the Far West was still in doubt. Spain was out, Russia had backed up to 54° 40', but England, the United States, and Mexico still had their stake. When the Republic of Texas was created, it, too, developed ambitions for a frontage on the Pacific.

The uncertainty was removed by the settler. Fur men and Santa Fe trader were followed into the alluring regions by land-hungry Americans. All that had gone before, all the colonial and international drama of the centuries, was the background into which fitted the relentless westward movement of the farmer frontier.

By 1820 the United States had achieved stability and confirmed its independence from Europe. The next two decades witnessed the rise of the great Middle West and the formation of a western democracy. It was a militant democracy, fully imbued with belief in manifest destiny. American institutions must embrace and regenerate the entire Western Hemisphere. A concrete application was to be found in the rich lands of Mexico and the disputed Oregon country, just beyond. So the shadow of Europe in the West now gave way to the shadow of the United States in the West—a shadow which all America and several European nations watched with anxiety, for nearly half of the northern continent was still at stake. Impelled by this expansion urge, Anglo-Americans drove a wide salient between Canada and Mexico, checking the expansion of the one, and absorbing half the territory of the other. This madness for conquest has been called by our naughty neighbors "the other side of the Monroe Doctrine."

Mexico, in spite of her turmoil, likewise felt the impulse of expansion. Settlers poured into her northern provinces at a rate unprecedented under Spain. The vast "Spanish Grants," as they are erroneously called, in Texas, New Mexico, Colorado, and California, were nearly all made during the Mexican régime. Part of the new settlers were Mexicans; part were foreigners. Spain had colonized Florida and Louisiana with Anglo-Americans. Mexico now made the same political mistake in Texas, New Mexico, and California.

Many factors aroused American interest in the Far West. Boston coast traders, overland fur men, Northwestern missionaries, and official explorers had spied out the land. Interest was stimulated by sectional rivalry, and by fear of England, France, or Russia. Pathfinders beckoned; government tried to follow. By diplomacy, through purchase from Mexico, and through compromise with England it essayed to acquire all the vast region between Louisiana and the Pacific. Mexico did not wish to sell, and England was "stubborn"—so our schoolbooks say. Canning put his heavy foot down on the Columbia, and there he stood; so Uncle Sam resorted to watchful waiting. We thank President Wilson for the phrase, for it precisely fits the case. Wilkes, Ap Jones, Larkin, and Frémont all typify the government's hope that something would "turn up."

While government watched, settlers moved in. Invited, Americans colonized Texas, arose in revolt, and sought annexation, alternating this ambition with dreams of possessing "the fine harbor of Monterey." Covered wagons creaked their way from the Middle West to Oregon; then England and the United States divided the disputed area. Uninvited, and long before the Gold Rush, other covered wagons invaded California, still a part of Mexico; their occupants obtained generous land grants, and then, imitating the Texans, set up the Bear Flag Republic. When something thus turned up, Frémont was on hand. Uninvited, Mormons poured into Utah, also Mexican territory. Uncle Sam's soldiers and diplomats now supplemented the work of the settlers. Texas was annexed; Mexico went to war, and was forced to yield half of her domain. The purchase of the Gadsden strip and of Alaska completed the story of Saxon growth on the western mainland. The contest for the continent was practically over.

This division of the western seaboard of North America was highly significant. It cut off from Spanish America the remaining borderland areas which had been only partly Hispanized and placed the boundary near the frontier of effective Spanish colonization. It gave both Canada and the United States frontage on the Pacific. It enabled them both to assimilate added millions of Europeans. Built on the national domain, in both countries the West became a powerful nationalizing force. The process of growth kept both nations young with continued frontier experience; it prolonged opportunity for social experimentation, and perpetuated early American and Canadian characteristics.

VI

On this long colonial and international background the subsequent development of the Western Hemisphere was founded. The nations had come into being. The outline of the map had been essentially completed. The territorial bases for the national system had been laid. The next phase was the filling in of the spaces with people, national unification, and economic growth. Like all the earlier phases, this, too, was not confined to one American nation, but was hemisphere wide.

In this whole process of national growth and unification in the nineteenth century the outstanding factors were boundless natural resources, foreign immigration, foreign capital, and expanding markets. Without these, none of the American nations would have come far on the road which they have traveled. No time is left me for detail. I can only indicate the broad lines. But if you are like my students, I am sure you will gladly forgive me for what I leave out.

The United States first got under way. Here territorial expansion was attended by growing pains. Tariffs, the slavery question, the acquisition of Texas, Oregon, and California aroused sectional jealousies. For thirty years peace between the sections was maintained by compromise. War followed, but the Union was preserved. It was then multiplied in strength by the peopling of the Far West. Wide flung and sprawling, it was welded by the building of transcontinental railroads, the economic reconstruction of the South, and the reorganization of industry on a national scale. In all this, European immigration and European capital played a decisive part. By the end of the nineteenth century both political and economic nationality had been achieved.

While the United States were gaining solidarity and power, the British provinces to the north were being similarly welded into a great dominion. The War of 1812 stimulated their sense of nationality, and British immigration lessened American influence. By 1850 the provinces had already won responsible government, but they were still detached entities. Like the United States, the Dominion was fashioned out of scraps of territory variously acquired.

Now the tide of federation set strongly in. Union was prompted by community of interests. Obstacles were met in local hostilities and racial suspicion. Federation found able champions and determined opponents. There were Hamiltons and Calhouns. In the Quebec Conference—as significant in Canadian history as the Constitutional Convention in the United States—the Dominion of Canada was born. One by one the older provinces joined. *A mari usque ad mare* became the slogan. Hudson's Bay Company relinquished its vast jurisdiction in the West, Manitoba and British Columbia entered the union, and the Dominion did indeed extend from sea to sea.

The loosely-knit federation, like its neighbor a little earlier, was now welded by transcontinental railroads and the development of the West. The American movement to the frontier was duplicated in Canada. European capital furnished the means. European immigrants thronged, Americans flocked across the border, new prairie provinces were formed, Winnipeg and Vancouver became boom towns. New railroads built up still more northerly cities, and mining rushes developed the yet more remote Northwest. Like California, Oregon, and Washington, British Columbia looks out across the Pacific.

The World War stimulated Canadian loyalism on the one hand, and English conciliation on the other. Canada now has full membership in the British Commonwealth. A fine sentiment binds her to the empire, but she is in all essentials an independent nation. From pole to pole American independence from Europe has been achieved.

Hispanic America has a similar tale of national growth to tell. Some of our southern neighbors have been moving rapidly along the same road as that traveled by the Anglo-American nations. The last half century has been remarkable especially for the emergence of the A B C powers—Argentina, Brazil, and Chile.

The essential factors in the recent development of these countries are much the same as those which have operated in Canada and the United States. Foreign capital and foreign immigration have been decisive. Italians, Spaniards, and Germans have come to the A B C countries by millions to make their homes. Railroads, plantations, stock ranches, nitrate works, mines, and oil wells have been developed by English and German capital. In business matters Uncle Sam has by no means had a monopoly there. Will Rogers, whom all will accept as an authority, wrote from Buenos Aires a few weeks ago, "Englishmen have got this country sewed up tighter than Borah has Idaho." Other indexes of material progress in that far Southland are the great modern cities, such as Santiago, Rio de Janeiro, and São Paulo. Cultural progress has followed material prosperity.

Buenos Aires, with its nearly three million inhabitants, is the third city in the Western Hemisphere, and one of the great ones of the world. Brazil, with a population of over forty millions, is the second power in America, a title which Argentina probably would contest. When a Brazilian boasted of his country's forty-three millions, an Argentinian retorted, "You must have counted all those who live in the trees."

"The first shall be last!" In the tropics and around the shores of the Caribbean there has been less material progress than in the temperate regions. The areas which were most developed in early colonial days are now most retarded.[7] Nevertheless, backwardness is only relative, and some of these tropical regions, with their fruit and oil, have recently attracted capital and been developed at a tremendous rate.

Mexico, our nearest Hispanic neighbor, has continued to have its ups and downs. The fall of Maximilian was followed by the rule of one of the remarkable men of all time. Porfirio Díaz, half-breed Zapotec Indian, and soldier hero, became president on the platform of no re-election—and then held office for seven terms in succession. He was a benevolent despot. He gave Mexico what it then most needed—good order and material progress. Foreign capital poured in, railroads were built, mines and oil wells opened. What had happened in the United States, Canada, and Brazil, was duplicated there. Díaz became a much eulogized world figure. Outsiders saw Mexico in a Golden Age.

But prosperity was one-sided. Vast estates were still intact while millions of people needed land. Foreigners and the old aristocracy flourished while peons were still bound to the soil. The kettle of unrest boiled, and the lid blew off. Madero gave the new *Grito*, Díaz fled the country never to return, Madero fell, Huerta was eliminated, Carranza put in power, and the new constitution installed. Socialistic and nationalistic in its aims, fifteen years have been spent putting it into operation. The declared objectives of the social revolution—for it is still going on—are Mexico for Mexicans, rights for the common man, and education for the common people—slogans

[7] This is true of British, Dutch, and French America also.

which sound familiar to Anglo-Americans. In so radical a program vested interests have suffered. In the struggle the Church has been involved. Critics maintain that some of the reforms are more apparent than real; but the same has been said of other countries.

VII

Progress toward nationality in the Western Hemisphere has been attended by international adjustments. The interrelations of Canada and the United States have always been close, as their development has been in many ways parallel. Loyalists never forget their expulsion from the home hearth, nor the attempted conquest of 1812. Fortunately, as the Canadians say, the Americans were always just exasperating enough to prevent an international marriage, thus preserving Canadian nationality. By 1846 the old boundary questions had been adjusted. The mid-century was sometimes disturbed by annexation talk that was seldom dangerous. The war between the states and Fenian raids caused irritation. Fisheries and the Bering Sea were bones of contention. Blaine enjoyed twisting the British Lion's tail. Trade relations have sometimes been troublesome. But eventually these matters have been amicably settled. All in all, with common boundaries unfortified for more than a century, Canada and the United States, in this world of turmoil, furnish a splendid example of neighborliness.

Of the Hispanic republics the most intimate international contacts have been with each other. Like good Irishmen, whom they greatly resemble, the Latins quarrel among themselves but show solidarity against outsiders who interfere. Bullets often fly. But boundary disputes on many borders have been settled by arbitration, in which Latin America has set an example before the world. With Europe there has been occasional friction, but much more conspicuous has been the peaceful intercourse of commerce, investment, immigration, and cultural contacts.

Hispanic dealings with the United States have generally been closest in the adjacent regions; and by the rest of Latin America, naturally, these dealings have been taken as an index. Early friendship soon cooled. When the United States seized half of Mexico's domain, that country became embittered and other Latins suspicious. In the mid-century relations with Mexico greatly improved, and the long reign of Díaz was the heyday of American investors south of the Rio Grande. After the fall of "El General," the story was one of frequent intervention. Huerta was eliminated and Carranza elevated largely through Wilson's aid. Villa-chasing and "saluting the flag" made Uncle Sam ridiculous. Mexico's new constitution threatened American investments and a decade of irritation followed. But this matter has been adjusted. In recent years the United States has had its most intimate relations with the Isthmus and the Caribbean area. In these regions the United States has exercised extensive super- visory functions. With South America, on the other hand, the ten- dency is toward recognition of the fullest autonomy. There the Monroe Doctrine is dead. The Southern Continent has grown up.

The essential unity of the Western Hemisphere was revealed by the Great War. Every nation had to answer the question of partici- pation or neutrality. Canada was in from the start; the United States moved more slowly. Until Uncle Sam joined the Allies, all Hispanic America held aloof. Then, of the twenty states to the south, eight joined the Allies, five broke relations with Germany, and seven re- mained neutral. It is a significant thing that all America, from the north pole to the south pole, was either on the same side of the great struggle or remained neutral. There was emphatic Western Hem- isphere solidarity.

The Americas have developed side by side. In the past their rela- tions have been close; in the future they may or may not be closer. In the colonial period Latin greatly outweighed Saxon America. In the nineteenth century the balance tipped decisively in the other direction. But it is swinging back. The importance of Hispanic Amer- ica as an economic unit and as a political factor is becoming greater from day to day. It is one of the great reservoirs of raw materials. It continues to attract foreign capital and foreign immigration. Saxon America, with its one hundred and forty millions of people, is practically closed to European settlers. Hispanic America, with its hundred millions, is wide open. A German colony of a whole million is right now being planned for the Upper Amazon—equipped with electric cooling plants and everything else up-to-date. It is entirely possible that within a short time Hispanic will outnumber Saxon America, and with continued immigration its race stock will be more and more largely European. Ever since independence there has been fundamental Western Hemisphere solidarity. Therefore, it is not a matter of indifference to know that European influence in South America today far outweighs that of Saxon America, and that Europe is bending every effort to draw the Southern continent more and more into the European circle and away from its northern neighbors.

VIII

In this imperfect way I have endeavored to indicate some of the larger historical unities and interrelations of the Americas. Those outlined are only a few out of the many that are patent at every turn. Cultural and intellectual relations are quite as close and fully as important as political, territorial, and economic contacts. What I have said is intended merely as an illustration.

In recent years the range of investigation in Western Hemisphere history has vastly broadened. This is due in no small part to the influence of Jameson's guides to foreign archives; to the work of American and Canadian scholars on British America; of the students of the Caribbean; of the historians of the frontier; of the whole galaxy of Hispanists; of the social, economic, institutional, cultural, and diplomatic historians, the international relationists, and a host of others. Our historical data have not only become greater in amount but much more complex in character. Phases and factors formerly undreamed of have come to light. Many of the new discoveries do not fit into the nationalistic pattern. In the old synthesis their significance is lost. In a larger framework, on the other hand, many things which have seemed obscure and secondary become outstanding and primary.

This applies especially to borderland researches. Brebner studied the institutional relations of New England and the Maritime Provinces of Canada, and concluded that the histories of Canada and the United States should be treated as one. Just as emphatically, those who have studied borderland areas between Saxon and Hispanic America are convinced that the two fields are inextricably linked together. Borderland zones are vital not only in the determination of international relations, but also in the development of culture. In this direction one of the important modifications of the Turner thesis is to be sought. By borderland areas not solely geographical regions are meant; borderline studies of many kinds are similarly fruitful.

It is not merely that a new framework will find a place for special researches that have already been consummated. Quite as important, a larger framework will call for data which we do not possess, and thus suggest a thousand new things to do. A classic example of the influence of a new synthesis is found in the multitude of investigators whom Turner set to work to fill out his elementary sketch. A report by a recent committee of historians complains that many doctoral thesis subjects in United States history have been cultivated past the point of diminishing returns. A larger synthesis of American history, I am sure, would do much to relieve this rather pathetic situation.[8] Who has written the history of the introduction of European plants and animals into the Western Hemisphere as a whole, or of the spread of cattle and horse raising from Patagonia to Labrador? Who has written on a Western Hemisphere scale the history of shipbuilding and commerce, mining, Christian missions, Indian policies, slavery and emancipation, constitutional development, arbitration, the effects of the Indian on European cultures, the rise of the common man, art, architecture, literature, or science? Who has tried to state the significance of the frontier in terms of the Americas?

A noted historian has written for us the *Epic of America*. In his title "America" means the United States. We need an Adams to sketch the high lights and the significant developments of the Western Hemisphere as a whole. Perhaps the person who undertakes the task, as a guarantee of objectivity ought to be an inhabitant of the moon. But such a synthesis, done with similar brilliancy, would give us the "Epic of *Greater* America."

[8] Before closing I wish to repeat with emphasis that I do not propose such a synthesis as a substitute for, but as a setting in which to place, any one of our national histories.

A BOLTON BIBLIOGRAPHY

THE BASIC WORK on the Bolton bibliography through 1932 was done by Mary Ross in her contribution "Writings and Cartography of Herbert Eugene Bolton," to *New Spain and the Anglo-America West: Historical Contributions Presented to Herbert Eugene Bolton* (2 vols., Los Angeles, 1932). The editors of *Greater America: Essays in Honor of Herbert Eugene Bolton* (Berkeley, University of California Press, 1945) carried the listings into the 1940's. Only a few major titles remained to be listed.

1902
" 'De los Mapas,' " Texas State Historical Association, *Quarterly*, VI (July, 1902), 69–70.
"Some Materials for Southwestern History in the Archivo General de México," Texas State Historical Association, *Quarterly*, VI (October, 1902), 103–12; VII (January, 1904), 196–213.

1903
"Tienda de Cuervo's Ynspección of Laredo, 1757," Texas State Historical Association, *Quarterly*, VI (January, 1903), 187–203.
Trans., documents on the Philippine Islands, in Emma Helen Blair and James Alexander Robertson, eds., *The Philippine Islands, 1493–1803* (55 vols.; Cleveland, Clark, 1903–1909): "Affairs in the Philipinas Islands, by Fray Domingo de Salazar" [1583], V, 210–55; "Two Letters to Felipe II" [Gerónimo de Guzmán, and Jhoan de Vascones, 1585], VI, 76–80.

1904
With Eugene Campbell Barker, *With the Makers of Texas: A Source Reader in Texas History* (New York, American Book Company, 1904).
Trans., documents on the Philippine Islands, in Emma Helen Blair and James Alexander Robertson, eds., *The Philippine Islands, 1493–1803* (55 vols.; Cleveland, Clark, 1903–1909): "Trade between

Nueva España and the Far East" [1617], XVIII, 57–64; "Events in the Filipinas Islands, from the Month of June, 1617, until the Present Date in 1618," XVIII, 65–92; "Description of the Philippinas Islands" [1618], XVIII, 93–106; "Relation of the Events in the Filipinas Islands and in Neighboring Provinces and Realms, from July, 1618, to the Present Date in 1619," XVIII, 204–34; "Letter from Francisco de Otaço, S.J., to Father Alonso de Escovar" [1620], XIX, 35–39; "Relation of Events in the Philipinas Islands and Neighboring Provinces and Kingdoms, from July, 1619, to July, 1620," XIX, 42–70.

1905

"The Spanish Abandonment and Re-occupation of East Texas, 1773–1779," Texas State Historical Association, *Quarterly*, IX (October, 1905), 67–137.

1906

"The Founding of Mission Rosario: A Chapter in the History of the Gulf Coast," Texas State Historical Association, *Quarterly*, X (October, 1906), 113–39.

"Massanet or Manzanet," Texas State Historical Association, *Quarterly*, X (July, 1906), 101.

"The Old Stone Fort at Nacogdoches," Texas State Historical Association, *Quarterly*, IX (April, 1906), 283–85.

1907

"Spanish Mission Records at San Antonio," Texas State Historical Association, *Quarterly*, X (April, 1907), 297–307.

1908

"Material for Southwestern History in the Central Archives of Mexico," *American Historical Review*, XIII (April, 1908), 510–27. Translated into Spanish by José Romero in the *Boletín de la Sociedad mexicana de geografía y estadística*, III (Mexico, 1909), Nos. 5 and 7.

"The Native Tribes about the East Texas Missions," Texas State Historical Association, *Quarterly*, XI (April, 1908), 249–76.

"Notes on Clark's 'The Beginnings of Texas,' " Texas State Historical Association, *Quarterly*, XII (October, 1908), 148–58.

Ed., "Papers of Zebulon M. Pike, 1806–1807," *American Historical Review*, XIII (July, 1908), 798–827.

1909

"Portolá's Letters Found," *San Francisco Call* (San Francisco, Calif.), October 17, 1909.

1910

"Records of the Mission of Nuestra Señora del Refugio," Texas State Historical Association, *Quarterly*, XIV (October, 1910), 164–66.

More than one hundred articles on Indian tribes of Texas and Louisiana, in Frederick Webb Hodge, ed., *Handbook of American Indians North of Mexico* (2 pts.; Washington, D.C., Government Printing Office, 1907–1910), Smithsonian Institution, Bureau of American Ethnology, Bulletin 30.

1911

Trans. and ed., "Expedition to San Francisco Bay in 1770: Diary of Pedro Fages," Academy of Pacific Coast History, *Publications*, II (July, 1911), 141–59.

"Father Kino's Lost History, Its Discovery and Its Value," Bibliographical Society of America, *Papers*, VI (1911), 9–34.

"The Jumano Indians in Texas, 1650–1771," Texas State Historical Association, *Quarterly*, XV (July, 1911), 66–84.

1912

"The Obligation of Nevada toward the Writing of Her Own History," Nevada Historical Society, *Third Biennial Report . . . , 1911–1912* (1913), pp. 62–79.

"The Spanish Occupation of Texas, 1519–1690," *Southwestern Historical Quarterly*, XVI (July, 1912), 1–26.

1913

Guide to Materials for the History of the United States in the Principal Archives of Mexico (Washington, D.C., Carnegie Institution of Washington, 1913). Carnegie Institution of Washington, Publication No. 163, Papers of the Department of Historical Research.

"The Admission of California," *University of California Chronicle*, XV (October, 1913), 554–66.

"New Light on Manuel Lisa and the Spanish Fur Trade," *Southwestern Historical Quarterly*, XVII (July, 1913), 61–66.

"Spanish Activities on the Lower Trinity River, 1746–1771," *Southwestern Historical Quarterly*, XVI (April, 1913), 339–77.

1914

Athanase de Mézières and the Louisiana-Texas Frontier, 1768–1780 (2 vols., Cleveland, Clark, 1914).

"The Founding of the Missions on the San Gabriel River, 1745–1749," *Southwestern Historical Quarterly*, XVII (April, 1914), 323–78.

"Mexico, Diplomatic Relations with" [the United States, 1821–1914], in Andrew Cunningham McLaughlin and Albert Bushnell Hart, eds., *Cyclopedia of American Government* (3 vols., New York, Appleton, 1914), II, 422–25.

1915

Texas in the Middle Eighteenth Century: Studies in Spanish Colonial History and Administration (Berkeley, University of California Press, 1915). University of California, Publications in History, Vol. III.

"The Location of La Salle's Colony on the Gulf of Mexico," *Mississippi Valley Historical Review*, II (September, 1915), 165–82. Also in the *Southwestern Historical Quarterly*, XXVII (January, 1924), 171–89.

1916

Spanish Exploration in the Southwest, 1542–1706 (New York, Scribner's, 1916).

"The Beginnings of Mission Nuestra Señora del Refugio," *Southwestern Historical Quarterly*, XIX (April, 1916), 400–404.

"The Writing of California History," *Grizzly Bear*, XIX (May, 1916), 4.

1917

Trans. and ed., "Explorers' Visits to San Diego Bay Told of in Diaries" [Cabrillo and Vizcaíno], *San Diego Union* (San Diego, Calif.), January 1, 1917.

"The Early Explorations of Father Garcés on the Pacific Slope," in Henry Morse Stephens and Herbert Eugene Bolton, eds., *The Pacific Ocean in History* (New York, Macmillan, 1917), pp. 317–30.

"French Intrusions into New Mexico, 1749–1752," in Henry Morse Stephens and Herbert Eugene Bolton, eds., *The Pacific Ocean in History* (New York, Macmillan, 1917), pp. 389–407.

"The Mission as a Frontier Institution in the Spanish-American Colonies," *American Historical Review*, XXIII (October, 1917), 42–61.

"The Spanish Missions of California: Their Relation to the General

Colonial Policy," *Oakland Tribune* (Oakland, Calif.), April 22, 1917.

1918

"Cabrillo and Vizcaíno Visit Catalina Island, 1542–1602," *The Islander* (Avalon, Santa Catalina Island, Calif.), July 16, 1918.

Ed., "General James Wilkinson as Advisor to Emperor Iturbide," *Hispanic American Historical Review*, I (May, 1918), 163–80.

1919

Kino's Historical Memoir of Pimería Alta: A Contemporary Account of the Beginnings of California, Sonora, and Arizona, by Father Eusebio Francisco Kino, S.J., Pioneer Missionary Explorer, Cartographer, and Ranchman, 1683–1711 (2 vols., Cleveland, Clark, 1919). Also in University of California, Semicentennial Publications, 1868–1918 (1919).

Trans. and ed., "Father Escobar's Relation of the Oñate Expedition to California," *Catholic Historical Review*, V (April, 1919), 19–41.

Ed., "The Iturbide Revolution in the Californias," *Hispanic American Historical Review*, II (May, 1919), 188–242.

1920

With Thomas Maitland Marshall, *The Colonization of North America, 1492–1783* (New York, Macmillan, 1920).

"The Old Spanish Fort on Red River," *Daily Oklahoman* (Oklahoma City), April 11, 1920.

1921

The Spanish Borderlands: A Chronicle of Old Florida and the Southwest (New Haven, Yale University Press, 1921). The Chronicles of America Series, Vol. XXIII.

1922

With Ephraim Douglass Adams, *California's Story* (Boston, Allyn and Bacon, 1922).

1924

"An Introductory Course in American History," *Historical Outlook*, XV (January, 1924), 17–20.

1925

Arredondo's Historical Proof of Spain's Title to Georgia: A Contribu-

tion to the History of One of the Spanish Borderlands (Berkeley, University of California Press, 1925).

With Mary Ross, *The Debatable Land: A Sketch of the Anglo-Spanish Contest for the Georgia Country* (Berkeley, University of California Press, 1925).

"The Mormons in the Opening of the West," *Deseret News* (Salt Lake City, Utah), October 24, 31, November 14, 25, 1925. Also in the *Utah Genealogical and Historical Magazine*, XVI (January, 1926), 40–72.

"Spanish Resistance to the Carolina Traders in Western Georgia, 1680–1704," *Georgia Historical Quarterly*, IX (June, 1925), 115–30.

1926

Historical Memoirs of New California, by Fray Francisco Palóu, O.F.M. (4 vols., Berkeley, University of California Press, 1926).

Palóu and His Writings (Berkeley, University of California Press, 1926).

"José Francisco Ortega," *Grizzly Bear*, XXXVIII (January, 1926), 1.

1927

Fray Juan Crespi, Missionary Explorer on the Pacific Coast, 1769–1774 (Berkeley, University of California Press, 1927).

A Pacific Coast Pioneer (Berkeley, University of California Press, 1927).

"Juan Crespi, a California Xenophon," *Touring Topics*, XIX (July, 1927), 23, 48.

1928

History of the Americas: A Syllabus with Maps (Boston, Ginn, 1928; new edition, 1935).

"Escalante in Dixie and the Arizona Strip," *New Mexico Historical Review*, III (January, 1928), 41–72.

Articles in the *Dictionary of American Biography* (20 vols.; New York, Scribner's, 1928–1936), on Juan Rodríguez Cabrillo, García López de Cárdenas, Francisco Vázquez Coronado, Juan Crespi, Eusebio Francisco Kino, Athanase de Mézières y Clugny, and Francisco Palóu.

1930

Anza's California Expeditions (5 vols.; Berkeley, University of California Press, 1930).

"Defensive Spanish Expansion and the Significance of the Borderlands," in James Field Willard and Colin Brummitt Goodykoontz, eds., *The Trans-Mississippi West: Papers Read at a Conference Held at the Uni-*

versity of Colorado, June 18–June 21, 1929 (Boulder, University of Colorado, 1930), 1–42.

1931

Font's Complete Diary: A Chronicle of the Founding of San Francisco (Berkeley, University of California Press, 1931).

Outpost of Empire: The Story of the Founding of San Francisco (New York, Knopf, 1931).

"Anza Crosses the Sand Dunes," *Touring Topics*, XXIII (May, 1931), 7.

"The Capitulation at Cahuenga," *Touring Topics*, XXIII (November, 1931), 7.

"Coming of the Cattle," *Touring Topics*, XXIII (March, 1931), 7.

"Coronado Discovers Zuñi," *Touring Topics*, XXIII (January, 1931), 8.

"The Founding of San Diego Mission," *Touring Topics*, XXIII (April, 1931), 7.

"Fremont Crosses the Sierra," *Touring Topics*, XXIII (October, 1931), 7.

"Gold Discovered at Sutter's Mill," *Touring Topics*, XXIII (December, 1931), 9.

"In the South San Joaquin Ahead of Garcés," California Historical Society, *Quarterly*, X (September, 1931), 211–19. First printed in the *Bakersfield Californian* (Bakersfield, Calif.), May 19–22, 1931. Also reprinted by the Kern County Historical Society, Bakersfield, California, May, 1935.

"Jedediah Smith Reaches San Gabriel," *Touring Topics*, XXIII (June, 1931), 7.

"Oñate in New Mexico," *Touring Topics*, XXIII (February, 1931), 8.

"Trapper Days in Taos," *Touring Topics*, XXIII (July, 1931), 7.

1932

The Padre on Horseback: A Sketch of Eusebio Francisco Kino, S.J., Apostle to the Pimas (San Francisco, Sonora Press, 1932). Translation, *El incansable jinete: Bosquejo de la vida del p. Eusebio Francisco Kino, S.J., apóstol de los Pimas* (Mexico, Buena prensa, 1940). Reprinted by the Loyola University Press, Chicago, in 1963, with an introduction by John Francis Bannon.

1933

"The Epic of Greater America," *American Historical Review,*

XXXVIII (April, 1933), 448–74. Translated by Carmen Alessio Robles, *La epopeya de la máxima América* (Mexico, Bosque, 1937), Instituto panamericano de geografía e historia, Publicación Número 30.

1934
"Pack Train and Carreta," *California Monthly*, XXXIII (November, 1934), 4, 6.

1935
"The Black Robes of New Spain," *Catholic Historical Review*, XXI (October, 1935), 257–82.

1936
Cross, Sword and Gold Pan (Los Angeles, Primavera Press, 1936).
Rim of Christendom: A Biography of Eusebio Francisco Kino, Pacific Coast Pioneer (New York, Macmillan, 1936).
"Archives and Trails," *California Monthly*, XXXVII (October, 1936), 19, 40–42.
"The Jesuits in America: An Opportunity for Historians," *Mid-America*, XVIII (October, 1936), 223–33.

1937
"Francis Drake's Plate of Brass," in *Drake's Plate of Brass: Evidence of His Visit to California in 1579* (San Francisco, California Historical Society, 1937), 1–16. California Historical Society, Special Publication, No. 13.

1939
Wider Horizons of American History (New York, Appleton-Century, 1939).
"Escalante Way—An Opportunity for the National Park Service," in Harlean James, ed., *American Planning and Civic Annual* (Washington, D.C., American Planning and Civic Association, 1939), 266–73.

1940
"Cultural Coöperation with Latin America," National Education Association, *Journal*, XXIX (January, 1940), 1–4. This article, sometimes under slightly different titles, was translated and published in Latin American newspapers and magazines, and appeared also in other United States periodicals, including the following: *Hispanic*

American Historical Review, XX (February, 1940), 3–11; *International Quarterly*, Vol. IV, No. 4 (autumn, 1940), 21–24, 59; and *Southwest Review*, XXV (January, 1940), 115–25.

Articles in the *Dictionary of American History* (6 vols.; New York, Scribner's 1940), on "Alta California," "California, Russians in," "California, Spanish Exploration of," "California Missions," "California under Mexico," and "California under Spain."

1949

Coronado, Knight of Pueblos and Plains (New York, Whittlesey House, 1949).

Coronado on the Turquoise Trail, Knight of Pueblos and Plains (Albuquerque, University of New Mexico Press, 1949). Volume I, Coronado Cuatro Centennial Publications, edited by George P. Hammond.

1950

"Pageant in the Wilderness: The Story of the Escalante Expedition to the Interior Basin, including the diary and itinerary of Father Escalante," Utah State Historical Society, *Quarterly*, XVIII (1950).

INDEX

As is evident to one reading these varied essays of Bolton's work, the index could, and possibly should, be very extensive. The editor feels that a selective index, noting some of the principal persons or topics frequently recurring, may be adequate and not unduly lengthy. Many personal and place names have been omitted; those which have been chosen will, it is hoped, be useful. After almost every entry that covering word *passim* might be added. Basically, this index is a reader, not a reference tool.